BRARY

PERCEPTUAL-MOTOR BEHAVIOR IN DOWN SYNDROME

Daniel J. Weeks
Simon Fraser University

Romeo Chua
University of British Columbia

Digby Elliott
McMaster University

Human Kinetics

Library of Congress Cataloging-in-Publication Data

Perceptual-motor behavior in Down syndrome / Daniel J. Weeks, Romeo Chua, Digby Elliott.
   p. cm.
   Includes bibliographical references and index.
   ISBN 0-88011-975-6
   1. Down syndrome. 2. Perceptual-motor processes. I. Weeks, Daniel J., 1956- II.
Chua, Romeo, 1967- III. Elliott, Digby, 1950-

   RC571.P45 2000
   616.85'8842--dc21

                                                                99-042474

ISBN: 0-88011-975-6

Acquisitions Editor: Judy Patterson Wright, PhD; **Managing Editor:** Cynthia McEntire; **Assistant Editors:** John Wentworth, Pam Johnson; **Copyeditor:** John Mulvihill; **Proofreader:** Erin Cler; **Indexer:** Betty Frizzell; **Permission Manager:** Heather Munson; **Graphic Designer:** Robert Reuther; **Graphic Artist:** Francine Hamerski; **Cover Designer:** Jack W. Davis; **Photographer (cover):** e.e.henry photographic arts. Eve Henry is an artist and photographer specializing in black and white, handtinted portraiture. As a mother, her primary focus is on children and maternity portraiture. Her studio is located in Vancouver, Canada; **Illustrators:** Kim Maxey, Kristin King; **Printer:** Versa/Dekker

Printed in the United States of America   10 9 8 7 6 5 4 3 2 1

Human Kinetics
Web site: http://www.humankinetics.com/

United States: Human Kinetics, P.O. Box 5076, Champaign, IL 61825-5076
1-800-747-4457
e-mail: humank@hkusa.com

Canada: Human Kinetics, 475 Devonshire Road Unit 100, Windsor, ON N8Y 2L5
1-800-465-7301 (in Canada only)
e-mail: humank@hkcanada.com

Europe: Human Kinetics, P.O. Box IW14, Leeds LS16 6TR, United Kingdom
+44 (0)113-278 1708
e-mail: humank@hkeurope.com

Australia: Human Kinetics, 57A Price Avenue, Lower Mitcham, South Australia 5062
(08) 82771555
e-mail: humank@hkaustralia.com

New Zealand: Human Kinetics, P.O. Box 105-231, Auckland Central
09-523-3462
e-mail: humank@hknewz.com

Contents

**PART II   Motor Development, Learning,
and Adaptive Change 149**

Preface

Thirty years after Esquirol (1838) first documented the characteristics of an individual with Down syndrome, John Langdon Down published the seminal paper "Observations on an ethnic classification of idiots" (1866). That paper would ultimately define the syndrome that results from the presence of all or a part of a third chromosome 21 in the genome. Over the past century, the study of Down syndrome has emerged as a multidisciplinary research effort directed at understanding the biological and behavioral consequences associated with the condition.

Statistical data indicates that Down syndrome occurs in approximately 1 of every 800 live births (Torfs & Christianson, 1998), making Down syndrome the most common organic form of mental retardation. Over the past few decades, biomedical advances have contributed to a significant increase in the life expectancy of persons with Down syndrome. As a consequence, it is important to detail the behavioral consequences of Trisomy 21 with the goal of circumventing, or at least minimizing, some of the general and specific information-processing challenges associated with the syndrome.

The thematic focus of the present volume involves aspects of perceptual-motor behavior, broadly defined. In this context, perceptual-motor behavior encompasses the sensory, cognitive, and movement processes that underlie goal-directed behavior. One point that surfaces throughout the chapters is that it may be neither theoretically nor empirically sufficient simply to view the perceptual-motor behavior of persons with Down syndrome as atypical relative to individuals without the syndrome. Rather, a growing consensus suggests that perceptual-motor behavior in this population is lawful, adaptive, and appropriate. Thus, a goal in creating this volume was to bring together a broad range of authorship and content related to perceptual-motor behavior.

Representing 10 different countries, the authors contributing to this volume have submitted theoretically-driven chapters on specific aspects of perceptual-motor behavior in infants, children, and adults with Down syndrome. Part I begins with a discussion of muscular activation patterns then moves to more complex manual, locomotor, and visuomotor themes, focusing on some of the underlying functional components of perceptual-motor behavior. Chapter 1 concerns the initiation of voluntary movements involving the upper limbs and provides a backdrop for understanding the integral movement elements for reaching, grasping, throwing, catching, and other manipulative skills. We then progress to a model of coordinated manual control in chapter 2 that captures the kinematic characteristics and neurological correlates of upper-limb control in prehension. The third chapter integrates "difference" and "development" perspectives to detail the variables that influence the organization and control of goal-directed movements. Chapter 4 uses a dynamic systems approach to explore the locomotor behavior of people with DS, examines the impact of behavioral constraints, and identifies modes of coordination and strategies of control. Chapter 5 forwards an approach in which ophthalmic function is viewed and examined as an integral modular component within motor behavior. Finally, the last chapter in part I considers some potential neuropsychological links between perceptual-processing abilities in Down syndrome and the motivational factors that might determine their application in the specific task of processing identity and expression information contained in faces and the relation to sociability and social understanding.

Within the context of maturation, learning, and adaptive change, part II offers four chapters that explore the characteristics of motor development in Down syndrome. Chapter 7 reviews the extent to which individuals with DS have specific sensorimotor deficits and whether intervention can be used to facilitate motor performance. Chapter 8 adopts a decidedly broad perspective of skill acquisition. After providing a review of the effects of practice on the performance of individuals with and without mental retardation, the chapter forges a link between the empirical research findings and the constructs of mental flexibility and rigidity and their relation to learning and performance. The next chapter points out that the effectiveness of movement coordination can only be evaluated in the context of the movement goals of the actor's central nervous system. The last chapter in part II provides a much-needed evaluation of the progressive attainment of perceptual-motor skills in individuals with Down syndrome.

Finally, theoretical advances and accompanying new research strategies are explored in the four chapters included in part III. It covers, in turn, information-movement coupling (chapter 11), dynamical systems (chapter 12), functional systems (chapter 13), and neurophysiological approaches to understanding perceptual-motor behavior in Down syndrome (chapter 14). These research paradigms will provide the foundation for research in the 21st century.

The material presented could serve as a text for a senior undergraduate or graduate seminar. The volume will also appeal to practicing professionals including physical and occupational therapists, health care aids, nurses, and physicians who work with individuals with Down syndrome. Over the years we have found that the parents of persons with Down syndrome are frequently well-informed and sophisticated consumers of scientific information. We hope that many of them will also find this book of interest.

Down, J.L. (1866). Observations on an ethnic classification of idiots. *London Hospital Clinical Lectures and Reports, 3*, 259-262.

Esquirol, J.E.D. (1838). *Des maladies mentales considérées sous les rapports médical hygiénique et médico-légal* [mental illness considered by the medical, health, and medical-legal reports]. Paris: Bailliere.

Torfs, C.P. & Christianson, R.E. (1998). Anomalies in Down syndrome individuals in a large population-based registry. *American Journal of Medical Genetics, 77* (5), 431-438.

Acknowledgments

For their support of our own research efforts over the past several years, we would like to thank the children and adults with Down syndrome and their families in the Hamilton-Wentworth and greater Vancouver areas. We also acknowledge the support of several granting agencies, including Natural Sciences and Engineering Research Council of Canada, Ontario Mental Health Foundation, Scottish Rite Charitable Foundation of Canada, Ontario Educational Research Council, Ontario Ministry of Community and Social Services, British Columbia Health Research Foundation, National Down Syndrome Society, National Institute of Child Health and Human Development, and the National Institute of Neurological Disorders and Stroke. Appreciation is also extended to Josephine Mills, Executive Director of the Down Syndrome Research Foundation and Resource Centre in Vancouver, for her assistance in identifying research participants. We thank all the colleagues, undergraduate students, and graduate students who collaborated with us over the past several years as well.

Finally, this volume would never have been completed without the support and commitment of Rainer Martens and his staff at Human Kinetics. In particular, we benefited from the patient assistance of Judy Patterson Wright, Acquisitions Editor, and Cynthia McEntire, Managing Editor.

PART

Characteristics of Perceptual-Motor Behavior Associated With Down Syndrome

The majority of individuals with Down syndrome have an extra 21st chromosome in every cell in their body (cf. mosaicism). This particular genotype expresses itself in a number of unique anatomical, physiological, and behavioral characteristics. In this section, six chapters examine the perceptual-motor differences and similarities between persons with Down syndrome and people with other disabilities and nondisabled people. While some chapters concentrate on behavioral differences/similarities, others examine some of the anatomical and physiological bases for the unique perceptual-motor performance of persons with Down syndrome.

1

Although in many cases the focus is on group differences, all authors provide a window into the behavioral variability exhibited by this special group of people.

In chapter 1, Greg Anson and Grant Mawston examine how the characteristics of the motor system in persons with Down syndrome affect their ability to prepare and execute a simple response to a sensory event. Their paper highlights the fact that perceptual-motor speed must be studied in the context of the entire system involved in producing the behavior.

Chapter 2 by Judith Charlton, Elfriede Ihsen, and Barbara Lavelle extends the examination of upper-limb movements to manual tasks that involve a high degree of cognitive, perceptual, and motor precision. The authors not only compare the developmental course of reaching and grasping behaviors in children with Down syndrome to people in other groups, but through both a quantitative and qualitative examination of group and individual differences in performance suggest instructional interventions that may facilitate skill acquisition.

In chapter 3, Tim Welsh and Digby Elliott make the argument that motor performance and learning in persons with Down syndrome often depend on whether the performance context involves visual or auditory/verbal mediation of the movement. They go on to suggest when general motor learning and performance principles will apply to persons with Down syndrome and when specific instructional strategies may prove useful.In their examination of lower-limb activity in chapter 4, Eliane Mauerberg-deCastro and Rosa Angulo-Kinzler seek to determine how children and adults with Down syndrome adapt their locomotor patterns. They conclude that, as in persons without Down syndrome, the locomotor patterns of persons with Down syndrome are uniquely influenced by a complex interaction of environmental and task constraints.

In chapter 5, Mark Mon-Williams, Anne Jobling, and John Wann consider whether general ophthalmic deficits, common to persons with Down syndrome, are a critical component underlying the motor problems associated with the syndrome. They suggest that while it may be tempting to assign a causal role to visual dysfunction in the movement challenges associated with Down syndrome, until further research is conducted the evidence presently restricts one to conclude that these factors are co-occurring products of the syndrome.

Finally, chapter 6 by Tom Pitcairn and Jennifer Wishart focuses on perceptual processing of identity and expression information in faces. The authors provide a neuropsychological foundation for the idea that children with Down syndrome have specific deficits in the capacity to process emotional information. They contribute to the theme of this volume by exploring how understanding others, through face processing, serves a fundamental role in the motivation and capacity for social understanding that underlies effective social and cognitive development.

CHAPTER

Patterns of Muscle Activation in Simple Reaction-Time Tasks

J. Greg Anson and Grant A. Mawston

School of Physical Education
University of Otago

Key words

simple reaction time ◆ reaction time ◆ electromyography ◆ Down syndrome ◆ motor programming ◆ muscle activation ◆ preparation ◆ proximal-to-distal ◆ distal-to-proximal ◆ strategy ◆ fractionation ◆ adaptive response ◆ timing

The most remarkable thing about moving is how easy it is. It is only when we watch someone who cannot move, perhaps after a stroke, or someone whose movements continually go wrong, . . . that we are reminded of the problems of movement control with which our nervous system copes so uncomplainingly. (Rothwell, 1994, p. 1)

But, just how is movement controlled? A vigorous debate has centered on two proposals: a "motor systems" explanation, and an "action systems" explanation. Curiously, these two explanations appear to have evolved principally from a single primary source, the remarkable work of Nikolai Bernstein, "The Co-Ordination and Regulation of Movements" (Bernstein, 1967 trans.). At a recent conference celebrating the centenary of Bernstein's birth (Latash, 1996), a satisfactory reconciliation of the two views appeared not to be on the horizon (see also Meijer, Wagenaar, & Blankendaal, 1988). Without question, such debate is healthy in pursuing an understanding and knowledge of movement control. However, the lack of agreement makes theoretically bounded comparisons of normal and other than normal movement behavior less clear cut.

The views expressed in this chapter imply that knowledge about the neuromotor system's structure and function can increase our understanding of the association between control of movement and Down syndrome (DS). The focus is on the initiation of voluntary movements, specifically those involving the upper limbs—the kind of movements that are the integral elements of reaching and grasping, throwing and catching, or participation in the popular environment of interactive video games. This chapter consists of four sections: (1) a brief review of DS, movement preparation, and simple reaction time; (2) the proximal-to-distal phenomenon with respect to control of upper-limb movement; (3) DS and patterns of muscle activation; and (4) concluding comments.

Movement Preparation and Simple Reaction Time

Although observed for almost 900 years, the clinical features of DS were reputedly described first in 1866 by Dr. J.H. Langdon Down (1828-1896), an English physician (Patterson, 1987). Down used the less appropriate term "mongolism" to label the disorder that now bears his name. Later the genetic etiology was determined, and a contemporary definition of DS resulted: "the set of physical, mental, and functional abnormalities that result from trisomy 21, the presence in the genome of three rather than the normal two chromosomes 21" (Epstein, 1987, p. 336). Etiological and neuropathological details of DS have been described elsewhere (see, e.g., Anson, 1992; Epstein, 1987; Patterson, 1987).

The individual with DS faces numerous movement control challenges. In addition to showing lengthened reaction time, individuals with DS may demonstrate diminished sensory acuity, hypotonia, altered postural responses to perturbations, and positive and/or neutral effects of practice (Anson, 1992; Latash, 1992). With one exception, there seems to be no clear systematic pattern of altered performance.

Extensive variability appears to be a hallmark signature. The one consistent observation has been a slowness of reaction time in individuals with DS (Anson, 1992; Berkson, 1960; Henderson, 1985; Inui, Yamanishi, & Tada, 1995). Reaction time is used frequently as a measure of the speed of information processing. It is often used in clinical settings to assess the integrity of cognitive functioning. In motor control research, it is a significant dependent measure for assessing the duration of movement preparation.

Movement Preparation

The idea that reaction time measures the speed of information processing is not new and has its origins in the 19th century in the works of Donders (1868), Helmholtz (1850), Wundt (1868/1912), and Woodworth (1899). In fact, the concept of reaction time can be traced to the astronomers of the 16th century and their efforts to accurately mark the transit of stars across the heavens (Woodworth, 1938). However, at least one source of current thinking, while not denying the existence of reaction time per se, would seriously challenge the information-processing model as applied to movement preparation. Proponents of the "action systems" view (e.g., Reed, 1988; Thelen, 1994; Turvey, 1990; Wade, 1994) would question the existence of representations (e.g., motor programs) as substrates of mental activity, the "stuff" of information processing. In a specific reference to DS, Wade (1994) expresses an "action systems" perspective of motor behavior, stating that "coordination arises via the system's capacity to self-organize, rather than being a slave to a central executive" (Wade, 1994, p. 98). According to Wade, individuals with DS experience motor control difficulties because they "fail to detect the dynamical properties represented in the perception-action cycle . . ." (Wade, 1994, p. 98). How the perception-action cycle occurs in the absence of information processing is not clear, and such a debate is beyond the scope of this chapter.

The alternative, some would say more "traditional," view of accounting for processes of movement preparation is represented by the "motor systems" model. The "motor systems" view accommodates information processing as the integration of sensory input, memory, cognition, and the processes of motor programming through which facilitation of movement preparation in advance of an expected stimulus can be achieved. Such information processing is the "work of the brain" and coordinates the preparation for voluntary movement (Ghez, 1991). In numerous studies this perspective has been taken into account along with known neuropathological consequences of DS in describing possible limitations for movement preparation associated with DS.

Two interpretations grounded in a "motor systems" view are noted. One posits that movement preparation deficits in DS are a function of mental retardation and structural alterations within the central nervous system. This interpretation is the theme of the extensive work of Digby Elliott and colleagues (Chua, Weeks, & Elliott, 1994; Elliott, Weeks, & Elliott, 1987; Elliott, Weeks, & Gray, 1990; Elliott

& Weeks, 1993; Elliott, Weeks, & Chua, 1994; LeClair, Pollock, & Elliott, 1993). Initially, Elliott, Weeks, and Elliott (1987), intrigued by the results from dichotic listening studies that reported reversed cerebral specialization (left-ear/right-hemisphere advantage) for speech perception in individuals with DS, proposed that production of movement sequences might be affected by atypical brain organization. But results from a study that examined production of movement sequences were not in agreement with the reversed cerebral specialization hypothesis. Elliott et al. (1987) suggested that there could be hemispheric dissociation between mechanisms for perception and production of speech in DS. Later, Elliott et al. (1990) investigated both oral and limb movement performance in discrete and sequential movement tasks following either verbal or visual (demonstration) cues. Both the mentally retarded (but not DS) group and the group with DS performed better with visual than with verbal cues. The difference between visual and verbal cuing was greater for the group with DS, particularly in the sequential movement task. Similar results favoring visual instruction over verbal were reported by Elliott and Weeks (1993). Despite the apparent preference for visual cuing, the deficit in movement preparation in DS was still characterized by significantly elevated reaction time and movement time. LeClair et al. (1993) used the parameter precuing model (Rosenbaum, 1980) to examine the temporal ordering of parameters likely to be used in motor program preparation. In three, two-choice reaction time conditions there were no differences in choice reaction time, a result consistent with the predictions of Hick's Law (Rosenbaum, 1991) but not with the predictions of the parameter precuing model. It appeared that individuals with DS were not able to take advantage of "hand" or "distance" precue information to facilitate faster processing and reduce reaction time. A caveat for this result is warranted, as there were only 12 trials per block for each precue condition.

In proposing a model to explain cerebral specialization in DS, Elliott and colleagues (Chua et al., 1994; Elliott et al., 1994) suggested that one difficulty in understanding movement preparation in DS involves determining whether DS results in brains that are organized differently or whether the difference is associated with the way in which information is organized by the brain. It is also possible that both outcomes are true. Contrary to earlier suggestions prompted by results from studies of speech perception using dichotic listening tasks, Chua et al. (1994) concluded that the pattern of lateral advantage in DS is similar to that for individuals without DS, and thus the major difference is most likely associated with differences in organization of information by the brain. This view appears to be supported by interpretations of auditory-evoked potential recordings from individuals with DS (Diaz & Zuron, 1995). However, a recent paper (Carlesimo, Marotta, & Vicari, 1997) suggested that altered neural structure is a predisposing factor explaining poorer memory in individuals with DS than in other individuals without DS who scored equally well on standardized mental-age tests. This argument questions the idea of a consistent etiology underlying mental retardation. Such interpretations make the modeling of cerebral specialization in DS even more challenging.

An alternative interpretation (Latash, 1992, 1994; Latash & Anson, 1996) suggests that in general the central nervous system is a "smart system," and while the movements produced by those with DS appear "clumsy," they can be viewed as "adaptive reactions" due to changed priorities within the central nervous system (Latash, 1994). The "smartness" of the central nervous system is able to generate solutions to provide movement outcomes acceptable to itself. This is analogous to the idea of detours providing access to villages along a flood-damaged highway. Sometimes the highway is clear (sometimes individuals with DS demonstrate entirely normal responses), and at other times the highway is impassable (frequently, individuals with DS produce erratic, highly variable responses), requiring a detour if access to the village is to be achieved.

The influence of DS on movement preparation is complex and yet to be adequately explained. In contrast, the effect on reaction time and movement time is exceptionally clear: both measures are significantly longer in almost every instance. Perhaps there are characteristics other than those directly involving movement preparation and information processing that can help explain the lengthened reaction time. Before examining other characteristics of DS that could cause a slowing of reaction time, we will clarify, for the purpose of the ensuing discussion, exactly what we mean by "reaction time."

Reaction Time

Reaction time (RT) is the duration between onset of an imperative stimulus and initiation of movement. Under conditions in which both temporal and event uncertainty are minimal, reaction time is described as "simple" (simple reaction time, or SRT). Examples of situations in which SRT would be measured include sprint starting in track and/or swimming events. In most SRT settings, the emphasis is on initiating the movement as fast and accurately as possible. In contrast, when temporal and, in particular, event uncertainty are increased, initiation of the response may require selection from one of two or more possible stimuli. In this situation, the measured delay is called "choice" reaction time (CRT). In this chapter, we limit our review primarily to studies in which SRT has been the principal dependent measure.

The observation that SRT is longer in participants with DS is not surprising in itself. Lengthened reaction time is frequently associated with mental retardation, a characteristic of DS. What is surprising, perhaps, is the finding that SRT in DS is substantially longer than in other individuals who have comparable levels of mental functioning and who are chronologically similar to those with DS. This observation, first reported by Berkson (1960), provided the impetus for our initial investigations of reaction time in DS (see Anson, 1992, pp. 396-398).

One explanation given for SRT being substantially shorter than CRT is that when temporal and event uncertainty are minimized, knowledge about the upcoming response can be used for advance preparation and preprogramming of responses. One question of interest to us was whether individuals with DS were failing to take advantage of the information available before stimulus onset, or whether despite taking advantage of the information, they were slowed by structural limitations of the neuromotor system. One possible way to answer this question is to examine the effect(s) of independent variables on fractionated SRT. Fractionated SRT uses electromyography (EMG) to separate the processes underlying SRT into two temporal components, as illustrated in figure 1.1.

Premotor time (PMT) is the interval between the imperative stimulus and the time of onset of significant change in the baseline of the electromyogram of the primary agonist muscle. Motor time (MOT) is the interval between the change in EMG and initiation of overt movement as measured by an electromechanical or infrared switch, or by onset of change in a movement sensor such as a potentiometer or accelerometer. Changes in PMT are considered to reflect changes in central or information-processing demands, while changes in MOT reflect changes due to peripheral or musculoskeletal factors. Changes, or more precisely, absence of changes, in EMG signals have often formed the basis of evidence supporting the existence of motor programming (Anson, 1982, 1989; DeLuca, 1997; Jeannerod, 1988; Latash, Almeida, & Corcos, 1993; Schmidt, 1988; Wadman, Denier van der Gon, & Derksen, 1980). However, relatively few studies (Anson, 1992; Anson, Lockie, & Mawston, 1994; Davis, Ward, & Sparrow, 1991; Mawston & Anson, 1994) have employed EMG to fractionate reaction time to investigate movement preparation in individuals with DS.

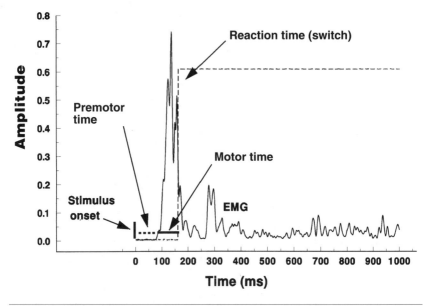

Figure 1.1 Reaction time is preceded by the onset of muscle activation (premotor time) and completed when sufficient force is generated such that the switch can be activated (motor time). Thus, reaction time = premotor time + motor time.

The Proximal-to-Distal Phenomenon

"All motions with the strongest joynts performe
    Lett the weaker second and perfect the same
The stronger joint its motion first most end
    Before the nixt to move in the least intend"

(Thomas Kincaid, 1687, cited by Herring & Chapman, 1992, p. 1173)*

The performance of fast reaching movements is commonly believed to occur in a proximal-to-distal manner. As the above quotation implies, this has been "known" for more than 300 years. However, Herring and Chapman state that "little theoretical or empirical evidence supports this theory" (Herring & Chapman, 1992, p. 1173). Three points are important: (1) The phenomenon of proximal-to-distal activation is a popular clinical entity with minimal empirical support (Horak, personal communication, November 1996); (2) most of the existing empirical support comes from biomechanical studies of kinetic and kinematic properties of the limb during throwing-type tasks (Herring & Chapman, 1992; Jöris, Edwards van Muyen, van Ingen Schenau, & Kemper, 1985; Putnam, 1993; Sørenson, Zacho, Simonsen, Dyhre-Poulsen, & Klausen, 1996); and (3) there is very little empirical data on proximal-to-distal initiation of movement citing reaction time and/or pattern of muscle activation (Karst & Hasan, 1991), although a recent model includes simulation of muscle activation (De Lussanet & Alexander, 1997).

Why the concern with the proximal-to-distal phenomenon? In our initial studies of reaction time and DS (see Anson, 1992, pp. 396-405), we used various forms of simple pointing tasks to none, one, or two large Styrofoam targets and recorded EMG from principal agonist muscles as well as reaction time from two locations: one behind the elbow, the second beneath the index finger. A typical setup for these experiments is illustrated in figure 1.2.

We were investigating movement complexity effects on reaction time in individuals with DS and used an experimental setup similar to that used by Anson (1982, 1989) in which a dental chair provided maximal postural support, minimizing the need to achieve stability prior to movement initiation. In all cases, participants in the control group demonstrated either a proximal-to-distal order of activation of anterior deltoid, biceps, and extensor indicis muscles accompanying an elbow-then-finger order of reaction time, or simultaneous activation of muscles and reaction-time switches. A typical example is shown in figure 1.3.

This result alone would have given no cause for surprise and probably would not have attracted further interest. However, when the results for the participants with DS were examined, we were indeed surprised! In the majority of trials the order of activation, both of the muscles and reaction-time switches, was reversed. This effect, represented by average premotor and switch reaction times for blocks of trials for the DS group, was accompanied by high variability but nonetheless was a consistent

---

* Thanks to Dave Goodman (personal communication, November 1996) for this reference.

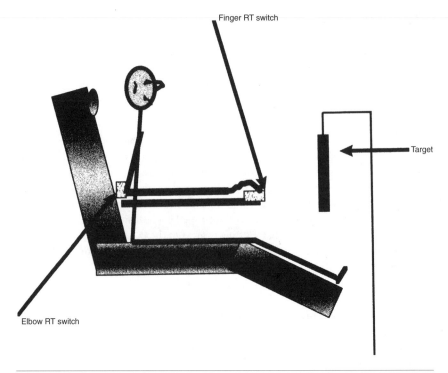

Figure 1.2 Experimental setup to measure segmental and fractionated reaction time.

finding. This surprising result led to two lines of inquiry: (1) to determine the origin and robustness of the proximal-to-distal phenomenon, and (2) to attempt to determine why individuals with DS demonstrated a reversed pattern of activation.

Empirical Support for the Proximal-to-Distal Phenomenon

De Lussanet and Alexander (1997) have proposed a simple model for fast planar arm movements and note that in fast movements a proximal-to-distal sequence of both joint velocity and muscle activation is usually found. However, the most compelling evidence for proximal-to-distal sequencing appears in a comprehensive investigation by Karst and Hasan (1991) in which timing and magnitude of EMG activity in two-joint arm movements in different directions was examined. Karst and Hasan noted that while the proximal-to-distal activation pattern was consistent, the differences in onset of muscle activation of muscles involved in the sequence were influenced by the direction required for the movement. As a general rule for upper-body movements, "initial agonist activations proceed sequentially from axial joints to peripheral ones" (Karst & Hasan, 1991, p. 1602). One reason, and a potential advantage of proximal-to-distal activation, is that it may provide the

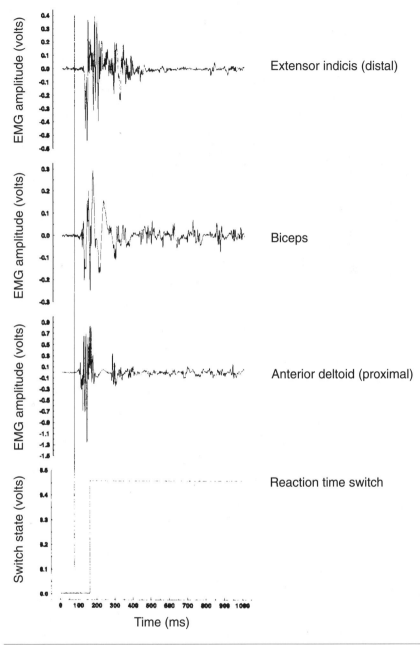

Figure 1.3   A typical example of the proximal-to-distal ordering of activation of agonist muscles during initiation of a fast pointing task made with the right arm. A "step" change in the finger-switch signal indicates reaction time; vertical line at approximately 100 ms indicates premotor time of anterior deltoid (proximal) muscle.

opportunity for on-line corrections or the chance to "fine-tune" the terminal phase of the response. Although we have investigated movement responses of limited direction and examined just a sample of possible muscles involved, our results (for participants in the control groups) are entirely consistent with those of Karst and Hasan (1991) and are in agreement with the predictions of the model proposed by De Lussannet and Alexander (1997), with data described by Jeannerod (1988), and with data for bilateral reaching movements (Tyler & Hasan, 1995).

Why Do Individuals With Down Syndrome Demonstrate a Distal-to-Proximal Pattern?

The answer at this time is that "We do not know!" Since our initial unexpected finding (Anson & Davis, 1988), we have observed distal-to-proximal patterns of activation in the data from each experiment we have completed. It does not appear to be specifically associated with movement complexity (Anson & O'Connor, 1989; Gorely & Anson, 1990) or visual feedback (Gorely & Anson, 1990). It is not removed with practice (Anson & Gorely, 1990), although a reduction of between-muscle activation latency was observed in one experiment (Mawston & Anson, 1994). In recent work (Anson et al., 1994; Mawston & Anson, 1994), we have measured nerve conduction velocity in the median nerve of five individuals with DS. Nerve conduction velocities for all participants were within the normal range (Taylor, personal communication, August 1994).

An investigation of the influence of attention on neuromotor reaction time has also been conducted (Mawston & Anson, 1994). Attention was assessed as the number of off-task glances per second during the preparatory interval between a verbally presented "ready" command and onset of an imperative auditory stimulus (between 1 and 4 s). Off-task glancing was measured from videotape records of each subject's eye movement during each trial. A summary of the results is presented in figure 1.4.

On average, off-task glancing (diverted attention) occurred in just 1% of trials for participants in the control group and in 76% of trials for participants in the DS group. Comparison between the fastest and slowest 25% of trials in the DS group revealed that a higher frequency of off-task glancing was generally associated with slower reaction time. In the same study, accuracy of performance was examined by varying the size (small, medium, large) of the Styrofoam targets to be hit. Reaction time among target sizes was not significantly different in either the control or the DS group, but movement time was faster to the large target. Regardless of condition (accuracy) or the attention result (off-task glancing), the distal-to-proximal pattern associated with DS remained a persistent feature of the data and was always accompanied by substantially lengthened reaction times (up to 100% greater than observed in participants in the control group).

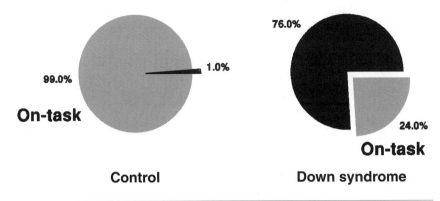

Figure 1.4   Diminished attention (off-task glancing) was characteristic of 76% of trials for the Down syndrome group but occurred in just 1% of trials for the control group.

Recently we investigated whether the distal-to-proximal effect in DS could be influenced by imposing a specific strategy on participants during an aiming task (Anson & Lockie, 1996; Anson et al., 1994). Results from other studies (Almeida, Corcos, & Latash, 1994; Latash et al., 1993) indicated that individuals with DS were able to adapt their responses to either a "react" or "let go" instruction in an elbow-positioning task. We varied the instruction to participants by informing them to either "move as fast as possible and hit the target" ("move fast" instruction) or "start as fast as possible and hit the target" ("react fast" instruction) to bias their preparation strategy. We also varied the target proximity (near or far, with target size adjusted to maintain a constant distance/width ratio) and measured the effects of both variables (strategy and target proximity) on fractionated simple reaction time. There were no significant effects of either strategy or target proximity on fractionated reaction time, but the distal-to-proximal pattern was once again present in the DS group (Anson & Lockie, 1996). In further analyses, trial-by-trial results for each group (control and DS) and for each condition were examined. The persistence of the distal-to-proximal outcome was consistently represented, as illustrated in figure 1.5. Note too that figure 1.5 also shows the consistency of the "normal" proximal-to-distal effect in the data from the control group.

To this point we have discussed results based on group averages. Given the substantial variability associated with the "averaged" DS data, it is possible that the distal-to-proximal effect is a consequence of the influence of a few extreme data points or the result of large effects contributed by one or two subjects. Therefore we thought that it would be informative to compare exemplar data from chronologically matched individuals representing the control and DS groups, respectively. This approach provides graphic evidence of intra-individual differences in performance.

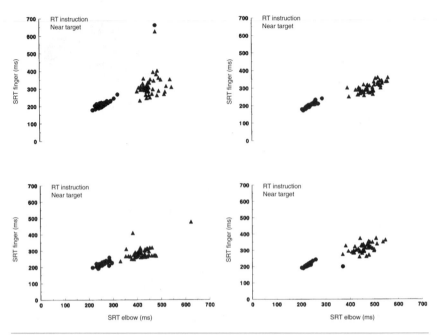

Figure 1.5 Scatterplots of elbow (proximal) versus finger (distal) reaction times of trial means for the control and Down syndrome groups in each of four strategy/target proximity experimental conditions. Several points to note: (1) Down syndrome reaction times (RTs) are consistently longer than those for the control group; (2) the shortest control group RTs show tight coupling (minimal difference) between elbow and finger RT measures; (3) in general, control group elbow RTs occupy a smaller range along the x-axis than finger RTs do on the y-axis, illustrating the proximal-to-distal pattern; (4) the shortest Down syndrome group RTs are measured at the finger (200-250 ms on the x-axis) and are paired with elbow RTs that begin more than 100 ms later (300-350 ms on the y-axis); (5) in general, Down syndrome finger RTs are dispersed over a narrower range on the y-axis than are the elbow RTs on the x-axis, emphasizing the predominant distal-to-proximal pattern of activation.

Performance Consistency and Patterns of Muscle Activation

Given the relatively narrow range of dispersion of group reaction-time data for the control group as pictured in figure 1.5, it should not be surprising to observe very consistent trial-to-trial performances by participants in the control group. To make individual trial comparisons clearer, the EMG data were demeaned, and the root mean square (RMS) computed using a 10 ms time constant. The examples displayed in figure 1.6 show that a 10 ms time constant allows the inherent

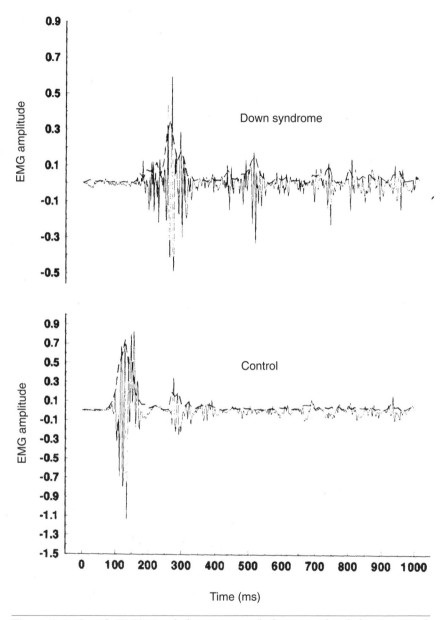

Figure 1.6   Sample EMG signals from one muscle for one trial each from a control group participant (lower panel) and participant with Down syndrome (upper panel). Solid lines represent the raw EMG signal. Dashed lines are the corresponding root mean square (RMS) values. The time constant for each RMS signal is 10 ms.

15

shape of the raw EMG signal to be preserved with no apparent biasing of the temporal changes in the signal. Thus for clarity in the figures that follow, the examples will contain just the RMS values of the EMG signal. For the control group, consistency of performance was a feature of the data and is clearly evident in the repeated measures for one participant over a block of 11 trials, as illustrated in figures 1.7a and 1.7b. Figure 1.8 shows the results of one participant with Down syndrome.

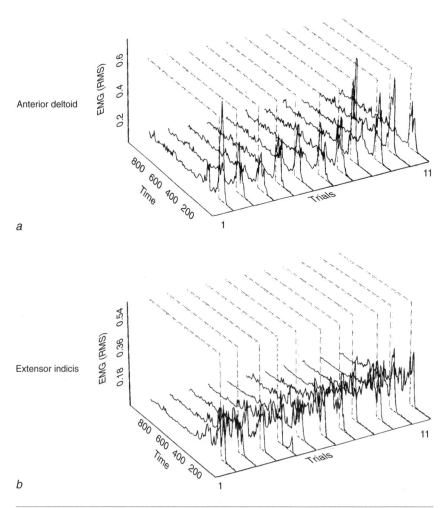

Figure 1.7 (*a*) Simple RT (elbow = dashed; finger = dotted) and EMG (RMS) for each of 11 trials for one control participant showing consistent trial-to-trial performance in the pattern of proximal muscle activation (anterior deltoid). (*b*) From the same subject in figure 1.7a. RT data are the same, but EMG (RMS) is from the distal muscle (extensor indicis).

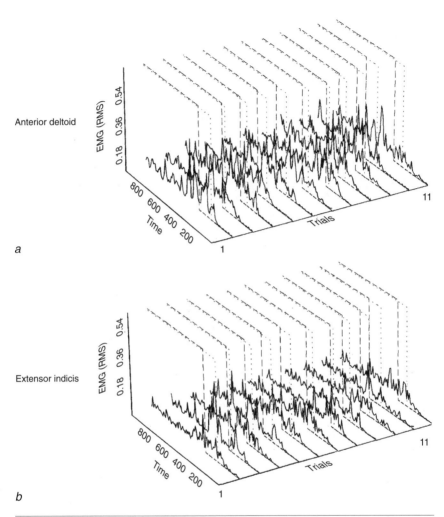

Figure 1.8   (*a*) Simple RT (elbow = dashed; finger = dotted) and EMG (RMS) for each of 11 trials for one participant with Down syndrome (chronologically age matched to the control participant whose data appears in figure 1.7a). EMG (RMS) data are from the proximal muscle (anterior deltoid) and show inconsistent timing, exemplified by the large range of differences between the RT measures at the finger and elbow. (*b*) From the same subject in figure 1.8a. RT data are the same, but EMG (RMS) is from the distal muscle (extensor indicis).

The data in figures 1.7a and 1.7b are from the same trials with EMG from the proximal muscle (anterior deltoid) shown in figure 1.7a and from the distal muscle (extensor indicis) in 1.7b. It can be seen that features of consistent performance include tight time-locking of the proximal (elbow) and distal (finger) simple reaction times and, with the exception of the 4th trial in figure 1.7b, smooth baseline EMG followed by a rapid transition to heightened muscle activity before activation of the reaction-time switches. In all trials, onset of activity in anterior deltoid occurs well in advance of switch activation. The pattern of activity in extensor indicis (figure 1.7b) is characterized by consistently longer duration of baseline EMG with onset of change from baseline in closer proximity to the time of switch activation. This pattern fits well with the predictions of Karst and Hasan (1991), suggesting that peripheral adjustments could be made on-line if a proximal-to-distal sequence was present.

Results for the same condition for the chronologically age-matched individual with DS are presented in figures 1.8a and 1.8b. Again, the data in figures 1.8a and 1.8b are from the same set of trials with EMG from anterior deltoid shown in figure 1.8a and that of extensor indicis in figure 1.8b. The differences in content between figures 1.7 and 1.8 are striking. Longer reaction times for elbow and finger switches are evident in all trials. In all cases in figure 1.8, "finger" reaction time precedes "elbow" reaction time, but the difference between each switch time varies substantially from trial to trial. For example, the reaction times in trials 2 and 7 appear relatively closely coupled compared to those in trials 1, 4, 5, 9, 10, and 11. Comparison of figures 1.7a and 1.8a reveals substantial differences in the EMG profiles for the pattern of anterior deltoid activation in control and DS, respectively. EMG associated with DS has a longer baseline (i.e., lengthened premotor time), and when active, the activation reflects several bursts of activity progressively increasing in magnitude. In contrast, the EMG profiles shown in figure 1.7a feature a single large burst of activity at the onset of change from baseline, consistent with rapid muscle activation in a fast response. However, it should be remembered that in DS, anterior deltoid is often not activated first, as generally "rapid" responses have been shown to be initiated in a distal-to-proximal order. Therefore, it might be expected that in DS the pattern of activity in extensor indicis would resemble, with respect to timing, the pattern seen in anterior deltoid muscle for the control group participant. Comparison of the EMG in figure 1.8b with that in 1.7a indicates no similarities in pattern of onset. The EMG profiles in figure 1.8b (extensor indicis for DS) are more like those in figure 1.8a. Although onset of extensor indicis activity (figure 1.8b) occurs earlier than in anterior deltoid (figure 1.8a), it too is polyphasic, often with a series of bursts slowly increasing in magnitude (see, e.g., trials 1, 3, 4, 5, 6, 9, and 10 in figure 1.8b).

In sum, the EMG patterns for anterior deltoid and extensor indicis of the control group participant show a "steplike" change in activation from baseline, whereas those of the DS participant are "ramplike." While we are not aware of a neurophysiological relationship between reaction time and "shape" of agonist EMG profiles, it is tempting to speculate that fast reactions would be more likely to accompany "steplike" than "ramplike" changes in muscle activation.

Conclusions

Normally, initiation of fast, accurate movements of the upper limb are facilitated by either proximal-to-distal or synchronous activation of the principal agonist muscles. We must also conclude that the proximal-to-distal phenomenon is frequently absent from the performance of rapid upper-limb movements by individuals with DS and replaced by a reversed distal-to-proximal pattern of muscle activation. We do not know why this occurs. It clearly does not occur in isolation from other events, as witnessed by the associated lengthened reaction time characteristic of DS. If the lengthened reaction time is in part a consequence of the generally reversed pattern of activation, it is not clear what the underlying mechanism connecting these two outcomes might be. Perhaps it is an "action system"!

The possibility that our results reflect the enforced laboratory task and procedures cannot be overlooked, although if this were a significant factor we might not expect to see the quite robust conventional proximal-to-distal pattern featured by participants in the control group. Perhaps, if the distal-to-proximal pattern could be recorded in DS during performance of an "everyday" reaching and grasping task (e.g., reaching to grab a falling object), additional credence for the result would be forthcoming. However, to test this idea, EMG needs to be recorded and this process itself could alter "normal" task performance.

An alternative explanation (Latash & Anson, 1996) would propose that the slow reaction time and distal-to-proximal behavior of individuals with DS are representative of an "adaptive reaction," a deliberate behavior resulting from a central nervous system that "realizes" its own limitations. For individuals with DS, performing fast and accurately may be defined by quite different benchmarks, in which generating a response in and of itself might be regarded as successful, independent of the "finer" issues of accuracy and speed. It is not difficult to imagine that survival can be sustained without depending on high levels of speed-accuracy performance. Certainly some tasks will be avoided—for example, driving a car may be ill advised. But task avoidance is not an uncommon feature of the human disposition. Children identified as "clumsy" may become adults who avoid motor control challenges requiring fast and accurate performance, yet survive extremely well in society. This observation does not escape the notion that survival may be at the cost of experiencing the full richness of motor opportunities. The "adaptive reaction" perspective provides a chance to see motor performance on one continuum linked to a parallel continuum that reflects the status of the organism's central nervous system. CNS status provides a means of adapting the organism's motor control to facilitate the best possible movement outcome. Without doubt the quality of this movement outcome can be altered by clinical therapeutic intervention (Anson & Latash, 1996). From this perspective, comparing the performance of individuals with DS with samples from various control populations might be, in functional terms, nonsense and irrelevant. However, this view would be counterproductive and could deny the value and validity of attempting to determine what makes motor control in DS different. The creation of new knowledge is of paramount importance; without the knowledge base already developed, there would be no basis on which to initiate an "adaptive reaction" discussion.

There are, in fact, several specific unanswered questions associated with mechanisms underlying DS that may contribute to a greater understanding of altered reaction time and EMG activation patterns. For example: what is the relationship between memory demands and reaction time given that DS appears to affect memory retrieval without altering scores on standardized IQ tests (Carlesimo et al., 1997)? Further, it is possible that the issues raised by Elliott et al. (1994) concerning brain structure versus organizational capacity can be evaluated within a parameter precuing paradigm (Rosenbaum, 1980) employing fractionated reaction time. In a recent study of information-processing strategies in "clumsy" children (Anson, 1997; Higgott & Anson, 1995), we used the parameter precuing technique with some success. Although clumsiness was observed to be associated with longer reaction times, these were linked to precue predictions indicating that these children demonstrated appropriate response organization but needed more time to accomplish the processing of information prior to initiating the response. Numerous questions about motor control in DS remain unanswered and offer exciting opportunities for further research.

Summary

For most of us, movement is a virtually effortless undertaking. In contrast, scientists who study the nature of motor control have yet to agree on how human movement is controlled. Current debate centers on two quite different perspectives. The "action systems" perspective argues that control of movement is best understood by examining the interaction between the organism and its environment because motor control is a product of this interaction. On the other hand, the "motor systems" perspective proposes that control of movement can be best understood by knowing how the structure and function of the organism permits it to control movement within its environment.

In this chapter, a mostly "motor systems" view underlies our research into the influence of DS on the preparation and performance of simple movements for which success requires speed and accuracy. It is generally accepted that to perform a movement task fast and accurately the body needs to be stabilized before movement of the limb (or limbs) takes place. An outcome of this "stability-then-movement" principle is the idea that fast and accurate movements are performed in a proximal-to-distal sequence. Proximal refers to closeness to the body axis (near to the center), distal to away from the body axis (e.g., arms and hands). Thus, proximal muscles contribute more to stabilizing the body in preparation for movement and distal muscles are associated with determining the path of the limb through space, such as in a "reach-and-grasp" movement. We have used reaction time and electromyography (the recording of electrical activity from muscles) to examine the performance of fast, accurate movements by individuals with DS and from age-matched participants without DS whose data serve as a control or "normal" reference. The results of our research have verified that slow reaction time is one characteristic of motor control and DS. In addition, electromyographic measures have indicated that the sequencing of muscle activation is changed in DS; in fact, it frequently appears to be reversed. Instead of a proximal-to-distal sequence, the pattern of muscle activation occurs in a distal-to-proximal order. It seems that stabilization before rapid movement is not a high priority of the motor system when DS is involved. At this time we do not have a good explanation for this experimental result and will continue to seek answers to this challenging problem. It is likely that some of the answers may be dependent on improving our understanding of how DS affects the way the brain works, and how it alters the structure of the brain itself.

References

Almeida, G.L., Corcos, D.M., & Latash, M.L. (1994). Practice and transfer effects during fast single-joint elbow movements in individuals with Down syndrome. *Physical Therapy, 74*, 1000-1012.

Anson, J.G. (1982). Memory drum theory: Alternative tests and explanations for the complexity effects on simple reaction time. *Journal of Motor Behavior, 14*, 228-246.

Anson, J.G. (1989). Effects of moment of inertia on simple reaction time. *Journal of Motor Behavior, 21*, 60-71.

Anson, J.G. (1992). Neuromotor control in Down syndrome. In J.J. Summers (Ed.), *Approaches to the study of motor control and learning* (pp. 387-412). Amsterdam: Elsevier.

Anson, J.G. (1997). Clumsy children. *New Zealand Science Monthly, 8*, 8-9.

Anson, J.G., & Davis, S.A. (1988). Neuromotor programming and Down syndrome. *International Journal of Neuroscience, 40*, 82.

Anson, J.G., & Gorely, P.J. (1990). Down syndrome: Movement control and performance variability [Abstract]. *Commonwealth and International Conference on Physical Education, Sport, Health, Dance, Recreation and Leisure.*

Anson, J.G., & Latash, M.L. (1996). Toward peaceful coexistence of adaptive central strategies and medical professionals. *Behavioral and Brain Sciences, 19*, 94-106.

Anson, J.G., & Lockie, R.M. (1996). Neuromotor reaction time in young adults with Down syndrome [Abstract]. *Bernstein's Traditions in Motor Control International Conference*, 26.

Anson, J.G., Lockie, R.M., & Mawston, G.M. (1994). Down syndrome: Persistence of distal-to-proximal sequencing. In M.L. Latash (Ed.), *Proceedings of the Second International Conference of Motor Control in Down Syndrome* (pp. 24-27). Chicago, IL: Rush-Presbyterian St. Luke's Medical Center.

Anson, J.G., & O'Connor, H.M. (1989). Down syndrome: Initiation of discrete rapid movements. *International Journal of Neuroscience, 46*, 36.

Berkson, G. (1960). An analysis of reaction times in normal and mentally retarded young men. III. Variation of stimulus and of response complexity. *Journal of Mental Deficiency Research, 4*, 69-77.

Bernstein, N.A. (1967). *The co-ordination and regulation of movements.* Oxford: Pergamon Press.

Carlesimo, G.A., Marotta, L., & Vicari, S. (1997). Long-term memory in mental retardation: Evidence for a specific impairment in subjects with Down's syndrome. *Neuropsychologia, 35,* 71-79.

Chua, R., Weeks, D.J., & Elliott, D. (1994). Cerebral specialization and motor control in adults with Down syndrome: II. Further examination and extension of the model. In M.L. Latash (Ed.), *Proceedings of the Second International Conference of Motor Control in Down Syndrome* (pp. 40-45). Chicago, IL: Rush-Presbyterian St. Luke's Medical Center.

Davis, W.E., Ward, T., & Sparrow, W.A. (1991). Fractionated reaction times and movement times of Down syndrome and other adults with mental retardation. *Adapted Physical Activity Quarterly, 8,* 221-223.

De Luca, C.J. (1997). The use of surface electromyography in biomechanics. *Journal of Applied Biomechanics, 13,* 135-163.

De Lussanet, M.H.E., & Alexander, R.M. (1997). A simple model for fast planar arm movements: Optimizing mechanical activation and moment-arms of uniarticular and biarticular arm muscles. *Journal of Theoretical Biology, 184,* 187-201.

Diaz, F., & Zuron, M. (1995). Auditory evoked potentials in Down's syndrome. *Electroencephalography and Clinical Neurophysiology, 96,* 526-537.

Donders, F.C. (1868). On the speed of mental processes. *Archives of Anatomy and Physiology,* 657-681. [referenced in Woodworth, R.S. (1938). *Experimental Psychology,* pp. 298-339. New York: Henry Holt & Co.]

Elliott, D., & Weeks, D.J. (1993). Cerebral specialization for speech perception and movement organization in adults with Down's syndrome. *Cortex, 29,* 103-113.

Elliott, D., Weeks, D.J., & Chua, R. (1994). Cerebral specialization and motor control in adults with Down syndrome: I. The development of a model. In M.L. Latash (Ed.), *Proceedings of the Second International Conference of Motor Control in Down Syndrome* (pp. 34-38). Chicago, IL: Rush-Presbyterian St. Luke's Medical Center.

Elliott, D., Weeks, D.J., & Elliott, C.L. (1987). Cerebral specialization in individuals with Down syndrome. *American Journal of Mental Retardation, 92,* 263-271.

Elliott, D., Weeks, D.J., & Gray, S. (1990). Manual and oral praxis in adults with Down's syndrome. *Neuropsychologia, 28,* 1307-1315.

Epstein, C.J. (1987). Down syndrome. In G. Adelman (Ed.), *Encyclopedia of neuroscience* (pp. 336-337). Boston, MA: Birkhauser.

Ghez, C. (1991). Voluntary movement. In E. Kandel, J.H. Schwartz, & T.M. Jessell (Eds.), *Principles of neural science* (3rd ed., pp. 609-625). New York: Elsevier.

Gorely, P.J., & Anson, J.G. (1990). Down syndrome: Fractionated simple reaction time and motor control [Abstract]. *Commonwealth and International Conference on Physical Education, Sport, Health, Dance, Recreation and Leisure.*

Helmholtz, H.v. (1850). *Philosophy Magazine,* 4, 6, 313-325. [referenced in Woodworth, R.S. (1938). *Experimental psychology,* pp. 298-339. New York: Henry Holt & Co.]

Henderson, S.E. (1985). Motor skill development. In D. Lane & B. Stratford (Eds.), *Current approaches to Down syndrome* (pp. 187-218). London: Holt, Rinehart & Winston.

Herring, R.M., & Chapman, A.E. (1992). Effects of changes in segmental values and timing of both torque and torque reversal in simulated throws. *Journal of Biomechanics, 25,* 1173-1184.

Higgott, J.M., & Anson, J.G. (1995). Effect of movement direction and extent on motor control in clumsy children. Programme and abstracts, "Understanding Movement Conference," School of Physical Education, University of Otago, 15.

Inui, N., Yamanishi, M., & Tada, S. (1995). Simple reaction times and timing of serial reactions of adolescents with mental retardation, autism, and Down syndrome. *Perceptual and Motor Skills, 81,* 739-745.

Jeannerod, M. (1988). *The neural and behavioural organization of goal-directed movements.* Oxford: Oxford University Press.

Jöris, H.J.J., Edwards van Muyen, A.J., van Ingen Schenau, G.J., & Kemper, H.C.G. (1985). Force, velocity and energy flow during the overarm throw in female handball players. *Journal of Biomechanics, 18,* 409-414.

Karst, G.M., & Hasan, Z. (1991). Timing and magnitude of electromyographic activity for two-joint arm movements in different directions. *Journal of Neurophysiology, 66,* 1594-1604.

Latash, M.L. (1992). Motor control in Down syndrome: The role of adaptation and practice. *Journal of Developmental and Physical Disabilities, 4,* 227-261.

Latash, M.L. (1994). What is clumsiness? *Proceedings of the Second International Conference of Motor Control in Down Syndrome* (pp. 68-71). Chicago, IL: Rush-Presbyterian St. Luke's Medical Center.

Latash, M.L. (Ed.). (1996). Program and abstracts, "Bernstein's Traditions in Motor Control International Conference," Pennsylvania State University, University Park, PA.

Latash, M.L., Almeida, G.L., & Corcos, D.M. (1993). Preprogrammed reactions in individuals with Down syndrome: The effects of instruction and predictability of the perturbation. *Archives of Physical Medicine and Rehabilitation, 74,* 391-399.

Latash, M.L., & Anson, J.G. (1996). What are "normal movements" in atypical populations? *Behavioral and Brain Sciences, 19,* 55-94.

LeClair, D.A., Pollock, B.J., & Elliott, D. (1993). Movement preparation in adults with and without Down syndrome. *American Journal on Mental Retardation, 97,* 628-633.

Mawston, G.A., & Anson, J.G. (1994). Down syndrome: Attention and neuromotor reaction time. *International Journal of Neuroscience, 74,* 158.

Meijer, O.G., Wagenaar, R.C., & Blankendaal, F.C.M. (1988). The hierarchy debate: Tema con veriazioni. In O.G. Meijer & K. Roth (Eds.), *Complex movement behaviour: 'The' motor action controversy* (pp. 489-561). Amsterdam: North-Holland.

Patterson, D. (1987). The causes of Down syndrome. *Scientific American, 257,* 2, 42-48.

Putnam, C.A. (1993). Sequential motions of body segments in striking and throwing skills: Descriptions and explanations. *Journal of Biomechanics, 26*(Suppl. 1), 125-135.

Reed, E.S. (1988). Applying the theory of action systems to the study of motor skills. In O.G. Meijer & K. Roth (Eds.), *Complex movement behaviour: 'The' motor action controversy* (pp. 45-86). Amsterdam: North-Holland.

Rosenbaum, D.A. (1980). Human movement initiation: Specification of arm, direction, and extent. *Journal of Experimental Psychology: General, 109,* 444-474.

Rosenbaum, D.A. (1991). *Human motor control.* Santiago, CA: Academic Press.

Rothwell, J. (1994). *Control of human voluntary movement* (2nd ed.). London: Chapman & Hall.

Schmidt, R.A. (1988). Motor and action perspectives on motor behaviour. In O.G. Meijer & K. Roth (Eds.), *Complex movement behaviour: 'The' motor action controversy* (pp. 3-44). Amsterdam: North-Holland.

Sørenson, H., Zacho, M., Simonsen, E.B., Dyhre-Poulsen, P., & Klausen, K. (1996). Dynamics of the martial arts high front kick. *Journal of Sport Sciences, 14,* 483-495.

Thelen, E. (1994). Infant motor skills: Lessons for typical and atypical development. *Proceedings of the Second International Conference of Motor Control in Down Syndrome* (pp. 84-86). Chicago, IL: Rush-Presbyterian St. Luke's Medical Center.

Turvey, M.T. (1990). Coordination. *American Psychologist, 45*, 938-953.

Tyler, A.E., & Hasan, Z. (1995). Qualitative discrepancies between trunk muscle activity and dynamic postural requirements at the initiation of reaching movements performed while sitting. *Experimental Brain Research, 107*, 87-95.

Wade, M.G. (1994). Aperiodic motor behavior in Down's syndrome: A diminished capacity to self organize. *Proceedings of the Second International Conference of Motor Control in Down Syndrome* (p. 98). Chicago, IL: Rush-Presbyterian St. Luke's Medical Center.

Wadman, W.J., Denier van der Gon, J.J., & Derksen, R.J.A. (1980). Muscle activation patterns for fast goal-directed arm movements. *Journal of Human Movement Studies, 6*, 19-37.

Woodworth, R.A. (1899). The accuracy of voluntary movement. *Psychological Review, 3*(Suppl. 2).

Woodworth, R.A. (1938). *Experimental psychology* (pp. 228-339). New York: Henry Holt & Co.

Wundt, W. (1912). *Lectures on human and animal psychology* (J.E. Creighton & E.B. Titchener, Trans.) (pp. 266-281). London: George Allen & Co. (Original work published 1868).

Author Note

Preparation of this chapter was supported in part by a grant to J. Greg Anson from the Down's Syndrome Research Fund, Chicago, Illinois. Our gratitude is expressed to the participants in the many experiments and to the following student researchers involved at various stages of this project: Suzanne Wildboar (Davis), Helen O'Connor, Patricia Gorely, Christine Worsfold, Rachel Lockie, Mark Hollands, Justine Higgott, and Clare Register.

2

CHAPTER

Control of Manual Skills in Children With Down Syndrome

Judith L. Charlton

Institute of Studies in Disability
Deakin University

Elfriede Ihsen

Swinburne University of Technology

Barbara M. Lavelle

Deakin University

Key words

manual skills ◆ prehension ◆ grasping ◆ brain structure ◆ motor learning ◆ movement planning ◆ movement kinematics

It is widely accepted that individuals with Down syndrome (DS) experience diffi-culty performing motor skills. The impact of these performance difficulties is wide-spread, affecting achievement in academic settings in tasks such as writing and using a keyboard, and compromising efficiency in employment and recreational opportu-nities. One of the strong motivations for our program of research on motor behavior in children with DS is the maximization of participation of individuals in school, home, and community life. Our work has been concerned with everyday manipu-lative skills and their adaptive performance under different contextual conditions, which, arguably, are critical for achieving independence and full participation in all aspects of life. This work has explored the fundamental nature of movement diffi-culties in DS within the framework of a Coordinated Control Program for reach-to-grasp actions (Arbib, 1981; Hoff & Arbib, 1993) and has been guided by current research describing the kinematic characteristics and neurological correlates of upper-limb control in prehension (Jeannerod, 1981, 1984, 1997; Jeannerod & Rosetti, 1993). Later in this chapter we introduce the model of coordinated control for reaching and grasping and describe its application to the study of motor difficulties in DS. First, we provide a brief overview of development across a number of do-mains, highlighting the nature of the developmental path, areas of atypicality, and the influence of multiple constraints on motor performance in individuals with DS.

Development of Abilities in Children With Down Syndrome

A widely held view in the literature on people with DS is that their motor skills are *quantitatively* different from age-matched, normally developing peers, leading to the premise that in DS, motor skills are, quite simply, developmentally delayed. A contrasting perspective is that motor performance in DS is *qualitatively* different. In much of the literature describing motor control in individuals with DS, proponents of both views have hinted at specific delay or deficits in the motor system per se, while others have speculated that difficulties in movement performance are associ-ated with, and consequential to, cognitive delay or dysfunction (e.g., Latash, 1993). Our approach takes the view that the acquisition and performance of motor skills in everyday life are influenced by a complex interplay between domains intrinsic to the individual (e.g., biomechanical properties of the performer, the state of the central nervous system and its constituent cognitive, perceptual, and motor capaci-ties) as well as external variables in the individual's environment, such as the context within which the performance occurs and the richness of the learning environment. In the following review, we present representative work that touches on some of the cognitive, perceptual, and motor variables that interact to create a complex pattern of development in individuals with DS.

Developmental psychologists and clinicians involved in early intervention have long been interested in the achievement of developmental milestones. For example, it is generally acknowledged that 90% of normally developing infants can sit without support by 7.8 months and can stand alone by 13.0 months (Sigelman & Shaffer, 1995). By age 4 to 5 months, successful visually guided reaching emerges from the more primitive and spontaneous prereaching movements of the neonate (Hofsten 1984; Hofsten & Ronnqvist 1993; Thelen, Corbetta, Kamm, & Spencer, 1993). Around 9 months, infants begin to use limb gestures as part of their vocabulary of communication: first reaching, then indicative pointing (Berndt, 1997). Such achievements in normally developing infants are commonly used for comparative and diagnostic judgments in assessing children with disabilities. Literature describing the development of children with DS abounds with comparative information on achievement of milestones. For example, in a longitudinal study of infants with DS from 4 weeks of age, Cunningham (1979, cited in Thombs & Sugden, 1991) reported marked delays in development of accurate reaching. Cunningham also reported that infants with DS were less likely to manipulate and explore objects once grasped and that they were less adept at adjusting hand shape to match object size and shape. These qualitative differences were attributed to differences in use of visual feedback. Hogg and Moss (1983) have demonstrated that this pattern of development of hand function persists into childhood years in DS, with delayed acquisition of a mature precision grasp reported across the age span from 15 to 44 months.

In the gross motor domain, Ulrich and Ulrich (1993) have reported delays in the emergence of alternating stepping patterns prior to unassisted walking. They suggest that this may in part be attributed to asynchronous development of contributing action patterns such as diminished spontaneous leg kicking observed in infants aged 4 to 7 months. Infants with DS are also reported to be delayed by 6 months in sitting, and an even greater lag of 10 months is evident in unsupported standing (Cowie, 1970). Cowie's findings reflect a common theme reported across many areas of cognitive and motor development, that children with DS lag further and further behind their normally developing peers as they get older (Block, 1991; Henderson, 1985; Hodapp & Zigler, 1990).

The lag in achievement of postures has been variously attributed to hypotonicity (flaccidity) of muscles (Henderson, 1985) and to impaired visual and vestibular processes specifying autonomous control of postural stability (Cichetti & Beeghly, 1990). However, in the light of evidence for diminution in hypotonicity with increasing age (Morris, Vaughan, & Vaccaro, 1982; Owens, Dawson, & Losin, 1971), it is unlikely that muscle flaccidity alone explains early motor delays, nor the persistence of motor coordination difficulties and widening gap in motor performance with increased age.

This developmental disparity between DS and normally developing children is likely to have far-reaching consequences and is a matter of concern for educators. For example, delayed postural and locomotor skills, in addition to cognitive delays, may further limit the child's ability to interact with the environment and to explore space and manipulate objects from a stable frame of reference (Cichetti & Beeghly, 1990). Moreover, there is a likelihood that delays in postural development may impinge on aspects of intellectual development such as the understanding of properties and uses of objects. This strongly points to a need for intensive intervention very early in infant development and urges researchers to continue the search for an explanation of the sources of such delay.

While recognizing the delay in the development of a number of milestones, many researchers have claimed that milestones nevertheless emerge in an orderly and typical sequence across several domains of sensorimotor functioning, including the motor domain (Hodapp & Zigler, 1990). However, there is an increasing awareness that the pattern of cognitive and motor skills development in DS is almost certainly more complex than this. In the motor domain, Dyer and colleagues have reported evidence that children with DS achieve some motor milestones in a different sequence from that of normally developing infants (Dyer, Gunn, Rauh, & Berry, 1990). The authors attributed this atypical sequence to impairment of prerequisite skills (standing, locomotion, etc.) that are dependent on muscle strength and balance and that are likely to be influenced in a detrimental way by hypotonia and joint hypermobility.

There is also considerable evidence for wide individual differences in motor development among children with DS. For example, while we might expect a normally developing child to walk sometime between the ages of 9 and 17 months (Berk, 1996), for children with DS the age of mastery of walking is highly variable, between 13 and 48 months (Henderson, 1985). In their analysis of motor milestones leading to mature locomotion patterns, Lienert and Rauh (1993) found large individual differences in time intervals between stages of development, particularly in the transition from locomotion close to the ground to unassisted walking. Furthermore, the authors report that some infants with DS used very different forms of locomotion, such as rolling and shuffling while sitting, before achieving a more mature pattern.

The complexity of this developmental pattern is also exhibited in what is described as differences in the *structure* of cognitive and sensorimotor functioning. That is, children with DS have been found to exhibit particular difficulties in certain areas (e.g., linguistic skills; visual scanning; and the ability to attend to, discriminate, and encode complex stimuli) compared with their overall level of mental functioning (Hodapp & Zigler, 1990). Hogg and Moss (1983) found that while children with DS attained the same scores as mental age-matched peers on the Bayley Scales of Infant Development, their pattern of performance across test items was quite different, with children with DS performing relatively well on language and less well on fine motor items. An earlier study (Moss & Hogg, 1981) found that this unevenness across language and motor performance had disappeared by age 7 years. Work by Cobo-Lewis, Oller, Lynch, and Levine (1996) also illustrates this lack of uniformity in the development of motor and vocal skills in infants with DS. They showed severe delays in stepping, standing, creeping, and rolling and reaching, but less severe delays in rhythmic behaviors such as babbling and hand-banging.

Recent research using systematic longitudinal methods has also contributed to our understanding of the complex structure of development in DS and has questioned the long-held view of an orderly sequence. For example, Dunst (1990) and

Wishart (1993) have shown that children with DS exhibit a significant lack of stability in achieving sensorimotor skills and cognitive skills such as development of object concept. Object concept, referring to knowledge about object properties and the principles governing simple events involving objects, is thought to be a key predictor of subsequent developmental rate. In the study by Wishart, she reports that after demonstrating success in finding a hidden object, infants with DS showed frequent failures. Thus, new skills had been acquired but could not be reliably produced. In contrast, normally developing children rarely showed reversals in competence following acquisition. It is possible that there may be a connection between unstable patterns of performance reported in these studies of early development and evidence for high within-subject variability in performance of motor skills reported in adults with DS, and in our own work with children with DS (e.g., Anson, 1989, 1992; Charlton, Ihsen, & Oxley, 1996, 1998). Together, these findings suggest a pattern of inefficient learning and developmental instability that "undermine[s] the progress of development in DS and result[s] in their development following markedly different pathways to those seen in normal development" (Wishart, 1993, p. 393).

Other work by Wishart and colleagues (Franco & Wishart, 1995) confirms the notion of atypical structure of development of intelligence in DS and casts further doubt on the idea of an orderly sequence of development in DS. Their longitudinal studies of gestural communication skills showed that children with DS exhibited the same patterns of pointing and reaching behaviors but at a later chronological age compared to normally developing children. However, compared to developmental age-equivalent peers, children with DS showed advanced use of gesture and checking behavior (i.e., frequent use of head/eye orienting to check if the recipient is attending) for communication. The authors proposed that this may reflect a chosen strategy to maximize efficiency in gestural communication to compensate for an absence of expressive language skills. This study also highlights the interaction of development in the cognitive and motor domains and illustrates how an understanding of the purpose and consequence of one's voluntary actions can influence the frequency of and presumably the level of success in skill performance.

Brain Structure and Function in Down Syndrome

The pattern of delay and unequal development of skills in different domains is consistent with emerging evidence from the neurosciences demonstrating atypical brain structure and organization in individuals with DS. New techniques in neuroimaging have begun to reveal an intricate pattern of differences in cerebral structure in DS. This work adds an important dimension to our understanding of brain-behavior relations in general and of cognitive and motor difficulties in DS in particular.

Recent studies using magnetic resonance imaging (MRI) scans have revealed that individuals with DS typically have a smaller overall brain volume, including significant reductions in both cerebrum and cerebellum (Aylward, Habbah, War-ren, Pulsifer, Barta, Jerram, & Pearlson, 1997; Jernigan & Bellugi, 1990; Jernigan, Bellugi, Sowell, Doherty, & Hesselink, 1993). Neuropathological evidence sug-gests that observed differences in brain structure are not present in utero but rather emerge during early development due to retarded growth patterns (Raz, Torres, Briggs, Spencer, Thornton, Loken, Gunning, McQuain, Driesen, & Acker, 1995). One feature of this early delay in neural development is a delay in myeli-nation of neurons in the central nervous system. The functional importance of myelin is to enhance the speed and efficiency of transmission of information along neural pathways. Using MRI scans, Koo and colleagues reported a delay in my-elination of approximately 9–11 months in an infant with DS (Koo, Blaser, Harwood-Nash, Becker, & Murphy, 1992). Typical development of myelination has been well documented, with the pattern proceeding from posterior to anterior and inferior to superior brain areas, and with maturation being achieved between 18 and 24 months. In the 18-month-old child studied by Koo and colleagues, myeli-nation had developed only in the brain stem, cerebellum, corpus callosum, and parts of the internal capsule, but not in the cerebral cortex. The authors noted that the degree of myelination delay correlated well with the observed cognitive delay. It is also noteworthy that delayed myelination in the cortex, reported in this study, implicates transcortical pathways, and it is possible that this delay might underlie atypicality in the development of motor milestones in children with DS. While the authors did not identify specific cortical pathways that may be affected, these are likely to include connections from visual, auditory, and somasthetic modalities to the prefrontal cortex and connections between prefrontal, premotor, and primary motor cortex, all of which play an important role in motor control of hand func-tion. These claims warrant further investigation with larger samples of subjects using longitudinal neurobehavioral studies across the age span when key motor skills are emerging.

Other white matter anomalies in individuals with DS also have been reported, including narrower corpus callosum (Wang, Doherty, Hesselink, & Bellugi, 1992). Wang and colleagues propose that this may have significance for the transfer of semantic information across hemispheres. They also note that the corpus callosum provides important projections to the frontal lobe and suggest that differences in its structure may account for frontal dysfunctions reported in the literature, such as poor verbal fluency, perseveration, and difficulty in problem-solving.

Differences in cortical volume and pathways noted above may also underlie the model of atypical cerebral organization of language and motor skills, put forward by Elliott and Weeks and their colleagues (Elliott & Weeks, 1993; Elliott, Weeks, & Chua, 1994; Elliott, Weeks, & Elliott, 1987; Weeks, Chua, Elliott, Lyons, & Pollock, 1995). Based on evidence from a series of experiments manipulating mode of information input for performance, their model proposes that while left-hemi-sphere specialization for organization and control of sequential motor response is similar in DS and in nondisabled adults, there appears to be an atypical left-ear/right-hemisphere advantage for the perception of speech sounds in DS. In one study, the authors describe a discrepancy between motor performance to verbal instruction compared with motor performance to visual demonstration (Elliott, Weeks, & Gray, 1990). These findings have significant consequences for motor skill acquisition and important implications for instructional strategies for individuals with DS.

A key feature of brain structure associated with DS is that neural deficits are multifocal rather than generalized (Raz et al., 1995). This is consistent with evidence of unequal pockets of skill development described in the developmental literature. Several studies have reported localized areas of reduced volume, including frontal cortex, limbic areas, cerebellum, and hippocampus and significant left-right cerebral asymmetries in the limbic region and a larger parahippocampal gyrus (Jernigan et al., 1993; Kesslak, Nagata, Lott, & Nalcioglu, 1994; Raz et al., 1995). The significance of differences in brain volume of these structures is currently not well understood. However, frontal findings are consistent with neurobehavioral evidence for abnormalities in event-related potentials over frontal cortex in children with DS, implicating frontal-attentional processes for visual tasks (Karrer, Wojtascek, & Davis, 1995). Similarly, atypical hippocampal volume is consistent with RT and ERP findings showing slowed speed of orienting to and categorizing auditory information, and impairments in immediate auditory memory (Lincoln, Courchesne, Kilman, & Galambos, 1985). Raz and colleagues have also reported that while overall brain volume is not significantly correlated with intelligence and linguistic performance, a strong negative relation exists between volume of the parahippocampal gyrus and Performance IQ.

The findings from neurological studies reported above leave little doubt that there are significant structural differences in the central nervous system associated with DS. Nevertheless, there are many gaps in our understanding of the functional significance of these neurological anomalies. Moreover, atypical cerebral structure accounts only in part for atypical motor performance in DS. We emphasize, as have others who take an ecological perspective (e.g., Thelen et al., 1993), the importance of other influences, such as the environmental context within which the individual moves and the accumulated past experiences the performer brings to the learning setting. An example of this is the obvious and documented benefits that enriched environments (e.g., home versus institutional care) have on the development and functioning of individuals with DS (see Dunst, 1990, for a review).

Notwithstanding the complexities of the influence of central and environmental factors on behavior, the atypicalities in brain structure and function described above contribute substance to the proposition that the pattern of development in DS is not simply delayed in a uniform way, but is *different* than that of other children. Both behavioral and biological evidence suggests a patchwork of atypicality in structure and function in individuals with DS across the childhood and adult years. Notably, we see that delay in development across different skill domains is by no means equivalent. A lack of stability in achievement of milestones (e.g., Dunst, 1990; Wishart, 1993) and individual differences in skill acquisition and performance are also noteworthy features (Henderson, 1985).

Much of the research on development of children with DS has been influenced by traditional approaches in developmental and cognitive psychology. The primary focus of this work has been the development of sensorimotor stages and cognitive and language functions. In the motor domain, although we have learned a great deal from systematic observations and descriptive accounts of achievement of motor milestones, the sensitivity of motor measures used has been relatively crude. With the development over the past two decades of paradigms and measurement tools arising from motor learning and motor control theory, it is now possible to provide insights into the mechanisms and processes underlying motor skill development in DS. We outline some of the important findings from this area in the following section.

Motor Learning and Motor Control in Down Syndrome

A pervasive feature of motor skill performance in children with DS, and which persists through adulthood, is slowness of movement (e.g., Davis & Kelso, 1982; Henderson, Morris, & Frith, 1981; O'Brien & Hayes, 1989). In general, although children with DS learn to walk, reach and grasp objects, feed themselves, and many other fundamental skills, their movements lack precision, appear poorly coordinated, and are less efficient than movements of normally developing children (Block, 1991; Henderson, 1985). Compared to normal controls, children and adults with DS have been found to be slower and more variable in reaction time tasks (Anson, 1989, 1992; O'Brien & Hayes, 1989) and are less able to modulate actions under changing task conditions, such as grasp forces and postural responses (Cole, Abbs, & Turner, 1988; Shumway-Cook & Woollacott, 1985). Individuals with DS also exhibit aberrant sequencing of movements of different parts of the arm and hand (Anson, 1992) and have poorer control of the timing and force production of actions (Davis & Kelso, 1982; Latash & Corcos, 1991).

A number of hypotheses have been suggested to explain differences in motor function in DS. One popular claim is that the source of motor difficulties in DS may be attributed to a deficit in the central representation of actions. This hypothesis was investigated by Henderson and colleagues who compared the performance of children with DS; non-DS retarded children; and normally developing, mental age-matched controls on continuous tracking and drawing tasks (Henderson et al., 1981). Their findings showed that children with DS had no difficulty with spatial aspects of the task, but showed significant impairment in temporal features of tracking. The results were not consistent with an overall slowness of movement. Rather, it was suggested that difficulties exhibited by children with DS were likely to result from an inability to use regular and predictable environmental information to form an accurate internal model.

The weight of evidence from studies of motor performance and development, reviewed above, suggests a diverse pattern of motor difficulties in DS. However, it is unlikely that we will find an explanation for these performance deficits by searching for isolated features of atypicality, such as poor muscle tone or localized central deficits in perceptual and cognitive processing. A more useful theoretical framework for the study of motor problems associated with DS involves the idea that actions are controlled by a number of functional systems distributed in the central nervous system and that they may be differentially influenced by the environmental context in which they are performed.

In the next section of the chapter, we review current theoretical perspectives on motor control of hand function. We present a well-known model of coordinated control for reaching and grasping actions (Arbib, 1981) and review some of the empirical work on which the model is based and other work describing the characteristics of the reach-to-grasp in individuals with and without impairments. We explain how we have used the model to guide our own work in seeking to understand the control mechanisms and the effects of contextual cues that might underlie poor manipulative skills in children with DS.

A Model for the Reach-to-Grasp Action

Over the last decade there has been a great deal of interest in the control characteristics of the reach-to-grasp action. Much of this work has stemmed from the seminal studies of Jeannerod (1981, 1984), who first described prehension actions in terms of two component parts: a transport component, bringing the hand to the vicinity of the target object, and a manipulation component in which fingers opened in preparation for and then closed to form a grasp enabling pickup of the object. The transport component includes an initial ballistic, preprogrammed phase prior to peak velocity. This is followed by a low-velocity phase as the hand homes in on the object, during which small adjustments (reaccelerations) are observed in the hand trajectory. It is frequently assumed that these adjustments are the result of on-line use of visual information. However, corrections have been reported even in the absence of vision, or when the target object is visible but the hand is not, suggesting a role of other modes of sensory feedback (e.g., haptic and proprioceptive) (Chua & Elliott, 1993; Jeannerod, 1984; Pratt & Abrams, 1996).

An important contribution to our understanding of these processes is provided in Arbib's (1981) model of a coordinated control system describing Jeannerod's empirical data. Arbib postulated that perceptual schemas serve to provide information about object location in space and about object properties of size and shape and object orientation in relation to the grasping hand. These perceptual schemas activate motor schemas, corresponding to the reach (transport) and grasp (preshape and hand orientation) subcomponents of prehension.

Intuitively, the reach and the grasp must be coordinated in space and time to the extent that the fingers do not close before the hand reaches the object. The early version of the Coordinated Control Program for prehension (Arbib, 1981, 1985) described a temporal relation between reach and grasp schema. This was based on Jeannerod's early work showing a correlation between the slow phase of the hand transport (reach) and the final phase of the manipulation component (grasp) as the fingers enclosed the object. Support for the proposition of a time-based mechanism connecting reach and grasp components has eluded researchers. Furthermore, such a mechanism likely involves both spatial and temporal elements. Evidence for this kind of coordination comes from research showing that when performers reach for objects quickly, they open their fingers wider than when reaching at a slow pace (Wing, Turton, & Fraser, 1986).

Recent studies involving the perturbation of task information relevant for either the reach (object location) or the grasp (object size) have shown convincing evidence for a bidirectional time-based relation between the two components. For example, Paulignan and colleagues showed that perturbation of object location at movement onset results in corrections (prolongation) not only in the limb transport component, but also in temporal aspects of grasping, with finger closure time significantly reduced. Similarly, parameters of both the reach and grasp were modified when object size was perturbed (Paulignan, Jeannerod, MacKenzie, & Marteniuk, 1991; Paulignan, MacKenzie, Marteniuk, & Jeannerod, 1991). Based on this evidence, Hoff and Arbib (1993) refined Arbib's earlier model to include a two-way interaction between control of the reach and grasp schemas. Essentially, the new model proposes that the component that is predicted to take longer (i.e., either the reach or grasp schema), as determined by feedback controllers, is given the full time it needs while the other is slowed down.

Much of our understanding of the control of prehension has come from the study of visuomotor control of hand function in animals and humans with localized brain lesions and in healthy individuals. Converging evidence from this work points to the organization of control for reach-to-grasp actions being distributed across multiple domains within the central nervous system. Key cortical areas include (1) *motor cortex*, implicated in the control of independent finger movement required for grasping; (2) *prefrontal cortex*, which forms part of a circuit thought to be involved in planning of goal-directed actions based on intentions, prior knowledge, and instructions; (3) *premotor cortex*, in which neurons encode both performance and observation of others' performance of specific types of grasp, as well as the semantic context of action sequences (e.g., see Rizzolatti, Fadiga, Gallese, & Fogassi, 1996); and (4) *parietal cortex*, which plays a role in control of the reach and preshaping of the hand (see Jeannerod, 1997, for a comprehensive review).

Jeannerod and Rosetti (1993) have proposed two visuomotor channels linking important posterior and anterior cortical regions involved in reach-to-grasp actions. One channel is associated with the reach component and provides relevant information corresponding to the extrinsic properties of objects, such as location in space and speed of motion. These properties are required for computation of distance and direction of points in space with respect to the performer's body and are critical for accurately specifying the ballistic component directing the limb to the target. The second channel provides information relating to intrinsic object properties of size, texture, shape, and other features relevant to the control of preshaping the fingers for preparation and execution of the grasp. Neural correlates of the two visuomotor systems have been proposed, with fundamental reliance on "dorsal" pathways linking posterior parietal cortex with the premotor cortex. Pathways for reaching connect the parieto-occipital extrastriate area with the dorsal premotor cortex in area 6. The pathway for grasping connects the dorsal extrastriate cortex and ventral premotor cortex in area 6 (Jeannerod, 1997).

Evidence for the dissociation of pathways for control of reaching and grasping actions comes from recent work by Chieffi and colleagues (Chieffi, Gentilucci, Allport, Sasso, & Rizzolatti, 1993), Goodale and colleagues (Goodale, Meenan, Bulthoff, Nicolle, Murphy, & Racicot, 1994), and Jeannerod, Decety, and Michel (1994). In patient MM, who had a right parietal lesion and left-sided neglect, Chieffi's group demonstrated significant deviations in the reaching trajectory but no change in the kinematics of grasp properties. In contrast, patients RV (Goodale et al., 1994) and AT (Jeannerod et al., 1994), who both had bilateral occipito-parietal lesions, exhibited relatively well-preserved reaching kinematics but significant difficulties in grasping, especially evident when picking up small objects. Awkward grasp patterns were reported, with an exaggerated aperture and object contact occurring on the underside of the digits or palm rather than fingertips. These difficulties stood in contrast to preserved ability to make perceptual judgments of object size and shape. Jeannerod proposed that the grasp deficits of AT were specific to dorsal pathways for goal-directed grasping under visual guidance, rather than to cortical areas involved in object discrimination per se. Furthermore, because AT and RV had recovered from earlier reaching deficits, it was claimed that the grasping deficit could not merely be a consequence of a reaching deficit. Rather, this was a distinguishable deficit in its own right.

An interesting observation made in Jeannerod's study was that patient AT performed significantly better when grasping real, familiar objects rather than cylinders, suggesting a role of stored information about object properties of size, shape, and function. Jeannerod and others have described this distinction between simple, "pragmatic" tasks (e.g., grasping different cylinders) and functional tasks that are centrally represented at a symbolic or "semantic" level (Jeannerod, 1997; Jeannerod et al., 1994). The latter are likely to rely on pathways connecting intraparietal cortex and ventral premotor areas (Grafton, Fagg, Woods, & Arbib, 1996).

A critical feature of mature reaching and grasping is the ability to adapt our actions to suit the context of the task. Arbib's model (1981; Hoff & Arbib, 1993) predicts how intrinsic properties of objects specify the most appropriate type of grasp (e.g., small objects require precision grasps while larger objects might demand a whole-hand grasp). Semantic knowledge of task goals and object properties might also determine the posture of our hand as we grasp an object in preparation for subsequent use (e.g., a pen is likely to be grasped differently for writing than when the intention is to move it from one side of our desk to another). Several researchers have explored the constraints that influence the reach-and-grasp action in normal, healthy adults as well as in groups with specific brain lesions (e.g., Gentilucci, Castiello, Corradini, Scarpa, Umiltà, & Rizzolatti, 1991; Marteniuk, MacKenzie, Jeannerod, Athenes, & Dugas, 1987). Compared with earlier studies that simply monitor measures of movement outcome (e.g., reaction time, movement time, and error scores), these studies used kinematic measures to provide a detailed analysis of the reach and grasp in space and time. Therefore they tell us more about the quality of the movement of the hand and fingers. Trajectories can be compared across different task conditions, across groups of individuals with and without impairment, and across repeated trials, providing information about the impact of various constraining factors on movement.

One of the key findings, first reported by Marteniuk et al. (1987), is known as the "precision effect." It is characterized by a longer proportion of total movement time the hand spends in decelerating toward the object, a widening of the maximum grasp aperture (gap between the thumb and index fingers), and an increase in time to complete grasp closure. These effects have been demonstrated across a wide range of object and task variables: for example, small compared to large objects, more fragile objects compared with nonfragile objects, and tasks requiring careful placing rather than throwing following object pickup (Marteniuk et al., 1987; Marteniuk, Leavitt, MacKenzie, & Athenes, 1990).

We have used an adaptation of these techniques and paradigms to guide our studies of reaching and grasping in children with DS. Details of these studies are reported elsewhere (Charlton et al., 1996, 1998). In the following section we provide a summary of this work as well as some new results based on further analyses of the same studies and from work in progress.

Performance of Reaching and Grasping in Individuals With Down Syndrome

In ongoing work in our laboratories, we are investigating reach-to-grasp actions in children with DS (age 8-10 years) and in two control groups of normally developing children matched in developmental age and chronological age. Reach-and-grasp trajectories are tracked using a 3-D Optotrak optical motion tracking system and a 2-D videotape camera system. In two studies reported to date (Charlton et al., 1996, 1998), we have manipulated intrinsic properties of objects (small and large size) and task goals—that is, what must be done with the object once it is grasped (e.g., pick up object, place object in designated position, or throw object into a large container). Following the work of Marteniuk and colleagues (1987, 1990), the resulting six experimental conditions reflect differences in precision demands (small versus large objects and placing versus throwing) as well as in the level of contextual cues available. For example, in our first experiment, a stick to be picked up provided minimal contextual information about task goal compared with a peg and pegboard and a rocket of the same size that was to be thrown into a box decorated to represent "outer space." This distinction between grasping a stick and the two conditions involving pegs and rockets also allowed us to examine performance of pragmatic versus semantic or symbolic tasks (Jeannerod, 1997).

Our studies predicted that evidence for adaptive control would be seen in systematic changes in reaching and grasping that are appropriate to critical object properties and task goals in the same way as has been described for adult prehension. The general assumption underlying these studies is that if children with DS have difficulty accessing or using information about object or task-specific cues, they might resort to a generalized schema for all reaching and grasping actions. Alternatively, children with DS may show random variation in reaching and grasping movements from trial to trial, with no evidence of use of an effective schema.

Additionally, following the theme elaborated in an earlier section of this chapter, we were interested in whether children with DS would show patterns of reaching and grasping that were *qualitatively different* from those of normally developing children, or alternatively, whether their actions would merely show *delay*. In particular, we proposed to further explore the findings of key studies of hand function in which individuals with DS have been found to exhibit delays in achieving a mature precision grasp and deficits in the ability to adapt grasp shape and grip forces to critical object properties (Cole et al., 1988; Cunningham, 1979; Hogg & Moss, 1983). Lastly, our experimental measures allowed us to examine whether differences or delays are more prominent in features of the transport component or the grasp component, which might provide some insight into the two underlying channels for visuomotor control for reach and grasp schemas.

Results for Reaching

First, we present a summary of the findings for the transport component of the initial reach-to-grasp action in our studies. Results from our two studies show that compared to control children, children with DS reach and grasp more slowly, with longer overall movement times and reduced peak speed. Performance of children with DS was more like that of the developmentally equivalent group. In addition, we found that measures of intra-subject variability in movement time were significantly greater in children with DS compared with both young and older control groups. In our first experiment (Charlton et al., 1996), movement times for reaching movements of all children were influenced by object properties and task goals, but there were no clear and consistent group differences. Movements for all children were faster for the large object and when precision demands of the task goal were lowest (i.e., throwing the large rocket following pickup). Children with DS were also found to be least variable in peak speed for the actions involving pickup of the rocket.

In general, our finding for slowness of reaching in the overall movement time indicates a delay consistent with developmental age. Additional support for this was shown in a recent longitudinal study comparing reaching kinematics in infants with and without DS (Cadoret & Beuter, 1997). This study showed that while performance of disabled infants was similar to normally developing infants matched in developmental age at 7 and 5 months, respectively, an increasing lag was observed in the ability of infants with DS to generate arm velocity across the age span 7-11 months.

Earlier in this chapter we noted that slowness appears to be a pervasive feature of DS in a range of motor tasks. Thus, our findings of overall slowing and reduced peak speeds in reaching were not especially surprising. However, our findings extend previous work by showing that in children with DS, overall timing of the reach appears to be influenced by object properties and task goals in much the same way as in normally developing children, with some evidence for more typical performance when precision demands were relatively low.

Of greater interest, we suggest, are the internal timing parameters of the reach—that is, time before and after peak speed. These measures are important because they reflect the symmetry of the trajectory. After time-normalizing the trajectories to account for significant discrepancies in overall movement time of DS and control groups, we looked for differences in the relative proportions of time spent in the ballistic, preprogrammed phase, and the deceleration phase. In our first study (Charlton et al., 1996), we found that children with DS spent a greater time in deceleration than both younger and older control children (58%, 52%, and 41%, respectively), although differences between those with DS and participants of a similar developmental age did not reach significance. Intra-subject variability mirrored this same pattern of results across groups. We failed to find differences for time in deceleration for object size or task context, with the exception that children with DS seemed to perform more consistently when reaching for the object to be thrown. The absence of a precision effect on this internal timing parameter may be partly explained by insufficiently distinct grasping surfaces of the two object sizes used. That is, differences in precision demands associated with object size were not as great as those used in adult reach-to-grasp studies (Marteniuk et al., 1987). In our second study (Charlton et al., 1998), using the similar experimental manipulations as described for our first study, we adopted two disks of substantially different sizes (a lolly, 1.5 cm in diameter, and a biscuit, either 7 cm and 9 cm in diameter, assigned according to subject's hand size). Here, we found the expected precision effects in the relative time spent in deceleration in normally developing children. However, preliminary analyses for two children with DS showed no clear pattern of performance across contextual conditions. This is likely to be explained by the considerable within-subject variability and individual differences in their trajectory formation.

In both studies, we have found that reaches of the older control children were smooth during deceleration time. That is, additional accelerations and decelerations or movement units following peak speed were rarely observed. In contrast, trajectories of the reaching movements of children with DS were extremely jerky and highly variable from trial to trial (based on analyses of standard deviations across nine trials for each condition). Movements of the younger control children were somewhat smoother than those of children with DS but more irregular than those of older children. Latash (1993) reported similar findings for adults with DS who exhibited very different kinematic trajectories on consecutive trials on a simple, single-joint motor task: some smooth and others with many irregularities.

Our data for children with DS showing slowness, extended time in deceleration, and jerkiness of limb transport are consistent with the interpretation that they are unable to generate an appropriate schema for reaching. Consequently they are unable to execute efficient and accurate reaches. Their reaches are spatially variable and inaccurate, and therefore are likely to require greater reliance on feedback guidance to correct spatial inaccuracies. This, in turn, may account for increases in the duration of the reach and, more particularly, the duration of the deceleration phase.

We investigated the possibility of spatial error in the path of the hand during reaching by examining variability in end-point accuracy. These analyses of reaching data from our early study, not previously published, showed significantly higher end-point variability across all conditions in children with DS compared with both younger and older control children. Differences between young and older children were not reliable (70 mm, 38 mm, and 19 mm for the DS, the developmentally young, and the older control subjects, respectively). Thus, end-point variability is a prominent feature of reaching behavior in children with DS, with significant differences much greater than what would be predicted for their developmental age. This finding contrasts the work by Latash (1993), who found smaller end-point variability in adults with DS than in nondisabled control subjects for single-joint elbow-flexion tasks. It is possible that differences in the two sets of findings may be accounted for by (1) different task goals—for example, differences in precision demands and the requirements for manipulation of objects; (2) differences in task complexity (single- versus multijoint actions); and/or (3) differences in participant characteristics such as chronological and mental age.

Based on Arbib's model, the spatial variability described in our study fits comfortably with the notion of a deficit in reaching schema that relies on extrinsic object properties specifying object location. An alternative explanation that we previously proposed to explain our reported differences in temporal aspects of reaching is that slowness and longer deceleration time might be a manifestation of a primary deficit in grasping (Charlton et al., 1996, 1998). This would be predicted by the time-based interaction component of prehension described by Hoff and Arbib (1993). For example, one might expect that increased spatial variability of reaching might be associated with a wider maximum grasp aperture and longer time in grasp closure. That is, a wider opening of the fingers may compensate for errors in direction of the reach. In our second study, we have not found any evidence to support this. In fact, maximum aperture and time in closure in children with DS were almost always smaller than in both young and older children. However, this is not to say that, as illustrated in the case of patients AT and RV described earlier, deficits in reaching and grasping may occur in their own right (Goodale et al., 1994; Jeannerod et al., 1994). These competing hypotheses need to be explored further in two ways: first looking at spatial variability at the end of each movement unit to determine whether the first, preprogrammed phase is responsible for the spatial error; and second, using systematic perturbations of object location as well as object size, as described by Paulignan and colleagues (1991, 1991).

Results for Grasping

In our initial reaching study, we did not measure kinematic characteristics of the grasp. We have, however, conducted further testing and analyses of videotaped performances of grasping patterns from this study, which have not been reported previously. These analyses involved the classification of grasp styles (precision grasp versus whole-hand grasp) by two independent raters. In total, approximately 50 grasps were analyzed for each of 12 children with DS (age 8-10 years), 6 normally developing children matched for developmental age (4-5 years of age), and 8 older control children matched for chronological age. Overall, children with DS used a pincer grasp less frequently than children of the same chronological age (70% and 91%, respectively), but their performance was similar to that of younger children (63%). A further analysis of performance across the six task conditions revealed interesting similarities and differences between groups. For example, older children used a pincer grasp on approximately 95% of trials for both small and large objects in the tasks involving placement or throwing following pickup. This probably reflects their awareness that a precision grasp would allow greater flexibility for the fingers to manipulate the object in order to complete the second phase of the action (place or throw). Similarly, both children with DS and younger control children adopted a precision grasp on almost 90% of placing and throwing trials using the small object. However, for the large object, these two groups used a precision grip on fewer than half the trials (47% and 43% for DS and younger control children, respectively). Only 2 of the 12 children with DS and 1 of the 6 young children did not show this pattern. This finding suggests that with respect to the *selection* of grasp type, both DS and younger children were more influenced by the intrinsic property of object size (i.e., they predominantly selected precision grasps for small objects and whole-hand grasps for larger objects) rather than by current contextual cues (or stored prior knowledge) about semantic features such as the function of the object and task goals.

These results are consistent with other studies examining patterns of grasping in younger children with DS. Moss and Hogg (1981) found that children with DS (up to 4 years of age) used mature precision grasps only about half as frequently as their age-matched peers. In a second study, Hogg and Moss (1983) compared performances of children with DS (15-44 months) and mental age-matched peers on the same peg grasp-and-place task. The results of this study showed little difference between the two groups in the emerging use of the mature precision grasp, suggesting that, at least in the early childhood years, there is a delay rather than difference in the development of hand function. Our findings suggest that this delay persists into middle childhood years.

In our second study we analyzed kinematic features of the grasp component for 16 normally developing children (8 younger and 8 older) and two children with DS. As described above, children performed reach-to-grasp actions with two sizes of objects, a small lolly (a Smartie) and a large biscuit, and, following pickup, either carefully placed the object in a designated position or dropped it into a container.

Kinematic analyses of grasps showed that all children adjusted the size of their grasp appropriate to object size. This adds support to the findings for grasp selection and suggests that children with DS are able to use intrinsic properties of object size, at least for some spatial aspects of the grasp. In addition, the normally developing children exhibited the classic precision effect in the temporal components of the grasp. That is, they spent a relatively longer time in closure of the fingers following maximum aperture for small than for large objects and for placing compared with throwing following pickup. In general, compared with both young and older normally developing children, the two children with DS spent a considerably smaller proportion of time in grasp closure. Both children exhibited a high degree of variability from trial to trial in the timing of grasp preshape, and also showed a number of irregularities (opening and closing the grasp aperture) reflecting corrections in the grasp size throughout the action. This was particularly evident when grasping the small object. Thus, notwithstanding the findings that children with DS were able to select grasp type and make spatial adjustments of grasp aperture appropriate to object size, the multiple corrections and small but variable time in grasp closure lend support to the suggestion that they may be inefficient in temporal aspects of the grasp schema.

Further support for grasping difficulties can be seen in our analyses of videorecordings of these grasping performances. In work published to date (Charlton et al., 1998), we have reported individual differences in grasping patterns of two case studies of children with DS. Specifically, we described one child with DS (DS1) who showed an awkward grasp and atypical finger posture upon object contact and another child with DS (DS2) who showed a more typical grasp (see figure 2.1). We have continued to examine grasping actions in ongoing work in a total of five children, and our analyses to date suggest that the unusual grasp posture reported for DS1 is not unique. The unusual grasping style of DS1, observed in approximately 50% of trials with the Smartie, was also seen in one other of the five children. This child used an atypical grasp in the majority of trials with both Smarties and biscuits. It is worthy of note that the atypical grasp of these two participants with DS is very similar to that described in patients AT and RV (Goodale et al., 1994; Jeannerod et al., 1994). That is, we see an awkward finger positioning with a significant overshoot of the fingertips beyond the object, so that contact is made on the underside of the fingers rather than the fingertips. However, unlike AT and RV, our subjects did not adopt a wider maximum aperture compared with control subjects.

In addition to the marked grasping impairment described above, we observed many other examples of atypical finger postures in all except one of the five children with DS. In approximately 50% of over 200 grasps observed, and across all task conditions, we found unusual finger postures, including positioning of fingers on top of the biscuit, readjustment of finger position after pickup, a small number of gropes and fumbles, and even one or two cases of use of the nonpreferred limb. Although the majority of these unusual grasp postures were generally less prominent than those described for DS1, the data suggest a pattern of individual differences and variability in performance of grasping in children with DS. At least in

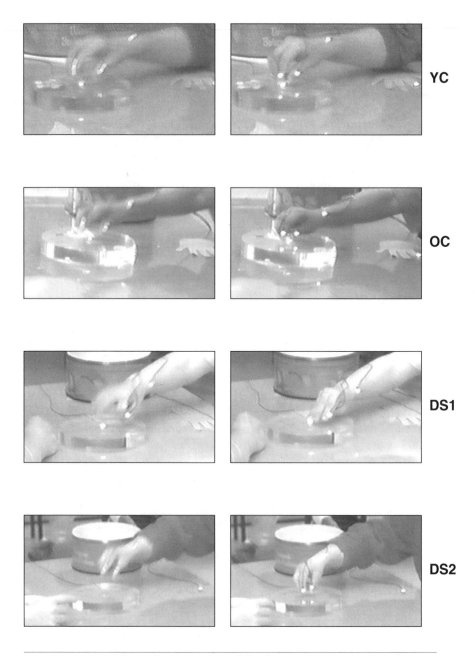

Figure 2.1   Hand shapes during preshape (left column) and at completion of grasp (right column) for children with Down syndrome (DS1 and DS2) and normally developing children, matched in chronological age (OC) and developmental age (YC).

some children with DS, grasping patterns are qualitatively different from those of their normally developing peers, suggesting some fundamental difficulties in the development of a grasping schema.

Conclusions

The results of our studies suggest that there may be both quantitative and qualitative differences between prehension skills of children with DS and normally developing children. Reach-and-grasp actions were clearly delayed compared with those of their peers of the same chronological age. However, while children with DS performed more like control children of the same developmental age, their performances were less proficient on many measures. This, we propose, suggests a developmental progression that is more severely delayed than would be predicted by developmental age.

In addition, evidence of variability in performance in spatial and temporal measures of the reach and in timing of grasp closure suggests that children with DS go about the task differently than normally developing children. We propose that ineffective generation of a reach schema explains their performance variability and spatial inaccuracies requiring a longer deceleration phase to correct the movement path. It is possible that these inaccuracies may be attributed to difficulties in using extrinsic information about object location. Our grasping data suggest that children with DS are able to select the appropriate type of grasp and adjust their fingers appropriate to object size. However, unlike their age-matched peers, they seem to have some difficulty in selecting a grasp that is appropriate to task goals. This also appears to be a characteristic of normally developing children of the same developmental age.

Other findings for the grasp component suggest differences rather than developmental delay in motor control characteristics of DS children. For example, timing of the grasp was not adjusted in any systematic way for object size or task goal, and individual differences were observed in the ability to use effective finger postures. These data might be explained by a deficit in some aspects of the grasp schema, which relies on information about the intrinsic properties of objects and semantic properties specifying the task goal. In future studies we will explore the underpinnings of these delays and differences in reach and grasp with larger numbers of children. In particular, we are keen to tease out potential differences in the ability to use pragmatic and semantic information relevant to prehension.

Finally, we consider how these findings might guide strategies for assessment and interventions to enhance motor development and control. In view of the variability and individual differences reported in our own results and other studies, we suggest that assessment should be conducted in different task contexts using objects differing in shape and size. Although most motor assessment batteries for children rarely require more than one or two performances, we suggest that it is critical that skills are measured over several trials. Lastly, we emphasize the importance of identifying individual differences in children with DS, so that specialized interventions can be offered to suit individual needs.

With respect to the question of whether interventions are appropriate for individuals with DS, and if so, how and when they should be delivered, we are guided by evidence from studies reviewed earlier in this chapter as well as our own findings. First, evidence from neurological studies suggests that some aspects of the central nervous system are typical at birth but differences emerge early in development. Similarly, findings from behavioral studies suggest that there are increasing performance gaps between those with DS and normally developing children in many areas of cognitive and motor development, including reach-to-grasp actions. A number of studies have examined the effectiveness of an enriched learning environment and early intervention on the enhancement of cognitive and motor skills in children with DS (see Dunst, 1990, for a review). Some authors have demonstrated that early intervention minimizes the decline typically seen with increased age (e.g., Connolly, Morgan, Russell, & Fulliton, 1993). This leads us to think that early interventions specifically targeting reaching and grasping may be useful in ameliorating the delays and difficulties observed in our studies. Our findings of variability in both reaching and grasping characteristics suggest that the schemas for these components are poorly formulated. Schema consolidation is thought to be achieved through experience and practice so that, over time, more efficient and reliable links are formed between object and task recognition criteria for the perceptual schema and the motor schema.

Program content for such intervention might include arranging the performance environment to promote chances of selection of the most appropriate grasp and correct finger positioning. For example, if a precision grasp is required, a target object could be placed in a container that permits only the tips of the index finger and thumb to reach inside. In addition, our findings suggest that children with DS might benefit from an enhancement of the stimulus value of important contextual cues. This might be done, for example, by practicing with very large versus very small objects, and with tasks requiring powerful whole-hand grasps versus delicate precision grasps. Lastly, we suggest the use of learning by observation. This method may be particularly useful for two reasons. The first concerns recent findings of Rizzolatti et al. (1996), who have shown that premotor neurons responsible for performance of grasping are also activated when observing another individual performing a grasping action. Hence, visual demonstrations might facilitate access to grasp schema. Secondly, in view of their relatively poor language development and atypical auditory functions, children with DS might best take advantage of practice if instructors provide visual rather than verbal instructions (e.g., Elliott et al., 1990).

References

Anson, J.G. (1989). Down syndrome: Neuromotor programming and fractional reaction time. In M.L. Latash (Ed.), *Proceedings of the Second International Conference of Motor Control in Down Syndrome* (pp. 6-13). Chicago, IL: Rush-Presbyterian St. Luke's Medical Center.

Anson, J.G. (1992). Neuromotor control and Down syndrome. In J.J. Summers (Ed.), *Approaches to the study of motor control and learning* (pp. 387-412). Amsterdam: North-Holland.

Arbib, M.A. (1981). Perceptual structures and distributed motor control. In V.B. Brooks (Ed.), *Handbook of physiology, Section 1: The nervous system, Vol. 2: Motor control* (pp. 1449-1480). Baltimore: Williams & Wilkins.

Arbib, M.A. (1985). Schemas for temporal organization of behaviour. *Human Neurobiology, 4,* 63-72.

Aylward, E.H., Habbah, R., Warren, A.C., Pulsifer, M.B., Barta, P.E., Jerram, M., & Pearlson, G.D. (1997). Cerebellar volume in adults with Down syndrome. *Archives of Neurology, 54,* 209-212.

Berk, L.E. (1996). *Infants, children and adolescents* (2nd ed.). Boston: Allyn & Bacon.

Berndt, T.J. (1997). *Child development* (2nd ed.). Madison, WI: Brown & Benchmark.

Block, M.E. (1991). Motor development in children with Down syndrome: A review of the literature. *Adapted Physical Activity Quarterly, 8,* 179-209.

Cadoret, G., & Beuter, A. (1997). Early development of reaching in Down syndrome infants. *Early Human Development, 36,* 157-173.

Charlton, J.L., Ihsen, E., & Oxley, J. (1996). Kinematic characteristics of reaching and grasping in children with Down syndrome. *Human Movement Science, 15,* 727-743.

Charlton, J.L., Ihsen, E., & Oxley, J. (1998). The influence of context in the development of reaching and grasping: Implications for assessment of disability. In J.P. Piek (Ed.), *Motor behavior and human skill. A multidisciplinary approach* (pp. 283-302). Champaign, IL: Human Kinetics.

Chieffi, S., Gentilucci, M., Allport, A., Sasso, E., & Rizzolatti, G. (1993). Study of selective reaching and grasping in a patient with unilateral parietal lesion. *Brain, 116,* 1119-1137.

Chua R., & Elliott, D. (1993). Visual regulation of manual aiming. *Human Movement Science, 12,* 365-401.

Cichetti, D., & Beeghly, M. (1990). An organizational approach to the study of Down syndrome: Contributions to an integrative theory of development. In D. Cichetti & M. Beeghly (Eds.), *Children with Down syndrome. A developmental perspective* (pp. 29-62). Cambridge: Cambridge University Press.

Cobo-Lewis, A.B., Oller, D.K., Lynch, M.P., & Levine, S.L. (1996). Relations of motor and vocal milestones in typically developing infants and infants with Down syndrome. *American Journal on Mental Retardation, 100,* 456-467.

Cole, K.J., Abbs, J.H., & Turner, G.S. (1988). Deficits in the production of grip forces in Down syndrome. *Developmental Medicine and Child Neurology, 30,* 752-758.

Connolly, B.H., Morgan, S.B., Russell, F.F., & Fulliton, W.L. (1993). A longitudinal study of children with Down syndrome who experienced early intervention programming. *Physical Therapy, 73,* 170-181.

Cowie, V.A. (1970). *A study of the early development of mongols.* Oxford: Pergamon Press.

Cunningham, C.C. (1979). *Aspects of early development of Down's syndrome infants.* Unpublished doctoral dissertation, University of Manchester.

Davis, W.E., & Kelso, J.A.S. (1982). Analysis of 'invariant characteristics' in the motor control of Down's syndrome and normal subjects. *Journal of Motor Behavior, 14,* 194-212.

Dunst, C.J. (1990). Sensorimotor development of infants with Down syndrome. In D. Cichetti & M. Beeghly (Eds.), *Children with Down syndrome. A developmental perspective* (pp. 180-230). Cambridge: Cambridge University Press.

Dyer, S., Gunn, P., Rauh, H., & Berry, P. (1990). Motor development in Down syndrome children: An analysis of the Bayley Scales of Infant Development. In A. Vermeer (Ed.), *Motor development. Adapted physical activity and mental retardation: Vol. 30. Medicine Sport Science* (pp. 7-20). Basel, Switzerland: Karger.

Elliott, D., & Weeks, D.J. (1993). Cerebral specialization for speech perception and movement organization in adults with Down's syndrome. *Cortex, 29,* 103-113.

Elliott, D., Weeks, D.J., & Chua, R. (1994). Anomalous cerebral lateralization and Down syndrome. *Brain and Cognition, 26,* 191-195.

Elliott, D., Weeks, D.J., & Elliott, C.L. (1987). Cerebral specialization in adults with Down syndrome. *American Journal on Mental Retardation, 92,* 263-271.

Elliott, D., Weeks, D.J., & Gray, S. (1990). Manual and oral praxis in adults with Down's syndrome. *Neuropsychologia, 12,* 1307-1315.

Franco, F., & Wishart, J.G. (1995). Use of pointing and other gestures by young children with Down syndrome. *American Journal on Mental Retardation, 100,* 160-182.

Gentilucci, M., Castiello, U., Corradini, M.L., Scarpa, M., Umiltà, C., & Rizzolatti, G. (1991). Influence of different types of grasping on the transport component of prehension movements. *Neuropsychologia, 29,* 361-378.

Goodale, M.A., Meenan, J.P., Bulthoff, H.H., Nicolle, D.A., Murphy, K.J., & Racicot, C.I. (1994). Separate neural pathways for the visual analysis of object shape in perception and prehension. *Current Biology, 4,* 604-610.

Grafton, S.T., Fagg, A.H., Woods, R.P., & Arbib, M.A. (1996). Functional anatomy of pointing and grasping in humans. *Cerebral Cortex, 6,* 226-237.

Henderson, S.E. (1985). Motor skill development. In D. Lane & B. Stratford (Eds.), *Current approaches to Down's syndrome* (pp. 187-218). London: Holt, Rinehart & Winston.

Henderson, S.E., Morris, J., & Frith, U. (1981). The motor deficit in Down's syndrome children: A problem of timing? *Journal of Child Psychology and Psychiatry, 22,* 233-245.

Hodapp, R.M., & Zigler E. (1990). Applying the developmental perspective to individuals with Down syndrome. In D. Cichetti & M. Beeghly (Eds.), *Children with Down syndrome. A developmental perspective* (pp. 1-28). Cambridge: Cambridge University Press.

Hoff, B., & Arbib, M.A. (1993). Models of trajectory formation and temporal interaction of reach and grasp. *Journal of Motor Behavior, 25,* 175-192.

Hofsten, C. von. (1984). Developmental changes in the organization of prereaching movements. *Developmental Psychology, 20,* 378-388.

Hofsten, C. von, & Ronnqvist, L. (1993). Preparation for grasping an object: A developmental study. *Journal of Experimental Psychology: Human Perception and Performance, 14,* 610-621.

Hogg, J., & Moss, S.C. (1983). Prehensile development in Down's syndrome and non-handicapped preschool children. *British Journal of Developmental Psychology, 1,* 189-204.

Jeannerod, M. (1981). Intersegmental coordination during reaching at natural visual objects. In J. Long & A. Baddeley (Eds.), *Attention and performance IX* (pp. 153-168). Hillsdale, NJ: Erlbaum.

Jeannerod, M. (1984). The timing of natural prehension movements. *Journal of Motor Behavior, 16*, 235-254.

Jeannerod, M. (1997). *The cognitive neuroscience of action.* Cambridge, MA: Blackwell.

Jeannerod, M., Decety, J., & Michel, F. (1994). Impairment of grasping movements following a bilateral posterior lesion. *Neuropsychologia, 32*, 369-380.

Jeannerod, M., & Rosetti, Y. (1993). Visuomotor coordination as a dissociable visual function: Experimental and clinical evidence. *Bailliere's Clinical Neurology, 2*, 439-460.

Jernigan, T.L., & Bellugi, U. (1990). Anomalous brain morphology on magnetic resonance images in Williams syndrome and Down syndrome. *Archives of Neurology, 47*, 529-533.

Jernigan, T.L., Bellugi, U., Sowell, E., Doherty, S., & Hesselink, J.R. (1993). Cerebral morphologic distinctions between Williams and Down syndromes. *Archives of Neurology, 50*, 186-191.

Karrer, R., Wojtascek, Z., & Davis, M.G. (1995). Event-related potentials and information processing in infants with and without Down syndrome. *American Journal on Mental Retardation, 100*, 146-159.

Kesslak, J.P., Nagata, S.F., Lott, I., & Nalcioglu, O. (1994). Magnetic resonance imaging analysis of age-related changes in the brains of individuals with Down's syndrome. *Neurology, 44*, 1039-1045.

Koo, B.K.K., Blaser, S., Harwood-Nash, D., Becker, L.E., & Murphy, M.B. (1992). Magnetic resonance imaging evaluation of delayed myelination in Down syndrome: A case report and review of the literature. *Journal of Child Neurology, 7*, 417-421.

Latash, M.L. (1993). *Control of human movement.* Champaign, IL: Human Kinetics.

Latash, M.L., & Corcos, D.M. (1991). Kinematic and electromyographic characteristics of single-joint movements of individuals with Down syndrome. *American Journal on Mental Retardation, 96*, 189-201.

Lienert, C., & Rauh, H. (1993). Entwicklung der Fortbewegung bei Kindern mit Down-Syndrom. *Kindheit und Entwicklung, 2*, 227-238.

Lincoln, A.J., Courchesne, E., Kilman, B.A., & Galambos, R. (1985). Neuropsychological correlates of information-processing by children with Down syndrome. *American Journal of Mental Deficiency, 89*, 403-414.

Marteniuk, R.G., Leavitt, J.L., MacKenzie, C.L., & Athenes, S. (1990). Functional relationships between grasp and transport components in a prehension task. *Human Movement Science, 9*, 149-176.

Marteniuk, R.G., MacKenzie, C.L., Jeannerod, M., Athenes, S., & Dugas, C. (1987). Constraints on human arm movement trajectories. *Canadian Journal of Psychology, 41*, 365-378.

Morris, A.F., Vaughan, S.E., & Vaccaro, P. (1982). Measurement of neuromuscular tone and strength in Down's syndrome children. *Journal of Mental Deficiency Research, 26*, 41-46.

Moss, S.C., & Hogg, J. (1981). The development of hand function in mentally handicapped preschool children. In P. Mittler (Ed.), *Frontiers of knowledge in mental retardation* (pp. 35-44). Baltimore: University Park Press.

O'Brien, C., & Hayes, A. (1989). Motor development in early childhood of clumsy, intellectually disabled and Down's syndrome children. Guidelines for adapted motor activity program. *The Australian Council for Health, Physical Education and Recreation National Journal*, June, 15-19.

Owens, D., Dawson J.C., & Losin, S. (1971). Alzheimer's disease in Down's syndrome. *American Journal of Mental Deficiency, 75*, 606-612.

Paulignan, Y., Jeannerod, M., MacKenzie, C.L., & Marteniuk, R.G. (1991). Selective perturbation of visual input during prehension movements. 2. The effects of changing object size. *Experimental Brain Research, 87*, 407-431.

Paulignan, Y., MacKenzie, C.L., Marteniuk R.G., & Jeannerod, M. (1991). Selective perturbation of visual input during prehension movements. 1. The effects of changing object position. *Experimental Brain Research, 83*, 502-512.

Pratt, J., & Abrams, R.A. (1996). Practice and component submovements: The roles of programming and feedback in rapid aimed limb movements. *Journal of Motor Behavior, 28*, 149-156.

Raz, N., Torres, I.J., Briggs, S.D., Spencer, W.D., Thornton, A.E., Loken, W.J., Gunning, F.M., McQuain, J.D., Driesen, N.R., & Acker, J.D. (1995). Selective neuroanatomic abnormalities in Down's syndrome and their cognitive correlates: Evidence from MRI morphometry. *Neurology, 45*, 356-366.

Rizzolatti, G., Fadiga, L., Gallese, V., & Fogassi, L. (1996). Premotor cortex and the recognition of motor actions. *Cognitive Brain Research, 3*, 131-141.

Shumway-Cook, A., & Woollacott, M. (1985). Dynamics of postural control in the child with Down syndrome. *Physical Therapy, 65*, 1315-1322.

Sigelman, C.K., & Shaffer, D.R. (1995). *Life-span human development* (2nd ed.). Pacific Grove, CA: Brooks/Cole.

Thelen, E., Corbetta, D., Kamm, K., & Spencer, J.P. (1993). The transition to reaching: Mapping intention and intrinsic dynamics. *Child Development, 64*, 1058-1098.

Thombs, B., & Sugden, D. (1991). Manual skills in Down syndrome children ages 6 to 16 years. *Adapted Physical Activity Quarterly, 8*, 242-254.

Ulrich, B.D., & Ulrich, D.A. (1993). Dynamic systems approach to understanding motor delay in infants with Down syndrome. In G.J.P. Savelsbergh (Ed.), *The development of coordination in infancy* (pp. 445-459). Amsterdam: North-Holland.

Wang, P.P., Doherty, S., Hesselink, J.R., & Bellugi, U. (1992). Callosal morphology concurs with neurobehavioral and neuropathological findings in two neurodevelopmental disorders. *Archives of Neurology, 49*, 407-411.

Weeks, D.J., Chua, R., Elliott, D., Lyons, J., & Pollock, B.J. (1995). Cerebral specialization for receptive language in individuals with Down syndrome. *Australian Journal of Psychology, 47*, 137-140.

Wing, A.M., Turton, A., & Fraser, C. (1986). Grasp size and accuracy of approach in reaching. *Journal of Motor Behavior, 18*, 245-260.

Wishart, J.G. (1993). The development of learning difficulties in children with Down's syndrome. *Journal of Intellectual Disability Research, 37*, 389-403.

Author Note

The authors wish to thank the children and their parents who have given their time generously and participated enthusiastically in our research program. We also acknowledge the valuable contribution of our two research assistants, Marika Jagow and Jennie Oxley. Research by the authors, summarized in this chapter, was supported by Faculty of Health and Behavioural Sciences and School of Studies in Disability Research Grants and an ARC Infrastructure Grant.

3

CHAPTER

Preparation and Control of Goal-Directed Limb Movements in Persons With Down Syndrome

Timothy N. Welsh and Digby Elliott

Department of Kinesiology
McMaster University

Key words

perceptual-motor speed ◆ movement preparation ◆ reaction time ◆
precuing ◆ lateralization ◆ feedback ◆ movement kinematics ◆
aiming ◆ attention ◆ verbal-mediation ◆ motor learning

It is well known that adolescents and young adults with Down syndrome (DS) are slower and more variable in initiating and completing goal-directed movements than nonhandicapped persons of a similar chronological age (see Anwar, 1981, for a review). Although the findings are not as robust, there is also evidence that persons with DS are disadvantaged in rapid limb control relative to persons of a similar mental age (i.e., chronologically younger persons without DS and persons with another handicapping condition of a similar chronological age). Process-oriented researchers interested in perceptual-motor behavior and DS have attempted to determine how these movement preparation and control problems can best be characterized.

Drawing on information-processing models of perceptual-motor behavior that distinguish between the structural constraints of a system and control processes developed to optimize the use of a system's "hardware," researchers have attempted to identify processing differences that might lead to the performance deficiencies evident in persons with DS. Investigators taking a "difference" or "deficit" approach to the problem have attempted to isolate specific structural components of the system that may be responsible for slower, more variable performance. In terms of specific information-processing models, this is akin to identifying the weak link in a chain of information-processing events. Too often this approach to research is associated with the old medical model of intellectual impairment (Grossman, 1977), which emphasizes identification or diagnosis of perceptual-motor difficulties without necessarily providing a framework for remediation (see Elliott, 1990, and Hoover & Wade, 1985, for reviews). From an information-processing view, the emphasis has often been on serial, additive, and rather static descriptions of how the human system operates. More often than not, the neural correlates of perceptual-motor behavior have been ignored.

In response to this extremely limited "difference" or "deficit" approach, a developmental orientation to understanding perceptual-motor behavior in persons with DS has dominated over the last two decades. This research paradigm is more optimistic in that the emphasis is placed on identifying control processes or strategic shortcomings amenable to change rather than structural deficits. Thus, part of the research approach has involved identifying and introducing specific task strategies or behaviors that will improve perceptual-motor performance and learning (e.g., Reid, 1980). The disappointing aspect of this work has been that the strategies adopted to improve performance are often extremely task specific, and usually do not generalize beyond the specific performance/learning context under consideration (Brown & Campione, 1986). It is our view that at least some of this problem stems from the assumption that common facilitory strategies will apply to heterogeneous groups of individuals, who will come to the performance/learning situation with a variety of perceptual-motor and learning problems. In terms of the development versus difference issue, we suggest that more attention needs to be paid to the interaction between the constraints provided by individual differences and the motor performance/learning context.

This chapter deals with research on the organization and control of goal-directed limb movements in persons with DS from both a difference and a developmental perspective. By examining some of the general and specific perceptual-motor problems experienced by persons with DS, we will show that while a developmental model is often appropriate for understanding individual differences within a given etiology, a specific difference model can prove fruitful, both for the identification and remediation of difficulties, when that model is "nested in an overall developmental approach" (Elliott, 1990, p. 202).

Perceptual-Motor Speed: A Review of Reaction Time and Movement Preparation Literature

When crossing the street; operating machinery; participating in sport; or performing any number of daily living, work, or recreational activities, it is often necessary to make rapid decisions about the appropriate movements to perform based on either anticipated or unexpected environmental events. In the laboratory, investigators have attempted to simulate these rapid processing situations using a reaction time paradigm. In the typical reaction time protocol, a participant is first given a warning signal such as a tone, a light, or simply a verbal "ready" command. After a foreperiod, which may vary from several hundred milliseconds to several seconds, a stimulus event (e.g., a tone or a light) occurs and the participant must make a simple predetermined response such as a button press, a finger lift, or a one-syllable vocalization. In what has been termed a "simple" reaction-time situation, there is only one possible stimulus and one possible response. Here the researcher is interested in the time required for very fundamental sensory-motor processing. Typically, in a simple reaction-time situation, a variable foreperiod is used to prevent the participant from anticipating the temporal onset of the imperative stimulus.

When an investigator is interested in more complex decision-making, a "choice" reaction-time protocol is employed. In this paradigm, there are two or more possible stimuli (e.g., lights of different colors or in different locations) that each specify a particular response (e.g., which finger to move). In a choice reaction-time situation, the foreperiod can be variable or fixed because the response required for a particular trial is specified by the imperative stimulus, thus making it difficult for the performer to anticipate a particular response. Investigators manipulate the complexity of the decision-making by varying the number of stimulus-response alternatives, and sometimes other factors such as the spatial mapping between the stimuli and response possibilities.

It has long been known that there is a moderate to strong relation between mental age and speed of processing as indexed by reaction time (Eysenck, 1967). Thus, people who are developmentally young due to mental handicaps exhibit longer simple reaction times than nonhandicapped individuals. In terms of choice reaction time, individuals of a lower mental age also exhibit greater increases in reaction time with increases in the number of stimulus-response alternatives than control participants who are of the same chronological age (Vernon, 1986; Wade, Newell, & Wallace, 1978).

Because individuals with DS often share the same work or learning environments as other persons with handicapping conditions, it is important to determine if the same information-processing principles apply. If, for example, there are differences between persons with DS and individuals with other developmental handicaps, then it may be necessary to make adaptations to the learning and work environments to accommodate members of the two groups. In this section, we will discuss both the similarities and differences between these two groups in their ability to respond rapidly and accurately in different reaction time contexts.

Reaction time studies comparing individuals with undifferentiated developmental handicaps to persons with DS have provided differing results. Some investigators have reported that persons with DS are slower than other individuals of the same mental age, while others have not. To our knowledge, there are no reports of persons with DS being faster than other mentally handicapped individuals.

Davis, Sparrow, and Ward (1991) employed a simple reaction-time paradigm to determine if the processing disadvantage sometimes associated with DS is due to central-processing differences or simply muscular-mechanical factors perhaps related to hypotonia in DS (Davis & Kelso, 1982). Adults with DS and peers matched for mental or chronological age responded with a right arm elbow extension in a variety of stimulus situations (i.e., a light, a tone, or both). In order to isolate the central and peripheral components of the response, Davis et al. (1991) recorded the onset of muscle activity from the medial head of the triceps brachii (the prime mover) in order to fractionate reaction time into premotor and motor components. The former is the time from stimulus onset until the first sign of muscle activity and reflects central-processing time, while the time remaining until response initiation (i.e., motor time) is associated with the neuromuscular and mechanical properties of the effector that have their impact at a more peripheral level. Overall, participants with DS were slower than participants in both control groups. There was, however, no reliable difference between participants with DS and mentally handicapped participants without DS for movement time. Interestingly, although both handicapped groups exhibited longer premotor times than their nonhandicapped peers, the participants with DS also took longer for central processing than the persons in the other handicapped group, but only for the tone and the light plus tone stimulus conditions. When the imperative stimulus was a light alone, participants with DS engaged in central processing just as rapidly as other participants of the same mental age. This finding may indicate a specific auditory-processing deficit in persons with DS, since people are typically faster with an auditory stimulus than a visual stimulus (see Posner, Nissen, & Klein, 1976, for a review). In this study, the auditory advantage was experienced by both control groups, but not participants with DS (Davis et al., 1991).

Hermelin (1964) also reported simple reaction-time differences between persons with DS and individuals with undifferentiated developmental handicaps. In this case, the difference was mediated not only by the nature of the imperative stimulus, but also by the type of warning signal given to participants. Similar to Davis et al. (1991), persons with an undifferentiated developmental handicap and nonhandicapped control participants reacted more quickly to a tone than to a light, while participants with DS exhibited the reversed pattern of performance. Moreover, it was also found that the modality of the warning signal also had a differential effect on the reaction time of participants in the DS group. Specifically, individuals with an undifferentiated handicap were fastest when a visual warning signal preceded the auditory stimulus and next fastest when both signals were auditory. When the imperative stimulus was visual, persons in the undifferentiated group were slower regardless of the warning signal. Persons with DS were fastest when an auditory warning signal was followed by a visual stimulus and next fastest when both signals were visual. They took the most time to react when both signals were auditory. Once again this suggests that sound (e.g., a tone or a verbal "ready" signal) may not have the same alerting properties for persons with DS as for other individuals (see also Berkson, 1960; Mack & MacKay, 1989; MacKay & Bankhead, 1983; cf. Henderson, Morris, & Frith, 1981).

Given that the specific simple reaction-time deficit in persons with DS appears to be associated with the auditory modality, it is interesting that event-related brain potential studies involving persons with DS (e.g., Miezejeski, Heaney, Belser, & Sersen, 1994) have reported aberrant lateralization of brain stem auditory-evoked responses. Our colleagues at Simon Fraser University have reported similar findings at the cortical level using magnetoencephalography (Weeks, Chua, Elliott, Weinberg, Cheyne, & Lyons, 1997).

Perhaps atypical brain organization for auditory processing in persons with DS sets the developmental stage for the unique pattern of cerebral specialization these individuals show for receptive language including speech perception (Elliott & Weeks, 1993). As discussed in chapter 13, this "difference" may be responsible for verbal-motor integration problems that affect perceptual-motor performance in a wide variety of simple tasks.

The essence of the simple reaction-time paradigm is that the performer knows what to expect, and as such has the opportunity to prepare his or her response in advance of the movement imperative (i.e., preprogram the movement). When one compares the performance of persons with and without DS in a choice reaction-time context, the situation becomes more complicated. This is particularly true if partial information is provided about the probability of specific responses.

In a study conducted in our laboratory, LeClair, Pollock, and Elliott (1993) had participants with and without DS perform right- or left-hand aiming movements to targets that were positioned close to or further away from the start position. By providing participants with either complete advance information, partial advance information, or no advance information, participants essentially performed in simple, two-choice, and four-choice reaction-time situations. In this experiment, both the precue (which provided advance information and also served as a warning signal) and the imperative stimulus were visual. Although mentally handicapped participants with and without DS were slower to respond than nonhandicapped participants, performers with DS showed no disadvantage relative to control participants of the same mental age. Individuals in both handicapped groups as well as the control group exhibited an increase in reaction time with the number of stimulus-response alternatives. Interestingly, all participants were faster when responding with their left hand (see Carson, 1996).

In a follow-up study, LeClair and Elliott (1995) employed a variation of the cost-benefit (Posner, 1978) or reprogramming (Lee, Elliott, & Carnahan, 1987) paradigm in order to examine the ability of persons with and without DS to prepare movements on the basis of visual and verbal advance information. In this study, participants moved the right hand from a central microswitch to red or blue target lights located to the right and the left of the participant's midline. On what is termed a neutral trial, both movements were equally probable. In this situation, participants were cued either verbally by the experimenter saying "red or blue" or visually by the brief illumination of both target lights. Following a foreperiod, one of the lights would again illuminate, serving as the imperative stimulus. On other sets of trials, only a single target would be precued; for example, the experimenter might say "red" or the red target light would be briefly illuminated. On the majority of these single precue trials, the cue would be valid (e.g., the red target was precued and also served as the imperative). However, on 20% of the trials, the precue was invalid and the other target served as the imperative. This experimental protocol was used to determine whether or not participants with DS were able to benefit from a valid cue (i.e., use advance information about the probability of a response), as well as whether or not any savings in reaction time depended on the nature of the cue (i.e., visual versus verbal). Also of interest was the temporal cost associated with an invalid cue, and how that might change as a function of cue type.

The reaction time results revealed that although visual cues improved the performance of participants in all groups equally, participants with DS did not show as much benefit as nonhandicapped (NDH) and handicapped (UDH) participants without DS when the cue was verbal (see figure 3.1). Surprisingly, persons with DS were disrupted to the same extent by invalid visual and verbal precues. While this study once again provides support for the idea that persons with DS have specific difficulty preparing movements on the basis of auditory/verbal information, it should be pointed out that the reaction time differences associated with the nature of the precue were small (25-40 ms) compared to the overall latency differences between nonhandicapped control subjects and participants in the two handicapped groups (>200 ms). This suggests that there is a more general processing deficiency associated with mental age.

Although more work needs to be conducted, it appears that at least some of the reported differences in reaction time between persons of the same mental age with and without DS may be due to the nature, perhaps modality, of the signal or advance information. However, the question still remains as to why individuals with lower intelligence quotients have longer simple and choice reaction times than nonhandicapped persons of a similar chronological age. Based on fractionated simple reaction-time studies (e.g., Davis et al., 1991), it is tempting to conclude that the difference is the result of a slower rate of sensory processing. However, in a review of the reaction time work, Nettlebeck and Brewer (1981) pointed out that at one time or

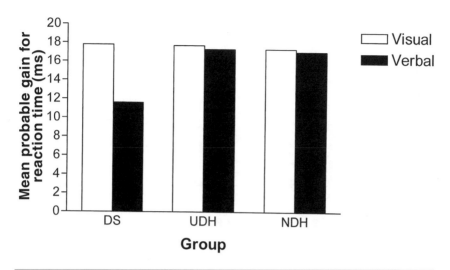

Figure 3.1   Mean probable gain for reaction time as a function of group and type of precue. Probable gain was calculated as follows: Probable gain = (.80 × RT benefit) – (.20 × RT cost), where .80 and .20 are the probabilities of a valid and invalid precue, RT benefit is the difference in ms between the neutral precue condition and the valid precue condition, and RT cost is the difference between the invalid condition and the neutral condition.

Reprinted, by permission, from D.A. LeClair and D. Elliott, 1995, "Movement preparation and the costs and benefits associated with advance information for adults with Down Syndrome," *Adapted Physical Activity Quarterly* 12(3): 239-249.

another all stages of information processing have been implicated in the psychomotor slowness associated with mental retardation. Drawing on some ideas developed by Rabbitt (1979, 1981) to explain the psychomotor slowing associated with aging, Brewer and Smith (1982) have suggested that the differences in reaction time may be more a function of how the performer approaches the reaction time task than of any weak link in an information-processing chain.

Taking this approach, it is first important to realize that the reaction time differences between persons with and without intellectual handicaps are not restricted to mean reaction time. In figure 3.2, we present two idealized reaction-time distributions based on many trials for a typical handicapped and nonhandicapped individual (see Baumeister & Kellas, 1968). Although the mean reaction time is certainly longer for the individual of the younger mental age, there are other differences as well. For example, this person also exhibits much more trial-to-trial variability and the distribution has a more pronounced positive skew. Notice that on "fast" trials, the developmentally young performer is just as "fast" as the other individual, while the outliers at the high end of the distribution have a profound effect on mean reaction time. How do distributions like these develop over several thousand trials?

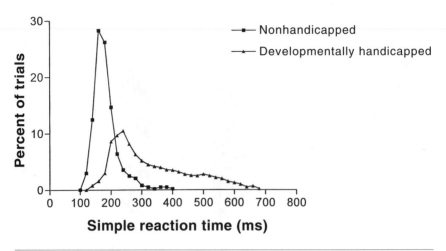

Figure 3.2   Two idealized reaction-time distributions for a typical individual with and without disabilities.

According to Rabbitt (1979), in order to understand the shape of the distribution it is important to first consider the nature of the reaction time task. As an example, the performer may be faced with a two-choice, equal probability situation in which the illumination of one stimulus light (right side) requires a right-hand response, and the illumination of the only other light (left side) requires a left-hand response. The experimenter instructs the participant to respond as rapidly as possible, but not to make errors (e.g., lift the right hand in response to the left light). The performer then is faced with the task of determining how fast he or she can respond without making an error. A trial-to-trial analysis of reaction times usually reveals that a participant will start out fairly slowly in order to be safe, but over trials will attempt to move more and more quickly. The idea is that the performer is involved in a problem-solving exercise that entails discovering a safe (error-free) but fast responding zone (see figure 3.3a). When an error is made, there is typically an adjustment (i.e., a longer response time), after which the performer attempts to creep up to the "safe but fast" zone once again.

Rabbitt (1981) demonstrated that elderly adults have greater difficulty than young adults in tracking this safe but fast reaction-time zone, and Brewer and Smith (1982, 1984) hypothesized that individuals with intellectual disabilities may have the same problem. Brewer and Smith (1984) conducted a series of studies involving trial-by-trial analysis of the serial choice reaction trials of adults with undifferentiated mental handicaps and found at least partial support for their proposal. Specifically, while they found that participants with intellectual handicaps were able to recognize their errors, as evidenced by an increase in reaction time following an error, they were less able to use error and performance feedback over a number of trials to track the safe-fast performance zone. A typical trial-to-trial profile of performance is depicted in figure 3.3b.

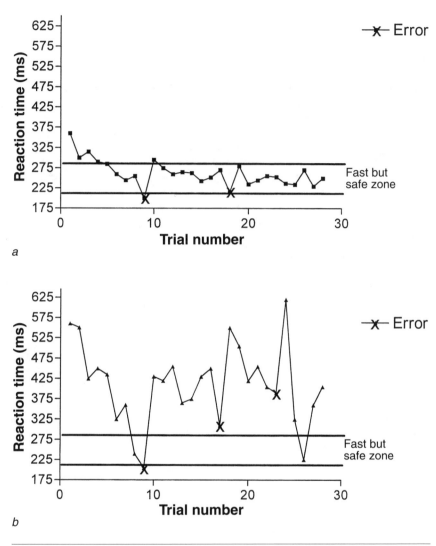

Figure 3.3   Two idealized reaction-time-by-trial functions for *(a)* a typical non-handicapped and *(b)* a typical handicapped individual.

Thus, it appears that while persons with DS may exhibit some specific information-processing difficulties with movement preparation on the basis of auditory and verbal information, they can also be expected to show more general developmental problems related to the control processes used to optimize performance. What remains to be determined is how amenable these more general perceptual-motor problems are to training (see Hoover, Wade, & Newell, 1981), as well as how they might influence the actual execution of movements more complex than a simple button press. The latter issue serves as the basis for the next section of this chapter.

Rapid Limb Control: Vision and Kinesthesis in On-Line Regulation

An issue of central importance to motor control researchers is the relative importance of advance preparation and planning in limb control and the on-line regulation of movement through the use of response-produced feedback (e.g., Carlton, 1981; Elliott & Allard, 1985; Woodworth, 1899). Although a number of researchers have speculated about how persons with DS might control rapid limb movements, very few studies have directly tackled the issue of advance planning versus on-line control.

Frith and Frith (1974) suggested that the movement clumsiness often associated with DS is the result of an inability to adequately plan or program limb movements. This proposal was based on a between-task comparison of finger-tapping rate and pursuit-rotor performance. Specifically, compared to autistic participants of the same mental age, adults with DS tapped more slowly and failed to improve their pursuit-tracking performance even when tracking a completely predictable pattern. These apparent deficits were taken to reflect difficulty in structuring a precise series of muscle commands that could be used to centrally direct the movements. It was argued that this "motor programming" deficit made persons with DS more dependent on visual and kinesthetic information for limb control. However, given both the control group and the between-task nature of the comparison, Frith and Frith's (1974) conclusions are questionable.

LeClair et al. (1993) examined the issue of movement preparation more directly using the movement precuing paradigm developed by Rosenbaum (1980). Mentally handicapped participants with and without DS as well as nonhandicapped persons of a similar chronological age performed a four-alternative aiming task. Movements could be made with either the right or left hand to either near or far targets. Advance information about the movement to be completed on a given trial was manipulated via the use of a precue. Specifically, the experimenter provided either no advance information (4 possible targets), complete information (1 possible target), or partial information (2 possible targets). In the partial precue situations, the advance information could specify hand or distance or provide an ambiguous two-alternative precue (e.g., right hand—near or left hand—far). The goal of this study was to determine if persons with DS display an ability to use the available information to either partially or completely prepare their movements in advance of a response imperative. Although participants in the two handicapped groups exhibited longer reaction times and movement times than the control participants, they exhibited the same pattern of results across the various precue conditions. That is, both handicapped groups were able to use advance information to reduce movement preparation time. In contrast to Rosenbaum (1980; but see Goodman & Kelso, 1980), all groups were able to benefit from advance information about distance regardless of whether or not hand was specified. This latter finding indicates that the movement preparation process was not limited to a fixed order, and that, while slower, participants with mental handicaps display the same degree of programming flexibility as nonhandicapped individuals.

Many studies on rapid limb control have been conducted using some variation of Fitts's reciprocal (Fitts, 1954) or discrete (Fitts & Peterson, 1964) target-aiming task. In this paradigm, the difficulty of an aiming movement is manipulated by varying target size, movement amplitude, or both. As the difficulty of the movement increases (i.e., smaller targets and larger amplitudes), it is generally assumed that the performer becomes more dependent on response-produced visual feedback to complete the aiming task (see Carlton, 1992). Target-aiming studies involving heterogeneous groups of individuals with mental handicaps have shown that as the difficulty of the aiming task increases, movement times increase at a faster rate than for individuals without an intellectual handicap (Wade et al., 1978). While this extra time may reflect an overdependence on time-consuming feedback-based control, it could also be the case that individuals who are mentally handicapped simply require more time to process the same amount of visual or other information. Inferences about feedback utilization require experiments in which the availability of feedback is actually manipulated.

Anwar (1981; Anwar & Hermelin, 1979) has reported mixed evidence regarding the dependence of persons with DS on visual feedback utilization. In a study that involved straight-ahead pointing (Anwar & Hermelin, 1979), the performance of children with DS was compared to that of other mentally handicapped individuals, as well as to that of nonhandicapped persons of either a similar mental or chronological age. When vision of the aiming limb and target was occluded with a blindfold, the children with DS were as precise as nonhandicapped children of the same chronological age and better than the other mentally challenged participants. Although this suggests that persons with DS are not overly dependent on visual feedback, Anwar (1981) also reported that mentally handicapped persons with and without DS were more disrupted by the removal of vision than nonhandicapped participants of a similar mental age. In this study, however, the visual manipulation included the covariation of on-line visual feedback and visual knowledge of results. This confound makes it impossible to determine if group differences were due to differences in performance within or between aiming trials. This distinction is particularly salient when one considers that many of the reaction time differences between individuals with and without mental handicaps may be related more to trial-to-trial monitoring of performance than any processing deficit per se (e.g., Brewer & Smith, 1982, 1984).

A study conducted a few years ago in our laboratory provides the clearest picture of visual feedback utilization in the control of goal-directed limb movements in persons with DS (Hodges, Cunningham, Lyons, Kerr, & Elliott, 1995). A computerized aiming task (Chua & Elliott, 1993) was employed in which participants moved a mouse on a graphics tablet in order to displace a cursor the same distance on a computer monitor. On a given trial, the participant was required to move the cursor from a home position to a small target as rapidly and accurately as possible. During some trial blocks, participants were able to see both the target and the cursor over the entire course of the movement, while on other trial blocks the cursor disappeared on movement initiation. In both cases participants received visual feedback about the movement outcome when the movement was complete (cf. Anwar, 1981).

As well as allowing examination of aiming performance in terms of time and endpoint error, the experimental setup allowed us to examine the spatiotemporal characteristics of the movement trajectories. "By examining the pattern and consistency of subjects' velocity and acceleration profiles," the experimenters hoped to "gain insight into the movement control processes as well as how these processes change with the elimination of response-produced visual feedback" (Hodges et al., 1995, pp. 178-179).

In terms of movement time, participants with DS took twice as long as nonhandicapped participants to complete their movements. They were also significantly slower than participants from a heterogeneous group of persons with mental handicaps. The variable error results are redrawn in figure 3.4. It is apparent that although withdrawing vision had a profound overall effect on performance, individuals with DS exhibited a proportional increase in error similar to the nonhandicapped participants. Contrary to Frith and Frith's (1974) proposal, participants from the heterogeneous handicapped group were most affected by the removal of vision.

More interesting than the performance results were the group differences in the shape and variability of the velocity and acceleration profiles. Although nonhandicapped participants typically exhibited a primary movement (i.e., acceleration and

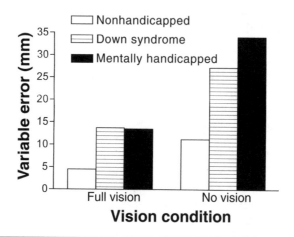

Figure 3.4 Variable error (mm) as a function of group and vision condition.

Reprinted, by permission, from N.J. Hodges, S.J. Cunningham, J. Lyons, T.L. Kerr, and D. Elliott, 1995, "Visual feedback processing and goal-directed movement in adults with Down Syndrome," *Adapted Physical Activity Quarterly* 12(2): 176-186.

deceleration) that undershot the target and one or two corrective movements to bring the cursor onto the target, the participants in both mentally handicapped groups exhibited greater than three corrective submovements on the majority of their aiming trials (DS = 88.5%, non-DS = 78.2%, nonhandicapped control participants = 25.3%). Discontinuities in the trajectory (see figure 3.5) occurred regardless of whether or not visual feedback from the cursor was available. Thus, it appears that when vision was not available, participants in the two handicapped groups attempted to adjust their movements on the basis of kinesthesis or some other information source rather than rely on the initial movement plan. This was not a successful strategy. However, the variability in peak velocity and the time to peak velocity data indicate that a more open-loop approach to the task also would not have been successful.

The focus of the Hodges et al. (1995) study was on movement execution, and for that reason participants were aware of the movement goal in advance and were allowed as much time as necessary to prepare their movements. One way to examine the interplay between advance preparation and on-line control is to create

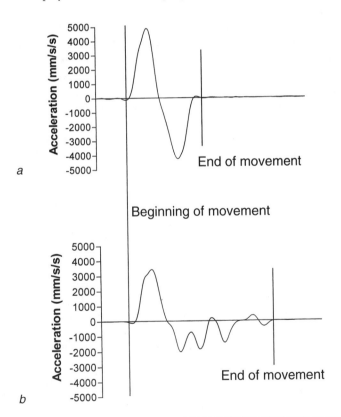

Figure 3.5 Typical acceleration profiles for a single rapid aiming movement for (a) a nonhandicapped subject and (b) a subject with Down syndrome (e.g., Hodges et al., 1995).

movement uncertainty and limit the time an individual has for movement preparation. Recently, Kulatunga-Moruzi and Elliott (1999) borrowed a paradigm that has been used to study selective attention and control of goal-directed movement in order to examine movement preparation and on-line control in adults with DS.

In this study, young adults with and without DS performed rapid three-dimensional aiming movements to small red targets that could appear to the right or the left of the midline. On some trial blocks, participants performed the task with the right hand, while on other blocks they used their left hand. On some trials a yellow "distractor" light also appeared in addition to the red target light. The distractor, which participants were told to ignore, could appear in the same hemispace as the target (i.e., beside it) or in exactly the same position in contralateral space. The purpose of the distractor was to provide a competing response and perhaps disrupt movement preparation or execution.

Overall, participants with DS were slower at initiating and executing their movements than the nonhandicapped control participants. As in the Hodges et al. (1995) study, much of the extra time was due to the many adjustments that were made to the movement trajectory after reaching peak velocity. This suggests that persons with DS may rely heavily on visual and other sources of feedback to successfully complete their movements. Interestingly, the distractors had no impact on the time it took either group to prepare and initiate their movements. However, both groups did exhibit prolonged movement times when distractors were present, particularly when the distractor appeared to the right of the subject. This indicates that both groups of participants were exhibiting a rather "risky" strategy in the face of uncertainty; that is, they would initiate the movement quickly and then decide where they were going. Presumably the control participants were able to make this decision and arrive at the target more quickly.

Taken together, these two kinematic studies of limb control in young adults with DS indicate that they are more reliant on response-produced feedback than nonhandicapped persons of the same chronological age (Hodges et al., 1995; Kulatunga-Moruzi & Elliott, 1999). This feedback-based approach to limb control is also seen in children at approximately 7 and 8 years of age (see Hay, 1990, for a review), elderly adults (Lyons, Elliott, Swanson, & Chua, 1996), and other intellectually challenged persons without DS (Hodges et al., 1995). Although one might try to argue that closed-loop control reflects a "play-it-safe" strategy (see Latash & Anson, 1996), the Kulatunga-Moruzi and Elliott (1999) study indicates that persons with DS are no more conservative in their strategy than everyone else. A better argument might be that persons with DS and other intellectual handicaps use feedback out of the necessity borne of a highly variable and imprecise initial movement toward the target. It may also be the case that these individuals have difficulty monitoring their trial-to-trial behavior (see reaction time literature) and thus depend exclusively on concurrent feedback for setting acceptable speed-accuracy performance levels. In order to evaluate this second possibility, trial-to-trial analyses of movement time-error relations need to be done (see Brewer & Smith's 1984 work on reaction time).

The Verbal Mediation of Goal-Directed Movement

Generally, the research on the visual regulation of goal-directed movement by persons with DS supports a developmental model of motor performance. That is, young adults with DS perform in a manner similar to other individuals with mental handicaps, as well as nonhandicapped children of a similar mental age. Specific differences between persons with DS and other individuals of the same mental age do emerge, however, when the organization and control of limb and oral movements depend on verbal mediation.

The initial research on this issue (Elliott & Weeks, 1990) involved the use of an apraxia battery developed to examine the execution of simple limb and oral movements (Kools, Williams, Vickers, & Caell, 1971). The battery required participants to complete individual limb movements (e.g., clap your hands, put your finger in your ear) or oral movements (e.g., blow out a match, stick out your tongue) following either verbal instruction or demonstration. The movements of mentally handicapped adults with and without DS were filmed and a two-point scoring system was used to evaluate each movement on the basis of several movement dimensions (e.g., amplitude, accuracy, overall pattern). Participants without DS performed equally well in the verbal instruction and demonstration conditions, while participants with DS made more oral and limb errors when attempting to produce movements following verbal direction. In a follow-up study, Elliott and colleagues found that this specific verbal-motor problem became more pronounced when the oral and manual gestures involved two and three movement components (Elliott, Weeks, & Gray, 1990). This difficulty was not related to an understanding of the verbal instructions or, in the case of the movement sequences, a verbal memory problem because participants with DS were able to point to pictures of an experimenter performing the appropriate task just as well as control participants, regardless of whether the movement(s) was (were) prompted visually or verbally (Elliott et al., 1990). As outlined in chapter 13, this specific verbal-motor processing difference may be related to a pattern of brain organization unique to persons with DS.

Following the use of this clinical tool (e.g., Kools et al., 1971), verbal-motor processing in persons with DS was examined using more controlled procedures. To this end, Elliott and Weeks (1990) constructed a movement-sequencing apparatus that consisted of three manipulanda that each afforded a distinct movement (i.e., a lever to shift, a headlight switch to pull, and a knob to turn). The three devices were arranged vertically 10 cm apart on a panel 30 cm in front of a home position at the participant's midline. On a given trial, the participant's task was to move from the home position and complete the three activities as quickly as possible. The order in which the tasks were to be completed varied from trial to trial and the order was cued either visually or verbally. On visual trials this cue was provided by the sequential illumination of small light-emitting diodes located next to each device on the panel. The verbal cue specified the location of each device (e.g., "bottom, top, middle"), and was provided at the same cadence by the experimenter. Immediately following the cues specifying movement order, a tone sounded signaling the participant to complete the task as rapidly as possible. The experimenters partitioned the time to complete the task into reaction time and movement time. Although reaction time was not affected by cue condition for either participants with DS or nonhandicapped control participants, an interaction between group and cue similar to the apraxia study was evident in the movement time analysis. Specifically, control participants performed equally well with a verbal or visual cue, but persons with DS were more than 300 ms faster when completing the sequence on the basis of visual as opposed to verbal information. This same pattern of findings was also apparent in the within-subject movement time variability analysis. That is, participants with DS were extremely inconsistent when they were required to complete a movement sequence on the basis of verbal direction. Once again, this study provides evidence for a specific verbal-motor impairment in young adults with DS.

Motor Learning

The studies reviewed up to this point in the chapter have all been concerned with perceptual-motor performance. Measures of performance such as reaction time, movement time, and movement accuracy provide motor control researchers with information about how an individual or group of individuals behaves (moves) at a single point in time. With respect to skill development and remediation, of greater concern is how motor skills are acquired over time. Motor learning is usually associated with relatively permanent improvements in motor performance that occur as a result of practice or experience. Although it is tempting to make inferences about the best way to teach a particular group of individuals based on performance data, it has been known for a number of years that the principles associated with optimal performance do not always apply to learning (see Salmoni, Schmidt, & Walter, 1984, for a review).

A good example of the performance versus learning distinction comes from the literature on practice structure. If an individual has more than one motor skill to learn, is it better to attempt to master the skills one at a time or to vary practice during a particular instructional session? In the motor learning literature, these practice schedules are referred to as blocked practice and random practice, respectively. The answer to the question about whether blocked or random practice is more effective depends on whether the instructor and the learner are interested in transient short-term performance gains or long-term retention of the motor skills (i.e., learning). Specifically, blocked practice facilitates the former, while random practice facilitates the latter (e.g., Lee & Magill, 1983; Shea & Morgan, 1979). This phenomenon is generally referred to as the contextual interference effect, and it appears to apply to both motor and nonmotor skills.

A learning environment high in contextual interference facilitates long-term retention or learning, because the interference creates a situation in which the learner must continually be involved in active problem-solving. If, for example, you were teaching someone to add (e.g., what is 33 + 8?), it would not be beneficial to ask the same addition question two times in a row. If you did, on the second occasion the learner would simply repeat the answer (41) rather than solve the problem. The introduction of a new activity (interference), even if it is just a different addition problem, interferes with the learner's ability to simply recall the solution and on a subsequent attempt the problem must be solved a second time. Likewise in a motor learning situation, it is important that the learner engages in new and different cognitive problem-solving activities as often as possible rather than simply repeating the same movement solution over and over. By varying the schedule of skill execution, an instructor creates this learning situation by taking advantage of contextual interference.

Interestingly, the idea that random practice facilitates long-term retention of motor skills is at odds with the traditional, but unsubstantiated, wisdom that individuals with intellectual handicaps will benefit most from a systematically ordered, repetitive schedule of skill instruction. In a study designed to examine skill acquisition in adolescents with DS, Edwards, Elliott, and Lee (1986) used a laboratory, anticipation-timing task that simulates batting a baseball or returning a tennis serve. Participants were situated at the end of a long runway of lights that were illuminated sequentially, resulting in the apparent motion of a target object toward the subject. The task of each participant was to knock down a barrier with a swing of their hand coincident with the virtual object arriving at the end of the runway. Timing error could be determined to the nearest millisecond. All subjects practiced four different runway speeds (3, 4, 6, and 7 mph) in either a blocked or random practice schedule, and then following a retention interval attempted to perform three novel runway speeds (2, 5, and 8 mph). Adult participants with DS and nonhandicapped children of a similar mental age exhibited the same pattern of benefit due to the random practice schedule. Contrary to the typical contextual interference findings, random practice was superior for both performance at the end of acquisition and for learning, which in this case involved performance at the new runway speeds after a retention interval.

Although the majority of the work involving persons with intellectual handicaps has not been limited to DS, the findings are surprisingly consistent. Specifically, conditions involving variability of practice and contextual interference that necessitate active problem-solving by the learner enhance both the long-term retention of specific skills and transfer of training to motor skills of the same type (Painter, Inman, & Vincent, 1994; Poretta, 1982, 1988). These findings involving adults with intellectual handicaps are consistent with learning studies conducted with children and thus are in line with a developmental approach to skill acquisition (e.g., Shapiro & Schmidt, 1982). From a practical point of view, they "suggest that a drill-type approach to motor skill instruction may not be the best approach when dealing with young children" or persons with DS and other handicapping conditions (Edwards et al., 1986, p. 256).

Although under most circumstances persons with DS can be expected to learn a novel motor task just as well as other individuals of the same mental age, there is some evidence that the verbal-motor performance problems exhibited by persons with DS also extend to motor learning. Using the same sequencing apparatus discussed earlier (Elliott & Weeks, 1990), Elliott, Gray, and Weeks (1991) taught participants with and without DS a novel limb movement sequence using a verbal protocol. Although all participants improved at the task over practice, the participants with DS had more difficulty with the task than either mentally handicapped or nonhandicapped control participants after a retention interval during which the verbal cues specifying the sequence were withdrawn. Group differences were particularly profound for movement initiation. This suggests that participants with DS had difficulty internalizing the verbal instructions that were available during acquisition. While the results of this study suggest that the verbal-motor problems associated with DS generalize to skill acquisition, a similar study needs to be conducted in which the instructional mode is visual or verbal. This type of study could help educators develop instructional protocols designed to circumvent some of the specific (perhaps structural) information-processing constraints associated with DS. As well as examining the learning of discrete sequential movements, it will also be important to consider verbal versus visual instructional protocols for the acquisition of continuous movement coordination patterns, as well as complex skills with both continuous and discrete components (Chua, Weeks, & Elliott, 1996). In our future work, we intend to move outside of the laboratory and tackle the problem of motor skill instruction in a typical educational or rehabilitation context.

Conclusions

Research from our laboratory at McMaster University indicates that the developmental approach to perceptual-motor performance in persons with DS breaks down when the motor control or motor learning context involves the verbal, or perhaps even auditory, mediation of movement. In these situations, persons with DS not only exhibit specific difficulties relative to other individuals of the same mental age, but the extent of the "difference" also appears to depend on the complexity of the motor behavior under consideration. Although more research needs to be conducted, it is probably safe to say at this point that the principles/rules of motor behavior that apply to other developmentally young persons do not always apply to persons with DS when the verbal mediation of motor behavior is necessary. In this case, specific differences may require specific strategies for motor skill instruction.

Summary

In this chapter, we argued that persons with DS perform and learn goal-directed movements in a manner similar to other individuals at the same developmental level if the motor behavior under consideration occurs in visually mediated conditions. Given this context, variables such as the availability of visual and kinesthetic feedback, advance information, task difficulty, response competition, and practice structure can be expected to affect the motor performance of persons with DS in the same way as with other individuals of a similar mental age. This suggests that a developmental model of information processing and skill acquisition should be used to guide the instructional protocols used by clinicians, teachers, and parents attempting to optimize skilled performance in this population.

We took a reasonably empirical/descriptive approach to the development versus difference issue of perceptual-motor behavior in persons with DS. However, much of the research we reviewed on the verbal mediation of movement has been driven by a theoretical model of brain organization in persons with DS that also has its roots in our laboratory. The model is presented in detail in chapter 13 (see also Chua et al., 1996). The model, as it currently stands, is far too simple to explain all the complex variations in behavior reviewed here and elsewhere in this book. It has, however, provided a direction for our research program, and together with the empirical work presented here, indicates that neither a developmental nor difference approach in isolation provides adequate answers to our questions about perceptual-motor behavior in DS. In the long term, our research program will focus not only on the constraints imposed by a modified neurobiological system, but also on how those constraints can be circumvented.

References

Anwar, F. (1981). Motor function in Down syndrome. In N.R. Ellis (Ed.), *International review of research in mental retardation: Vol. 10* (pp. 107-138). New York: Academic Press.

Anwar, F., & Hermelin, B. (1979). Kinesthetic movement after-effects in children with Down's syndrome. *Journal of Mental Deficiency Research, 23,* 147-155.

Baumeister, A.A., & Kellas, G. (1968). Distribution of reaction times of retardates and normals. *American Journal of Mental Deficiency, 72,* 715-718.

Berkson, G. (1960). An analysis of reaction time in normal and mentally deficient young men: III. Variation of stimulus and of response complexity. *Journal of Mental Deficiency Research, 4,* 69-77.

Brewer, N., & Smith, G.A. (1982). Cognitive processes for monitoring and regulating speed and accuracy of responding in mental retardation: A methodology. *American Journal of Mental Deficiency, 87,* 211-222.

Brewer, N., & Smith, G.A. (1984). How normal and retarded individuals monitor and regulate speed and accuracy of responding in serial choice tasks. *Journal of Experimental Psychology: General, 113,* 71-93.

Brown, A.L., & Campione, J.C. (1986). Training for transfer: Guidelines for promoting flexible use of trained skills. In M.G. Wade (Ed.), *Motor skill acquisition of the mentally handicapped* (pp. 257-271). Amsterdam: North-Holland.

Carlton, L.G. (1981). Visual information: The control of aiming movements. *Quarterly Journal of Experimental Psychology, 33A,* 87-93.

Carlton, L.G. (1992). Visual processing time and the control of movement. In L. Proteau & D. Elliott (Eds.), *Vision and motor control* (pp. 3-31). Amsterdam: North-Holland.

Carson, R.G. (1996). Putative right hemisphere contributions to the preparation of reaching and aiming movements. In D. Elliott & E.A. Roy (Eds.), *Manual asymmetries in motor performance* (pp. 159-172). Boca Raton, FL: CRC Press.

Chua, R., & Elliott, D. (1993). Visual regulation of manual aiming. *Human Movement Science, 12*, 365-401.

Chua, R., Weeks, D.J., & Elliott, D. (1996). A functional systems approach to understanding verbal motor integration in individuals with Down syndrome. *Down Syndrome: Research and Practice, 4*, 25-36.

Davis, W.E., & Kelso, J.A.S. (1982). Analysis of 'invariant characteristics' in motor control of Down's syndrome and normal subjects. *Journal of Motor Behavior, 14*, 194-212.

Davis, W.E., Sparrow, W.A., & Ward, T. (1991). Fractionated reaction times and movement times of Down syndrome and other adults with mental retardation. *Adapted Physical Activity Quarterly, 8*, 221-233.

Edwards, J.M., Elliott, D., & Lee, T.D. (1986). Contextual interference effects during skill acquisition and transfer in Down's syndrome adolescents. *Adapted Physical Activity Quarterly, 3*, 250-258.

Elliott, D. (1990). Movement control and Down's syndrome: A neuropsychological approach. In G. Reid (Ed.), *Problems in movement control* (pp. 201-216). Amsterdam: North-Holland.

Elliott, D., & Allard, F. (1985). The utilization of visual feedback information during rapid pointing movements. *Quarterly Journal of Experimental Psychology, 37A*, 407-425.

Elliott, D., Gray, S., & Weeks, D.J. (1991). Verbal cuing and motor skill acquisition for adults with Down syndrome. *Adapted Physical Activity Quarterly, 8*, 210-220.

Elliott, D., & Weeks, D.J. (1990). Cerebral specialization and the control of oral and limb movements for individuals with Down's syndrome. *Journal of Motor Behavior, 22*, 6-18.

Elliott, D., & Weeks, D.J. (1993). Cerebral specialization for speech perception and movement organization in adults with Down's syndrome. *Cortex, 29*, 103-113.

Elliott, D., Weeks, D.J., & Gray, S. (1990). Manual and oral praxis in adults with Down's syndrome. *Neuropsychologia, 28*, 1307-1315.

Eysenck, H.J. (1967). Intelligence assessment: A theoretical and experimental approach. *British Journal of Educational Psychology, 37*, 81-98.

Fitts, P.M. (1954). The information capacity of the human motor system in controlling the amplitude of movement. *Journal of Experimental Psychology, 47*, 381-391.

Fitts, P.M., & Peterson, J.R. (1964). Information capacity of discrete motor responses. *Journal of Experimental Psychology, 67*, 103-112.

Frith, U., & Frith, C.D. (1974). Specific motor disabilities in Down's syndrome. *Journal of Child Psychology and Psychiatry, 15*, 293-301.

Goodman, D., & Kelso, J.A.S. (1980). Are movements prepared in parts? Not under compatible (naturalized) conditions. *Journal of Experimental Psychology: General, 109*, 475-495.

Grossman, H.J. (1977). *Manual on terminology and classification in mental retardation.* Washington, DC: American Association on Mental Deficiency.

Hay, L. (1990). Developmental changes in eye-hand coordination behaviors: Preprogramming versus feedback control. In C. Bard, M. Fleury, & L. Hay (Eds.), *Development of eye-hand coordination across the life span* (pp. 217-244). Columbia: University of South Carolina Press.

Henderson, S.E., Morris, J., & Frith, U. (1981). The motor deficit in Down's syndrome children: A problem of timing? *Journal of Child Psychology and Psychiatry, 22*, 233-245.

Hermelin, B. (1964). Effects of variation in the warning signal on reaction times of severe subnormals. *Quarterly Journal of Experimental Psychology, 16*, 241-249.

Hodges, N.J., Cunningham, S.J., Lyons, J., Kerr, T.L., & Elliott, D. (1995). Visual feedback processing and goal-directed movement in adults with Down syndrome. *Adapted Physical Activity Quarterly, 12*, 176-186.

Hoover, J.H., & Wade, M.G. (1985). Motor learning theory and mentally retarded individuals: A historical review. *Adapted Physical Activity Quarterly, 2*, 228-252.

Hoover, J.H., Wade, M.G., & Newell, K.M. (1981). The trainability of reaction time and movement time in moderately mentally handicapped workers. *American Journal of Mental Deficiency, 85*, 389-395.

Kools, J.A., Williams, A.F., Vickers, M.J., & Caell, A. (1971). Oral and limb apraxia in mentally retarded children with deviant articulation. *Cortex, 7*, 387-400.

Kulatunga-Moruzi, C., & Elliott, D. (1999). Manual and attentional asymmetries in goal-directed movements for adults with Down syndrome. *Adapted Physical Activity Quarterly, 16*, 138-154.

Latash, M.L., & Anson, J.G. (1996). What are "normal movements" in atypical populations? *Behavioral and Brain Sciences, 19*, 55-106.

LeClair, D.A., & Elliott, D. (1995). Verbal and visual advance information in the preparation of movement in adults with Down syndrome. *Adapted Physical Activity Quarterly, 12*, 239-249.

LeClair, D.A., Pollock, B.J., & Elliott, D. (1993). Movement preparation in adults with and without Down syndrome. *American Journal on Mental Retardation, 97*, 628-633.

Lee, T.D., Elliott, D., & Carnahan, H. (1987). The preparation of actions and parameters of action: A fixed or variable process? *Acta Psychologica, 66*, 83-102.

Lee, T.D., & Magill, R.A. (1983). The locus of contextual interference in motor skill acquisition. *Journal of Experimental Psychology: Learning, Memory and Cognition, 9*, 730-746.

Lyons, J., Elliott, D., Swanson, L.R., & Chua, R. (1996). The use of vision in manual aiming by young and older adults. *Journal of Aging and Physical Activity, 4*, 165-178.

Mack, P., & MacKay, D.N. (1989). Reaction times of Down's syndrome and other mentally retarded individuals. *Perceptual and Motor Skills, 69*, 430.

MacKay, D.N., & Bankhead, L. (1983) Reaction times of Down's syndrome and other mentally retarded individuals. *Perceptual and Motor Skills, 56*, 266.

Miezejeski, C.M., Heaney, G., Belser, R., & Sersen, E.A. (1994). Aberrant lateralization of brainstem auditory evoked responses by individuals with Down syndrome. *American Journal on Mental Retardation, 98*, 481-489.

Nettlebeck, T., & Brewer, N. (1981). Studies of mild mental retardation and timed performance. In N.R. Ellis (Ed.), *International review of research in mental retardation: Vol. 10* (pp. 62-106). New York: Academic Press.

Painter, M.A., Inman, K.B., & Vincent, W.J. (1994). Contextual interference effects in acquisition and retention of motor tasks by individuals with mild mental handicaps. *Adapted Physical Activity Quarterly, 11*, 383-395.

Porretta, D.L. (1982). Motor schema formation by EMR boys. *American Journal of Mental Deficiency, 87*, 164-172.

Porretta, D.L. (1988). Contextual interference effects on the transfer and retention of a gross motor skill by mildly mentally handicapped children. *Adapted Physical Activity Quarterly, 5*, 332-339.

Posner, M.I. (1978). *Chronometric exploration of the mind.* Hillsdale, NJ: Erlbaum.

Posner, M.I., Nissen, M.J., & Klein, R.M. (1976). Visual dominance: An information processing account of its origins and significance. *Psychological Review, 83*, 157-171.

Rabbitt, P.M.A. (1979). How old and young subjects monitor and control responses for accuracy and speed. *British Journal of Psychology, 70,* 305-311.

Rabbitt, P.M.A. (1981). Sequential reactions. In D.H. Holding (Ed.), *Human skill* (pp. 147-170). London: Wiley.

Reid, G. (1980). The effects of memory strategy instruction in the short-term motor memory of the mentally retarded. *Journal of Motor Behavior, 12,* 221-227.

Rosenbaum, D. (1980). Human movement initiation: Specification of arm, direction, and extent. *Journal of Experimental Psychology: General, 109,* 444-474.

Salmoni, A.W., Schmidt, R.A., & Walter, C.B. (1984). Knowledge of results and motor learning: A review and critical reappraisal. *Psychological Bulletin, 95,* 355-386.

Shapiro, D.C., & Schmidt, R.A. (1982). The schema theory: Recent evidence and developmental implications. In J.A.S. Kelso & J.E. Clark (Eds.), *The development of movement control and coordination* (pp. 113-150). New York: Wiley.

Shea, J.B., & Morgan, R.L. (1979). Contextual interference effects on acquisition, retention and transfer of motor skill. *Journal of Experimental Psychology: Human Learning and Memory, 5,* 179-187.

Vernon, P.A. (1986). Speed of information-processing, intelligence, and mental retardation. In M.G. Wade (Ed.), *Motor skill acquisition of the mentally handicapped* (pp. 113-129). Amsterdam: North-Holland.

Wade, M.G., Newell, K., & Wallace, S.A. (1978). Decision time and movement time as a function of response complexity in retarded persons. *American Journal of Mental Deficiency, 83,* 135-144.

Weeks, D.J., Chua, R., Elliott, D., Weinberg, H., Cheyne, D., & Lyons, J. (1997). The use of magnetoencephalography (MEG) to investigate cerebral specialization in Down syndrome. *Journal of Sport & Exercise Psychology, 19,* S117.

Woodworth, R.S. (1899). The accuracy of voluntary movement. *Psychological Review, 3* (Monograph Suppl. 2), 1-119.

Author Note

The preparation of this chapter and our latest empirical studies were supported by the Scottish Rite Charitable Foundation of Canada.

4
CHAPTER

Locomotor Patterns of Individuals With Down Syndrome: Effects of Environmental and Task Constraints

Eliane Mauerberg-deCastro
Universidade Estadual Paulista
Rio Claro, Brazil

Rosa M. Angulo-Kinzler
University of Michigan

Key words

locomotion ◆ phase portraits ◆ task constraints ◆ environmental constraints ◆ forward locomotion ◆ backward locomotion ◆ running ◆ coordination ◆ dynamical systems ◆ organismic constraints ◆ phase angles

Much has been written about individuals with Down syndrome (DS) and their motor deficits (Haley, 1986; Latash, Almeida, & Corcos, 1993; Shumway-Cook & Woollacott, 1985), developmental delays (Block, 1991; Parker, Bronks, & Snyder, 1986; Parker & James, 1985), health impairments, neurological abnormalities, and deteriorations such as those caused by associations with Alzheimer's disease (Percy, Dalton, Markovic, McLachlan, Hummel, Rusk, & Andrews, 1990). Much of the literature has placed importance on the identification of the impairing factors leading to limitations in development and the learning of functional skills in individuals with DS.

In the area of motor behavior, the control and coordination capabilities of people from special populations often are explained using concepts built on unfair comparisons to normally developing individuals. However, individuals with DS develop specific behaviors based on pertinent solutions, the result of an interplay between their biological inheritance and environmental and task demands.

Recently, researchers appear to be more interested in looking for mechanisms of motor control and coordination using a process-oriented analysis (Thelen & Smith, 1994; Ulrich & Ulrich, 1995; Ulrich, Ulrich, Collier, & Cole, 1995). That is, rather than employing a product-oriented analysis that focuses on final behaviors, these researchers are examining the process of change in emergent behaviors of infants with DS. They argue that individual differences and variability can result from a wide spectrum of motor choices available to these individual infants (Ulrich & Ulrich, 1995; Ulrich, Ulrich, Angulo-Kinzler, & Chapman, 1997). These choices are dependent on their intrinsic dynamics (i.e., behavioral possibilities that result from organismic constraints—neural networks; muscle, joint and tendinous elements) and on the context demands (i.e., environmental and task constraints).

Sparrow (1992) mentioned that studies in motor behavior have often included single-case research because detailed movement pattern measures are obtained to capture the process of change in control and coordination. In the area of human gait analysis, for example, continuous change in intralimb coordination is captured via dynamic tools such as angle-angle diagrams (Sparrow, 1992), phase portraits (Beuter & Garfinkel, 1985; Clark & Phillips, 1991), or phase angles (Clark, Truly, & Phillips, 1993; Kelso, Saltzman, & Tuller, 1986). These tools provide qualitative analyses necessary for a dynamic systems approach.

This chapter takes a dynamic systems approach to examining the locomotor behaviors of individuals with DS. Moreover, the chapter is concerned with the impact of different constraints on the behaviors of individuals with DS and how their modes of coordination and strategies of control can be identified. Here, following a process-oriented analysis, we provide a qualitative analysis utilizing dynamic tools such as *phase portraits* and *phase angles* to explain how and why locomotion patterns of children and adults with DS adapt under task and environmental constraints. In the first section we present definitions and explanations of some dynamic systems terms such as *intrinsic dynamics* and *constraints*. The next section includes details on the analysis of locomotion using dynamic systems tools such as phase portraits and phase angles. The "methods" section describes the assessment of walking and running behaviors of children and adults with DS. In our "results and discussion" section we present the patterns, captured via phase portraits, of walking and running by these individuals. We also present their patterns of walking on different support surfaces. Finally, we examine the effects of change in direction (i.e., backward and forward walking and running) on the resultant locomotion patterns and relative intralimb coordination.

Dynamic Principles in Locomotion Behavior and Sources of Constraints

When an organism's subsystems set limits or boundaries on behavior, we refer to them in dynamic systems terms as *constraints* (Mauerberg-deCastro, Ulrich, & Angulo-Kinzler, 1995). Constraints arise not only from the elements or subsystems of an organism (neural networks, muscle, skeletal structure, joint and tendinous elements), but also from contexts, where tasks and environments change according to the perspective of a given organism. Constraints set the boundaries of the system's behavior, leading to the emergence of semipredictable, patterned behaviors. At the same time, constraints are flexible enough to maintain the system's sensitivity to its own changes as well as changes in context (Saltzman & Kelso, 1987). Thus, even though invariant patterns can be found in human behavior repertoires, rapid behavioral modulations can take place in response to subtle environmental changes (or new task demands). When these modulations go too far beyond a system's preferred behavioral mode, transitions to a new behavioral form can occur. These concepts may help us to understand how the locomotor behaviors of individuals with DS become patterned and predictable, yet remain flexible and adaptive.

The acquisition of bipedal locomotion allows humans not only to explore exterior spaces, surfaces, and surrounding objects (e.g., avoid obstacles, go over objects, pass through openings, etc.), but also to explore alternatives with regard to their own intrinsic dynamics. When compared to a normally developing child, for example, a child with cerebral palsy has a unique intrinsic dynamic because she or he has to deal with the organismic constraints typical for that condition.

Biologically, humans demonstrate multiple levels of reorganization or varied levels of flexibility. Consequently, adaptation is possible. Adaptation, as a result of effective experience, can be observed by looking at the similarities within a species' behavior. It can also be observed by looking at differences in individual behaviors in a given species. For example, the architecture of legs, muscles, and neurons guarantees that walking has an invariant pattern among healthy humans. After some practice, human infants can exhibit, as their adult peers do, predictable patterns of locomotion (Clark & Phillips, 1991). However, opportunity for practice is a potential source of individual differences. According to Ulrich (1997), opportunity for practice is a key component for the emergence and organization of behavioral patterns because it provides the needed interplay between the acting system and its sources of constraint (i.e., the organism itself, the environment, and task demands).

Environmental constraints such as texture, deformability, and the inclination of surfaces influence how an individual tunes his or her system and subsystems (e.g., neuromusculoskeletal components) so that a reliable, adaptive, and functional behavior can occur. In real life, the environment is not always stable and predictable. For example, given unfamiliar surfaces of support, an older person using a cane to assist walking may slow down to prevent falls.

In addition to environmental constraints, it is important to note that task constraints such as speed, direction, and movement magnitude are important variables that impact movement patterns. For example, if a person is required to increase walking speed on an elastic surface such as a trampoline, the steps will gradually increase in amplitude and velocity due to the propulsion created by the deformation of the elastic surface. If no attempts are made to dampen or stop movement, the person may start running or have his or her body projected forward and upward. If in addition the person has balance problems, these organismic constraints will start to contribute to changes in locomotor behavior. This person may fall forward and, eventually, down. Thus, efficiency and adaptability depend on the three-way interplay among environment, task, and organismic constraints.

The Analysis of Locomotion in Down Syndrome

The developmental course of disabilities intrigues researchers because it raises questions about the diversity of adaptation and the unique solutions available to disabled organisms. However, the challenges facing researchers are, first, to identify impacting constraints (e.g., a damaged brain structure) and, second, to measure their contribution to the actual status of behavior (e.g., the correlation between the extent of brain damage and dysfunction). In general, associations between structure and function derived from sophisticated measures (i.e., CAT scan, functional MRI) can indicate how important a particular constraint is to a given behavior. However, the contribution of a constraint can also be determined by examining changes in behavior. Behavioral change can be reflected in levels of stability/instability or the emergence of new behaviors. Therefore, researchers manipulate constraints and observe the consequent changes in the system's behavior to better understand the adaptive interplay between organism and environment. For example, we would expect a blindfolded individual walking through an obstacle course to have initial collisions and use exploratory patterns during the course of walking. Through these exploratory strategies, subjects learn and decrease their frequency of collisions.

However, experimental manipulations or imposed changes in constraints may not have a significant impact on the system's behavior. A consistent behavioral pattern that is not easily disrupted is said to have *structural stability* (Clark et al., 1993).

The system's behavior can be qualitatively assessed in its level of stability and also in its mechanisms of control so that the impact of constraints can be observed. Those parameters that best represent a system's behavior can rely on as few as two kinematic parameters: *angular position* and *angular velocity*. Plots of these two variables in a Cartesian coordinate system yield a simple tool, a *phase portrait* (Abraham & Shaw, 1984), that can be used to model dynamic systems. Rhythmical and cyclical leg actions during locomotion are referred to as *limit cycle oscillators* (Clark et al., 1993) or *attractors*, and can have their topologies represented in phase portraits. Phase portraits are constructed from *dependent variables* (i.e., angular velocity and angular position) and can be affected by various *independent variables* (i.e., experience, motivation, developmental level, presence of a disability), which act as constraints during the simple behavior of walking.

Phase Portraits

A phase portrait that captures the cyclical behavior of a system is constructed by plotting angular position against the angular velocity of a segment. The topographic quality of a phase portrait, or its dimensionless qualitative aspects (i.e., low-dimensional dynamics), allows us to analyze the continuous intralimb process of coordination during walking and running. Phase portraits also allow us to identify control strategies individuals use when perturbed by different contexts, when at different developmental levels, or when faced with disabling conditions.

Phase portraits have been used to study control and coordination in individuals with disabilities (Beuter & Garfinkel, 1985; Heriza, 1988), analyze task dynamics (Saltzman & Kelso, 1987), verify developmental changes on the gait of new walkers (Forrester, Phillips, & Clark, 1992), and identify the impact of environmental constraints on stepping behavior (Mauerberg-deCastro et al., 1995).

Based on Abraham and Shaw's work (1984), Winstein and Garfinkel (1989) provided interesting descriptions of the geometry (or shapes) of phase portraits. They include the following:

- *Round shape:* reflects a pendulum motion.
- *Steep positive slopes:* indicate ballistic action requiring fast acceleration.
- *Squared corners:* indicate movement with a constant velocity preceded or followed by ballistic motion.
- *Loops:* reflect reversals of movement within a cycle. A sequence of two reversals, backward-to-forward and vice versa, creates one loop.
- *Inward/outward inflection:* with or without reversals of direction, means that a sudden reduction and resumption of velocity occurred. Inflections often occur during the support phase or near a footstrike. If a stepper stops his or her movement at the middle of the swing phase, a sharp inflection will result, with the velocity dropping to zero.

Phase Angles

Another tool used to describe the low dimensionality of a dynamic system is the phase angle. A phase angle provides a description of the relative coordination between adjacent segments (i.e., intralimb coordination) during locomotion and their phase locking (i.e., in- and out-of-phase relation) for individual cycles.

To construct a phase angle, each point in a phase portrait is converted from a fixed coordinate system (i.e., Cartesian system) to a moving coordinate system (i.e., a polar coordinate system) (Meriam, 1966). The phase angle's reference system relies on a polar vector, and the direction of motion conventionally begins at 0° along the horizontal axis and proceeds clockwise. Figure 4.1 represents the conventional transformation of information from a Cartesian coordinate system into a polar coordinate system.

Plotting the phase angles of two adjacent segments permits us to visualize the coordination relation of two coupled systems (i.e., two segments of a limb during locomotion) across relative time (i.e., one cycle duration). There are portions of the cycle in which the shank and thigh segments move in-phase with regard to each other and other portions of the cycle in which they move out-of-phase. If plots of the trajectories of the two segments during walking run parallel to each other, they are in-phase. Alternatively, if the plots run in opposite directions, they are out-of-phase.

Both phase portraits and phase angles are used as a collective variable (Clark et al., 1993), which represents the complex processes underlying coordinated human movement (Thelen & Smith, 1994). Questions about coordination can be addressed differently through both methods of data reduction.

In the sections that follow, we present some preliminary work for the purpose of demonstrating and discussing aspects of adaptation and strategies of control during locomotion by individuals with Down syndrome while under task and environmental constraints. Our first goal was to highlight the status of locomotion of individuals with DS. Second, we sought to determine the impact of different environmental constraints on the pattern of locomotion. Our final goal was to determine the impact of task constraints on the locomotion patterns. By using concepts and tools offered by a dynamic systems approach (i.e., phase portraits and phase angles), we were able to represent and analyze the low-dimensional dynamics of the locomotion typical of individuals with DS, and their adaptations to imposed constraints.

Preliminary Work

Five children with DS, ages 4 to 9 years, and three adults with DS, ages 30 to 38 years, were selected from larger samples of individuals with mental retardation who are participants in other studies currently underway in our laboratory. Participants included males and females who attended the same institution in Rio Claro, São Paulo, Brazil (APAE, Associação de Pais e Amigos do Excepcional). One 22-year-old normal participant (CAR) volunteered to be used as a reference for normal locomotion behavior.

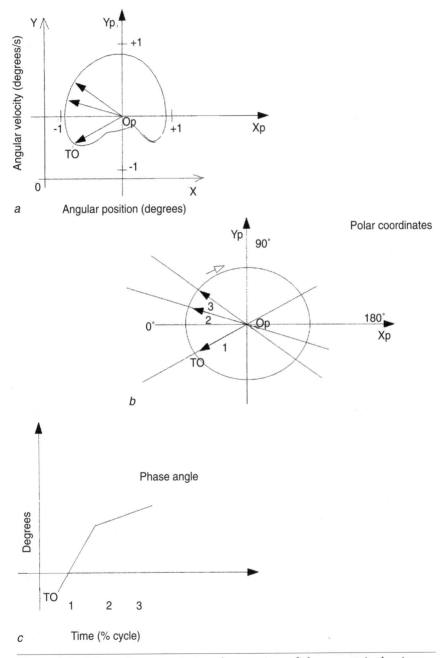

Figure 4.1 Schematic representation of conversions of phase-portrait plots into phase-angle plots: (*a*) normalization of parameters in Cartesian coordinates; (*b*) transformation from Cartesian into polar coordinates; (*c*) phase angles (degrees) across time (% of cycle). (TO = toeoff.)

Procedure

For each participant the following anatomical joints were marked with black and white circle Band-Aid pads: ankles (lateral malleolus), knees (lateral epicondyle of femur), and hips (greater trochanter of femur). Kinematic analyses were performed for the two segments—shank and thigh—and the knee joint. Subjects were requested (verbally or by demonstration) to walk and run at their preferred pace along a corridor. Some participants needed the aid of an assistant to perform the tasks.

The environmental constraints were slightly different between the groups of children and adults with DS because they belonged to two different studies. The environmental contexts included the following:

- *Hard surface:* Children and adults walked and ran with bare feet on a concrete floor.

- *Elastic surface:* Children walked with bare feet on a trampoline, and adults walked with bare feet on 7 cm thick pads placed on the walkway.

- *Beam surface:* Children and adults walked on a 7 cm × 4 m beam placed on the walkway.

The reference participant was tested in the same environmental conditions as both DS groups, including the two elastic surfaces.

Some of the children with DS were unable to perform some of the walking tasks (i.e., walking on the beam and backward walking) without the support of an assistant. In such cases, an assistant supported the subject by holding the subject's hands as he or she walked. Six trials of five or more steps for walking and three or more steps for running were videotaped. The two locomotion behaviors were performed in both forward and backward directions. While the adults with DS performed both forward and backward running, none of the children with DS were able to run backward. One child was unable to walk on the trampoline.

The sagittal view of the participants was videotaped and joint mark points subsequently digitized. Figure 4.2 represents the resulting angles for segmental and joint angles.

The angles were calculated with respect to the horizontal line of reference for the shank and thigh segments and the anatomical joint at the knee. The knee joint measurements were derived from the thigh and shank angles. When the knee was fully extended, the angle had a value of 180°. Using the angular position, angular velocity was then calculated.

For each participant, phase portraits were plotted using angular position as the x-axis and angular velocity as the y-axis. The phase portraits were plotted in a clockwise direction for forward locomotion and counterclockwise for backward locomotion. In addition, angular position and angular velocity were normalized in order to calculate the phase angle-time history of shank and thigh segments for comparisons among the DS participants and the reference participant.

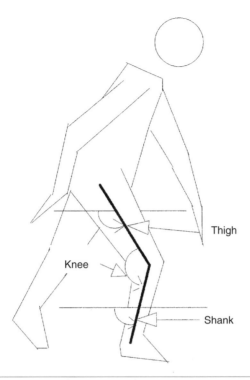

Figure 4.2 Representation of angle calculations for the shank and thigh segments and the knee joint in the sagittal plane.

Patterns of Walking

The walking patterns of the five children with DS were very similar to those of the adults with DS and to that of the reference participant. Figure 4.3 shows an example of a phase portrait of one of the adults with DS (subject ROB). The movements of both joints show very smooth trajectories and resemble a typical adultlike pattern of walking (see Clark & Phillips, 1991). Some variability, probably due to modulation of speed, was seen for one of the adults with DS.

The ranges-of-motion (r-o-m) of the children with DS were slightly more variable than those of the adults with DS. Their mean values for angular position were 70° for the shank segment and 36° for the thigh segment. The adults' mean values for the same segments were 78° and 42°, respectively. The smaller r-o-m for the shank by the children with DS was mostly due to a lesser degree of extension at the hip level. However, during walking, the children were elevating their thighs (average 82° flexion), so that they had different reversal points than those of the adults with DS (average 71° flexion). At the same time, they took shorter steps than those of their older peers. Small and fast steps were the strategies observed here. In fact, the mean peak velocities for the shank and thigh of the children, 464°/s

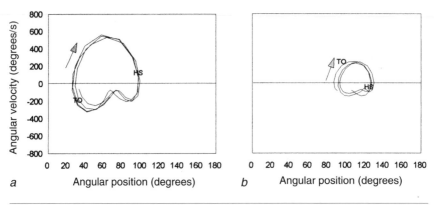

Figure 4.3 Phase portraits of one adult with DS (ROB) walking on a hard surface: (*a*) shank; (*b*) thigh. (HS = heelstrike; TO = toeoff.)

and 192°/s, respectively, confirm this observation. The adults' mean peak velocities were 356°/s and 174°/s, respectively.

According to these results and despite some spatiotemporal differences between participants and groups, commonalities rather than differences were observed in all of the walking cycles, reflecting similar coordination patterns among children with DS, adults with DS, and our normal adult.

Patterns of Running

Four of the five children with DS were able to run, although none of them consistently exhibited a phase in which both feet came off the ground (flight phase). Some of their steps exhibited a momentary double support that lasted at least 33 ms, which was our camera's sampling resolution. The adults with DS had no problem running. The children's inability to maintain the flight phase consistently throughout the trials reflects a developmental delay typical for this population. However, their patterns of coordination did not differ from our normal participant. Everyone, including the adults with DS, exhibited a smooth and pendular type of activity for both segments.

In general, the children with DS exhibited varied r-o-m and velocities during running, probably due to the eventual emergence of double support (since they were oscillating between flight and double-support phases). The mean r-o-m values for both children and adults with DS were closer to their own walking r-o-m than the normal participant's r-o-m for running. The r-o-m of the shank segments of the children with DS were limited to 73°, and for the adults with DS to 78°. The normal participant's r-o-m was 88°.

The major indicator of differences in patterns of running between the two groups with DS and our normal participant was knee activity. During locomotion, activity at the knee joint reveals levels of damping that are represented by the inner loops formed in the phase portraits. By examining the size of the typical inner loop, one can make inferences about the magnitude of damping (Forrester, et al., 1992). According to Davis and Sinning (1987), damping is an internal frictional force indicated by the extension of oscillation of a joint with respect to its final resting position. These authors suggest that decreased levels of stiffness and damping can be characteristics of muscle hypotonia, a common motor deficiency in individuals with DS. However, their results showed that measures of stiffness were not significantly different among DS, non-DS mentally handicapped, and nonhandicapped subjects. Davis and Kelso (1982) also found no difference between individuals with DS and nonhandicapped individuals with regard to measures of stiffness. However, the individuals with DS were less capable of voluntary increases in levels of stiffness as well as presenting underdamped muscle-joint systems.

Figure 4.4 shows knee phase portraits of four children with DS. The inner loops are very small when compared to the inner loop found in the phase portrait for our normal adult during running (see the left side of figure 4.11a, page 92). Although these phase portraits exhibit a large overall trajectory, it is not necessarily related to the amount of damping, but instead to high velocities of segmental oscillation during the fast and short steps taken by this group during running.

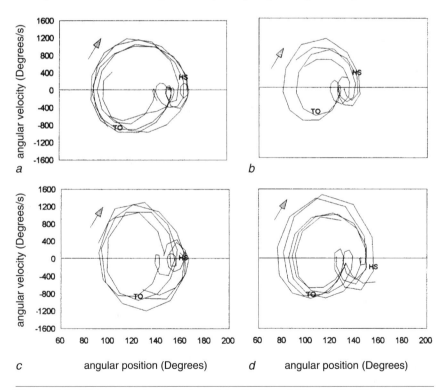

Figure 4.4 Phase portraits of the knee joint for four children with DS running: (*a*) WAM; (*b*) SER; (*c*) WER; (*d*) ALE. (HS = heelstrike; TO = toeff.)

The adults with DS revealed segmental running patterns similar to those of the children with DS but with slightly larger inner loops in the knee phase portraits. As stated earlier, these adults consistently demonstrated all phases characteristic of mature running even though their r-o-m here was similar to that of walking.

Impact of Surfaces on Walking Behavior

The use of different surfaces as sources of constraint is a viable method for identifying levels of stability in fundamental motor skills such as walking. Also, by assessing walking on different surfaces of support, we can identify strategies of control typical of individuals with DS and perhaps better understand their adaptive processes.

Even though both surfaces were considerably different in their elastic properties, the use of the trampoline for children with DS and a pad surface for the adults with DS as soft surfaces was an effective way to demonstrate how these individuals responded differently to environmental constraints.

The trampoline surface provided the children with DS with a very dynamic medium during the support phase and therefore acted as a source of energy for subsequent steps. The elastic surface propelled the children, thereby causing them to speed up successive steps. This propulsion can be observed in the phase portraits of both shank and thigh segments during trampoline walking shown in figure 4.5.

The progressive expansion of orbits indicates that the children were walking progressively faster as they moved across the surface of the trampoline. The only limitation to the emergence of running seems to be the short distance across the trampoline. Indeed, after seven or eight steps, the children were forced to break their movement pattern. The shank phase portrait for WAM (figure 4.5a) illustrated a quick increase in rotational velocity just after the heelstrike (i.e., beginning of the support phase). During walking on a hard surface there is a large dissipation of energy visible in the shank phase portrait at the initiation of the support phase. As a consequence, rotational velocity tends to drop to near zero, causing an inflection in the lower part of the phase portrait. Due to the nature of the elastic surface of the trampoline at the support phase, WAM (figure 4.5a) exhibited phase portraits with shapes characteristic of both shank and thigh segments with very subtle inward inflections and high negative velocity (see also WER's thigh phase portrait, figure 4.5c, right column). The common aspect among all the children was the progressive increases in velocity and r-o-m across cycles and, more notable, the small degree of shank rotation at the backward-to-forward rotation (approximately 20° or less). This means that, as a result of the propulsion created by the elastic surface when the foot left the surface, the shank was almost parallel with the horizontal line. (Remember, when the shank is perpendicular to the ground, it is at a 90° angle with respect to the horizontal line.)

The knee phase portraits for all of the children indicate, by small or absent inner loops, that the damping process during walking on the trampoline was not the same

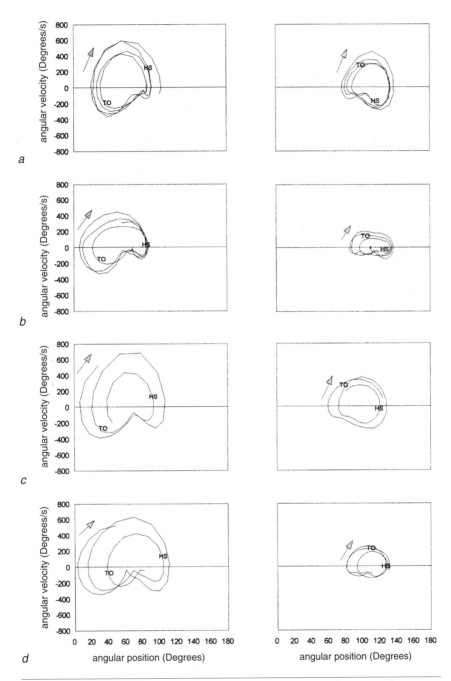

Figure 4.5 Phase portraits of four children with DS walking on a trampoline: shank (left column); thigh (right column); *(a)* WAM; *(b)* SER; *(c)* WER; *(d)* ALE. (HS = heelstrike; TO = toeoff.)

as for walking on hard surfaces (see figure 4.6). In fact, demands for damping at the knee during walking on the trampoline are probably unnecessary. The moment the heel strikes, the elastic surface deforms and displaces with the foot. When the surface of the trampoline reaches its maximum stretch, the leg motion reverses and travels in the opposite direction (i.e., upward).

The finding of consistently small or absent inner loops in knee phase portraits during walking on a trampoline supports the notion that strategies of control rely on information about surface properties. Damping is provided externally by deformation of the trampoline surface. Consequently, the children are relying on this kind of information and move with different strategies. However, sensitivity to this kind of information certainly depends on experience so that modulations or strategies are appropriate. Remember that one child with DS was unable to walk on the trampoline without falling. Perhaps a person who has balance problems and is concerned for his or her safety would not take advantage of an elastic surface in the same manner as a more secure child. Instead he or she would try to control fast-growing steps generated from external constraints (i.e., the elastic properties of the

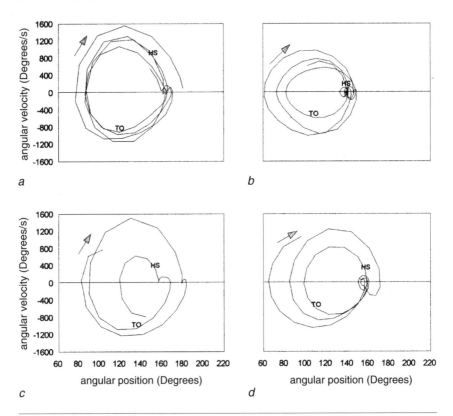

Figure 4.6   Knee phase portraits of four children with DS walking on a trampoline: (*a*) WAM; (*b*) SER; (*c*) WER; (*d*) ALE. (HS = heelstrike; TO = toeoff.)

surface dynamically changing with leg displacement and gravity) in an attempt to avoid falls. It would be interesting to see if the adults with DS would be as carefree as the children seemed to be in walking on the trampoline.

When the adults with DS walked on the pad surface, they experienced a momentary downward displacement as the foot struck the surface until the pad compressed against the ground. The limited deformability and propulsion of this surface were probably the causes of more restricted ranges of movements and lower velocities by these individuals. Also, instability was evident in the phase portrait trajectories for two out of three adults with DS, suggesting that these individuals could be experiencing balance problems as they walked on the pad. Perhaps slow and limited motion were strategies adopted by these individuals to prevent falls.

Figure 4.7 represents the shank, thigh, and respective knee phase portraits of two adults with DS. It is interesting to note that, for these individuals, both shank and thigh phase portraits are relatively small and quite similar in shape and location in state space. Also, the relatively small size of the knee phase portrait (compared to other examples of knee phase portraits used throughout this chapter) indicates that little activity is taking place at this joint because both segments are oscillating at similar amplitudes and directions.

The limited action of the knee in adults with DS could be due to an augmented level of stiffness. In another study examining the stepping patterns of infants with DS, we found that limited knee action in prewalkers could be an important factor in the existing number of degrees of freedom. In some of our findings, the similarity of phase portrait shapes between segments and locations in state space, as well as reduced sizes of knee phase portraits, led us to speculate that a degree of freedom was missing. That is, two segments oscillated with the same r-o-m and at the same rate, configuring a single- rather than a double-pendulum mechanism. This means that there was no activity at the knee level; instead, it acted as a locked joint rather than as a hinge (Mauerberg-deCastro et al., 1995).

Both groups were exposed to the beam surface, although none of the children were able to walk without the support of an assistant. Perhaps the most common aspect of an altered topology in their walking was instability throughout trajectories. The unstable support phase showed the most pervasive evidence regarding the degree of difficulty experienced by these children (see figure 4.8).

Pendular action—a round and smooth trajectory—was observed during the swing phase of the shank segment for three of five children, although not necessarily observed for the adjacent thigh segment. It seems apparent that poor balance and, at the same time, voluntary attempts to place the foot on the beam made the thigh more susceptible to variability. Smaller and slower steps, which resulted in smaller phase portraits, reflected higher levels of control during walking.

The adults with DS walked on the beam without any help. Similar to the children with DS, the adults were unstable and exhibited smaller phase portraits than when walking on a hard surface.

Similar to our previous findings for the pad surface, the size of knee phase portraits was reduced as a consequence of reduced knee action on the beam surface.

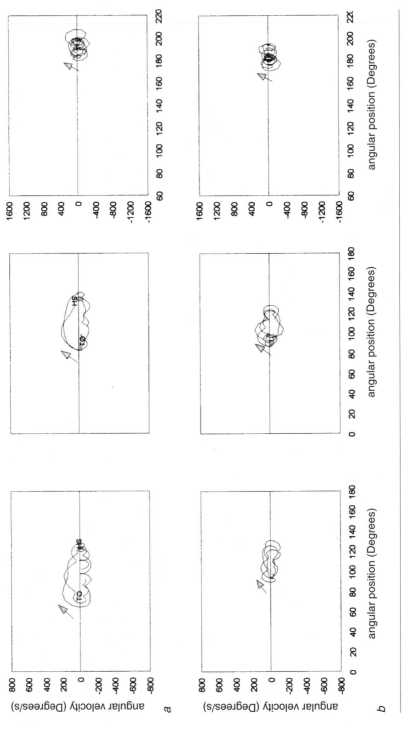

Figure 4.7 Phase portraits of two adults with DS walking on a pad surface: shank (left column), thigh (center column), and knee (right column); (*a*) ROB; (*b*) MIG. (HS = heelstrike; TO = toeoff.)

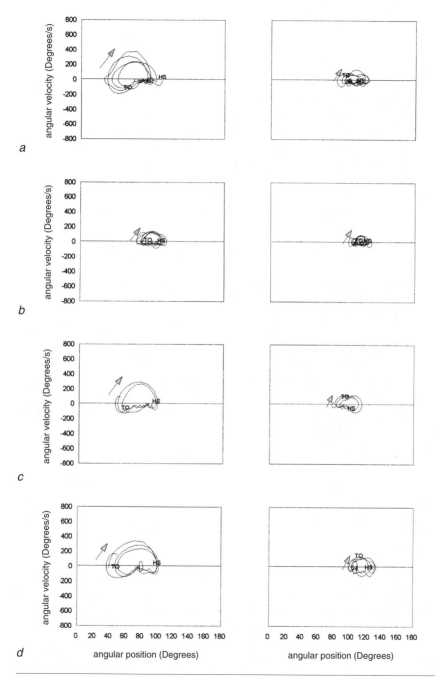

Figure 4.8 Phase portraits of four children with DS walking on a beam: shank (left column) and thigh (right column); *(a)* WAM; *(b)* SER; *(c)* WER; *(d)* ALE. (HS = heelstrike; TO = toeoff.)

Here, the three adults with DS also exhibited similar patterns for both shank and thigh segments simultaneously, which resulted in small knee phase portraits.

In summary, it seems apparent that the different surfaces influenced walking such that different strategies of control emerged that were contingent upon the context and properties of the environment. Although trampoline and pad surfaces share some elastic properties, they have different levels of resistance and influence children and adults differently. However, the beam surface was a very restrictive environment to both groups. Instability was common to both children and adults with DS. The limited knee action for the adults with DS reflected the individual strategies these individuals used to maintain their balance. This strategy could have been used to minimize vertical displacements of their bodies. Conversely, the children with DS, also with balance problems, had choices about when and where to place their feet on the beam, because they were assisted with external support.

Backward Locomotion: Coordination Styles

In general, people have little opportunity to practice backward locomotion except when sitting down or changing directions, which requires minimum displacements. Backward locomotion is an activity customarily performed by athletes playing field or court sports, although even athletes still experience it less than forward locomotion.

According to Devita and Stribling (1991), the study of backward locomotion is useful in identifying the neural functions underlying movement and, also, as an alternative modality for training and rehabilitation. For example, they reported that the large knee movement in backward running could increase knee extensor torque capabilities through systematic training.

Walking. Backward walking has been a controversial issue among researchers. Some suggest that the movement trajectories of backward walking essentially mirror those of forward walking, with movements simply occurring in the reversed direction (Thorstensson, 1986). However, for some authors like Vilensky, Gankiewicz, and Gehlsen (1987), backward walking is not simply the reverse of walking forward. Between forward and backward walking, they found notable differences in the ranges of motion and patterns of the hip, knee, and ankle joints, although temporal parameters (i.e., swing and stance duration) were the same.

Winter, Pluck, and Yang (1989) argued that forward and backward walking are somewhat different from a biomechanical and anatomical perspective because both modes must cope with postural and balance requirements and also provide propulsion and absorption power from the lower limbs in different ways. However, from experimental observations these authors found almost identical, but reversed, biomechanical motor patterns for the two directions of walking. Thus, it appears that the same neurons are controlling both modes of walking, although with different levels of tonic control.

The results of our kinematic parameters, represented in phase portraits, helped us to better visualize how patterns in both forward and backward directions develop. In some cases, the results we found in the plots of knee phase portraits led us to opt for another tool to represent the coordination phenomena: phase angles. By deriving our kinematic data into phase angles, we restored relative time (i.e., the relative cycle duration) so that both shank and thigh segments could be compared to each other. In what follows, we present both phase portraits and phase angles.

Figure 4.9 contains examples of phase portraits of the shank and thigh segments and of the knee joint for one child with DS walking forward and backward on a hard surface. This participant's segmental patterns during backward walking were very similar to his patterns during forward walking. However, the knee pattern is drastically different between the two directions. That is, the overall pattern of the knee phase portrait during backward walking lacks the inner loop characteristic of forward walking.

During backward walking, no research participant, including the normal participant, exhibited an inner loop. Instead they demonstrated one or more inflections toward zero angular velocity at the support phase. The lack of an inner loop was not due to knee inactivity; rather, it was a consequence of a different mechanism for damping. Perhaps this mechanism leads to differential activity in other joints (i.e., hip and ankle). Thorstensson (1986) pointed out in his study about backward walking that knee flexion during support was absent in backward walking. Vilensky et al. (1987) also found that the knee flexion is reduced during backward walking, as is the r-o-m.

The consistent pattern for the knee during backward walking led us to suspect that the coordination profile was a result of a different phase relation between the shank and thigh. To verify this intralimb phase relation, we derived phase angles. Figure 4.10 shows an example of the normal adult and two adults with DS walking forward and backward.

The two adults with DS show that for backward walking the phasing of shank and thigh is reversed for most of the cycle compared to forward walking. In the former situation, the shank is moving slightly ahead of the thigh. Further, during the duration of the swing phase, the segments are rotating in-phase. This in-phase relation takes approximately 40 to 50% of the cycle, and reversals (i.e., inward and outward inflections) are not evident until 60% of the cycle's total duration has passed.

During walking forward, subject MAD (figure 4.10c, left column) exhibits a clearer out-of-phase relation at 20% of her cycle than her peer MIG (figure 4.10b, left column), who shows an overlap of the two lines at the heelstrike. The out-of-phase relation means that the thigh reverses its direction of rotation before the shank. The temporal difference for these segment rotations creates the inner loop at the knee level. During backward walking, the parallel lines for the shank and thigh segments are an indication that these segments are reversing at the same time, especially at the toestrike.

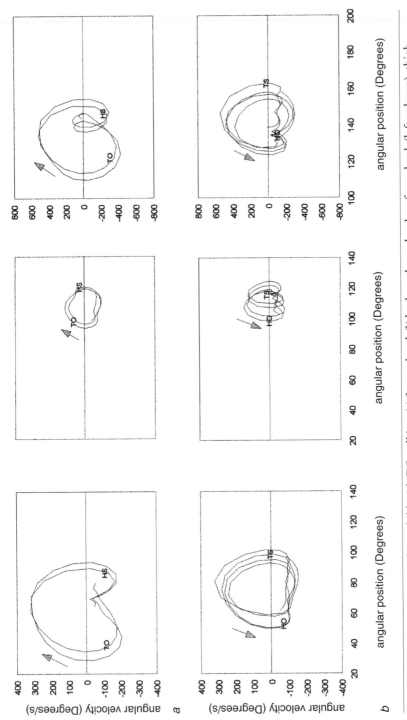

Figure 4.9 Phase portraits of one child with DS walking (*a*) forward and (*b*) backward on a hard surface: shank (left column), thigh (center column), and knee (right column). (HS = heelstrike; TO = toeoff; HO = heeloff; TS = toestrike.)

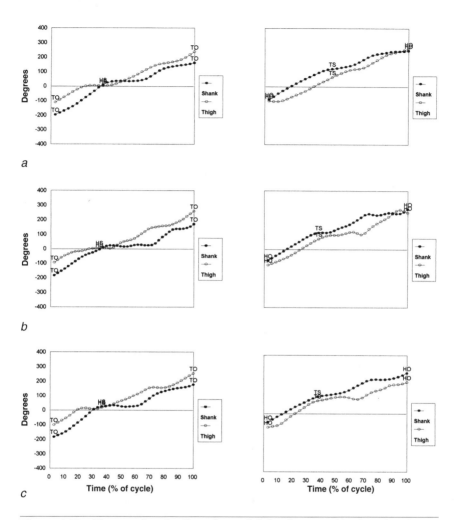

Figure 4.10   Phase angles of walking forward (left column) and backward (right column) on a hard surface: (*a*) normal adult, CAR; (*b*) adult with DS, MIG; (*c*) adult with DS, MAD. (HS = heelstrike; TO = toeoff; HO = heeloff; TS = toestrike.)

Running.   The adults were the only participants with DS able to run backward. Patterns of segmental activity were very similar between the adults with DS and with the normal adult for both forward and backward running (not depicted here), although their individual speeds differed. However, during backward running the knee phase portraits for the normal participant exhibited the inner loop typically found during forward running, while those of adults with DS did not (see figure 4.11).

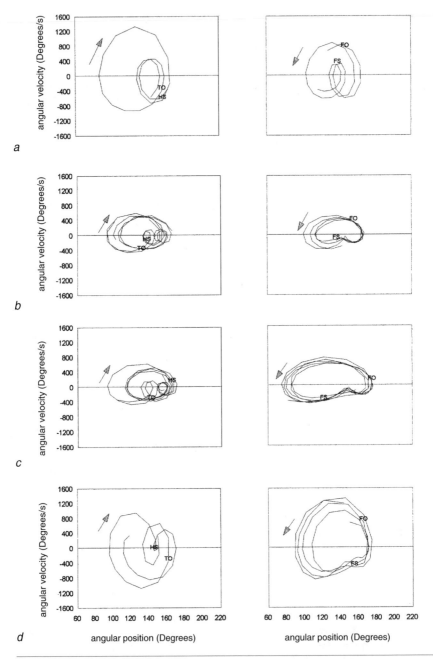

Figure 4.11 Knee phase portraits of one normal adult and three adults with DS running forward (left column) and backward (right column): (*a*) normal adult, CAR; (*b*) adult with DS, MIG; (*c*) adult with DS, ROB; (*d*) adult with DS, MAD. (HS = heelstrike; TO = toeoff; FO = footoff; FS = footstrike.)

The absence of the inner loop in the knee phase portrait observed during backward walking by the adults with DS persists in backward running. In order to understand the way the participants coordinate segments during backward running, we utilized the phase angle technique. Figure 4.12 presents samples of one cycle of backward running for each adult with DS and for the normal adult.

Indeed, the typical in-phase relation seen during backward walking seems to remain during backward running for the adults with DS but not for the normal adult. The coordination style utilized by the adults with DS is different from that used by the normal adult. In the case of the normal adult, backward running seems

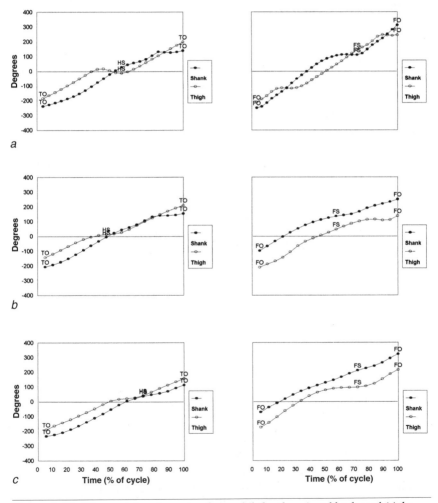

Figure 4.12 Phase angles of running forward (left column) and backward (right column): *(a)* normal adult, CAR; *(b)* adult with DS, ROB; *(c)* adult with DS, MAD. (HS = heelstrike; TO = toeoff; FO = footoff; FS = footstrike.)

to be a simple reversal of forward running, at least at this level of analysis. Perhaps, in the case of the adults with DS, backward running might have developmental stages that resemble characteristics of backward walking. Unfortunately, this is only speculation because we did not perform a thorough developmental analysis with data from longitudinal or cross-aged groups. Further studies may focus on adaptations across age and special populations to test some hypotheses about control and coordination with regard to task constraints such as direction of motion (e.g., backward and forward locomotion).

Conclusions

The utility of the qualitative approach presented here lies in its potential for revealing underlying control mechanisms and levels of stability of a system challenged by different sources of constraint. Here, common patterns of coordination typical for walking and running by both children and adults with DS were captured in the phase portraits.

According to Ulrich et al. (1997), infants with Down syndrome seem to have poor ability to differentiate responses to perturbations. This could lead to reduced sensitivity to their own movements and their consequences (i.e., intrinsic dynamics). This situation, according to those authors, could explain why infants with DS take more time to learn functional skills.

Perhaps, in addition to the fact that motor impairments are common in DS, the reduced sensitivity regarding their own intrinsic dynamics may lead to failures or unstable adaptations to dynamic environmental demands. For example, the elastic surface of the trampoline during locomotion affects the organism because its physical properties retroact and induce inevitable changes in the leg action. Thus, the organism and the environment are mutually interchanging status.

The fact that the children with DS progressively accelerated their steps on the trampoline could be an indication of reduced sensitivity to this situation. Perhaps this reflects an inability to control their movements to make the journey safely. Alternatively, they may simply be motivated to play with the surface and not be concerned with falls. Whatever their motivations or inabilities, they seemed to respond differently in terms of coordination between segments (the absence of inner loops or small inner loops in their knee patterns). This means that they modulated their actions based on their contexts. We do not know if these changes were functional, but certainly they reflect a kind of adaptation. One of the children was unable to walk on the trampoline. It could be that to her, there was not enough security afforded by her feet and body. Thus, she preferred to crawl to the center of the trampoline, sitting, swinging, and touching the surface.

The adults with DS seemed to have their walking behavior challenged by the pad surface even though a padded surface offers some level of security: if a person falls on a padded surface, the chance for injury is less than with a hard surface. They walked at slower paces and, more importantly, exhibited unstable patterns of coordination. They responded similarly to the beam surface.

The effect that environmental constraints had on the individuals with DS, both children and adults, was reflected at the knee action, although the other joints may also have had their patterns modified by these constraints. As mentioned earlier, the limited knee action of both adults and children with DS, represented by the small-size phase portraits, could be due to an augmented level of stiffness. Stiffness could be a strategy they use to minimize vertical sway so that they do not lose their balance. Latash et al. (1993) found that vertical displacements of the head are minimized during walking by individuals with DS. He argues that the inability of these individuals to stabilize their heads causes them to compensate with postural corrections that make their gaits resemble a person who is gliding or cross-country skiing. This strategy would minimize vertical displacements of the trunk, which would otherwise contribute to loss of balance.

Stiffness could also be a result of reduced sensitivity to the structure of the surface, which led participants to freeze their degree of freedom at that joint. If this pattern of behavior is an adaptive response due to Down syndrome's intrinsic dynamics, it certainly raises questions about the course of development (e.g., changes from spontaneous to functional activity) and the course of emergence of atypical responses and behavior.

Angulo-Kinzler and Romack (1996) suggest that the inability to appropriately adjust stiffness underlies the motor dysfunction common in infants with DS. In their study examining leg quasi-stiffness to load perturbation, they found that infants with DS tended to increase their interlimb stiffness when weight was added to one ankle. This was different than for normal infants whose interlimb quasi-stiffness asymmetry was reduced. Although the interlimb quasi-stiffness in infants with DS was different than that of normal infants, the overall level of interlimb activity was preserved. Interlimb activity is a fundamental motor strategy that infants use to control their movements and quasi-stiffness and, according to those authors, is a measure of the quality of their movements.

Young, developing infants with DS face the dilemma of transforming spontaneous and uncoordinated activity (i.e., stepping) to a task-specific action (i.e., prewalkers reducing the abduction of their hips during stepping with weights attached to their legs). This transformation supports the notion of freezing and unfreezing degrees of freedom and confirms that, as it evolves, an organism explores possible motions under its own architecture and environmental settings (Mauerberg-deCastro et al., 1995).

The question here is: if old, primitive, or atypical patterns evolve to compensate for limitations an organism faces in unfamiliar environments, could the process that governs the emergence of functional skills be the same process that governs the emergence of impaired skills?

To assess the status of coordination and control in individuals with disabilities, normal functional skills and their expected patterns of behavior are arbitrarily applied as a norm for classification, with deviations or delays used as gauges of disability. However, so-called atypical behaviors can, in fact, be viable and optimal solutions. Individuals with disabilities adapt differently than "normal" individuals due to their own intrinsic dynamics, challenged by task and environmental constraints. Often the tools used in formal assessments ignore the impact that these constraints have on the profiles of motor skills. As a result, scores from these assessments are rigid and artificial. When studying or assessing individuals whose behaviors are developing or delayed because of some disabling condition, one should include manipulations involving a variety of constraints (e.g., surface of support or changes in direction of locomotion). This could help us learn more about the abilities of these people to adapt and why they respond in certain ways.

As was evident in our direction of locomotion results, children and adults with DS responded differently to backward walking and running compared to the forward direction. During backward walking, they exhibited patterns similar to those of the normal adult. During backward running, however, they maintained similar patterns to backward walking, contrary to what the normal adult exhibited. Our findings for both forward and backward locomotion certainly contribute to the debate about the pattern configurations of both modes of locomotion (Bates, Morrison, & Hamill, 1984; Devita & Stribling, 1991; Winter et al., 1989). The coordination modes of backward walking presented by both children and adults with DS and our normal adult are an indication that a different phasing relation between the shank and thigh segments exists. The in-phase relation found for backward walking can be demonstrated via knee phase portraits and via phase angles of the shank and thigh segments.

Summary

In summary, we found that patterns of walking and running by individuals with DS resemble normal adultlike patterns and that environmental constraints affected their individual patterns in unique ways. These include differentiated amounts of damping at the knee joint on the elastic surface of the trampoline; instability of trajectories of the shank and thigh segments; and loss of a degree of freedom at the knee joint during walking on the pad and the beam surfaces. The task constraint, characterized in this study by the direction of locomotion, provides us with insights about coordination modes—that is, how the segments coordinate (i.e., in- and out-of-phase). In contrast to forward motion, backward walking and backward running by individuals with DS result in predominantly an in-phase mode throughout the cycle's duration. The normal individual, however, exhibited this type of mode only for backward walking.

Dynamic systems concepts and tools provide us with a comprehensive approach to studying the phenomena of coordination and control of locomotion by individuals with DS. In the future, researchers in motor behavior should concentrate their efforts on providing experimental evidence about the adaptability of these individuals' behavior as a consequence of their flexible and coherent interplay with sources of constraint. By doing so, we might change our perception about attributes such as atypical, abnormal, or impaired behavior.

References

Abraham, R.H., & Shaw, C.D. (1984). *Dynamics—The geometry of behavior.* Santa Cruz, CA: Aerial Press.

Angulo-Kinzler, R.M., & Romack, J.L. (1996). Changes in leg quasi-stiffness as a result of load perturbations in infants with and without Down syndrome. *Brazilian International Journal of Adapted Physical Education Research, 3,* 25-46.

Bates, B.T., Morrison, E., & Hamill, J. (1984). A comparison between forward and backward running. *The 1984 Olympic Scientific Congress Proceedings* (pp. 30-31) Eugene, OR: Microform Publications.

Beuter, A., & Garfinkel, A. (1985). Phase plane analysis of limb trajectories in nonhandicapped and cerebral palsied subjects. *Adapted Physical Activity Quarterly, 2,* 214-227.

Block, M.E. (1991). Motor development in children with Down syndrome: A review of the literature. *Adapted Physical Activity Quarterly, 8,* 179-209.

Clark, J.E., & Phillips, S.J. (1991). The development of intralimb coordination in the first six months of walking. In J. Fagard & P.H. Wolff (Eds.), *Temporal organization in coordinated actions* (pp. 245-260). Amsterdam: North-Holland.

Clark, J.E., Truly, T.L., & Phillips, S.J. (1993). On the development of walking as a limit cycle system. In L. Smith & E. Thelen (Eds.), *A dynamic systems approach to development: Applications* (pp. 71-93). Cambridge, MA: MED Press.

Davis, W.E., & Kelso, J.A.S. (1982). Analysis of "invariant characteristics" in motor control of Down's syndrome and normal subjects. *Journal of Motor Behavior, 14,* 194-212.

Davis, W.E., & Sinning, W.E. (1987). Muscle stiffness in Down syndrome and other mentally handicapped subjects: A research note. *Journal of Motor Behavior, 19,* 130-144.

Devita, P., & Stribling, J. (1991). Lower extremity joint kinetics and energetics during backward running. *Medicine and Science in Sport and Exercise, 23,* 602-610.

Forrester, L.W., Phillips, S.J., & Clark, J.E. (1992). Locomotor coordination in infancy: The transition from walking to running. In G. Savelsbergh (Ed.), *The development of coordination in infancy* (pp. 359-393). Amsterdam: Elsevier.

Haley, S.M. (1986). Postural reactions in infants with Down syndrome: Relationship to motor milestone development and age. *Physical Therapy, 66,* 17-22.

Heriza, C.B. (1988). Comparison of leg movements in preterm infants at term with healthy full-term infants. *Physical Therapy, 64,* 1831-1838.

Kelso, J.A.S., Saltzman, E.L., & Tuller, B. (1986). The dynamical perspective on speech production: Data and theory. *Journal of Phonetics, 14,* 29-59.

Latash, M.L., Almeida, G.L., & Corcos, D.M. (1993). Preprogrammed reaction in individuals with Down syndrome: The effects of instruction and predictability of the perturbation. *Archives of Physical Medicine and Rehabilitation, 74,* 391-399.

Mauerberg-deCastro, E., Ulrich, B.D., & Angulo-Kinzler, R. (1995). *Environmental constraints on treadmill stepping patterns of infants with Down syndrome: A dynamic systems perspective.* Technical report for grant by the Conselho Nacional de Desenvolvimento Científico e Tecnológico/Brazil, State University of São Paulo.

Meriam, J.L. (1966). *Dynamics.* London: Wiley.

Parker, A.W., Bronks, R., & Snyder, C.W. (1986). Walking patterns in Down syndrome. *Journal of Mental Deficiency Research, 30*, 317-330.

Parker, A.W., & James, B. (1985). Age changes in the flexibility of Down syndrome children. *Journal of Mental Deficiency Research, 29*, 207-218.

Percy, M.E., Dalton, A.J., Markovic, D.R., McLachlan, C., Hummel, J.T., Rusk, A.C.M., & Andrews, D.F. (1990). Red cell superoxide dismutase, glutathione peroxidase and catalase in Down syndrome patients with and without manifestations of Alzheimer disease. *American Journal of Medical Genetics, 35*, 459-467.

Saltzman, E.L., & Kelso, J.A.S. (1987). Skilled actions: A task-dynamic approach. *Psychological Review, 94*, 84-106.

Shumway-Cook, A., & Woollacott, M.H. (1985). Dynamics of postural control in the child with Down's syndrome. *Physical Therapy, 65*, 1315-1322.

Sparrow, W.A. (1992). Measuring changes in coordination and control. In J.J. Summers (Ed.), *Approaches to the study of motor control and learning* (pp. 147-162). Amsterdam: Elsevier.

Thelen, E., & Smith, L.B. (1994). *A dynamic systems approach to the development of cognition and action*. London: MIT Press/Bradford.

Thorstensson, A. (1986). How is the normal program modified to produce backward walking? *Experimental Brain Research, 255*, 1-5.

Ulrich, B. (1997). Dynamic systems theory and skill development in infants and children. In K. Connolly & H. Forssberg (Eds.), *Neurophysiology and neuropsychology of motor development* (pp. 319-345). London: Mac Keith Press.

Ulrich, B.D., & Ulrich, D.A. (1995). Spontaneous leg movement of infants with Down syndrome and nondisabled infants. *Child Development, 66*, 1844-1855.

Ulrich, B.D., Ulrich, D.A., Angulo-Kinzler, R., & Chapman, D.D. (1997). Sensitivity of infants with and without Down syndrome to intrinsic dynamics. *Research Quarterly for Exercise and Sport, 68*, 10-19.

Ulrich, B.D., Ulrich, D.A., Collier, D.H., & Cole, E.L. (1995). Developmental shifts in the ability of infants with Down syndrome to produce treadmill steps. *Physical Therapy, 75*, 14-23.

Vilensky, J.A., Gankiewicz, E., & Gehlsen, G. (1987). A kinematic comparison of backward and forward walking in humans. *Journal of Human Movement Studies, 13*, 29-50.

Winstein, C.J., & Garfinkel, A. (1989). Qualitative dynamics of disordered human locomotion: A preliminary investigation. *Journal of Motor Behavior, 21*, 373-391.

Winter, D.A., Pluck, N., & Yang, J.F. (1989). Backward walking: A simple reversal of forward walking? *Journal of Motor Behavior, 21*, 291-305.

Author Note

We thank Sandra de Oliveira, Adriana I. de Paula, and the graduate and undergraduate students under the supervision of Eliane Mauerberg-deCastro at the Laboratory of Action and Perception, State University of São Paulo, for their invaluable assistance during data collection and the digitizing process of this study. We also thank Debra Campbell for her editorial comments and gracious assistance with this manuscript. Finally, we thank the editors whose comments and suggestions helped to improve this chapter.

5

CHAPTER

Ophthalmic Factors
in Down Syndrome:
A Motoric Perspective

Mark Mon-Williams

School of Psychology
University of St. Andrews

Anne Jobling

Schonell Special Education Research Centre
University of Queensland

John P. Wann

Department of Psychology
University of Reading

Key words

ophthalmic factors ◆ oculomotor control ◆ refractive error ◆
vergence ◆ accommodation ◆ eyesight ◆ visual acuity ◆ conjugate
eye movements ◆ ophthalmic care

No unique ophthalmic features are associated with Down syndrome (DS). On the other hand, the prevalence of ophthalmic disorders in people with DS is far higher when comparisons are made with general population norms (e.g., Woodhouse, 1998). It is widely accepted that the primary purpose of vision is to enable action—it may be possible to have perception without action (see Milner & Goodale, 1995), but it is not possible to have skilled (learned) action in the absence of perception. If vision is one of the primary senses that underpins skilled movement, then it seems reasonable to posit that deficits in movement may be linked to ocular dysfunction. We suggest, however, that although poor eyesight may impact motor control in people with DS, it is important to avoid the temptation of inferring a causal relation between ocular disorder and movement dysfunction. We have previously argued that a distinction must be made between *processes* that may underpin control (the process approach) and *modules* that must be implicated in coordination (Wann, Mon-Williams, & Carson, 1998). Despite the everyday nature of many tasks (e.g., picking up an object), successful task completion may require a complex interaction of various skills. If we are to understand why complex skills break down, it is necessary to determine the essential components that allow for successful task completion. It is also necessary to assess what information is perceptually available to someone demonstrating poor movement control in order to determine whether a poorly coordinated movement is an adequate response to inadequate information, an inadequate response to adequate information, or whether problems arise from the interface between perception and action. This statement may seem to converge on the process approach, but the important difference is that it avoids hypothetical presuppositions. If someone with DS fails to catch a ball, it is a simple act of decomposition to state that this may have been due to an error of visual perception, an error of limb positioning, or an error of grasp timing (synchronization of the grasp to the perceived time of arrival). It is thus possible to identify modular areas such as visual perception, trajectory formation, and interlimb coordination and to suppose that these modules are the building blocks of a specific skill—without slipping toward hypothetical processes. An approach that decomposes complex tasks into modular components has the advantage that intervention can be directed at those areas of control that most restrict performance for an individual. In this chapter we will argue that ophthalmic function should be viewed as one module within the multi-faceted nature of motor behavior.

The usefulness of classifying vision as a module is illustrated when we begin to consider what is meant by *vision*. When referring to vision, it is typical to lump eyesight together with other aspects of visual function such as eye movements. It is important to remember, however, that many aspects of vision are motoric in nature. For example, the accommodation and vergence systems (see pages 109-115) are responsible for the provision of clear and single vision, respectively; but both of these systems require a skilled motor action in response to perceptual (retinal) information. In this sense, many functions that we consider to be vision are actually perceptual-motor skills in their own right. This consideration leads to the conclusion that attempts to construct simple causal relations on the basis of finding abnormal movement control co-occurring with visual perceptual problems are doomed to failure.

The close interaction between perception and action in ocular-motor control is illustrated by some aspects of ophthalmic development. One important physiological consequence of this tight coupling is highlighted by the sensory condition of amblyopia and the motoric condition of strabismus. Amblyopia refers to a condition of reduced eyesight despite optimal refractive correction in the absence of any overt pathology. Its etiology is well understood—cells within primary visual cortex (V1) require retinal stimulation in the earliest period of life in order to develop their optimum functional capacities (see Daw, 1994, for a comprehensive review). If retinal stimulation is removed, the cortical cells do not properly develop and reduced eyesight results. The most common forms of amblyopia are not due to pathological conditions but are caused by either high refractive errors and/or strabismus. Strabismus (or squint) is the term used to describe closed-loop vergence bias (a misalignment of the visual axes under normal viewing conditions—see page 111). In strabismus, binocular fixation of an object results in the fovea of only one eye being aligned with the object—the image is located away from the fovea of the other eye. The developmental consequence of this nonfoveal fixation is amblyopia—so that the consequence of the motoric deficit is sensory dysfunction. We will later review the numerous studies that have shown that DS is associated with a high incidence of refractive error and strabismus. These studies will form the basis for our assertion that infants with DS must receive prompt ophthalmic attention to ensure that amblyopia does not result.

This chapter will look at various aspects of vision from a motoric perspective. The basic notion is to provide a brief summary of terminology and some tutorial-type material prior to a discussion of how these factors impact people with DS. The chapter will not focus on specific pathological conditions that will affect only a small number of people with DS, but rather will consider dysfunction of basic visual functions common to the majority of those with DS. We should point out that there are large discrepancies between the estimates of incidence for the various ophthalmic disorders provided by extant studies. The discrepancies are hardly surprising when one considers the large differences between the studies, including the sample size, the age of the participants, and the origin of the sample (e.g., an ophthalmic outpatient sample versus a general pediatric population). Although studies vary in their estimates, all are in broad agreement that the incidence of ophthalmic disorder is high in people with DS. We will therefore not attempt to provide precise figures on the incidence of a particular ophthalmic problem but rather try to elucidate the impact of the ocular disorder on the individual.

Pathological Conditions

It has been well established (and extensively documented) that people with DS are subject to a large number of pathological ocular conditions (e.g., Eissler &

Longnecker, 1962; Frantz, Insler, Hagenah, McDonald, & Kaufman, 1990; Ginsberg, Ballard, Buchind, & Kinkler, 1980; Hestnes, Sand, & Fostad, 1991; Lowe, 1949). This chapter will not provide a detailed consideration of ocular pathology, but we will take this opportunity to make a couple of general points. First, we believe that the high incidence of pathological conditions associated with DS makes our arguments regarding continuous assessment from the earliest age even more apposite. Second, as we have already outlined, we believe that it is important to understand how a given deficit within the visual modality may impact an individual's movement performance so that intervention may contribute to the realization of a person's full potential for movement.

Eyesight

We will use the term eyesight to describe the clarity of the retinal image, since the terms *vision* and *visual acuity* have specialist meanings within the ophthalmic literature: *vision* refers to uncorrected eyesight, while *visual acuity* describes the level of eyesight obtained with optimum refractive correction. Eyesight is typically assessed with some form of chart and expressed as a fraction where the numerator refers to the distance of the chart and the denominator refers to the distance at which the smallest visible letter subtends 5' of arc. The standard clinical chart is placed at 6 m (or 20 ft), and a person with good eyesight is expected to read letters that subtend 5' of arc at that distance. If someone can read the small letters near the bottom of a chart, then they will typically have eyesight equal to 6/6 or better (20/20 in imperial measures), but if only the large letter on top of the chart can be read, then the eyesight is equal to 6/60 (6/12 occurs about halfway down).

Traditional (Snellen) eyesight charts have major disadvantages for scientific studies. These disadvantages relate to (1) the lines changing in unequal step sizes and (2) the lines having an unequal number of letters. These two facts make it impossible to validly report statistics for Snellen eyesight measures. Another major problem with Snellen charts is the fact that they rely on letter recognition. There are, however, a number of methods of subjectively assessing eyesight that both yield scientifically valid measures and are suitable for use in special-need populations (see Haegerstrom-Portnoy, 1993). One test that has proved to be suitable for measuring the eyesight of infants and children with DS is the Teller acuity test (e.g., Courage, Adams, Reyno, & Kwa, 1994; Woodhouse et al., 1996).

It should be noted that ophthalmic charts typically measure high contrast eyesight (i.e., a well-defined black shape or letter against a bright white background). The problem with such charts is that they do not indicate how well the visual system can process retinal information at different spatial frequencies (e.g., how well someone can see when contrast is low). A number of methods do exist, however, that allow eyesight to be assessed over a range of spatial frequencies.

Childhood development is normally marked by a rapid increase in the level of eyesight. A newborn baby's eyesight may be compared to viewing a scene through a thick mist—the outline of shapes is indistinct, brightness sensitivity is reduced, and colors appear unsaturated (McCulloch, 1998). Over the first few months of life, the improvement in eyesight is remarkable—as if the mist were rapidly dissipating. Typical figures suggest that a newborn baby has Snellen vision somewhere between the range of 6/400 and 6/60, but by the time the baby reaches 6 months, eyesight will fall within the range 6/40 and 6/6 (McCulloch, 1998). It is important to realize that this rapid increase in eyesight depends on retinal stimulation and must happen over these first few months if it is to happen at all (Daw, 1994). In normal development, the rate of eyesight improvement slows down after the first 6 months and gradually approaches adult levels over the period between 6 months and 6 years.

Evidence is starting to emerge that although children with DS show the normal rapid improvement in eyesight over the first 2 years of life, the subsequent refinement in eyesight appears to be missing (Woodhouse, 1998). Cross-sectional data have consistently suggested that people with DS have eyesight that is below the norm (e.g., Courage et al., 1994; Roizen, Mets, & Blondis, 1994; Woodhouse et al., 1996). These data are difficult to interpret, however, because of the distinct possibility that the reduced eyesight might have been caused by uncorrected refractive error during childhood. The data of Woodhouse (1998) are different because they are longitudinal and control for childhood refractive error. These data are important because they suggest that one factor contributing to the reduced eyesight (about 6/12) found in older children and adults with DS might be a difference in the architecture of primary visual cortex. Further evidence that suggests fundamental differences in the ophthalmic neural circuitry comes from the work of Hall (1993, cited in Roizen et al., 1994), who has shown that infants and children with DS show reduced sensitivity to all spatial frequencies—this result suggests that neural factors are affecting the eyesight, as optical blur reduces only sensitivity to high spatial frequencies.

Refractive Error

It is possible to think of the eye as an optical system where the cornea and crystalline lens have a certain refractive power with a corresponding focal length (the distance from the optical system to a principal focal point), as illustrated in figure 5.1. The length of the eye can be considered independent of the power of the optical system. If the length of the eye is such that the retina is at the focal length of the optical system, then the eye is described as *emmetropic*. If the retina is closer than the focal length, then the eye is described as *hypermetropic*. And if the retina is beyond the focal length, then the eye is described as *myopic*. It is possible for the optical system of the eye to cause two separate focal planes, which can both fall behind, both fall in front, or fall on either side of the retina. Such eyes are described as *astigmatic*. (It is easiest to think of the astigmatic optical system being shaped like an egg instead of a sphere.) Eyes that are myopic, hypermetropic, or astigmatic are described as having

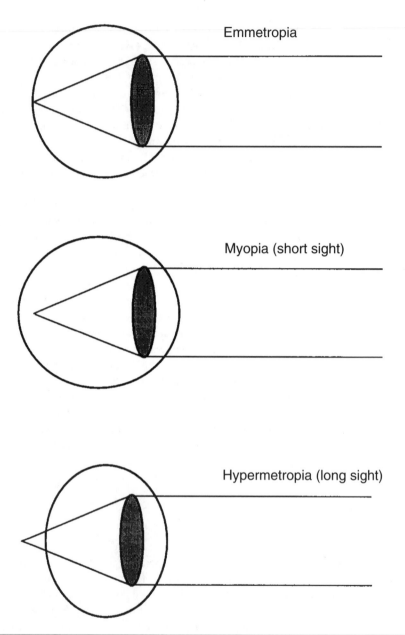

Figure 5.1   The eye is an optical system where the cornea and crystalline lens have a certain refractive power with a corresponding focal length (the distance from the optical system to a principal focal point). Emmetropia (upper panel) results if the length of the eye is such that the retina is at the focal length of the optical system. Myopia (short sight; middle panel) results if the retina is beyond the focal length. Hypermetropia (long sight; lower panel) results if the retina is closer than the focal length.

refractive error. The refractive error refers to the extent to which the eye is too long or too short for the power of the optical system, and is described in terms of diopters, the reciprocal of the refractive error in meters. It is normal to express the refractive error in terms of the lens that needs to be placed in front of the eye to correct for the refractive error—myopia requires a concave (negative) lens, while hypermetropia requires a convex (positive) lens.

It is important to realize that an eye's refractive state is not constant over the life span. It has been well established that newborn babies are born with hypermetropia (approximately 2-3 diopters) and astigmatism. Over the first 6 months of life, however, the hypermetropia and astigmatism disappear, and the majority of children end up being emmetropic. This progression from hypermetropia to emmetropia is known as *emmetropisation* and is widely held to be a process under active neural control (see Saunders, 1995). It has been demonstrated that some infants with DS do not show the normal shift in refraction (hypermetropia to emmetropia), while other infants show shifts in the correct direction but continue to progress through emmetropia to myopia (Woodhouse et al., 1998). Woodhouse et al.'s (1998) finding that the emmetropisation process does not function normally in people with DS may explain the distribution of refractive error across people with DS. It is typically found that the median refractive error of a population of people with DS is consistent with the median error within the general population, but the range of error is far greater, so that people with DS are far more prone to high refractive errors (e.g., Woodhouse, Meades, Leat, & Saunders, 1993).

The change in refraction with age poses some difficulties in deciding when a given refractive error is within normal limits. The generally accepted rule of thumb is that refractive error in the range –0.5 to +3.0 diopters is normal for children under 3 years of age, but that refractive measurements should fall between emmetropia and +2.0 diopters for children older than 3 years. Interocular differences in refractive error greater than 1.5 diopters and astigmatism greater than 1.5 diopters are also considered abnormal. The issue of when to correct refractive error is somewhat controversial, as there is a concern that correcting refractive error in young infants (<12 months) may interfere with the normal emmetropisation process (McCulloch, 1998). On the other hand, most authorities seem to agree that refractive errors that are well (1.0 diopter) outside of the normal range should at least be partially corrected (Atkinson et al., 1996). After the first 12 months of life, the general consensus seems to be that any refractive errors outside of the normal range should be corrected (McCulloch, 1998). It seems sensible to advocate the adoption of similar criteria for the correction of refractive error in children with DS. There is certainly no scientific basis for supposing that different criteria should be applied.

The previous discussion raises the question of how refractive error can be assessed in populations with limited communication. Two principal methods may be employed to objectively assess refractive error: photorefraction (Atkinson & Braddick, 1982) and retinoscopy. Bailey, Gunn, Tovey, and Jobling (1989) directly compared the efficacy of these two techniques for assessing refractive error in a population of

116 children with DS aged between 6 and 19 years. They concluded that the advantages of retinoscopy far outweighed any benefits of the photorefractive technique. The standard retinoscopy technique involves shining a light into the eye while viewing the resultant retinal reflection (the red eye observed in flash photography) along the visual axis through a semisilvered mirror. The practitioner then rotates the retinoscope and observes the resulting movement of the beam. If there is no resultant movement, then there is no refractive error. If the reflex moves in the same direction as the retinoscope (with), then the eye is hypermetropic; and if the reflex moves in the opposite direction, the eye is myopic. A number of studies have successfully used retinoscopy to assess the refractive status of people with DS (Bailey et al., 1989; Roizen et al., 1994; Woodhouse et al., 1993).

One important issue is whether the retinoscopy is carried out with the ciliary muscle paralyzed (cycloplegia). It is often advantageous to use a cycloplegic agent (cyclopentolate hydrochloride is generally the drug of choice) in order to remove any unwanted effects of accommodation when assessing refractive state (hypermetropia can be masked by active accommodation). One disadvantage of cycloplegic refraction is the possibility of a side effect to the drug. It has been suggested that cholinergic hypersensitivity in DS makes a reaction to cycloplegia more likely in these children (Coleman & Lenz, 1985). On the other hand, the huge advantages of refraction carried out under cycloplegia appear to far outweigh any potential disadvantages. We would argue that examination under cycloplegia is an important first step in providing ocular care for people with DS. We will later discuss pertinent research findings, however, that suggest that people with DS have reduced accommodative facility. As assessment of accommodative facility is important, and as such assessment requires knowledge of the refractive state of the eye, we would argue that at least two examinations (one under cycloplegia and a follow-up visit where cycloplegia is not administered) are necessary in the initial stages of providing ophthalmic care for someone with DS.

Conjugate Eye Movements

Horizontal movements of the two eyes may be considered either conjugate, when the eyes move in the same direction, or disconjugate, when the eyes move in opposite directions. These two types of eye movement are commonly referred to as version and vergence movements, but we will use the term *conjugate* rather than version. Conjugate eye movements are responsible for maintenance of static fixation (gaze holding), rapidly changing eye-fixation position (saccadic movement), or continuously maintaining fixation on a moving object (pursuit), as illustrated in figure 5.2.

Despite the primary nature of eye movements, remarkably little is known about the kinematics of eye movement control in people with DS. This lack of knowledge is very disappointing at both a clinical and a research level. It seems reasonable to suggest that a deficit in eye movement control might have an impact upon various

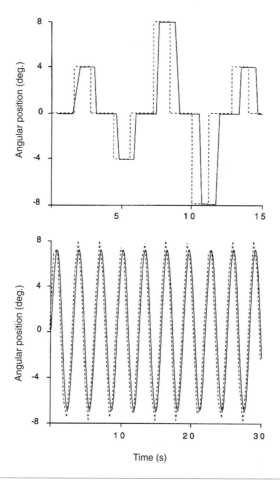

Figure 5.2   Conjugate eye movements are responsible for maintenance of static fixation (gaze holding), rapidly changing eye-fixation position (saccadic movement), or continuously maintaining fixation on a moving object (pursuit). The figures plot eye position (ordinate) against time (abscissa). Upper panel: saccadic eye movements; lower panel: pursuit.

movement skills. For example, catching or hitting a ball often requires locking gaze onto the ball's trajectory. A deficit in ocular pursuit (independent from other aspects of the skill such as grasp formation) may prevent the accurate tracking required for the task. If it was established that someone with DS had a problem making pursuit eye movements, therapeutic intervention might usefully be directed toward this modular skill. Furthermore, if a child with DS lacked the ability to make smooth pursuit movements, this might hinder his or her acquisition of more complex skills. In other words, the development of complex movement might await the development of basic ocular-motor control.

When one considers the generally poor movement found in people with DS, it seems reasonable to speculate that poor ocular-motor control might also be present. Cunningham (1982) has found that children with DS do not visually track objects until the age of 3 years, whereas infants normally show this behavior at 1+ years of age. We have previously investigated horizontal pursuit eye movements in two separate studies of children with special needs: one group exhibited Developmental Coordination Disorder (DCD) (n = 8), while another group of children (n = 8) were born prematurely (Langaas, Mon-Williams, Wann, Pascal, & Thompson, 1998). Both studies found a reduced gain in pursuit eye movements when the respective populations were compared to control groups (see

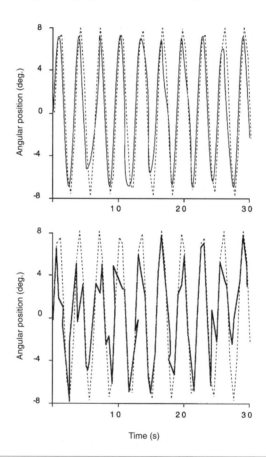

Figure 5.3   Pursuit performance of a 7-year-old control child (upper panel) and of a 7-year-old child with DCD (lower panel). The stimulus (dotted line) is tracked well by the control child, but the child exhibits some jumps in pursuit performance. The child with DCD attempts to track the stimulus but fails to match the velocity, invariably falls behind the stimulus, and has difficulty catching the target with a saccadic adjustment.

figure 5.3). A difference was also found in the ability of the children with special needs to temporally synchronize their tracking response to the stimulus, indicative of poor predictive control rather than lags in the control system. These results suggest that horizontal eye movements may be a sensitive indicator of more general motor deficits during childhood development. We suggest that the examination of ocular-motor control in people with DS might prove to be a fruitful area for future research.

At a clinical level, it is relatively easy for a practitioner to assess the status of eye movement control. The head can be gently held by a parent or helper when assessing ocular-motor control independent of head movements, although it may also be desirable to assess eye-head coupling. An interesting target can be shown to the person with DS and the stability of fixation monitored. Moving the target from side to side will allow an assessment of the tracking ability. The tracking should be smooth; jerky movements indicate a following strategy based on saccades rather than refined pursuit. Two laterally separated squeaky toys are useful for examining the quality of saccadic movements. If problems are found with eye movement control, then intervention can be directed toward helping the refinement of these basic skills within an overall movement program. Intervention strategies include games that involve the interception of slowly moving balls, allowing the refinement of pursuit eye movements in conjunction with the development of other aspects of ball skill.

Vergence and Accommodation

We will briefly describe the components of the ocular-motor system that are responsible for providing clear and single vision (accommodation and vergence eye movements, respectively). If an observer wishes to change fixation from a distant object to a near one (or vice versa), the retinal image of the target object is initially defocused (*blur* describes this error of focus), and there is a fixation error between the target and the angle of ocular vergence (*disparity* refers to this error of fixation). In order to bring clarity to the retinal image, the eye must focus in a process known as accommodation; and to overcome disparity, the eyes must change vergence angle to maintain fixation within corresponding retinal areas (if noncorresponding points of the retinae are stimulated, then double vision will result). We will use a graphical representation of accommodation and vergence in order to describe the most salient features of these systems (figure 5.4 modified from Schor & Kotulak, 1986). Figure 5.4 illustrates that accommodation is driven through blur, while vergence responds to disparity (see Schor, 1983 and 1986, for a comprehensive overview). An initial change in vergence angle or accommodative state is initiated by a phasic element within the vergence and accommodation system, respectively. The phasic controller acts to rapidly eliminate blur and disparity in order for a clear and single image to be achieved. A tonic controller in the vergence and accommodation system then adapts to reduce any steady-state demands placed upon the

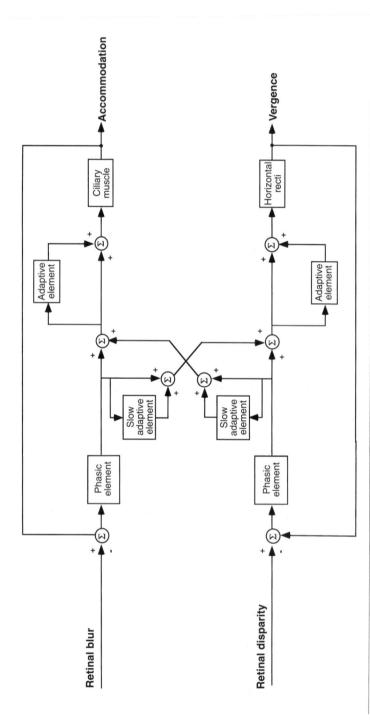

Figure 5.4 A heuristic model of the vergence control system. In normal situations, the system relies on negative feedback with a phasic element in the feed-forward pathway, rapidly eliminating disparity. A tonic controller is also present, and this adapts to reduce any steady-state demands placed upon the phasic response component. The tonic controller ensures that the vergence system is kept in the middle of its functional range. The negative-feedback loop to vergence may be opened by removing disparity (e.g., by covering one eye). The open-loop vergence bias is known as heterophoria (see text for details).

phasic response component (e.g., Carter, 1965; Schor, 1979). The tonic controller ensures that the accommodation and vergence systems are kept in the middle of their functional ranges. In order to further maximize system efficiency, the accommodation and vergence responses are neurally cross-linked (see Schor, 1986) so that accommodation produces vergence eye movements (accommodative vergence) while vergence causes accommodation (vergence accommodation). Accommodative vergence is normally expressed in terms of its ratio with accommodation (the AV/A ratio), and vergence accommodation is expressed in terms of its ratio with vergence (the VA/V ratio).

Vergence Status

We are not aware of any studies that have researched the dynamics of vergence eye movements in people with DS. It is possible, however, to consider the stationary properties of the vergence control system. Binocular fixation of a stationary object requires that both visual axes be aligned with an object of interest in order for double vision to not result. Examination of the muscular and neurological systems involved in the coordination of the two eyes can be carried out using a cover test. The *cover test* consists of the covering and uncovering of each eye in turn while the fellow eye maintains fixation on a target. Any movement of the eye when its fellow is being covered indicates the presence of heterotropia (commonly referred to as strabismus or squint). Strabismus can be either convergent (esotropia) or divergent (exotropia) and can affect either eye (e.g., right esotropia). The primary sensory effect of strabismus is amblyopia in the nonfixating eye.

The majority of human observers do not have strabismus (i.e., no bias is present in closed-loop situations) but do show open-loop vergence bias. It is possible to measure the constant resting point (or bias) that exists within the vergence system by opening the normal feedback loop to vergence (e.g., by removing any disparity information). Open-loop vergence bias is known as heterophoria and may be defined as a slight deviation from perfect binocular positioning apparent only when the eyes are dissociated. Esophoria refers to convergent visual axes when the eyes are dissociated and exophoria to divergent axes (see figure 5.5). The subjective assessment of heterophoria might be problematic in people with DS, as typical measurement procedures require judgments of the relative alignment of targets. In contrast, the objective assessment of heterophoria should pose few difficulties to an experienced practitioner—it simply requires carrying out the cover test in good illumination. Any movement of the nonfixating eye when it is uncovered during the test indicates the presence of heterophoria.

A qualitative appraisal of closed-loop vergence eye movements can be readily carried out by slowly moving a target in the sagittal plane and observing the quality (smoothness and synchronization) of the tracking in depth. Intervention can again be carried out if it is felt that a deficit in vergence control is impacting the acquisition of other requisite movement skills.

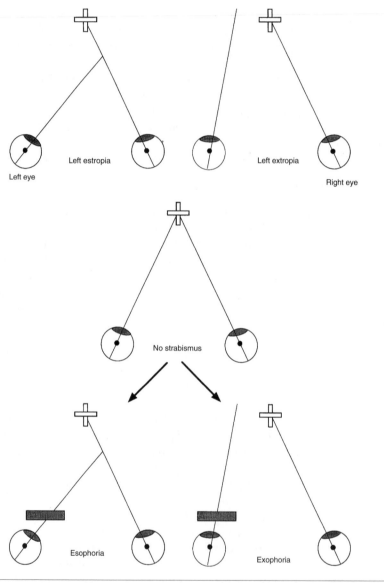

Figure 5.5 In normal binocular viewing, the visual axes of both eyes are in alignment with a fixated target (middle panel). If the axes are not in alignment, then the system is described as strabismic or heterotropic. Upper-left panel: esotropia (convergent visual axes); upper-right panel: exotropia (divergent visual axes). It is possible to measure the constant resting point (or bias) that exists within the vergence system in people without strabismus by opening the normal feedback loop to vergence (e.g., by covering one eye). Open-loop vergence bias is known as heterophoria. Lower-left panel: esophoria (convergent visual axes when the eyes are dissociated); lower-right panel: exophoria (divergent axes).

112

Accommodative Status

We are unaware of any studies that have looked at the kinematics of accommodation in DS. This is not surprising, as the dynamic recording of accommodation is technically demanding (in contrast to the relatively straightforward techniques available for recording eye movements). It is possible, however, to use the retinoscope (see the section on refractive error, page 103) to determine the level of accommodation that occurs in response to a proximal target. Despite the relatively straightforward nature of these measurements, only relatively recently has the status of accommodation in people with DS been assessed.

Margaret Woodhouse of Cardiff University has clearly shown that children with DS have a reduced accommodative response to proximal targets (Woodhouse et al., 1993, 1996). Similar findings have been reported for children with cerebral palsy (Leat, 1996; Shentall & Hosking, 1986). These findings are important because they suggest that children with DS (and cerebral palsy) may not be able to see small proximal targets. This has obvious implications for the ontogeny of prehensile behavior in DS. Furthermore, Woodhouse et al. (1996) have found evidence of poor accommodative control in infants as young as 3 months of age. More recent findings (Cregg et al., 1998; Woodhouse, 1998) have shown that the poor accommodative performance is not due to the peripheral musculature but rather is caused by dysfunction of the neural control processes. In the next section we speculate on how dysfunction of the neural cross-links between accommodation and vergence might give rise to the data reported by Woodhouse et al. (1993, 1996, 1998).

At a clinical level, the finding that the reduced accommodative facility is due to dysfunction of the neural control processes is unfortunate, as it rules out a simple therapy based on prescribing optical lenses. Woodhouse (1998) has found that prescribing convex lenses (which decrease the accommodative demand) does not result in an appropriate accommodative response—after prescription of the lenses, the children show the same reduced levels of accommodation when fixating a proximal target. This suggests that alternative therapies need to be developed to tackle the reduced accommodation (see page 114).

Interactions Between Accommodation and Vergence

It is impossible to know why DS is associated with (1) a high incidence of strabismus; (2) poor accommodative control; (3) a lack of response to the prescription of corrective lenses for accommodative dysfunction; and (4) dysfunction of the normal mechanisms of emmetropisation. It is possible, however, that all of these ophthalmic features may have a common causal mechanism. As we have already outlined, the accommodation and vergence systems are neurally cross-linked. Woodhouse et al. (1998) have suggested the possibility that "a weak link between convergence and accommodation is preventing the children exhibiting an accurate near response" (p. 151).

Woodhouse et al. (1998) did not expand on this notion, so we will consider how abnormalities in the cross-links might lead to the observed data. Quick, Newbern, and Boothe (1994) have found that monkeys with esotropia show either a reduced or an abnormally high AV/A ratio. Moreover, Parks (1958) has reported a high incidence of abnormal accommodative vergence in adult humans with strabismus. Let us suppose that the incidence of cross-link abnormalities is high in people with DS. This supposition may have some physiological basis: it seems likely that the cerebellum plays a role in coordinating the vergence and accommodation response (see Maxwell & Schor, 1994), and it is known that the cerebellum is lighter in weight in people with DS (e.g., Crome, Cowie, & Slater, 1966). In line with the anatomical findings, a reasonable amount of evidence exists to show that normal cerebellar functions may be impaired in people with DS (see Henderson, 1985). The high incidence of esotropia in infants with DS might therefore be explained by cerebellar dysfunction giving rise to abnormal gains in the cross-links between accommodation and vergence.

If this supposition is correct, then it may explain why accommodation is found to be abnormal in people with DS. It has been established that the tonic components of vergence and accommodation adapt independently of one another and that the gains of the cross-links are inversely related to the respective gains of the tonic components (Schor & Tsuetaki, 1987). One consequence of abnormal cross-links would be an increase in the demands placed on the disparity-driven component of the vergence system. It follows that the tonic component of the disparity system might increase its adaptability to cope with these pressures.

The following working hypothesis can thus be proposed: abnormal cross-link gains occur in infants with DS, giving rise to a high incidence of esotropia. Whether or not esotropia occurs, the high demands placed upon the tonic component of vergence will ultimately lead to a high adaptability of the vergence tonic component relative to accommodation. This might explain why optical correction does not increase the maximum amplitude of near accommodation in children with DS: decreasing the accommodation demand relative to vergence requires the system to adapt if the learned relation between these two motor responses is to be maintained. If the vergence tonic component adapts, then this would allow the normal relation between accommodation and vergence to be maintained and would result in the same amount of accommodation per unit change in vergence. If this hypothesis is correct, it follows that rather than attempting to prescribe corrective lenses for close work, orthoptic treatment (eye exercises) aimed at promoting neural adaptation might be beneficial for people with DS who demonstrate reduced accommodation. A considerable degree of ingenuity would be required to devise suitable orthoptic exercises that are both beneficial and interesting for the person with DS, but such exercises may well prove to be a rewarding venture.

We will conclude by noting that the idea of dysfunctional cross-links in DS may provide a basis for explaining the high degree of refractive error found within this population. A number of researchers have speculated that a breakdown in the emmetropisation process may be linked to abnormalities in the cross-links between accommodation and vergence (e.g., Jiang, 1995). It may ultimately prove that the high incidence of refractive errors found in people with DS is related to a dysfunctional relation between accommodation and vergence.

Implications for Movement

We have thus far reviewed a number of ophthalmic disorders that are prevalent in a population of people with DS. We will now consider the implications of these disorders for general movement skills. We first suggest that any clinician or researcher who is concerned with motor skills in people with DS should ensure that their patient/participant has had a thorough eye examination recently. In the case of research, it is clearly important that the researcher has established that an ophthalmic problem is not a confounding factor (e.g., that the participants can see a ball approaching in a study on catching). This suggestion seems obvious, but a number of studies have shown that visual integrity cannot be assumed in people with DS (e.g., Bailey et al., 1989; Roizen et al., 1994; Woodhouse et al., 1993). It follows that good lines of communication will need to exist between those responsible for ophthalmic care and those who are concerned with movement skill—Woodhouse (1998) has suggested that "it is therefore a large part of the responsibility of the Optometrist to explain the implications of the [ophthalmic] defects, and to offer advice on the best ways of coping with the level of residual vision" (p. 152). In turn, it is the responsibility of the movement clinician/researcher to communicate with the eyecare practitioner regarding the areas of movement that may be being hindered by poor ocular function, in order for the best ophthalmic care to be provided. If someone with DS wears spectacles, it is important that the movement clinician/researcher discovers what the spectacles have been prescribed for. For example, if the spectacles have been prescribed for reading alone, then it is important that they are not worn for tasks that require fixation of distant objects (e.g., catching a ball).

If someone with DS has ocular pathology, the pathological condition will need to be considered in any program aimed at improving general movement skills. For example, if someone with DS has corneal pathology (it has been estimated that 6% of people with DS have a corneal abnormality called keratoconus), then he or she may well be sensitive to bright lights (e.g., Frantz et al., 1990). A movement program that has that person participating outside would have to be aware of the need for adequate ocular sun protection.

In contrast to ocular pathology, it is relatively straightforward to deal with uncorrected refractive error. Undoubtedly a disservice is being done to someone with DS who is not provided with optimal refractive correction. It should be noted that some thought will need to be given to any optical correction for close work (Woodhouse, 1998). As we have discussed, it is possible that people with DS will have moderately reduced levels of eyesight even after optimal refractive correction. It seems likely, however, that although the level of reduction may place some constraints on some movement tasks, the general level of deficit (eyesight at an approximate level of 6/12) should not greatly restrict a large number of movement skills. It certainly seems hard to believe that the gross motor impairment demonstrated by many people with DS can be explained by reduced eyesight. In support of this contention, we note that evidence of movement problems in DS appears in the first two years—a period in which the level of eyesight is comparable with the general population. We would further argue that the poor manual control evidenced by a number of people with DS cannot simply be explained by poor eyesight resulting from reduced accommodation—the level and nature of the manual control problems are not consistent with those one would expect from a relatively slight reduction in eyesight. Similar arguments may be advanced for the deficit that is likely to result from strabismus—a large number of people have strabismus in the general population (estimates vary between 5 and 10%) and yet have no evidence of movement problems. We do believe, however, that the generally reduced eyesight makes it imperative that people with DS have the optimum possible optical correction. It is necessary for those concerned with general movement skills to realize the constraints the poor eyesight will place on various movements (e.g., picking up small objects). It is also important that programs aimed at improving movement skills make allowance for the reduced levels of eyesight (e.g., use large, brightly colored balls for catching practice) and provide the participants with strategies to cope with this additional handicap.

Conclusions

People with DS do not get adequate ophthalmic care. This lack of care is a global phenomenon, with at least three recent studies reporting large numbers of undetected ophthalmic disorders in their research populations: 35% (n = 77) of an American population (Roizen et al., 1994); 17% (n = 116) of an Australian population (Bailey et al., 1989); 23% (n = 26) of a British population (Woodhouse et al., 1993). All of these studies drew attention to the fact that simple refractive correction could have made a large difference to the people involved. For example, Bailey et al. (1989) found one child who had uncorrected myopia of –13.00 diopters and another with –5.00 diopters myopia. These uncorrected refractive disorders caused the children to have grossly impaired eyesight for distant objects. The implications of drastically reduced eyesight are obvious for a number of perceptual-motor skills. We would therefore strongly urge those clinicians and/or researchers concerned with investigating skilled movement behavior to ensure that their patients/participants have received adequate ophthalmic care recently.

Bailey et al. (1989) have presented some individual case studies to emphasize the poor provision of ophthalmic care in DS. In one case, the parents of a child with –3.00 diopters of detected myopia were advised by an ophthalmologist that their child did not need refractive correction "at this time" (Bailey et al., 1989). It seems inconceivable that such advice would have been provided to the parents if their child had not had DS. Bailey et al. speculated that the ophthalmologist either believed that the child would not be able to cope with wearing spectacles or felt that someone with DS would not benefit from good eyesight. The provision of spectacles proved that both of these assumptions were fallacious (Bailey et al., 1989).

As recently as 1996, the following advice appeared in the official newsletter of some DS associations:

> If a child starts to squint she should be referred for an eye test as soon as possible. For children with Down syndrome without any obvious problems, I recommend screening between 1 year and 18 months and again at 4 years, prior to starting school. . . . During the school years the children should be checked regularly at least every 2 to 3 years. If any disorder is found, the children are usually seen more frequently, often once or twice a year. This assumes that the child will also have developmental checks by a pediatrician who would also refer her if a problem were suspected. (Crofts, 1996, p. 11)

We are unable to find any scientific justification for these recommendations. As we have highlighted during this chapter, it is imperative that the eyes be checked at the earliest possible age—recommending that screening occur between 12 and 18 months of age has no scientific rationale. We are also disturbed by the fact that only screening is recommended. We would suggest that the potential number of ophthalmic disorders certainly necessitates a full ophthalmic examination. Moreover, the assumption that pediatric developmental checks will pick up any ophthalmic disorder is contrary to the findings of Roizen et al. (1994) who reported that 35% of children who had normal results on general pediatric examination were found to have ocular problems when examined by a pediatric ophthalmologist. On the basis of this finding, they recommend that "every child with DS should be evaluated by a pediatric ophthalmologist as part of standard practice" (p. 597).

One of the recurring conclusions of the numerous studies into the ophthalmic status of people with DS is that it is relatively straightforward to carry out a comprehensive eye examination with a few simple adaptations to routine examination procedures (e.g., the use of a squeaky toy or colored light) when necessary. These findings remove any excuses for not providing adequate ophthalmic care to those with DS. One interesting feature of studies that have recorded the ophthalmic status of people with DS is the lack of information that these studies provide regarding heterophoria or color vision. Information regarding the incidence and magnitude of heterophoria in people with DS might prove to be useful when considering the pathogenesis of binocular disorders. Measurements of heterophoria may be reasonably obtained by objective observation with the cover test. It would also be interesting to know the status of color processing when one considers the evidence for differences in primary cortical processing of visual information in DS. One problem with obtaining measures of color vision is the need for subjective responses, but innovative techniques are available and these could provide an insight into this aspect of visual processing (see Haegerstrom-Portnoy, 1993). It should also be noted that knowing the status of color vision in someone with DS may have important implications for approaches that use color discrimination to aid cognitive learning.

Within this chapter we have attempted to highlight the importance of providing good ophthalmic care for people with DS. It may therefore appear somewhat paradoxical that we have also been warning against the temptation to explain poor movement control on the basis of reduced visual function. The danger of constructing simple causal hypotheses is that they suggest equally simplistic therapeutic interventions that focus on only one aspect of skilled movement behavior. If proper care is to be provided for someone with DS, it is important to evaluate the extent to which any visual impairment will impact the *individual's* movement. A blanket style approach to remediating problems and structuring environments will inevitably fail because people with DS are individuals. It should further be noted that ophthalmic factors change over the life span—poor eye movements may be a primary concern in a young child with DS, whereas the early development of cataracts (e.g., Robb & Marchevsky, 1978) may be of greater importance later in life.

A number of investigations have been directed toward discovering whether a perceptual problem (kinesthetic or visual) lies at the root of the movement problems found in DS (see Henderson, 1985). We would suggest that such an approach is too poorly defined to yield useful results. If we are to understand why children with DS have poor movement control, we should explore what components of a particular movement skill cause problems for the individual. We must also be precise about what is meant by a visual perceptual problem. If we merely mean that the child has problems using the available visual information to guide action, then we have not gone beyond restating that the child has movement problems. On the other hand, if we were able to establish that a child has problems with a particular aspect of visual processing (e.g., egocentric distance perception), then we might make some progress in understanding one of the underlying factors contributing to the movement deficit and be able to design a principled intervention strategy accordingly.

Summary

In conclusion, it is important to emphasize that a causal relation has not been established between the ophthalmic disorder and the motor dysfunction found in DS. A causal relation can be established only when empirical evidence exists to show that the occurrence of ocular deficit is either necessary (or at least sufficient) for the presence of the movement problem (for an excellent discussion, see Henderson, Barnett, & Henderson, 1994). Although gross visual impairment is sufficient to cause difficulties in skilled movement, no evidence has been provided to support the notion that the general ophthalmic deficit observed in DS is a necessary or sufficient feature of the movement problems associated with the condition. Although ophthalmic dysfunction is prevalent in DS, such deficit should not be ascribed a causal role and must be regarded as a co-occurrent feature of the syndrome, albeit a feature that warrants meticulous attention.

References

Atkinson, J., & Braddick, O. (1982). The use of isotropic photorefraction for vision screening in infants. *Acta Ophthalmologica (Copenhagen), 157*(Suppl.), 36-45.

Atkinson, J., Braddick, O., Bobier, B., Anker, S., Ehrlich, D., King, J., Watson, P., & Moore, A. (1996). Two infant screening programs—Prediction and prevention of strabismus and amblyopia from photorefractive and videorefractive screening. *Eye, 10,* 189-198.

Bailey, N., Gunn, P., Tovey, C., & Jobling, A. (1989). Screening the vision of special school children with Down syndrome. *Australian and New Zealand Journal of Developmental Disabilities, 15,* 49-55.

Carter, D.B. (1965). Fixation disparity and heterophoria following prolonged wearing of prisms. *American Journal of Ophthalmology, 42,* 141-151.

Coleman, M., & Lenz, G. (1985). *A program of preventive medicine for Down's syndrome individuals of all ages.* College Park: Down's Syndrome Center, University of Maryland.

Courage, M.L., Adams, R.J., Reyno, S., & Kwa, P. (1994). Visual acuity in infants and children with Down syndrome. *Developmental Medicine and Child Neurology, 36,* 586-593.

Cregg, M., Woodhouse, J.M., Pakeman, V.H., Gunter, H.L., Parker, M., Fraser, W.I., & Sastry, P. (1998). Visual development in children with Down's syndrome: Accommodation [Abstract]. *Ophthalmic and Physiological Optics, 18,* 384.

Crofts, B. (1996, September/October). Eye problems in children with Down syndrome. *Official Newsletter of the Down Syndrome Association of Queensland Inc.,* 9-11.

Crome, I., Cowie, V., & Slater, E. (1966). Statistical note on cerebellar and brain stem weight in mongolism. *Journal of Mental Deficiency Research, 10,* 1969-1972.

Cunningham, C.C. (1982). *Down's syndrome: An introduction for parents.* London: Souvenir Press.

Daw, N.W. (1994). Mechanisms of plasticity in the visual cortex. *Investigative Ophthalmology and Visual Science, 35,* 4168-4179.

Eissler, R., & Longnecker, L.P. (1962). The common eye findings in mongolism. *American Journal of Ophthalmology, 54,* 398-406.

Frantz, J.M., Insler, M.S., Hagenah, M., McDonald, M.B., & Kaufman, H.E. (1990). Penetrating keratoplasty for keratoconus in Down's syndrome. *American Journal of Ophthalmology, 109,* 143-147.

Ginsberg, J., Ballard, E.T., Buchind, J.J., & Kinkler, A.K. (1980). Further observations of ocular pathology in Down's syndrome. *Journal of Pediatric Ophthalmology, 17,* 166-171.

Haegerstrom-Portnoy, G. (1993). New procedures for evaluating vision functions of special populations. *Optometry and Vision Science, 70,* 306-314.

Hall, E.J. (1993). *The assessment of contrast sensitivity in children with Down syndrome.* Unpublished thesis, Memorial University of Newfoundland.

Henderson, S.E. (1985). Motor skill development. In B. Stratford & B. Lane. (Eds.), *Current approaches to Down's syndrome* (pp. 187-218). London: Cassell Road Limited.

Henderson, S.E., Barnett, A., & Henderson, L. (1994). Visuospatial difficulties and clumsiness: On the interpretation of conjoined deficits. *Journal of Child Psychology and Psychiatry, 35,* 961-969.

Hestnes, A., Sand, T., & Fostad, K. (1991). Ocular findings in Down syndrome. *Journal of Mental Deficiency, 35,* 194-203.

Jiang, B. (1995). Parameters of accommodative and vergence systems and the development of late-onset myopia. *Investigative Ophthalmology and Visual Science, 36,* 1737-1742.

Langaas, T., Mon-Williams, M., Wann, J.P., Pascal, E., & Thompson, C. (1998). Eye movements, prematurity and developmental coordination disorder. *Vision Research, 263,* 1817-1826.

Leat, S.J. (1996). Reduced accommodation in children with cerebral palsy. *Ophthalmic and Physiological Optics, 16,* 385-390.

Lowe, R.F. (1949). The eyes in mongolism. *British Journal of Ophthalmology, 33,* 131-174.

Maxwell, J., & Schor, C.M. (1994). Mechanisms of vertical phoria adaptation revealed by time-course and two-dimensional spatiotopic maps. *Vision Research, 34,* 241-251.

McCulloch, D.L. (1998). The infant patient. *Ophthalmic and Physiological Optics, 18,* 140-146.

Milner, A.D., & Goodale, M.A. (1995). *The visual brain in action.* Oxford: Oxford University Press.

Parks, M.M. (1958). Abnormal accommodative convergence in squint. *Archives of Ophthalmology (AMA), 59,* 364-380.

Quick, M.W., Newbern, J.D., & Boothe, R.G. (1994). Natural strabismus in monkeys: Accommodative errors assessed by photorefraction and their relationship to convergence errors. *Investigative Ophthalmology and Visual Science, 35,* 4069-4079.

Robb, R.M., & Marchevsky, A. (1978). Pathology of the lens in Down syndrome. *Archives of Ophthalmology, 96,* 1039-1042.

Roizen, N.J., Mets, M.B., & Blondis, T.A. (1994). Ophthalmic disorders in children with Down syndrome. *Developmental Medicine and Child Neurology, 36,* 594-600.

Saunders, K.J. (1995). Early refractive development in humans. *Survey of Ophthalmology, 40,* 207-216.

Schor, C.M. (1979). The influence of rapid prism adaptation upon fixation disparity. *Vision Research, 19,* 757-765.

Schor, C.M. (1983). The Glenn A. Fry Award Lecture: Analysis of tonic and accommodative vergence disorders of binocular vision. *American Journal of Optometry and Physiological Optics, 60,* 1-14.

Schor, C.M. (1986). The Glenn A. Fry Award Lecture: Adaptive regulation of accommodative vergence and vergence accommodation. *American Journal of Optometry and Physiological Optics, 63,* 587-609.

Schor, C.M., & Kotulak, J.C. (1986). Dynamic interactions between accommodation and vergence are velocity sensitive. *Vision Research, 26,* 927-942.

Schor, C.M., & Tsuetaki, T.K. (1987). Fatigue of accommodation and vergence modifies their mutual interactions. *Investigative Ophthalmology and Visual Science, 28,* 1250-1259.

Shentall, G.A., & Hosking, G. (1986). A study of the visual defects detected in children with cerebral palsy and children with Down's syndrome. *British Orthoptics Journal, 43,* 22-25.

Wann, J.P., Mon-Williams, M., & Carson, R.G. (1998). Assessing manual control in children with coordination difficulties. In K. Connolly (Ed.), *The psychobiology of the hand* (pp. 213-339). Cambridge: Cambridge University Press.

Woodhouse, J.M. (1998). Investigating and managing the child with special needs. *Ophthalmic and Physiological Optics, 18,* 147-152.

Woodhouse, J.M., Meades, J.S., Leat, S.J., & Saunders, K.J. (1993). Reduced accommodation in children with Down syndrome. *Investigative Ophthalmology and Visual Science, 34,* 2382-2387.

Woodhouse, J.M., Pakeman, V.H., Saunders, K.J., Parker, M., Fraser, W.I., Lobo, S., & Sastry, P. (1996). Visual acuity and accommodation in infants and young children with Down's syndrome. *Journal of Mental Deficiency Research, 40,* 49-55.

Author Note

Production of this manuscript was supported by grants from the Australian Research Council; National Health and Medical Research Council, Australia; Engineering and Physical Research Council, UK; Action Research, UK.

6

CHAPTER

Face Processing in Children With Down Syndrome

T.K. Pitcairn
University of Edinburgh

Jennifer G. Wishart
University of Edinburgh

Key words

face processing ◆ social understanding ◆ social development ◆ prosopagnosia ◆ brain function ◆ stereotypes ◆ mental rotation ◆ emotion perception ◆ perceptual matching

Down syndrome (DS) is a uniquely interesting developmental disability but one that is largely ignored by mainstream psychology. The syndrome arises from the presence of an additional whole or part copy of chromosome 21, one of the smallest of the 22 human autosomes. Chromosome 21 is now believed to contain around 1,000 of the total human complement of 100,000 genes, and mapping studies have demonstrated that only a section estimated to contain fewer than 650 genes is in fact implicated in the characteristic DS phenotype. Despite this relatively tiny increase in genetic material, DS severely disrupts many aspects of physical and mental development, with cognitive development in particular presenting major challenges to those affected by the syndrome.

Intellectual disability of some degree is invariably present in DS, but, unusual for any major chromosomal disorder, levels of impairment vary greatly across individuals. Most of those with DS fall within the moderate to severe range of disability, but some show levels of cognitive abilities that are borderline normal while others experience profound mental retardation. IQ scores in adult and child samples, for example, typically range over 50-60 IQ points (Carr, 1995), a similar spread to that found within the general population, albeit displaced to the lower end of the normal distribution. Broader measures of social, cognitive, and adaptive skills show similarly wide variation in achievement levels (for overviews, see Cicchetti & Beeghly, 1990; Stratford & Gunn, 1996).

It is this variability in developmental outcome—and its lack of any strong correlation to genetic and family factors such as parental IQ and socioeconomic status—that makes DS so intriguing. It is clear that in itself the extra chromosome does not place an immutably low ceiling on development and that environmental factors and learning experiences must play a crucial role in determining final outcomes. However, surprisingly little is known yet about the specific nature of developmental processes in children with DS, and we still have few clues as to why some individuals manage to acquire quite reasonable levels of skills while others struggle to gain even simple everyday living skills.

Children with DS face enormous difficulties in most areas of their learning, and the last few decades have seen the investment of considerable effort and resources into early intervention in an attempt to raise achievement levels. Early intervention is very popular with parents and is clearly here to stay, but evidence of its long-term efficacy is still disappointingly weak (Gibson & Harris, 1988; Spiker & Hopmann, 1996; Wishart, 1998). In developed countries, inclusive education has widely replaced schooling in segregated settings. This undoubtedly has had important social benefits for children with DS and their families. However, evidence is still thin that there has been a significant impact on academic achievement levels beyond primary years (Carr, 1995; Casey, Jones, & Watkins, 1988; Sloper, Cunningham, Turner, & Knussen, 1990; Sloper & Turner, 1994). As a result, some concern is now being expressed among special educators that an uncritical belief in the efficacy of early intervention and in the benefits of inclusive education may result in an underestimation of the level of special educational needs likely to be experienced at older ages. There is also concern that inclusive education may lead to specialist resources and expertise being spread too thinly across too many schools.

The hard fact remains that the majority of children with DS still have great difficulty attaining many of the basic skills normally acquired in childhood, and most reach adulthood without sufficient skills to enable them to live independently (see, e.g., Carr, 1994; Irwin, 1989; Thomson, Ward, & Wishart, 1995). Educational interventions, with only a few notable exceptions, have so far had disappointingly little effect on developmental outcomes. In training studies, where gains have been made, these have seldom been maintained over long periods of time (see, e.g., Duffy & Wishart, 1994; Wishart, 1986). This failure to produce lasting effects on developmental progress is perhaps not surprising given the paucity of our current knowledge of developmental processes and developmental mechanisms in DS. We are only now, for example, arriving at a more detailed understanding of how the extra copy of chromosome 21 impacts the development of neurological structures, the basic "tools" for learning (Bellugi, Bihrle, Neville, Jernigan, & Doherty, 1992; Epstein, Hassold, Lott, Nadel, & Patterson, 1995; Nadel, 1996), and we are still a long way from understanding exactly how these inherent limitations affect learning itself. Equally importantly, from a psychological viewpoint, we still have very little insight into how children with DS apply themselves to the task of learning about the social and physical world around them or how they perceive themselves as learners.

Longitudinal studies are beginning to provide some information on how children with DS use their emerging cognitive abilities, and there is now growing evidence that the children's development may be compromised by their adoption of a counterproductive learning "style" from a very early age. Findings indicate both a failure to consolidate new learning and a failure to apply newly acquired skills in related problem-solving contexts in which they could be helpful. There is also some evidence that children with DS may become increasingly reluctant learners as experience of difficulty in learning accumulates (Wishart, 1991, 1993a, 1993b, 1996). The overall effect is that although new skills continue to be added slowly to the repertoire, developmental rate typically declines with increasing age, and the potential for development evidenced at younger ages is not realized. This decline in developmental rate is one of the few robust findings in DS research, irrespective of whether studies were carried out in the 1960s, when many children were still being brought up in institutions, or in the 1990s, when almost all children would have been brought up in the parental home and have experienced some form of specialized educational input in early years (Carr, 1985, 1995; Rauh et al., 1991; Wishart, 1996).

This chapter will look at two interlinked aspects of the DS developmental jigsaw: perceptual-processing skills and the efficiency with which these skills are applied in childhood. Findings from some of our own studies will be used as illustrative examples of information-processing abilities in children with DS and will be set within the current literature. It is beyond the scope of this chapter to provide a comprehensive overview of perceptuomotor development in DS, but much of this material is covered admirably in a number of other chapters, and readers should consult these for further detail. This chapter will instead focus on exploring some of the possible neuropsychological links between perceptual-processing abilities in DS and the motivational factors influencing their application in specific tasks. Specifically, the chapter will focus on the ability to process identity and expression information contained in faces and its relation to sociability and social understanding. There is some evidence that production of social signals may also be problematic for children with DS, at least as reflected in the ability to convey information through facial expression. This problem will be touched on.

Social Understanding in Children With Down Syndrome

DS is one of the best known and most easily recognized mentally handicapping conditions, and most people, if asked, would claim to know something about both the syndrome and the children affected by it. Misconceptions about DS abound, however, in professionals and the general public alike. The most robust of these is undoubtedly the attribution of a stereotyped personality to children with DS (Gibson, 1978; Wishart & Johnston, 1990). Almost unfailingly, they are described as friendly, happy, and affectionate children; it is also generally believed that they all love music and are great mimics. They are seen as "easy" children, children who are often willing to turn on party tricks to amuse visitors and who respond to most problems with a happy smile, irrespective of their success or failure. Their social development is seen somehow as relatively intact, while their cognitive development is widely recognized to be greatly impaired. "Charming but none-too-bright" more or less sums up the public's view of children with DS.

This presumed sociability is often seen as compensating to some degree for the children's weaknesses in other areas of development. It has, however, no firm foundation in empirical studies, or at least no firm foundation in studies that have looked directly at behavior and personality characteristics in children with DS. Many studies of DS temperament have simply asked teachers, caregivers, or parents about the children, often requiring them to respond from a limited checklist of personality characteristics containing all of the old chestnuts given above. The very few studies that have looked more directly at temperament provide little support for the stereotype, finding evidence of considerable individual variation in personality characteristics, just as in typically developing children (e.g., Berger & Cunningham, 1983; Gunn & Berry, 1985a, 1985b). Nevertheless, children with DS are seen as inherently "sociable," as children whose social understanding and empathy for others greatly exceeds their cognitive ability.

Despite the stereotype's predominantly positive composition, parents of children with DS and teachers with experience of more than one child with DS are quick to refute the stereotype, pointing out that children with DS are as individual as any other group of children, that they respond in different ways in different situations, and that they can be just as difficult as the next child when it suits them. Experience in our own and other laboratories backs up these claims, while also pointing to some reasons why this positive stereotype may be so deeply entrenched in the public's mind. Our cross-sectional and longitudinal studies of early cognitive development in infants and young children with DS, for example, found many instances of "charming" and elaborate social behaviors produced during testing sessions. What distinguished these behaviors from those of the control children, however, was not their content or frequency but their timing, as they were most likely to be produced in midtrial, at times when the child was faced with a problem that was either well beyond his or her current capabilities or, paradoxically, had already been mastered. The end result all too often was that either an error was made or the trial was failed by default as no scorable response to test materials had been made. In marked contrast, difficult tasks were associated with increased concentration and effort and minimal midtrial social interaction in nondelayed children, and "easy" tasks were usually quickly and successfully solved, albeit sometimes in a very offhand and cursory manner. The social behaviors of the children with DS in these studies stood out because of their inappropriateness, not because they were necessarily more frequent or more advanced.

On closer inspection, some of these behaviors were not in any case truly "social" and showed little accommodation to the behavior of the supposed partner in the interaction. Looking at the other, for instance, is generally considered an archetypal social interaction and a prerequisite for the turn-taking behavior that characterizes successful communication. Attentional patterns in infants with DS are in this respect quite different from those of typically developing infants and also from other infants with developmental delay—they typically engage in visual fixation for longer periods, both to nonsocial objects (Cicchetti & Ganiban, 1990) and to social interactants (Landry & Chapieski, 1989, 1990). In particular, infants with DS find it difficult to engage in joint attention when required to switch attention among objects. Gunn, Berry, and Andrews (1982) found that infants with DS looked more at their mothers than at objects and suggested that they had a different priority in their use of attention, in that they are more engaged in interpersonal contact than the referential, information-gathering use of attention. However, other studies of infants with DS have shown that overall they produce fewer social behaviors and differ in the way that they use attention (McTurk, Vietze, McCarthy, McQuiston, & Yarrow, 1985). Attention, according to McTurk et al. (1985), seems to be the center of the behavioral organization of infants with DS, whereas social behavior is the center for nondelayed infants. This may be because infants with DS have a slower information-processing ability (Zelazo & Stack, 1997) and use attention mainly to gather information, rather than as a social tool. The children in our studies also made use of attention in totally different ways, often smiling and locking gaze with the experimenter but resisting any of her attempts to direct attention back to the test materials and the task in hand. Though such behaviors may be charming and cute, they clearly are dysfunctional at both the social and cognitive level. However, it is easy to see how such behavior could mislead the positively disposed observer into attributing to the child with DS social skills of a higher level than may be justified.

Research over the last two decades on the development of social understanding in children with DS provides little support for the belief that social skills are an area of particular strength in these children. Although it has been suggested that in the early years the acquisition of social skills may be less severely impaired than other areas of psychological functioning, there would seem to be important qualitative differences in how social skills emerge and how social interactions evolve. In addition to showing attentional differences, young children with DS are less likely, for instance, to initiate play and show significant weaknesses in nonverbal requesting skills (for overviews, see Hines & Bennet, 1996; Wagner, Ganiban, & Cicchetti, 1990). It has been suggested that these differences in social behaviors may stem from underlying deficits in information processing, including problems in attending, discriminating, and encoding social stimuli, but as yet there are few studies that have provided data to allow these questions to be directly addressed. Although the cognitive abilities of children with DS have been extensively examined, the development of social skills has not, perhaps because of the presumption of the "sociable" stereotype. As it is clear that this stereotype may well be misinformed, we need to reexamine the social as well as the cognitive abilities of children with DS in the light of this more recent evidence.

Understanding Others: Developing Face-Processing Skills

Arriving at a working understanding of the social world is fundamental to both social and cognitive development. One of the tools necessary in the process of communicating successfully with others is an understanding of facial expressions of emotion. The child must be able to produce expressions him- or herself and understand those that others produce. Although there have been a great many studies of conceptual development in children with DS, there have been surprisingly few studies of those aspects of perceptual development that are crucial to the successful elaboration of more advanced social constructs. Where perception in children with DS has been investigated, studies have typically looked only at infants or very young children and have therefore provided only limited information on developmental patterns of either the emergence or use of such skills (Wagner et al., 1990). Very few have examined perception in relation to its neurological substrate or cognitive sequelae.

Those few studies that have looked at the motoric aspects of expression of affect in children with DS indicate that even familiar adults can have difficulty interpreting the facial expressions of young children with DS (Berger & Cunningham, 1983). This, it has been postulated, is due to the "dampened" expression of affect by children with DS. As with all research in the area of face processing, the story is not as simple as it might first seem. Deficits in expressive emotion may be due to a lack of the necessary motor control or to a lack of the cognitive understanding that underpins social interchanges. We already know that there is relatively poor control of fine muscle systems in DS (see chapters 1, 2, 5, 7, 9), but the evidence to be presented suggests that the problems may be more centrally located in the "social brain", specifically in the amygdala, hippocampus, and frontal lobes.

This chapter will concentrate on face processing, a core skill in the processing of socially based and socially transmitted information. The ability to process emotional cues in faces is in particular assumed to be crucial to the development of appropriate social skills, although there is as yet surprisingly little empirical evidence of any direct connection between development in these two areas (Rojahn & Warren, 1996). Difficulties in relating well to others are among the central diagnostic criteria for intellectual disability, and developing social awareness and social competence is a major objective of many educational and community programs for those with such disabilities. Research in this area, however, has tended to examine practical social skills rather than underlying perceptual competencies. A number of studies have found significant correlations between performance on emotion-matching tasks and level of cognitive functioning in those with intellectual disabilities (Gioia & Brosgole, 1988; Gray, Fraser, & Leudar, 1983; Iacobbo, 1978; Maurer & Newbrough, 1987; McAlpine, Singh, Kendall, & Ellis, 1992; Rojahn, Kroeger, & McElwain, 1994). However, there is also evidence from studies of adolescents and adults with intellectual disabilities that difficulty in decoding emotions may not simply reflect diminished levels of cognitive ability, since deficits in decoding facially expressed emotions cannot be fully accounted for by mental-age differences (e.g., Hobson, Ouston, & Lee, 1989; Rojahn, Rabold, & Schneider, 1995). Some weaknesses in design limit interpretation, although these data generally support an emotion-specificity account of deficits in face-processing skills.

There are very few data on developmental aspects of the processing of emotional information in children with intellectual disabilities. Inter- and intrapersonal understanding, like other aspects of cognition, are usually developmentally delayed in children with severe learning disabilities, although in some syndromes they are relatively spared (as in William's syndrome) or especially impaired (as in autism). This has led to suggestions that there may be a "social module" for representing and processing stimuli relevant to other people, such as language, feelings, and beliefs (Karmiloff-Smith, Klima, Bellugi, Grant, & Baron-Cohen, 1995). Studies of children with autism have been central to the elaboration of modular theories, and there is strong evidence that such children suffer a severe impairment in their social understanding that is not found in children with DS (Baron-Cohen, Leslie, & Frith, 1985, 1986).

Despite recent claims to the contrary (Johnson, 1997), these studies showed no direct evidence of any impairment in face-processing skills in children with DS. There is in fact some evidence—and as we have seen a very robust stereotype (Wishart & Johnston, 1990)—to suggest that some aspects of social understanding, if not advanced, may at least be relatively protected in DS. Carr (1995), for example, found that social skills were often better developed in children with DS than in mental age-matched children with other learning disabilities, while Franco and Wishart (1995) observed toddlers with DS using fundamental social skills such as referential pointing to good effect to compensate for their lack of verbal communicative skills.

Understanding the Information Available in Faces

Studies on facial expressions of emotion have shown that expressions are species-specific indicators of particular emotional states (Ekman & Friesen, 1971). The ability to recognize these expressions is apparent in children from the age of 6 months or even earlier (Oster, Daily, & Goldenthal, 1989).

The task that is commonly used to examine the ability to perceive facial expressions is that of labeling a photograph of the appropriate expression. This technique has been used since Darwin (1872) and is found in a very wide range of research, from the cross cultural (Ekman & Friesen, 1971) to research with subjects with specific disabilities (Pitcairn & Yan, 1999). The inability to recognize or label pictures of emotional expressions, however, cannot in itself be taken as indicative of a decrement in emotional ability, as the perception of pictures per se may be the cause of the difficulty (Pitcairn, 1989). The task of labeling emotion is often therefore combined with a picture-labeling task, such as recognizing an individual from pictures of faces, either by naming an already known face, or by identifying a second (different) picture of the same target individual. Processing facial expressions of emotion is dissociable from processing facial identity (Young, Newcombe, de Haan, Small, & Hay, 1993), and therefore the use of the two tests ensures that poor facial or picture processing does not confuse the results for emotional processing.

The ability to discriminate among individuals has been demonstrated very early in infancy, and there has been considerable discussion of whether this ability is innate or not (Johnson & Morton, 1991). Yin (1969, 1970) found that the processing of identity from faces was considerably more disrupted than for comparably complex objects when turned upside down, and Carey, Diamond, and Woods (1980) have suggested that faces are processed configurally (from the relations among the component parts) only when upright, an ability that does not reach full adult levels until the onset of puberty. This evidence, of different processing of faces upright and upside down, has been used to suggest that recognizing identity from faces is a neurologically distinct module that is separate from other aspects of cognitive and perceptual functioning (Yin, 1970).

The neurological underpinnings of face processing are understood to some degree. Damage to the right, or possibly both, temporal lobe(s) will often produce an inability to recognize people by their face, a condition known as prosopagnosia (Damasio, Damasio, & van Hoesen, 1982; de Renzi, 1986). The neurology of emotion, on the other hand, is associated with the limbic system. Patients suffering from Parkinson's disease, which consists of a loss of the neurotransmitter dopamine in the limbic pathways through the basal ganglia, show a reduced ability to display expressions of emotion (Rinn, 1984; Pitcairn, Clemie, Gray, & Pentland, 1990) and also seem to suffer a loss in the degree to which they perceive other people and contexts as portraying or indicating emotion (Pitcairn & Yan, 1999). A number of studies have suggested a specific role for the amygdala in the expression and perception of emotions, specifically in the processing of anger and fear (Calder et al., 1996; le Doux, 1995). Huntington's disease affects predominantly the subcortical structures of the basal ganglia and amygdala, at least in its early stages, and Sprengelmeyer et al. (1996) have reported that persons suffering from the disease are selectively impaired in the facial and vocal perception of disgust. Gray, Young, Barker, and Curtis (1997) found that the facial recognition of disgust is selectively impaired in patients who are presymptomatic for the disease, strongly suggesting the involvement of the basal ganglia. The specification of areas associated with specific emotions is very much in its infancy, and these suggestions, though interesting, must be treated with some caution.

The adult DS brain shows defective tissue development in the frontal lobes (Jernigan, Bellugi, & Sowell, 1993; Raz, Torres, & Briggs, 1995) and reduced size of the brain stem (Benda, 1971), temporal limbic cortex of the forebrain (Jernigan et al., 1993), and hippocampus (Raz et al., 1995). The hippocampus, another forebrain structure associated with the amygdala and basal ganglia, also shows a reduced nerve cell density in adults with DS in comparison to typical development (Ball & Nuttall, 1981) and fewer dendritic spines (Ferrer & Gullota, 1990). Uecker, Mangan, Obrzut, and Nadel (1993) have argued that children with DS have reduced spatial representational abilities as a result of this reduction in efficiency of hippocampal functioning.

The combined effects listed above show the need for an investigation of social understanding in children with DS. As there is some doubt about the validity of the DS stereotype and given the nature of the neural impairments associated with DS, it seems likely that there might be specific impairments in their ability to process emotional information. The experiments described below were designed to investigate this hypothesis.

Face-Processing Ability in Children With Down Syndrome: Some Illustrative Experiments

In the two experiments to be described here, three groups of children took part: children with Down syndrome (DS), children with nonspecific developmental delay (NSD), and typically developing (TD) children (Wishart & Pitcairn, 1999). The children with DS and NSD attended two Scottish schools for children with moderate to severe learning difficulties and were aged between 8 and 14 years. All of the children with DS had standard trisomy 21, the most common form of the syndrome in which a third complete copy of chromosome 21 is present in all cells. The NSD group was composed of children for whom the etiology of intellectual disability was unknown and who had no family history of learning problems. The typically developing (TD) children came from the Department of Psychology Nursery at the University of Edinburgh and were between 3 and 5 years of age. Matching was based on performance on a basic face-recognition task similar to that which would be used in the experiments, the face-recognition subtest of the Kaufman Assessment Battery for Children (KABC) (Kaufman & Kaufman, 1983).

In the first experiment, 16 DS and 16 NSD children were tested. Although the DS and NSD groups had similar levels of intellectual disability and were matched for chronological age at entry to the study, a significant difference in basic recognition ability emerged between the two intellectually disabled groups on the performance pretest. A total of 23 TD children had to be tested before appropriate matches were achieved for each of the 16 children in the two disabled groups.

The two face-processing tasks required the children to match photographs of people they had not seen before, first for identity and then for facial expression. In a third task, the children also were required to match facial expressions to a brief verbal story told by the experimenter. All of the 5-by-7-inch, black-and-white photographs used in the three tasks came from the Ekman and Friesen (1976) set of "Facial Affect Slides." These show either a male or female adult face expressing one of six "primary" emotions: happiness, surprise, fear, anger, sadness, and disgust. Over the last 20 years, the Ekman and Friesen slides have been used extensively in research with children and adults on facial expression of emotion and have high inter-rater reliability.

Testing was broken down into two parts, each containing three trials on each of the three tasks. There were thus six identity, six expression, and six expression-to-story trials in total. All six expressions were represented in both the expression and expression-to-story matching tasks. The faces in the photographs were given names to aid the children's comprehension of the task and to make the procedure more interesting.

In the identity-matching task, the child was shown one picture and told, "This is a picture of Laura." Two further pictures were placed underneath, and then the child was asked, "Can you show me another picture of Laura?" The people in the pictures all had different facial expressions, and in order to ensure that we were testing for identity recognition rather than recognition memory skills, the photographs all remained on the table until the child gave his or her answer. The facial expression-matching task was constructed in a very similar way to the identity task. A picture was shown and the child was told, "This is a picture of Jonathan. Jonathan looks surprised, doesn't he?" Two more pictures were then placed underneath, and the child was asked, "Can you find me another picture of a man that looks surprised?" Care was taken to ensure that the child knew the new rules of the game and that a different question was being asked. In addition to the standard words used to describe the six expressions, "cross", "scared", and "yucky" were also used to describe the angry, frightened, and disgusted faces, respectively. On the third task, the expression-to-story matching task, a simple story was told: "These are three pictures of Sally. Sally has just been given a very nice present. What would Sally look like now?" In this task, the child had to choose from three pictures, all of the same individual but each portraying a different emotion. All testing sessions were videotaped for subsequent analysis.

Mean scores on all three tasks for each of the three subject groups are given in table 6.1. Although the children with Down syndrome scored lower than all other groups in all three face-processing tasks, the only significant difference in scores was on the second task, the expression-matching task (Mann-Whitney $U = 64.5, p < .02$). It should nevertheless be noted that although the children with Down syndrome were relatively poorer at recognizing facial expressions than either the typically developing children or those with nonspecific delay, they still performed above chance level for all expressions except surprise and fear on the expression-matching task (table 6.2). This difference among expressions was present in the DS group only ($\chi^2 = 5.1$, 5df, $p < .02$). The expressions of surprise and fear, therefore, were recognized significantly less well than other expressions and below the chance level of recognition. The other interesting finding was that, while there was a clear relation of overall performance to chronological age in both the NSD group ($r = .84, p < .001$) and even the nursery group, where the age range was much smaller ($r = .45, p < .025$), there was no relation between age and scores in the DS group ($r = .23, p > .05$).

Overall, then, the children with DS were not as good at matching expressions, but not significantly different at matching identity or, surprisingly, at matching an expression to a story. The significantly poorer performance found in the expression-matching

Table 6.1   Mean Scores per Trial for the Three Subject Groups on the Three Face-Processing Tasks (Maximum Possible Score = 6) in Experiment 1

	IDENTITY		EXPRESSION		STORY	
	Mean	*SD*	Mean	*SD*	Mean	*SD*
DS	3.69	1.25	3.38*	1.09	3.06	1.44
NSD	3.88	1.31	4.13	1.67	3.25	1.92
TD/DS-matched	3.94	1.53	4.56	1.41	3.75	1.34
TD/NSD-matched	3.38	1.50	4.69	1.40	3.75	1.34

* $p < .02$

Table 6.2   Total Scores for the Three Subject Groups on the Six Expressions Used in the Expression-Matching Task (Maximum Possible Score = 16) in Experiment 1

	Happy	Surprise	Sadness	Fear	Anger	Disgust
DS*	11	6	12	5	12	9
NSD	11	11	13	13	8	10
TD/DS-matched	14	12	13	13	13	10
TD/NSD-matched	14	14	13	12	12	10

* $p < .02$

task was unlikely simply to result from poor picture perception, as there was no corresponding reduction in the ability to find the correct match of pictures of unknown people in the identity-matching task. Poorer performance would therefore seem to reflect a more specific inability to recognize particular emotions. The specific expressions that were poorly recognized by the DS group were surprise and fear.

A second experiment was designed in which the effects of rotation of the face stimulus were investigated. Although visuospatial abilities seem generally to be preserved in DS (Wang, 1996), Uecker et al. (1993) have argued that there is an impairment in the ability of children with DS to cope with rotation of objects. When an object is rotated, it takes much longer to recognize that object. Children with DS in Uecker et al.'s studies did not significantly increase their processing time, however, when an object was rotated, unlike both TD and NSD children. Paradoxically, if the measure used was accuracy rather than reaction time, there was no difference between DS and NSD subjects when the object was rotated. This seems interesting, but the two findings are difficult to reconcile and clearly need further investigation. A rotation study has the further advantage that rotation of faces is known to make identification and recognition of expressions more difficult because it requires the use of a different visuospatial processing mechanism (Carey et al., 1980), and thus the effect of difficulty with emotional perception can more easily be dissociated from that of general cognitive functioning.

Fourteen DS, 14 NSD, and 14 TD children took part in the second experiment on face-processing abilities. The intellectually disabled children in this study were drawn from three local special schools and were aged between 5 and 12 years; the typically developing control children attended the Psychology Department nursery and were again 3-5 years old. As in the previous experiment, subject groups were matched on the basis of face-recognition ability using the KABC subtest. Forty-eight children had to be tested to achieve the 14 matches, with 6 children excluded on the basis of either being out of the required range on pretest performance or apparent inability to understand the task instructions.

This second experiment also focused on identity and expression recognition, but aimed to measure the effect of rotation on ability to match facial expression or individual identity. Rotation makes the matching task much harder for children, and so for the purposes of this experiment only the expressions of happiness or anger were used in the expression-matching task (with prints again taken from Ekman & Friesen, 1976). Children were asked to indicate whether the expression in the rotated or nonrotated photograph was happy or angry by pointing to an outline drawing of either a happy or angry expression. For the identity task, children had to indicate whether the rotated or nonrotated face was familiar or unfamiliar, and in this case the photographs represented adults who were either known or unknown to the child. Photographs were passport-style photographs of female staff drawn from the participating schools and nursery, reproduced as 5-by-7-inch color prints. The reminder of belonging used to prompt the children was a photograph of a familiar room in the school or nursery versus a large black cross. The task was to indicate whether the person in the photograph was known or unknown by pointing to or touching either the photograph of the schoolroom or the black cross. (In pilot trials, the original design of posting the photograph into one of two boxes, with familiar represented by a box with a photograph of the school at the head, was found to be too difficult for some of the children. The above procedure proved to be less motorically difficult and more comprehensible.)

Each child sat opposite the experimenter, and was given three practice trials in each condition (expression and identity), with the expression practice and test preceding the identity practice and test. In the expression condition, the child was shown the outline drawings of happy and angry expressions and asked to identify the expressions on the faces by pointing first to the happy one, and then to the angry one. The child was then shown an upright photograph of a happy face, and told, "This is a picture of Jim. Is Jim happy or angry? If you think Jim is happy, I want you to touch the happy picture here (indicate), and if you think he is angry I want you to touch the angry picture over here (indicate)."

If the child failed to respond correctly or looked blank, prompts were employed as follows:

1. "Is Jim angry and cross, or is he happy and pleased?"

2. "Does Jim look as if someone has just taken away his favorite toy and he is angry, or does he look as though he has been given a lovely new toy and is happy?"

Two further practices used photographs of an angry expression upright and then a happy expression at 180° (upside down). In each case, prompts were used as necessary. The child had to indicate the correct expression in all three practice trials (with or without prompts) before the experiment could proceed.

There were 12 test trials in which 6 photographs of women portraying either happy or angry expressions were shown to the child; each photograph was presented twice, with order of presentation randomized. There were four trials in each of three different orientations (0°, 90°, and 180°), with orientation randomized and counterbalanced across expressions. Position of the two outline face drawings used to elicit responses was counterbalanced over trials such that the correct one was equally often to the left or the right. The following verbal instructions were given: "Some of the people will look a bit funny, they might be upside down or on their side, but I want you to keep your head nice and straight while we play this game. Is this lady happy or angry? If you think she is happy, point to the happy picture. If you think she is angry, point to the angry picture."

For the identity task, each child was similarly given three practice trials with prompts if necessary. The children were first shown the picture of their school/nursery room, and told, "This is a picture of your school/nursery, isn't it? I'm going to show you some pictures of people, and I want you to tell me if you see these people in your school or not. Is this person in your school/nursery? Point to the school/nursery picture if you know this person from school/nursery. If you don't know this person, point to the big black cross."

The practice trials were a familiar face upright, an unfamiliar face upright, and a familiar face upside down, all with a neutral expression. The photographs of female staff from the other schools or the nursery in the study served as the unfamiliar faces. The prompts were the following:

1. Repeat the original question.
2. "Do you see this person when you are at school/nursery?"

The experimenter continued with the test only when it was clear that the child understood the questions and could perform the tasks.

All trials were videotaped for subsequent analysis. For each subject, time taken to complete each trial was measured as well as whether the response was correct or not. Two-way analysis of variance on the correct scores for both the expression and identity-matching tasks revealed the same results. In both cases there were main effects for group and for orientation, but no interaction between group and orientation (table 6.3). Newman-Keuls post-hoc tests showed that the specific significant differences were between the DS and TD groups ($q = 4.11, p < .05$) and 0° and 180° ($q = 5.0, p < .05$) for the expression task, and the DS and NSD and the DS and TD groups ($q = 3.19, p < .05$ in both cases) and 0° and 180° ($q = 3.31, p < .05$) for the identity task.

The response latencies were not significantly different among the groups or orientations. Although the mean response latencies for DS were much longer than those for the other groups for both expression and identity tasks, the variance among this group was very large indeed, rendering the results nonsignificant. These experiments give support to the conclusion that there is a decrement in children with DS in the ability to recognize facial expressions of emotion. In this experiment there was no possibility of assessing the effect of specific expressions, as only happy and angry expressions were used. It should be noted that the difference, although significant, did not mean that the children with DS could not distinguish happy from angry

Table 6.3   Two-Way Analysis of Variance (Group × Orientation) of Correct Scores on the Expression and Identity Tasks in the Three Subject Groups in Experiment 2

	EXPRESSION		IDENTITY	
	F	p	F	p
Group (A)	6.57	.004	3.60	.037
Orientation (B)	20.44	.000	8.23	.001
Interaction (A × B)	0.48	.751	0.48	.748

F = the F ratio from the analysis of variance

expressions; they were simply less proficient at it than the other groups. In the first experiment, it will be recalled, the scores for the DS group were also lower than for matched controls, although the major effect was for fear and surprise.

This diminished ability to differentiate emotional expressions does not seem to result from deficits in simple picture processing. Although in this experiment the children with DS were less successful in recognizing known faces, there was no evidence in Experiment 1 of any inability to recognize unknown faces. In addition, the performance of the DS group on known faces did not get relatively worse when the picture was rotated away from upright, further suggesting that there is a decrement in recognizing known faces rather than a basic inability to process pictures. These results are interesting to compare with the findings of Uecker et al. (1993) using nonsocial stimuli and rotated stick figures. In their studies, there was no evidence of any DS-specific drop in accuracy at a rotation of 180°. This may well have been because of a speed/accuracy trade-off in the children with DS: whereas the intellectually disabled and typically developing control children took significantly longer to process stimuli at orientations of more than 90°, the children with DS were quicker to respond than they had been at upright orientations.

The Nature of the Deficit

The deficit for affective processing evident in these experiments does not fit easily with the common perception of children with DS as being hypersocial when it comes to expressing affection and responding to others' emotions. The deficit, however, is somewhat specific, in that there was a greater reduction in the ability to label expressions of fear and surprise. Two different hypotheses could explain this difficulty. First, it could be that children with DS are exposed to a predominantly positive social environment, and learn to deal only with positive expressions. However, there is no evidence that children with nonspecific learning disorders, who would surely be expected to be similarly protected, show a similar deficit. In any case, the deficit was in processing both fear, a negative emotion, and surprise, a positive one. The children also showed no comparative difficulty with the negative emotions of anger and disgust.

The second hypothesis is that the deficits are due directly to the syndrome, a symptom of the neurological problems. A specific deficit is found in the recognition of disgust in patients with damage to the amygdala (Calder et al., 1996). We know from work by Jernigan et al. (1993) and others that there is a reduction in the volume of the limbic cortex in children with DS and a reduction in volume and cell complexity in the hippocampus. In our experiments, however, we found a reduction in the ability to recognize surprise and fear. This is particularly interesting in that anger is still recognized well, thus showing a dissociation between anger and fear, the components of emotion that have been classically associated with amygdala damage. The deficits were not only specific, but also there was no evidence of improvement in performance with increasing age, as was the case in both the TD and NSD children. This suggests even more strongly that the deficit is fixed, not changing with the increasing experience of the child.

Perceptual-Matching Ability in Children With Down Syndrome

Perceptual matching, the task that forms the main part of the experiments outlined above, is something that children with DS are clearly capable of doing. Pitcairn and Wishart (1994), for instance, found that children with DS as young as 3 years had little difficulty with a shape-sorting task that required each of three differently shaped objects to be posted into their correct holes. In addition, when presented with an "impossible" task—posting an object into a box that had a hole of the correct shape but the wrong size—the children with DS would choose the right shape of opening in their initial attempts; that is, they would choose the square-shaped hole for the square object. They persisted, however, in this and subsequent trials, in attempting to post the "impossible" object, going on to try other holes at random. When faced with the failure of this approach, some of the children then reverted to the sorts of socially based "switching out" strategies already evidenced in other experimental paradigms, misusing their social skills in an attempt to divert attention—their own and the experimenter's—to some less demanding task. By contrast the age-matched control children quickly learned that the task was impossible, often saying that the shape would not "go" or that there was no hole for it, either refusing to try to post it on the second trial or finding the alternative solution of opening the large front door of the posting box and placing the shape inside, a solution usually accompanied by a grin of triumph or occasionally of defiance. Children matched on mental age did initially try to post the impossible object, but on their second trial would very quickly report that the shape did not fit or give up.

Comparisons of the "on-task" and "off-task" behavior of these three groups of children during the "impossible" trials uncovered interesting differences in affective behavior (not reported in the 1994 paper). An analysis of variance of frequencies of facial expressions during task performance found no significant difference in the frequency of positive affect (e.g., smiles) among groups, but significantly more negative facial expressions in the chronologically age-matched (CA) children than in either the DS or mentally age-matched (MA) children ($\chi^2r = 7.7; p < .01$). Despite this lack of any great enthusiasm for the task, none of the CA children and only a very few of the MA children used distracting social behaviors to bring trials to an end. It is worth emphasizing that the children with DS were not simply "more social." The social behaviors produced were rather a specific response to the inability to meet the demands of the task.

The behavior seen in these matching studies mirrored responses in a number of other kinds of problem-solving situations, with poor motivation apparently a significant factor in depressing performance levels. This switching on of engaging but irrelevant social behaviors in challenging situations fits well with the long-established perception of children with DS as being none-too-bright but very sociable and affectionate. As already mentioned, research into the personalities and affective behavior of the children in fact provides little support for this stereotype (Berger & Cunningham, 1983; Gunn & Berry, 1985a, 1985b; Sorce & Emde, 1982). The robustness of the stereotype becomes more understandable, however, if children with DS respond to everyday problems with the same socially based "failure avoidance" strategies (Cromwell, 1967) observed in laboratory studies.

The response of the children with DS to the "impossible" trials obviously cannot simply be explained in terms of perceptual deficits. The children were perfectly able to discriminate perceptually the relation between object and location and could perform the basic task of matching an object to an appropriately shaped hole with much the same success rate, and in much the same time, as chronologically younger children of a similar mental age. If anything, they were slightly faster than the MA controls. They could easily match the object to the appropriate hole, but what they seemed unable to do was to make use of this information in deciding whether the task was possible or not. This was reflected not only in the lengths of time spent on the first presentation of the "impossible" shapes, but in the lack of any significant drop in persistence when given the same shape a second time.

Conclusions

Children with DS seem unable to integrate sets of information toward completion of a task. This fits with other observations of the children's failures to consolidate new skills and to transfer what has been learned to new contexts. Wishart (1996) has suggested that this also may explain some of the differences seen in longitudinal patterns of performance on object permanence tasks, with failures to build on existing knowledge possibly underlying the reversals found in the normally well established order of developmental difficulty. Successes at early ages in some object concept tasks also proved to be very unstable, leading to the suspicion that the strategies used for solving these tasks may have been less conceptually driven than at first thought. Object concept tasks that had been passed to strict statistical criteria over several sessions were often failed at later ages, even though the child was simultaneously "passing" tasks normally taken as representing achievement at a higher cognitive level.

Findings from a recent doctoral dissertation by Wright (1997) cast further doubt on the integrity of the conceptual underpinnings of some of the cognitive successes of young children with DS on traditional tests of conceptual development. When object concept search tasks were recast so that removing the occluding cup required an action that the child could imitate, success rates were high; if, however, this action prompt was removed, success rates fell significantly, suggesting there had been no real understanding of the underlying constructs that normally drive solutions to these tasks. In Wright's study, performance was evaluated on two versions of object concept tasks, one in which an imitative strategy would allow success, another in which it would not. In the former, imitation of the experimenter's hand movements while hiding the toy in the cup was possible; in the latter, the toy could be retrieved only by depressing a lever that would raise the cup and reveal the hidden object. Although the motor skills required to perform this act were demonstrably within the repertoire of the children with DS, performance on this task was significantly poorer than in the more standard version of the task. The performance of typically developing children was not significantly different.

As with the shape-sorting task, the children in Wright's experiment seemed to have a "bottom-up" approach to the solving of problems, an approach characterized by a lack of organization in cognitive functioning and a failure to integrate knowledge across tasks. The relevance of knowledge gained from performance on one task was simply not recognized or transferred to behavior in a second, related task. Learning in children with DS would appear to be qualitatively different. Such a difference might explain the failure to produce lasting effects in training studies and interventions predicated on the assumption that development in children with DS, except in rate and ceiling, is fundamentally the same as in other children.

The Wright (1997) studies are particularly interesting because of the central role imitation played in determining success rates in children with DS on tasks traditionally considered to be archetypal tests of cognitive development. Imitation is considered by many to be the foundation stone of social learning, but the patterns of performance on Wright's tasks suggest that success was tied to learning to copy the action of the experimenter, not driven by the kind of developing representations of the hidden object assumed in most theories to underpin search at different levels of object concept task. At best, success is being driven by imitative or "empirical" representations (Meltzoff & Gopnik, 1989), not by processes of deductive reasoning.

Children with the same level of cognitive ability—or the same level of cognitive impairment (at least as measured by traditional developmental tests), such as those with nonspecific learning difficulties—seem better able to make use of their abilities within the framework of the test and to bring them together to solve the task. All too often, the response of children with DS is some sort of "social" response. It is this that gets them the reputation of being very sociable children, who respond to all difficulties with a smile or charm. However, this performance often precludes further exploration of the problem and ultimately its solution. The performance itself also needs to be more closely examined. We have shown that children with DS do not recognize facial expressions of emotion as well as other children with learning difficulties. How, then, can these children be more strongly sociable? Two possible answers arise. Either the tests of facial expression recognition are not very good tests of sociability, or indeed the performance of the children is not as sociable as assumed.

The brief review of the literature given above detailed some of the differences observed in the social behaviors of young children with DS. For example, children with DS have been found to use gaze to monitor the other's performance, rather than as a social tool. At this point, all we can offer on the social behavior of the children in our experiments is anecdotal information, but it does seem that performance was often limited and fairly stereotyped; that is, the same set of actions would occur repetitively in different situations irrespective of their appropriateness. Performance sometimes took the form of "party tricks" that the child had learned would amuse the observer and get them "off the hook," the hook of solving the task at hand. Given the frustrations children with DS must experience in tackling many tasks, whatever the root of that difficulty, it is perhaps not surprising that they evidence a growing lack of enthusiasm for problem-solving. Repeated exposure to failure may also lead them to distrust their own solutions to problems and to rely instead on the external environment for cues, as Zigler suggested many years ago in his "outer-directedness" theory of learning in children with intellectual disabilities (Zigler, 1969).

Normally, there is a set of rules that governs exchanges in even quite young infants, in which the use of gaze (looking at the other) takes a conversational form (Trevarthen, 1993). Gaze is managed carefully, without long periods in which the interactants are mutually gazing at each other's face. It was quite common, however, for some of the children with DS in our studies to attempt to hold gaze for very extended, and indeed quite uncomfortably long, periods. This anecdotal evidence suggests that the social performance of children with DS is constrained in a similar way to their cognitive performance. They are good at picking up the elements of an interaction, using gaze and other components in a way that superficially makes them appear to be extremely competent socially. However, this behavior is mechanistic, in the sense that they are not able to adapt to changing circumstances or to integrate the performance into a coherent whole. This hypothesis clearly needs much closer examination, but at least allows us to bring together the results from various different areas of research into DS.

Summary

The evidence from our work, then, is that there may be a specific deficit in children with DS in processing facial expressions. That this is not due to a cognitive deficit is supported by the fact that there is no evidence that their performance is relatively any different from controls when the task is made harder—that is, when the task requires processing the faces upside down. This normally means that a different sort of processing will occur, a shift from configural to feature detection. There seems, therefore, to be a specific deficit in facial expression processing that is not related to a general cognitive deficit. This does not seem to be a general visuospatial problem, as there was little evidence of a decrement in ability to label unknown faces by identity and the deficit in the facial expression matching task was specific to fear and surprise. This specific deficit in the processing of particular expressions has been found to be associated with the amygdala in cases of neurological damage (Calder et al., 1996). This part of the limbic system is concerned with the control of emotion, and has specific connections to the hypothalamus. As we have seen, it is already known that children with DS have a reduced volume in the temporal limbic cortex of the forebrain (Jernigan et al., 1993) and in adults in the hippocampus (Raz et al., 1995).

It would therefore seem reasonable to suggest that the deficits in processing facial information can be linked to the neurology of Down syndrome. In addition, the reduced volume of the frontal lobes (Jernigan et al., 1993) suggests that children with DS may well exhibit the classic effects of frontal lobe syndrome—an increase in extraversion and a lack of awareness of the relevance of the response of others. This does indeed fit with the pattern of social response seen in many children with DS: patterns of attention are not focused on interpersonal relations, and the positive social behaviors produced may be repetitive and dysfunctional in problem-solving contexts. The inability of children with DS to produce associative solutions to problems may also be a product of reduced efficiency in the associative frontal cortex. Recent evidence from studies on infants with DS measuring event-related potentials lends some support to this hypothesis (Karrer, Karrer, Bloom, Chaney, & Davis, 1998).

References

Ball, M.J., & Nuttall, K. (1981). Topography of neurofibrillary tangles and granovacuoles in the hippocampi of patients with Down's syndrome: Quantitative comparison with normally aging and Alzheimer's disease. *Neuropathology and Applied Neurobiology, 7*, 13-20.

Baron-Cohen, S., Leslie, A.M., & Frith, U. (1985). Does the autistic child have a "theory of mind?" *Cognition, 21*, 37-46.

Baron-Cohen, S., Leslie, A.M., & Frith, U. (1986). Mechanical, behavioral and intentional understanding of picture stories in autistic children. *British Journal of Developmental Psychology, 4*, 113-125.

Bellugi, U., Bihrle, A., Neville, H., Jernigan, T., & Doherty, S. (1992). Language, cognition and brain organization in a neurodevelopmental disorder. In M. Gunnar & C. Nelson (Eds.), *Developmental behavioral neuroscience* (pp. 201-232). Hillsdale, NJ: Erlbaum.

Benda, C.E. (1971). Mongolism. In J. Minckler (Ed.), *Pathology of the nervous system: Vol. 2.* (pp. 1361-1371). New York: McGraw-Hill.

Berger, J., & Cunningham, C.C. (1983). Development of early vocal behaviours and interactions in Down's syndrome and non-handicapped infant-mother pairs. *Developmental Psychology, 19*, 322-331.

Calder, A.J., Young A.W., Rowland, D., Perrett, D.I., Hodges, J., & Etcoff, N.L. (1996). Facial emotion recognition after bilateral amygdala damage: Differentially severe impairment of fear. *Cognitive Neuropsychology, 13*, 699-745.

Carey, S., Diamond, R., & Woods, B. (1980). Development of face recognition—A maturational component? *Developmental Psychology, 16*, 257-269.

Carr, J. (1985). The development of intelligence. In D. Lane & B. Stratford (Eds.), *Current approaches to Down's syndrome* (pp. 167-186). London: Holt, Rinehart & Winston.

Carr, J. (1994). Long term outcome for people with Down's syndrome. *Journal of Child Psychology and Psychiatry, 35*, 425-439.

Carr, J. (1995). *Down's syndrome: Children growing up.* Cambridge: Cambridge University Press.

Casey, W., Jones, D., & Watkins, B. (1988). Integration of Down's syndrome children in the primary school. *British Journal of Educational Psychology, 58*, 279-286.

Cicchetti, D., & Beeghly, M. (Eds.). (1990). *Children with Down syndrome: A developmental perspective.* New York: Cambridge University Press.

Cicchetti, D., & Ganiban, J. (1990). The organization and coherence of developmental processes in infants and children with Down syndrome. In R.M. Hodapp, J.A. Burack, & E. Zigler (Eds.), *Issues in the developmental approach to mental retardation* (pp. 169-225). New York: Cambridge University Press.

Cromwell, R.L. (1967). Success-failure reactions in mentally retarded children. In J. Zublin & G.A. Jervis (Eds.), *Psychopathology of mental development* (pp. 147-160). New York: Grune & Stratton.

Damasio, A.R., Damasio, H., & van Hoesen, G.W. (1982). Prosopagnosia: Anatomical basis and behavioural mechanisms. *Neurology, 32*, 331-341.

Darwin, C. (1872). *The expression of the emotions in man and animals.* London: John Murray.

De Renzi, E. (1986). Current issues on prosopagnosia. In H.D. Ellis, M.A. Jeeves, F. Newcombe, & A. Young (Eds.), *Aspects of face processing* (pp. 243-252). Dordrecht: Nijhoff.

Duffy, L., & Wishart, J.G. (1994). The stability and transferability of errorless learning in children with Down's syndrome. *Down's Syndrome: Research and Practice, 2*, 51-58.

Ekman, P., & Friesen, W.V. (1971). Constants across cultures in the face and emotions. *Journal of Personality and Social Psychology, 17*, 124-129.

Ekman, P., & Friesen, W.V. (1976). *Facial affect slides.* Palo Alto, CA: Consulting Psychologists Press.

Epstein, C., Hassold, T., Lott, I.T., Nadel, L., & Patterson, D. (Eds.). (1995). *Etiology and pathogenesis of Down syndrome.* New York: Wiley-Liss.

Ferrer, L., & Gullotta, F. (1990). Down's syndrome and Alzheimer's disease: Dendritic spine counts in the hippocampus. *Acta Neuropathologica, 79*, 680-685.

Franco, F., & Wishart, J.G. (1995). The use of pointing and other gestures by young children with Down syndrome. *American Journal on Mental Retardation, 100*, 160-182.

Gibson, D. (1978). *Down syndrome: The psychology of mongolism.* Cambridge: Cambridge University Press.

Gibson, D., & Harris, A. (1988). Aggregated early intervention effects for Down's syndrome persons: Patterning and longevity of benefits. *Journal of Mental Deficiency Research, 32*, 1-17.

Gioia, J.V., & Brosgole, L. (1988). Visual and auditory affect recognition in singly diagnosed mentally retarded patients with autism and normal young children. *International Journal of Neuroscience, 43*, 149-163.

Gray, J.M., Fraser, W.L., & Leudar, I. (1983). Recognition of emotion from facial expression in mental handicap. *British Journal of Psychiatry, 142*, 566-571.

Gunn, P., & Berry, P. (1985a). Down's syndrome temperament and maternal response to child behaviour. *Developmental Psychology, 21*, 842-847.

Gunn, P., & Berry, P. (1985b). The temperament of Down's syndrome toddlers and their siblings. *Journal of Child Psychology and Psychiatry, 26*, 973-979.

Gunn, P., Berry, P., & Andrews, R.J. (1982). Looking behaviour of Down syndrome infants. *American Journal of Mental Deficiency, 87,* 344-347.

Hines, S., & Bennett, F. (1996). Effectiveness of early intervention for children with Down syndrome. *Mental Retardation and Developmental Disabilities Research Reviews, 2,* 96-101.

Hobson, R.P., Ouston, J., & Lee, A. (1989). Recognition of emotion by mentally retarded adolescents and young adults. *American Journal on Mental Retardation, 93,* 434-443.

Iacobbo, M.L. (1978). Recognition of affective facial expressions by retarded and nonretarded individuals across the lifespan. (Doctoral dissertation, George Peabody College for Teachers, Nashville, 1997). *Dissertation Abstracts International, 38,* 08B, p. 3885.

Irwin, K.C. (1989). The school achievement of children with Down's syndrome. *New Zealand Medical Journal, 102,* 11-13.

Jernigan, T.L., Bellugi, U., & Sowell, E. (1993). Cerebral morphological distinctions between William's and Down's syndromes. *Archives of Neurology, 50,* 186-191.

Johnson, M.H. (1997). *Developmental cognitive neuroscience: An introduction.* Oxford: Blackwell.

Johnson, M.H., & Morton, J. (1991). *Biology and cognitive development: The case of face recognition.* Oxford: Blackwell.

Karmiloff-Smith, A., Klima, E., Bellugi, U., Grant, J., & Baron-Cohen, S. (1995). Is there a social module? Language, face-processing and theory of mind in individuals with William's syndrome. *Journal of Cognitive Neuroscience, 7,* 196-208.

Karrer, J.H., Karrer, R., Bloom, D., Chaney, L., & Davis, R. (1998). Event-related brain potentials during an extended visual recognition memory task depict delayed development of cerebral inhibitory processes among six-month-old infants with Down syndrome. *International Journal of Psychophysiology, 29,* 167-200.

Kaufman, A.S., & Kaufman, N.L. (1983). *The Kaufman Assessment Battery for Children.* Circle Pines, MN: American Guidance Service.

Landry, S.H., & Chapieski, M.L. (1989). Joint attention and infant toy exploration: Effects of Down syndrome and prematurity. *Child Development, 60,* 103-118.

Landry, S.H., & Chapieski, M.L. (1990). Joint attention of six-month-old Down syndrome and preterm infants: 1. Attention to toys and mother. *American Journal on Mental Retardation, 94,* 488-498.

Le Doux, J.E. (1995). Emotion: Clues from the brain. *Annual Review of Psychology, 46,* 209-235.

Maurer, H., & Newbrough, J.R. (1987). Facial expressions of mentally retarded and nonretarded children: I. Recognition by mentally retarded and nonretarded adults. *American Journal of Mental Deficiency, 91,* 505-510.

McAlpine, C., Singh, N.N., Kendall, K.A., & Ellis, C. (1992). Recognition of facial expression of emotion by persons with mental retardation: A matched comparison study. *Behavior Modification, 16,* 543-558.

McTurk, R.H., Vietze, P.M., McCarthy, M.E., McQuiston, S., & Yarrow, L.J. (1985). The organization of exploratory behaviour in Down syndrome and non-delayed infants. *Child Development, 56,* 573-581.

Meltzoff, A.M., & Gopnik, A. (1989). On linking non-verbal imitation, representation and language learning in the first two years of life. In G.E. Speidel & K.E. Nelson (Eds.), *The many faces of imitation in language learning* (pp. 23-51). New York: Springer-Verlag.

Merighi, J., Edison, M., & Zigler, E. (1990). The role of motivational factors in the functioning of mentally retarded individuals. In R.M. Hodapp, J.A. Burack, & E. Zigler (Eds.), *Issues in the developmental approach to mental retardation* (pp. 114-134). New York: Cambridge University Press.

Nadel, L. (1996). Learning, memory and neural functioning in Down syndrome. In J.A. Rondal, J. Perera, L. Nadel, & A. Comblain (Eds.), *Down syndrome: Psychological, psychobiological and socio-educational perspectives* (pp. 21-42). London: Whurr.

Oster, H., Daily, L., & Goldenthal, P. (1989). Processing facial affect. In A. Young & H. Ellis (Eds.), *Handbook of research on facial processing* (pp. 107-162). Amsterdam: North-Holland.

Pitcairn, T.K. (1989). Origins and processing of facial expressions. In A. Young & H. Ellis (Eds.), *Handbook of research on facial processing* (pp. 171-176). Amsterdam: North-Holland.

Pitcairn, T.K., Clemie, S., Gray, J.M., & Pentland, B. (1990). Non-verbal cues in the self-presentation of Parkinsonian patients. *British Journal of Clinical Psychology, 29*, 177-184.

Pitcairn, T.K., & Wishart, J.G. (1994). Reactions of young children with Down's syndrome to an impossible task. *British Journal of Developmental Psychology, 12*, 485-489.

Pitcairn, T.K., & Yan, J. (1999). Emotional perception in Parkinson's disease; the effects of age and disease on judgement of emotion and intensity in facial and vocal expressions, and emotion-evoking pictures. Manuscript submitted for publication.

Rauh, H., Rudinger, G., Bowman, T.G., Berry, P., Gunn, P.V., & Hayes, A. (1991). The development of Down's syndrome children. In M.D. Lamb & H. Keller (Eds.), *Infant development: Perspectives from German-speaking countries* (pp. 320-355). Hillsdale, NJ: Erlbaum.

Raz, N., Torres, I.J., & Briggs, S.D. (1995). Selective neuroanatomical abnormalities in Down's syndrome and their cognitive correlates: Evidence from MRI morphometry. *Neurology, 45*, 356-366.

Rinn, W.E. (1984). The neuropsychology of facial expression: A review of the neuropsychological and psychological mechanisms for producing facial expressions. *Psychological Bulletin, 95*, 52-77.

Rojahn, J., Kroeger, T.L., & McElwain, D.C. (1994). Performance on the Penn Facial Discrimination Task by adults with mental retardation. *American Journal on Mental Retardation, 99*, 316-319.

Rojahn, J., Rabold, D.E., & Schneider F. (1995). Emotion specificity in mental retardation. *American Journal on Mental Retardation, 99*, 477-486.

Rojahn, J., & Warren, V.J. (1996). Emotion recognition as a function of social competence and depressed mood in individuals with intellectual disability. *Journal of Intellectual Disability Research, 41*, 469-475.

Sloper, P., Cunningham, C., Turner, S., & Knussen, C. (1990). Factors relating to the academic attainment of children with Down's syndrome. *British Journal of Educational Psychology, 60*, 284-298.

Sloper, P., & Turner, S. (1994). *Families of teenagers with Down's syndrome: Parent, child and sibling adaptation.* University of Manchester: Hester Adrian Research Centre. Final Report to ESRC.

Sorce, J.F., & Emde, R.N. (1982). The meaning of infant emotional expressions: Regularities in caregiving responses in normal and Down's syndrome infants. *Journal of Child Psychology and Psychiatry, 22*, 145-158.

Spiker, D., & Hopmann, M.R. (1996). The effectiveness of early intervention for children with Down syndrome. In M.J. Guralnick (Ed.), *The effectiveness of early intervention: Directions for second generation research* (pp. 271-306). Baltimore: Brookes.

Stratford, B., & Gunn, P. (Eds.) (1996). *New approaches to Down's syndrome*. London: Cassell.

Thomson, G.O.B., Ward, K., & Wishart, J.G. (1995). The transition to adulthood for children with Down's syndrome. *Disability and Society, 10,* 205-220.

Trevarthen, C.B. (1993). The self born in intersubjectivity: The psychology of an infant communicating. In U. Neisser (Ed.), *The perceived self: Ecological and interpersonal knowledge of the self* (pp. 121-173). New York: Cambridge University Press.

Uecker, A., Mangan, P.A., Obrzut, J.E., & Nadel, L. (1993). Down syndrome in neurobiological perspective: An emphasis on spatial cognition. *Journal of Clinical Child Psychology, 22,* 266-276.

Wagner, S., Ganiban, G.N., & Cicchetti, D. (1990). Attention, memory, and perception in infants with Down syndrome: A review and commentary. In D. Cicchetti & M. Beeghly (Eds.), *Children with Down syndrome: A developmental perspective* (pp. 147-179). New York: Cambridge University Press.

Wang, P.P. (1996). A neuropsychological profile of Down syndrome: Cognitive skills and brain morphology. *Mental Retardation and Developmental Research Reviews, 2,* 102-108.

Wishart, J.G. (1986). The effects of step-by-step training on cognitive performance in infants with Down's Syndrome. *Journal of Mental Deficiency Research, 30,* 233-250.

Wishart, J.G. (1991). Taking the initiative in learning: A developmental investigation of infants with Down's Syndrome. *International Journal of Disability, Development and Education, 38,* 27-44.

Wishart, J.G. (1993a). The development of learning difficulties in children with Down's syndrome. *Journal of Intellectual Disability Research, 37,* 389-403.

Wishart, J.G. (1993b). Learning the hard way: Avoidance strategies in young children with Down's syndrome. *Down's Syndrome: Research & Practice, 1,* 47-55.

Wishart, J.G. (1996). Avoidant learning styles and cognitive development in young children with Down's syndrome. In B. Stratford & P. Gunn (Eds.), *New approaches to Down's syndrome* (pp. 173-205). London: Cassell.

Wishart, J.G. (1999). Early intervention. In W.I. Fraser, D. Sines, & M. Kerr (Eds.), *Hallas' the care of people with intellectual disabilities* (9th ed., pp. 26-36). London: Butterworth Heinemann.

Wishart, J.G., & Johnston, F. (1990). The effects of experience on attribution of a stereotyped personality to children with Down's syndrome. *Journal of Mental Deficiency Research, 34,* 409-420.

Wishart, J.G., & Pitcairn, T.K. (1999). The recognition of identity and expression in faces by children with Down's syndrome. Manuscript submitted for publication.

Wright, I. (1997). *The development of representation in children with Down's syndrome.* Unpublished doctoral dissertation, University of Warwick, Coventry, UK.

Yin, R.K. (1969). Looking at upside-down faces. *Journal of Experimental Psychology, 81,* 141-145.

Yin, R.K. (1970). Face recognition by brain injured patients: A dissociable ability? *Neuropsychologia, 8,* 395-402.

Young, A.W., Newcombe, F., de Haan, D.H.F., Small, M., & Hay, D.C. (1993). Face perception after brain injury: Selective impairments affecting identity and expression. *Brain, 116,* 941-959.

Zelazo, P.R., & Stack, D.M. (1997). Attention and information processing in infants with Down Syndrome. In J.A. Burack & J.T. Enns (Eds.), *Infancy, attention and psycho-pathology* (pp. 123-146). New York: Guilford Press.

Zigler, E. (1969). Developmental versus difference theories of mental retardation and the problem of motivation. *American Journal of Mental Deficiency, 73,* 536-556.

Author Note

This work was carried out with the help of Alison Hamilton, Christine Johnstone, and Sarah Landew as part of their final year studies. The collaboration of the schools and children who took part in the studies is gratefully acknowledged, as is funding support to Jennifer Wishart from the Medical Research Council of Great Britain (grant no. 9311518N).

Motor Development, Learning, and Adaptive Change

While it is clear that persons with Down syndrome exhibit unique performance patterns in many perceptual-motor activities, the characteristics of their motor behaviors are not static. The four chapters in this section examine how perceptual-motor performance changes as a function of growth and development, and learning. As a result of both environment experience and development, persons with Down syndrome may incorporate into their movement repertoire many adaptive behaviors that help them deal with the special characteristics of their cognitive, perceptual, and motor systems. In this section, the focus is on developmental, experiential, and adaptive change.

In chapter 7, Gil Almeida, Nádia Marconi, Charli Tortoza, Sandra Ferreira, Gerald Gottlieb, and Daniel Corcos bridge the work presented in part I not only by reviewing some of the perceptual-motor similarities and differences exhibited by persons with Down syndrome, but also by outlining the implications of this work for therapeutic intervention. Even more importantly, the authors provide a compelling argument that some atypical motor behaviors are adaptive. In the case of these behaviors, the message is that the educator/clinician should take a hands-off approach and leave well enough alone.

Cynthia Dulaney and Phillip Tomporowski extend the scope of this volume by exploring broader aspects of cognition in the acquisition of skilled behavior. Specifically, chapter 8 provides strong empirical and theoretical justification for the implementation of extensive practice for effective development of the important information-processing components that contribute to perceptual-motor behavior.

In chapter 9, Mark Latash presents the strongest case that the perceptual-motor behavior of persons with Down syndrome should not be merely dismissed as atypical. Rather, given the unique characteristics of the central nervous system in persons with Down syndrome, such behavior is lawful, adaptive, and appropriate.

Finally, on the basis of their own longitudinal research, Anne Jobling and Mark Mon-Williams make the case for extending our attention to developmental motor issues in persons with Down syndrome beyond the period typical for persons without Down syndrome (chapter 10). They suggest that, in light of the fact that the timeline for motor development and the attainment of important motor milestones may continue into adolescence in persons with Down syndrome, it is important that intervention strategies for perceptual-motor skill acquisition also extend into young adulthood.

Sensorimotor Deficits in Down Syndrome: Implications for Facilitating Motor Performance

Gil Lúcio Almeida and Nádia F. Marconi

Departamento de Fisiologia e Biofísica
Universidade Estadual de Campinas
Campinas, Brazil

Charli Tortoza and Sandra M.S. Ferreira

Departamento de Educação Física
Instituto de Biociências, Universidade Estadual Paulista
Rio Claro, Brazil

Gerald L. Gottlieb

NeuroMuscular Research Center
Boston University

Daniel M. Corcos

School of Kinesiology and Department of Psychology
University of Illinois at Chicago
and Department of Neurological Sciences
Rush Medical College

Key words

sensorimotor ◆ clumsiness ◆ practice ◆ muscle activation ◆ synergy ◆ hypotonia ◆ reaction time ◆ movement sequences ◆ somatosensory information ◆ intervention ◆ decision-making

Casual observation of the everyday movements of individuals with Down syndrome (DS) gives the impression of "clumsiness" or even "extreme motor clumsiness" (Frith & Frith, 1974). Several studies have shown that the movements of individuals with DS are slower, less smooth, and more variable from trial to trial when compared with the movements of the overall population. Evidence of slowness and lack of smoothness has been observed even in simple elbow-flexion movements (Almeida, Corcos, & Latash, 1994; Latash & Corcos, 1991), as well as in multijoint pointing tasks (Aruin & Almeida, 1997). The difference in motor performance between neurologically normal individuals and individuals with DS suggests that individuals with DS might have specific, experimentally identifiable sensorimotor deficits. Examples include deficits in timing (Henderson, Morris, & Frith, 1981), deficits in motor programming (Frith & Frith, 1974), and deficits in the ability to adjust the rate at which grip force is generated (Cole, Abbs, & Turner, 1988).

On the other hand, it has also been argued that there are either no specific motor deficits associated with DS or that they are not really significant in comparison with the other deficits observed. For example, Wang (1996) has suggested that verbal short-term memory skills are diminished in individuals with DS compared to other individuals with mental retardation. However, visual-motor skills are comparatively well preserved. Based on this and other observations, including impaired verbal communication skills, he has suggested that individuals with DS should be taught sign language. Also, Latash and Anson (1996) have argued that the way in which the movements of individuals with DS are performed is a reflection of an impaired decision-making process and not necessarily a consequence of a primary motor deficit. Specifically they have suggested, "Our basic assumption implies that the CNS of a person whose decision-making component of the system for movement production is somewhat impaired, may 'prefer' to facilitate clumsy movements rather than risk total failure during motor performance" (p. 66). Their argument suggests that although movement patterns and muscle activation patterns may differ from those observed in neurologically normal individuals, they are optimal adaptations given a primary impairment of decision-making.

In this chapter, we will review the evidence that relates to whether individuals with DS have specific sensorimotor deficits. We shall first discuss similarities in the control of movement between neurologically normal individuals and those with DS, and then consider differences. We will use this analysis to draw conclusions about the extent to which intervention should be used to facilitate motor performance. Whenever possible we will refer to studies that have used electromyography. Electromyography enables one to determine whether the patterns of motor commands are the same or different between groups of individuals. Studies of movement kinematics alone do not allow one to distinguish between problems of how movements are represented and how they are implemented (Anwar, 1986).

Similarities to Individuals Without Down Syndrome

In the following review, we look at many studies that show consistent similarities between control subjects and individuals with DS in the control of movement distance and speed, in the improvement of motor performance with practice, and in linear synergy. In our research, we also have not found any evidence of a causal relation between hypotonia and motor impairment in individuals with DS.

Control of Movement Distance

Numerous studies have investigated the muscle activation patterns associated with movements of different extents in neurologically normal individuals (Benecke, Meinck, & Conrad, 1985; Gottlieb, Chen, & Corcos, 1996a; Wachholder & Altenburger, 1926). Typically, a biphasic or triphasic pattern of muscle activation is observed in which an agonist burst of muscle activation is followed by an antagonist burst, and then sometimes a second agonist burst. For movements of different distances, the first agonist and antagonist bursts scale in a very consistent way. For movements that exceed 10° to 15°, the angle, velocity, acceleration, and net joint torque all rise at similar rates at the beginning of the movement. The same is true for the agonist EMG (Pfann, Hoffman, Gottlieb, Strick, & Corcos, 1998). For short movements and very strong experimental subjects, the initial EMG activation and movement kinematics diverge at the onset (Pfann et al., 1998). The agonist EMG also increases in duration for longer movements. The antagonist EMG is delayed in time. This is true for movements that are constrained by a manipulandum (Gottlieb, Corcos, & Agarwal, 1989) and also movements that are not constrained (Almeida, Hong, Corcos, & Gottlieb, 1995).

Movements of different extents have been studied in individuals with DS by Latash and Corcos (1991). The angle, velocity, and acceleration traces rose at the same rate in several of the subjects in their study. The agonist muscles (biceps and brachioradialis) also rose at the same rate, and the EMG duration increased with distance. In a follow-up study (Almeida, Corcos, & Gottlieb, manuscript in preparation), individuals with DS were asked to perform movements over three different distances using the same paradigm as Almeida et al. (1995). The data in figure 7.1 illustrate the performance of an unconstrained single-joint elbow movement performed by an individual with DS. The agonist muscle (biceps) was activated generating a flexor torque that accelerated the limb toward the target. The initial rate of rise of the agonist EMG over the first 50 ms was independent of movement distance. The agonist EMG increased in both duration and area. After about 100 ms, the antagonist muscle was activated to decelerate the limb.

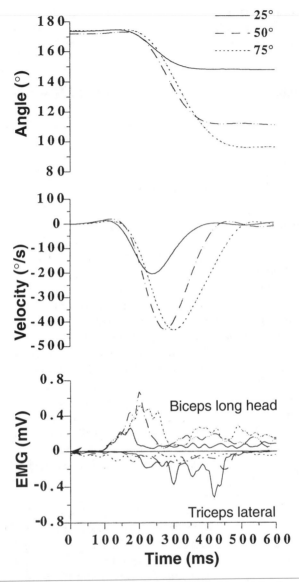

Figure 7.1 Elbow angle, velocity, and electromyographic activity (long head of biceps, agonist muscle, and lateral head of triceps, antagonist muscle) during unconstrained elbow-flexion movements performed in the vertical plane over three angular excursions (25°, 50°, and 75°). The time-series data are from an individual with DS, averaged across 11 trials and aligned according to the agonist (biceps) onset (100 ms). The EMG signals were smoothed by a 10 ms rectangular window. The subject was asked to move "as fast as possible."

Data taken from G.L. Almeida, D.M. Corcos, and G.L. Gottlieb. (manuscript in preparation). *Unconstrained single-joint movements of different distances in individuals with DS.*

Even though movement speed was slower for individuals with DS, the velocity increased for both groups of individuals with increasing angular excursion, as was also true in a previous study (Almeida et al., 1994). From three sets of studies, we can conclude that the capability of individuals with DS to modulate the agonist and antagonist EMG bursts is not impaired.

Control of Movement Speed

Several studies have shown that increases in movement speed are caused by increasing the intensity of excitation to the motoneuron pool of both agonist and antagonist muscles (Corcos, Gottlieb, & Agarwal, 1989; Mustard & Lee, 1987). This increase in neural excitation produces agonist and antagonist EMGs that have different slopes. The steeper the slope of the agonist EMG, the faster the rise of torque and, consequently, the faster the movement. Almeida et al. (1994) were interested in whether this ability to modulate the input to the motoneuronal pool is preserved in individuals with DS given that Cole et al. (1988) had previously reported that individuals with DS did not adjust the rate at which grip force was produced. The data in figure 7.2 depict angle, velocity, acceleration, and agonist and antagonist EMGs for one set of movements performed "as fast as possible" and another set of movements performed at a "comfortable speed" before and after extensive practice. Even prior to practice (see pretest), the pattern of muscle activation was very similar to that observed in individuals who are neurologically normal. Again, there was no obvious movement deficit in the neural activation of muscle.

Improvement of Motor Performance With Practice

It is well known that many individuals with DS have been institutionalized and that this can influence intellectual function (Wisniewski, Miezejeski, & Hill, 1988). As such, they may not have received the same environmental stimulation and opportunity to take part in physical activity as noninstitutionalized individuals. In addition, societal expectations of the capacity of individuals with mental retardation to take part in physical activity is often considerably less than the expectations for neurologically normal individuals. Therefore, part (maybe a large part) of the reduced performance that is observed in individuals with DS or other groups of individuals with mental retardation may be caused by their lack of experience: the so-called experiential hypothesis (Newell, 1989). Therefore, it is important to know the extent to which individuals with DS can improve their motor performance when given the opportunity for extensive practice.

Hulme and Mackenzie (1992) have suggested that individuals with DS have a selective deficit in acquiring motor programs because they showed less improvement across trials than other groups of children. This statement was based on a study by Frith and Frith (1974), who compared the performance of a group of normal individuals, autistic individuals, and individuals with DS on a pursuit-tracking task. Although it is true that the individuals with DS did not improve on the tracking task,

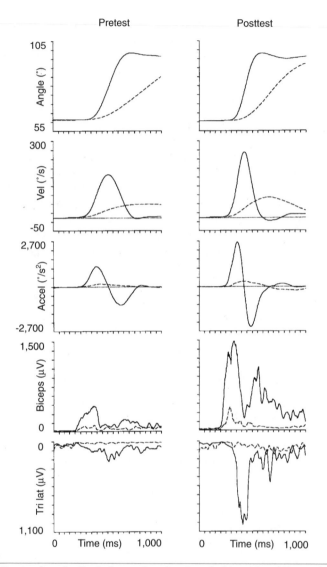

Figure 7.2 Angle, velocity (vel), acceleration (accel), biceps brachii muscle (biceps), and lateral head of triceps brachii muscle (tri lat) electromyographic (EMG) signals for elbow-flexion movements for the pretest and the posttest for subject S2. The EMG data have been filtered with a 25 ms moving average. The lateral head of triceps brachii muscle has been inverted. The subject was asked to move as fast as possible (solid line) and at a comfortable speed (broken line) over the same distance (36°). The data are averages of four and five trials, respectively, for the pretest and the posttest aligned at the onset of the agonist EMG activity (200 ms).

Reprinted from G.L. Almeida, D.M. Corcos and M.L. Latash, *Physical Therapy*, Alexandria, VA, American Physical Therapy Association, 1994, 1000-1012, with permission of the American Physical Therapy Association.

only two 3-minute sessions of practice with a 5-minute break were used. This is hardly sufficient time or practice to draw such a strong conclusion about impaired motor learning.

In contrast to this somewhat negative view of motor learning, Kerr and Blais (1985) had three groups of individuals (control, individuals with mental retardation, and individuals with DS) practice for several hundred trials on a discrete-tracking task involving movements over different distances and in different directions. The individuals with DS were slower than the other two groups of individuals. Also, as can be seen in figure 7.3, the individuals with DS were still improving their performance after 800 trials and showed no signs of reaching a plateau.

Improved performance as a result of practicing movements is not limited just to the limb practicing the task. Elliott (1985) had individuals practice tapping with one hand and showed there was a considerable increase in tapping speed in the nonpracticed hand for individuals with DS. Other studies have also shown that improved performance can result from practice (Kanode & Payne, 1989; Kerr & Blais, 1987).

Because individuals with DS can improve motor performance in a variety of motor tasks, the question arises as to whether they do so using normal patterns of

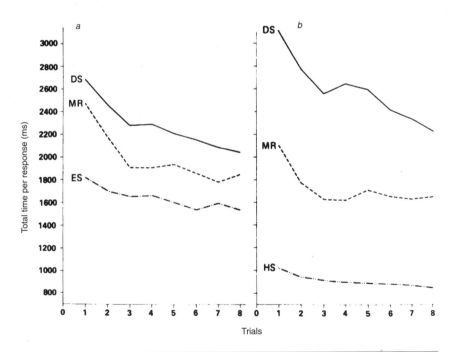

Figure 7.3   Total response time: (*a*) functional age match and (*b*) CA match. DS = Down syndrome, MR = mentally retarded, HS = high school, and ES = elementary school.

Reprinted, by permission, from R. Kerr and C. Blais, 1985, "Motor skill acquisition by individuals with Down Syndrome," *American Journal on Mental Deficiency* 90(3): 313-318.

muscle activation or whether they use different patterns of muscle activation. Almeida (1993) attempted to determine if movement slowness observed in individuals with DS is due to lack of experience or due to a specific inability to increase the intensity of neural activation to the motoneuron pool. He trained individuals with DS to perform a specific, 36° single-joint elbow-flexion movement. Even without training, individuals with DS can make movements at different speeds using "normal" patterns of muscle activation, as was shown in figure 7.2. However, before training, the total amount of EMG activity was small, which was reflected in a movement speed that was half of that observed for neurologically normal individuals (Corcos, Jaric, Agarwal, & Gottlieb, 1993). With extensive practice, all individuals increased movement speed substantially. They did so by learning how to increase the intensity with which the agonist and antagonist muscles were activated and by decreasing the antagonist latency as shown in figure 7.4. This was the same muscle activation pattern used by neurologically normal individuals who followed a similar training protocol (Corcos et al., 1993). More importantly, the movement speed of each of the eight individuals with DS improved, as shown in figure 7.5.

The movement accuracy of the individuals with DS was very high at the beginning of training and did not deteriorate with increasing speed. In other words, they did not trade off speed for accuracy with training (cf. Kerr & Blais, 1987). Five of the eight individuals did not display muscle coactivation. Three out of eight individuals who exhibited a pattern of muscle coactivation before training shifted to a reciprocal pattern of muscle activation after training. We can therefore conclude that individuals with DS do not have a neurological deficit in their ability to exhibit "normal" patterns of muscle activity. The remarkable improvement with training supports the idea that they can change from a pattern of muscle coactivation to a more universal reciprocal pattern of muscle activation (the posttest in figure 7.2). What was most impressive was that not only did performance improve at the practiced distance, it also improved at other distances that had not been practiced (18°, 54°, and 72°). This dramatic transfer in motor performance can be seen most clearly in figure 3 of Latash (1992), in which the performance of individuals with DS was compared to that of neurologically normal individuals.

The issue has been raised as to whether such dramatic performance improvement can occur only in artificial laboratory tasks (Connolly, 1994). In this context, a study by Perán, Gil, Ruiz, and Fernandez-Pastor (1997) is most revealing. They enrolled a group of 20 adolescents with DS in an extensive physical training program. The results were impressive. For example, the mean time to perform the 50 m dash dropped from 15.39 seconds to 10.69 seconds. Other measures of physical performance also improved dramatically. This study suggests that performance can dramatically improve in whole-body tasks that require balance and coordination.

Linear Synergy

The motor control studies that we have reviewed so far have all been restricted to single degree-of-freedom elbow joint movements. This raises the possibility that

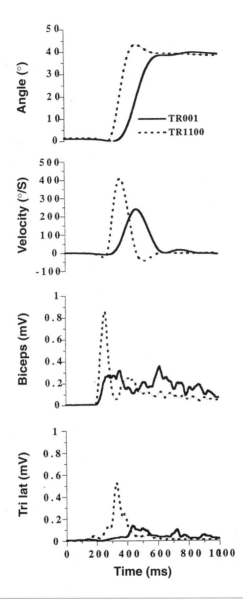

Figure 7.4 Elbow angle, velocity, and electromyographic activity (biceps long head, agonist muscle, and triceps lateral head, antagonist muscle) during constrained elbow-flexion movements performed over 36° "as fast as possible." The time-series data are from one individual with Down syndrome for the 1st and 1,100th trial. The data were aligned according to the agonist onset (200 ms). The EMG signals were smoothed by a 10 ms rectangular window.

Data taken from G.L. Almeida. 1993. Practice, transfer and performance enhancement of fast single-joint movements in individuals with Down syndrome. Unpublished. Ph.D. dissertation, Iowa State University.

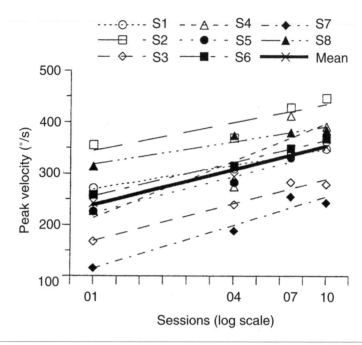

Figure 7.5 Increases in movement speed over the 1st, 4th, 7th, and 10th practice sessions. The data are for each of the eight individuals with Down syndrome and the group average (bold line) during the performance of the 36° movements. The data are plotted on a log scale.

Data taken from G.L. Almeida. 1993. Practice, transfer and performance enhancement of fast single-joint movements in individuals with Down syndrome. Unpublished Ph.D. dissertation, Iowa State University.

individuals with DS might have greater difficulty making movements that require the coordination of multiple joints since these are the types of movements that are generally performed in daily activities of living, such as buttoning one's clothes or drinking a glass of juice. It has been argued that in order to generate a multijoint movement, an internal model of the movement is necessary and that proprioception is necessary to continuously update this model (Ghez & Sainburg, 1995). Sainburg, Ghilardi, Poizner, and Ghez (1995) hypothesized that if proprioception was not available or was impaired, individuals would have difficulty performing reversal movements to targets. They hypothesized that the extent of the movement impairment would be related to the magnitude of the interaction torque generated during the movement. They had individuals who were neurologically normal and patients with large fiber neuropathy make reversal movements to six targets and found the greatest deviations from a straight-line path for movements at which the interaction torque was the greatest.

Given that there is very little evidence about the role of the proprioceptive system during movement in individuals with DS, Almeida, Corcos, and Hasan (manuscript in preparation) conducted a study similar to that of Sainburg and colleagues, in which subjects made reversal movements to a target in four different directions. Four target locations were employed for which the required elbow angular excursion was comparable, but the required shoulder excursion varied from 10° abduction to 75° abduction. The idea was that if individuals with DS have a proprioceptive deficit, they would not make the movements using a straight path. Instead, the path would be very erratic and similar to that observed by Bastian, Martin, Keating, and Thach (1996) in cerebellar patients and Sainburg et al. (1995) in patients with a proprioceptive deficit. In contrast to these studies, Almeida, Corcos, and Hasan (manuscript in preparation) found that the movement path of individuals with Down syndrome was not erratic. Shoulder and elbow torques were calculated and plotted against one another. Although the correlation of the joint torques was higher in individuals who are neurologically normal than in individuals with DS, the correlation was still high in individuals with DS. Also, the ratio of the joint torques changed systematically for movements of different directions. The fact that there was a high correlation between shoulder and elbow torque and that the ratio of joint torques changed with movement direction is consistent with a series of studies on pointing movements performed by Gottlieb and colleagues. They have shown that there is a very high correlation between shoulder torque and elbow torque for these movements and have referred to this relation as "linear synergy" (Gottlieb, Song, Hong, Almeida, & Corcos, 1996; Gottlieb, Song, Hong, & Corcos, 1996). They have also shown that the ratio of joint torques changes very systematically for movements of different directions (Gottlieb, Song, Almeida, Hong, & Corcos, 1997). As such, the findings by Almeida, Corcos, and Hasan (manuscript accepted pending revision) on reversal movements suggest that there is no clear movement impairment in individuals with DS for reversal movements that involve the coordination of two joints.

Torque, Angle Characteristic, and Hypotonia

Nearly every article or book chapter on DS refers to the fact that individuals with DS have reduced muscle tone, or hypotonia, especially during infancy (Coleman, 1978; McIntire, Menolascino, & Wiley, 1965). Whereas few would dispute that babies and young infants have clinically identifiable hypotonia, it is by no means clear that this is true of young adults. Part of the problem with investigating hypotonia is establishing an operational definition. If a muscle is pressed or lightly pinched, a certain amount of tissue deformation will be produced. This deformation is larger for individuals with DS, especially when young (Morris, Vaughan, & Vaccaro, 1982). However, the body type of individuals with DS is also different, with a much greater tendency to endomorphy (Perán et al., 1997), and this may partially account for the observation that there is greater deformation in their muscles when pinched. Although hypotonia has often been measured by palpation, we are unaware of any study that has explicitly related hypotonia measured by this method to impaired motor control in adolescents or adults with DS.

Other groups of investigators have investigated "muscle tone" in terms of segmental motoneuron pool excitability. Shumway-Cook and Woollacott (1985) investigated the postural control of individuals with DS by means of applying perturbations to individuals standing on a movable force platform. They reported the presence of monosynaptic reflex latencies in young children with DS and concluded that any balance problems are related to defects in higher level postural mechanisms and not to decreased segmental motoneuron pool excitability. Latash, Almeida, and Corcos (1993) measured the joint compliant characteristic of individuals with DS. They applied stretches to the biceps muscle by applying different torques at the elbow joint. The individuals were instructed "not to react" voluntarily. Then the amount of joint displacement was measured. The slope of the relation between angle and torque was used as a measure of "joint stiffness," and the values calculated for individuals with DS were similar to those calculated for neurologically normal individuals (Latash & Gottlieb, 1990). Unlike muscle palpation, stretching a muscle takes into account the integrity and functionality of the neural network acting on the muscle-joint complex in addition to the visco-elastic properties of the muscles. Given that measuring "muscle tone" through palpation has not been directly related to impaired motor control and that the studies of Shumway-Cook and Woollacott and Latash and colleagues suggest that the spinal neural networks are intact, we concur with Anson (1992): "In sum, the role of hypotonia in accounting for movement disorders in DS individuals can no longer be considered a default explanation when all alternatives fail" (p. 392).

Differences in Comparison to Individuals Without Down Syndrome

In the previous section, we reviewed the results from numerous studies that have shown no striking evidence for any motor abnormality in the control of movement. We have also found no evidence of a causal relation between hypotonia and motor impairment in individuals with DS. In this section, we highlight those differences that have been observed.

Slower Reaction Time

One frequently observed performance difference between individuals with DS and people with other forms of mental retardation is the slowed reaction time in the individuals with DS. Several studies have reported that the simple reaction time and choice reaction time for individuals with DS is longer than that of mentally retarded individuals (Berkson, 1960; Blais & Kerr, 1986; Henderson, Illingworth, & Allen, 1991; Kerr & Blais, 1987). As pointed out by Anson (1992) in a review of DS and reaction time, differences in simple reaction time have varied from 25% to greater than 300%. This slowness in reaction time can have two consequences. First, in all movements made in response to an external stimulus, the initiation of the movement is likely to be delayed and can therefore give the impression of movement slowness even if the actual movement itself is reasonably quick. For example, in the study by Blais and Kerr (1986), individuals with DS took 600 ms to react to a stimulus, whereas control subjects took about 300 ms. Second, when individuals with DS are asked to perform sequences of movements, if each movement in the sequence is treated as a separate movement the sequence will be performed extremely slowly because of the increased reaction time to program each component movement.

Higher Incidence of Muscle Coactivation

One finding that we have observed in our studies of individuals with DS that is different from what is seen in neurologically normal individuals is the extent to which muscles are coactivated. Instead of the biphasic pattern of muscle activity, subjects in several studies have shown a simultaneous pattern of activation (coactivation) of the agonist and antagonist muscles during constrained and unconstrained movements when the subject is seated (Almeida et al., 1994; Aruin, Almeida, & Latash, 1996; Latash & Corcos, 1991) and during unconstrained single-joint movements performed while standing (Aruin & Almeida, 1997). Further studies are required to determine whether muscle coactivation is task dependent or whether it is a preferred default strategy (Latash & Anson, 1996) used to perform unpracticed movements that have an element of uncertainty.

Slowness Becomes Accentuated at Longer Distances

Although we have shown that individuals with DS can make movements over different angular excursions using essentially normal patterns of muscle activation, there are clearly differences in performance that might be linked to differences in how muscles are activated. In three separate studies, we observed that the absolute difference in movement speed of individuals with DS and neurologically normal individuals is greater as angular excursion increases (Almeida, Corcos, & Gottlieb, manuscript in preparation; Almeida et al., 1994; Latash & Corcos, 1991). An example of this observation is shown in figure 7.6, in which we have plotted movement velocity, biceps long head, antagonist latency, and muscle torque for movements over three distances.

One implication of this observation is that the ability of individuals with DS to generate muscle force does not increase to the same extent for longer distances as it does in neurologically normal individuals. This relative decrease in muscle force could be a consequence of differences in modulating the intensity and/or duration of the agonist and antagonist EMG burst and/or the antagonist latency. As can be

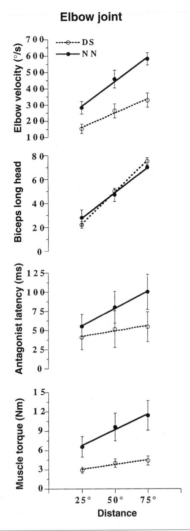

Figure 7.6 Changes in movement velocity, the total amount of agonist muscle activity, antagonist latency, and muscle torque for three different movement distances. The data were averaged across eight individuals with Down syndrome (broken line) and eight neurologically normal individuals (solid line) during the performance of unconstrained elbow movements over three different distances. Muscle torque is given in Newton meters, antagonist latency in milliseconds, and velocity in degrees per second. The amount of biceps long head muscle activity was normalized to the background EMG activity.

Data for the individuals with Down syndrome taken from G.L. Almeida, D.M. Corcos, and G.L. Gottlieb (manuscript in preparation). *Unconstrained single-joint movements of different distances in individuals with Down syndrome.* Data for the neurologically normal individuals taken from G.L. Almeida, D.A. Hong, D.M. Corcos, and G.L. Gottlieb. 1995. Organizing principles for voluntary movement: Extending single-joint rules. *Journal of Neurophysiology* 74:1374-1381.

observed in figure 7.6, the problem seems to be related to the modulation of the antagonist latency. Observe the similar slopes for elbow velocity and antagonist latency. In other words, even though both groups of individuals were able to modulate the duration of the agonist EMG burst, the individuals with DS turned on the antagonist earlier for longer distances compared with control subjects (figure 7.6). The result of this difference in EMG activity is a decreased gain in the net muscle torque with increasing movement angular excursion. Note the similarity between the slope of muscle torque and movement speed. These differences in the way individuals with DS activate their muscles might explain the relative decrease in the gain of movement speed for longer joint excursions, but not movement clumsiness itself.

Movement Sequences

Perhaps the simplest possible repetitive movement sequence, and easiest to perform, is finger-tapping. Frith and Frith (1974) showed that individuals with DS tap slowly, inconsistently, and sometimes just stop tapping. They also showed that a group of individuals with DS tapped more slowly than a group of individuals with autism. Seyfort and Spreen (1979) demonstrated that, when asked to tap between two different targets, not only were individuals with DS slow but they sometimes tapped the same target twice in succession. The individuals with DS in the Seyfort and Spreen (1979) study were tapping only about two times a second. Elliott (1985) replicated the study of Frith and Frith (1974), confirming that individuals with DS tap slowly. However, he also showed that there was no difference in tapping speed between individuals with DS and participants in a mentally handicapped control group, and that individuals with DS do not tap more quickly with their right hand than their left hand as do nonhandicapped individuals. In a follow-up study, Elliott, Weeks, and Jones (1986) showed that individuals with DS were slower to lift up their fingers than to press down. These four studies suggest that it would be most informative to investigate how individuals with DS learn and perform sequences of movement. All of the studies reviewed in the first section in this chapter, in which no deficits were postulated, used pointing movements to a target or reversal movements (movements with one change of movement direction). None of the movement tasks required continuous movements. The heightened variability in the tapping movements, coupled with the fact that releasing a key press takes longer in individuals with DS than in neurologically normal individuals, suggests that individuals with DS have greater difficulty performing sequences of movements than individual movements. They may find switching from one movement to another difficult, just as they find changing movement direction difficult when tracking a moving target (Henderson et al., 1981).

Movement sequences do not have to be long to show that individuals with DS find them very difficult to perform. Chiarenza (1993) had individuals with DS perform a task in which pressing a button with the left hand started the sweep of an oscilloscope and pressing a button with the right hand stopped the sweep. The button to stop the oscilloscope trace had to be pressed in the time interval of 40-60 ms following the start of the sweep. This task requires that individuals centrally program two separate movements with a time delay of no more than 40-60 ms. Initially, individuals with DS pressed the second button much too late. Although practice enabled them to learn to press the second button earlier, the majority of their performances had a time interval of about 200 ms. Analysis of the EMG activation of the hand that started the stimulus sweeping and the hand that stopped the stimulus sweeping showed only minor differences in comparison to the chronologically and maturationally matched control subjects. The rate of rise of the EMG of the stopping hand was reduced. What is most striking is that, "From a neurophysiological point of view, these behavioral patterns express themselves in reduced preparation of the movement, absent or very low Bereitschaftspotential, a lack of elaboration of the reafferent somatosensory information, absence of motor cortex potential, impairment of the processes involved during the evaluation of the outcome of the performance, and the presence of low skilled positivity" (Chiarenza, 1993, p. 464; see also chapter 14).

One possibility is that these difficulties in sequencing are simply due to an inability to sustain concentration on a task. These difficulties are also entirely consistent with the notion of an impaired central timekeeper (Ivry & Keele, 1989). In order to tap consistently with one limb or to generate one tap followed by another tap with a different limb, it has been argued that a clocklike mechanism is responsible for sending out periodic commands to muscles. The tapping data imply that in individuals with DS this central timer is slower, more variable, and cannot send commands to different sets of muscles with only a short time delay. One prediction is that if the tapping performance of individuals with DS was decomposed into a "motor component" and a "clock" component (Wing, Keele, & Margolin, 1984), it would be the clock component that would be impaired. This idea of a timekeeping problem is consistent with a study by Henderson and colleagues (1981). They had subjects perform four tasks. The first task involved subjects tracking a moving sinusoidal target. The second task was to continue tracking when the target was no longer present. The third task was to draw the sinusoidal track from memory. The fourth task was to track a sinusoidal target that increased in speed and decreased in amplitude. Individuals with DS could draw the sinusoidal track from memory, suggesting that they do not have a spatial or perceptual problem. The individuals with DS showed more undershooting at corners and had difficulty keeping up with the moving pattern in both sinusoidal tracking tasks. They could not continue to draw the sinusoid when it was no longer visually presented. This inability to keep drawing a sinusoid when the stimulus was no longer present suggests that individuals with DS have difficulty timing an internally generated sequence of movements. Given that Wang (1996) has argued in favor of teaching sign language to individuals with DS, further research is needed to determine how well individuals with DS can perform different internally generated sequences of movements.

Somatosensory Information

Almeida, Corcos, and Hasan (manuscript accepted pending revision) provide evidence with reversal movements that argues against a proprioceptive deficit influencing the control of movement. However, two studies suggest that tactile perception might be impaired in persons with DS. Cole, Abbs, and Turner (1988) showed that when individuals are asked to grip an object whose gripping surface and vertical load force were systematically manipulated, they did not change the rate at which grip force was generated, as was the case with normal control subjects. They also generated much more force than necessary to perform the task. One possibility is that there is an abnormality in the detection and processing of cutaneous afferent information. Brandt (1996) has shown that individuals with DS do not perform well in tactual perception tests. For example, the data in figure 7.7 show performance on a stereognosis test. Children were asked to feel a wooden object in a cloth bag. A formboard with holes of various shapes was then placed in front of the child, and the child was asked to indicate into which hole the object in the bag fit. As shown in figure 7.7, the children with DS did very poorly on this test. Clearly, further neurophysiological studies are required to discern which mechanisms are responsible for the impaired tactual perception and how this relates to the control of movement.

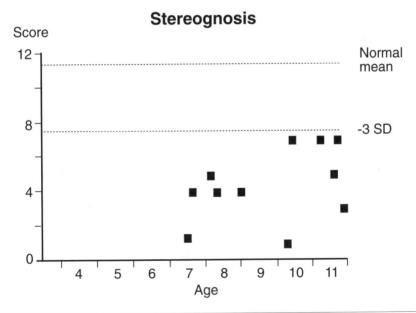

Figure 7.7   Results of the stereognosis test for 11 children with DS. Age and score are indicated for each individual (filled squares). Mean (upper broken line) and –3 SD (lower broken line) for normal children aged 7 years are shown for comparison.

Reprinted, by permission, from B.R. Brandt, 1996, "Impaired tactual perception in children with Down's syndrome," *Scandinavian Journal of Psychology* 32(4): 312-316.

Can Movement Clumsiness Be Attributed to Impaired Decision-Making in Down Syndrome?

Are the motor problems observed in individuals with DS specific to abnormal sensorimotor mechanisms or are they consequences of cognitive limitations that are associated with mental retardation? At one end of the spectrum is the argument that individuals with DS have severe motor problems. At the other end lies the view that their sensorimotor systems are intact, but they have decision-making problems that lead them to use conservative movement strategies adequate for most movement tasks but perhaps not optimal for any specific task. This raises the question of what is meant by "poor decision-making." If poor decision-making refers to task comprehension, this explanation does not always hold true. The reason for this can most easily be seen in the study by Almeida et al. (1994) in which subjects were asked to make movements over different speeds and also different distances (see sections on speed and distance earlier in this chapter, pages 153-155). Both types of movements were made with relatively normal patterns of muscle activation, suggesting that individuals with DS can decide between two tasks and can use relatively normal patterns of muscle activation to perform the tasks. It should be pointed out that these tasks were presented in a block of trials so the subjects knew exactly which movement they had to make. It would be interesting to replicate these studies in a choice reaction-time paradigm in which greater decision-making is required.

However, if impaired decision-making refers to the inability to rapidly distinguish between different movement possibilities, there is evidence to support the idea that appropriately timed patterns of muscle activation are not always used. Instead, muscle groups are often coactivated. In addition, there is considerable anecdotal evidence that individuals with DS may not interpret experimental instructions in the manner expected by the experimenter. For example, the instruction to move faster can result in subjects pressing down harder. Henderson and colleagues (1981) pointed out that when subjects were encouraged to go faster, subjects merely pressed harder on the paper they were tracking on. This difference in how instructions are interpreted is clearly a decision-making problem that can dramatically influence how some movement tasks are performed. However, just as Anson (1992) noted that hypotonia should not be considered the default explanation for impaired motor performance, neither should impaired decision-making be considered the default explanation for impaired motor performance. Careful experiments are required that manipulate both the complexity of the movement and the complexity of the decision-making to determine how impaired decision-making impacts the control of movement.

Conclusions

One therapeutic strategy that has been suggested for improving motor function in individuals with DS is to increase muscle tone. The logic behind this approach is the assumption that "normal" tone is a necessary condition for normal movement control. The cause of hypotonia has been linked to the reduced weight of the cerebellum of individuals with DS (Cowie, 1970; Crome, Cowie, & Slater, 1966). Also, Gilman, Bloedel, and Lechtenbers (1981) have shown in experiments on primates that a lesion in the cerebellum can produce cerebellar hypotonia. Therapeutic interventions for altering muscle tone include isometric exercise, training of muscle force, and tactile stimulation (Linkous & Stutts, 1990). The idea is that these interventions improve muscle activation and therefore muscle tone. As we have argued earlier in this chapter, individuals with DS can adjust patterns of muscle activation, and, in this sense, their motor control systems are functionally intact. At least adolescents and young adults with DS do not seem to have muscle hypotonia. This may explain the lack of notable success for drugs that are designed to increase muscle tone in DS (Coleman, 1978). It may also explain only the small gain in the acquisition of functional abilities with training designed to improve muscle tone (Shumway-Cook & Woollacott, 1985). In sum, we see no compelling reason to recommend any training based on increasing muscle tone to improve the control of voluntary movement (Blanche, Botticelli, & Hallway, 1995).

Despite the clear observation of movement slowness and increased variability, we have shown that the differences in motor performance between individuals with DS and neurologically normal individuals are very subtle for a variety of pointing movements and movements with a single reversal. We do not know at this point if there is a general impairment in proprioception that could account for the subtle differences in performance reported. Whether training to enhance proprioceptive acuity will lead to a decrease in movement clumsiness is an open question. We are not optimistic about this kind of treatment. Indeed, it would be difficult to explain the accuracy in movement experiments demonstrated by individuals with DS without assuming an intact proprioceptive system (Almeida, 1993).

The idea of a universal and invariant sequence of development, as advanced by Gesell (1925), had and still has a great impact on therapeutic intervention. The mapping of "normal" movement sequences and stages was argued to be the best framework for therapeutic approaches. Learning and practicing movements that obey this universal and invariant sequence would cause the client's movements to become as close as possible to "normal." Latash and Anson (1996) have criticized approaches that routinely try to normalize the control of movement. Because the mechanisms and priorities of normal motor control are generally unknown, they have argued for a "hands-off" approach and that "adaptive changes in motor patterns should be considered normal and, as such, should not be corrected" (p. 67). Given that we do not know the priorities of the CNS, it is only supposition that the CNS changes its priorities in certain situations. As such, the idea that the central nervous system of individuals with DS may "prefer" to use safer motor strategies that prevent failure might be as detrimental as the idea of imposing a "normal" pattern.

At this point we would like to offer our recommendations regarding therapeutic intervention. When we trained individuals with DS to move quickly, neither did we tell them which pattern of muscle activation to adopt, nor did we impose any kinematic pattern of normality (Almeida et al., 1994). Latash and Anson (1996) have argued that the considerable improvement we observed in individuals with DS could be attributed to the friendly and reinforcing environment offered during training. While we agree that a friendly environment is conducive to performance, individuals with DS may need considerably more practice to improve their ability to control everyday movements. They need more practice for two reasons. The first is that individuals with DS have less life experience, so that even if the experimental protocol gives equal formal practice, this is not enough to equalize the real experience of the two groups. The second is that they learn at a reduced rate and therefore need more practice. In our opinion, the biggest problem with the design of the studies investigating the motor performance of individuals with mental retardation is that they do not include practice sessions or refer to two 3-minute practice sessions as "learning" (Frith & Frith, 1974). Society does not treat its handicapped and nonhandicapped populations equally, and we should not assume that research participants have had the same opportunity for practice prior to arriving at the laboratory. Training can help to decrease the differences that might erroneously be attributed to structural or functional changes within the CNS, making comparisons more realistic. This effect of lack of prior experience, coupled with the benefits of practice shown in numerous studies that we have reviewed, suggests caution in implementing a hands-off approach.

One major contribution of the systematic study of motor control is to offer insight into when and how to intervene. We suggest a hands-on approach without imposing any "normal" pattern, just as we did with the single-joint flexion movements. One can then observe if normality comes naturally. The next step would be to determine if the subtle qualitative differences in the way individuals with DS control their muscles disappear with simple repetition of the motor task. The elbow-flexion training study suggested that all anatomical and neurophysiological differences that have been well documented in this population of individuals may not be detrimental to movement performance if appropriate training is provided (Almeida et al., 1994; Perán et al., 1997). However, care should be taken in drawing such a conclusion. We may discover that during more complex tasks, individuals with DS may be unable to couple the muscle forces across different joints even after extensive training. It may turn out that the coactivation strategy for postural muscles (Aruin & Almeida, 1997) does not change with practice. In such instances, it is preferable to structure therapeutic sessions in ways that allow the individual to master the task in his or her own preferred way as opposed to trying to teach one preferred way.

Summary

In summary, we suggest that a balanced approach is required when considering different therapeutic interventions for facilitating sensorimotor performance in individuals with DS. Although there are clear verbal, linguistic, and auditory-processing deficits (Wang, 1996; Wisniewski et al., 1988), individuals with DS do not seem to have any striking deficits in activating muscle. There is also such incredible diversity between different individuals with DS that physicians, therapists, and parental associations need to be very careful when making prognostications and giving advice. A message that is too negative can lead to reduced expectations, with the result that individuals with DS do not achieve their full potential. Similarly, an overly optimistic message can cause severe parental emotional stress if the individual is profoundly retarded and not capable of reaching expected functional levels (Gath, 1994).

However, the training and practice studies that we have reviewed show that large improvements in motor performance are possible. This fact, coupled with the fact that no clear muscle activation deficits have been identified, strongly suggests that active intervention may be very important and very beneficial. We have identified no study that has shown a decrease in performance after extensive practice. We concur that practice should not be directed at normalizing movement patterns (Latash & Anson, 1996), and clearly any vigorous hands-on approach should take into account potential problems (e.g., orthopedic, cardiac) of individuals with DS (Block, 1991). However, practice and training should be directed at improving performance, consistency, and generalizability of movement skills. In very rare cases, sustained practice at physical activity can lead to such high skill levels that an individual with DS has competed in mainstream open competition in gymnastics (Jones, 1994).

References

Almeida, G.L. (1993). *Practice, transfer and performance enhancement of fast single-joint movements in individuals with Down syndrome.* Unpublished doctoral dissertation, Iowa State University, Ames.

Almeida, G.L., Corcos, D.M., & Gottlieb, G.L. Unconstrained single-joint movements of different distances in individuals with Down syndrome. Manuscript in preparation.

Almeida, G.L., Corcos, D.M., & Hasan, Z. Horizontal-plane arm movements with direction reversals performed by normal individuals and individuals with Down syndrome. *Journal of Neurophysiology.* Manuscript accepted pending revision.

Almeida, G.L., Corcos, D.M., & Latash, M.L. (1994). Practice and transfer effects during fast single-joint elbow movements in individuals with Down syndrome. *Physical Therapy, 74,* 1000-1012.

Almeida, G.L., Hong, D.-A., Corcos, D., & Gottlieb, G.L. (1995). Organizing principles for voluntary movement: Extending single-joint rules. *Journal of Neurophysiology, 74,* 1374-1381.

Anson, J.G. (1992). Neuromotor control and Down syndrome. In J.J. Summers (Ed.), *Approaches to the study of motor control and learning* (pp. 387-413). Amsterdam: Elsevier Science.

Anwar, F. (1986). Cognitive deficit and motor skill. In D. Ellis (Ed.), *Sensory impairments in mentally handicapped people* (pp. 169-183). London: Croom Helm.

Aruin, A.S., & Almeida, G.L. (1997). A coactivation strategy in anticipatory postural adjustments in persons with Down syndrome. *Motor Control, 1,* 178-191.

Aruin, A.S., Almeida, G.L., & Latash, M.L. (1996). Organization of a simple two-joint synergy in individuals with Down syndrome. *American Journal on Mental Retardation, 101,* 256-268.

Bastian, A.J., Martin, T.A., Keating, J.G., & Thach, W.T. (1996). Cerebellar ataxia: Abnormal control of interaction torques across multiple joints. *Journal of Neurophysiology, 76,* 492-509.

Benecke, R., Meinck, H.-M., & Conrad, B. (1985). Rapid goal-directed elbow flexion movements: Limitations of the speed control system due to neural constraints. *Experimental Brain Research, 59,* 470-477.

Berkson, G. (1960). An analysis of reaction time in normal and mentally deficient young men: III. Variation of stimulus and of response complexity. *Journal of Mental Deficiency Research, 4,* 69-77.

Blais, C., & Kerr, R. (1986). Probability information in a complex task with respect to Down syndrome. *Journal of Human Movement Studies, 12,* 183-194.

Blanche, E.I., Botticelli, T.M., & Hallway, M.K. (1995). *Combining neuro-developmental treatment and sensory integration principles. An approach to pediatric therapy.* Tucson, AZ: Therapy Skill Builders.

Block, M.E. (1991). Motor development in children with Down syndrome: A review of literature. *Adapted Physical Activity Quarterly, 8,* 179-209.

Brandt, B.R. (1996). Impaired tactual perception in children with Down's syndrome. *Scandinavian Journal of Psychology, 37,* 312-316.

Chiarenza, G.A. (1993). Movement-related brain macropotentials of persons with Down syndrome during skilled performance. *American Journal on Mental Retardation, 97,* 449-467.

Cole, K.J., Abbs, J.H., & Turner, G.S. (1988). Deficits in the production of grip force in Down syndrome. *Developmental Medicine and Child Neurology, 30,* 752-758.

Coleman, M. (1978). Down's syndrome. *Pediatrics Annals, 7,* 36-63.

Connolly, B.H. (1994). Invited commentary. *Physical Therapy, 74,* 1012-1113.

Corcos, D.M., Gottlieb, G.L., & Agarwal, G.C. (1989). Organizing principles for single joint movements: II. A speed-sensitive strategy. *Journal of Neurophysiology, 62,* 358-368.

Corcos, D.M., Jaric, S., Agarwal, G.C., & Gottlieb, G.L. (1993). Principles for learning single-joint movements: I. Enhanced performance by practice. *Experimental Brain Research, 94,* 499-513.

Cowie, V.A. (1970). *A study of the early development of mongols.* Oxford: Pergamon Press.

Crome, L.C., Cowie, V., & Slater, E. (1966). A statistical note on cerebellar and brain stem weight in mongolism. *Journal of Mental Deficiency Research, 10,* 69-72.

Elliott, D. (1985). Manual asymmetries in the performance of sequential movement by adolescents and adults with Down syndrome. *American Journal of Mental Deficiency, 90,* 90-97.

Elliott, D., Weeks, D.J., & Jones, R. (1986). Lateral asymmetries in finger-tapping by adolescents and young adults with Down syndrome. *American Journal of Mental Deficiency, 90,* 472-475.

Frith, U., & Frith, C.D. (1974). Specific motor disabilities in Down's syndrome. *Journal of Child Psychology and Psychiatry, 15,* 293-301.

Gath, A. (1994). Down's syndrome. *Journal of the Royal Society of Medicine, 87,* 276-277.

Gesell, A. (1925). *The mental growth of the pre-school child. A psychological outline of normal development from birth to the sixth year, including a system of developmental diagnosis.* New York: Macmillan.

Ghez, C., & Sainburg, R. (1995). Proprioceptive control of interjoint coordination. *Canadian Journal of Physiology and Pharmacology, 73,* 273-284.

Gilman, S., Bloedel, J.R., & Lechtenberg, R. (1981). *Disorders of the cerebellum: Vol. 21.* Philadelphia: F.A. Davis.

Gottlieb, G.L., Chen, C.-H., & Corcos, D.M. (1996). Nonlinear control of movement distance at the human elbow. *Experimental Brain Research, 112,* 289-297.

Gottlieb, G.L., Corcos, D.M., & Agarwal, G.C. (1989). Organizing principles for single joint movements: I. A speed-insensitive strategy. *Journal of Neurophysiology, 62,* 342-357.

Gottlieb, G.L., Song, Q., Almeida, G.L., Hong, D., & Corcos, D. (1997). Directional control of planar human arm movement. *Journal of Neurophysiology, 78,* 2985-2998.

Gottlieb, G.L., Song, Q., Hong, D., Almeida, G.L., & Corcos, D.M. (1996). Coordinating movement at two joints: A principle of linear covariance. *Journal of Neurophysiology, 75,* 1760-1764.

Gottlieb, G.L., Song, Q., Hong, D.-A., & Corcos, D.M. (1996). Coordinating two degrees of freedom during human arm movement: Load and speed invariance of relative joint torques. *Journal of Neurophysiology, 76,* 3196-3206.

Henderson, S.E., Illingworth, S.M., & Allen, J. (1991). Prolongation of simple manual and vocal reaction times in Down syndrome. *Adapted Physical Activity Quarterly, 8,* 234-241.

Henderson, S.E., Morris, J., & Frith, U. (1981). The motor deficit of Down's syndrome children: A problem of timing? *Journal of Child Psychology and Psychiatry, 22,* 233-245.

Hulme, C., & Mackenzie, S. (1992). *Working memory and severe learning difficulties.* Hove, UK: Erlbaum.

Ivry, R.B., & Keele, S.W. (1989). Timing functions of the cerebellum. *Journal of Cognitive Neuroscience, 1,* 135-152.

Jones, S. (1994, October 25). Sisters unite to meet special needs. *Times,* p. 46.

Kanode, J.O., & Payne, V.G. (1989). Effects of variable practice on retention and motor schema development in Down syndrome subjects. *Perceptual and Motor Skills, 69,* 211-218.

Kerr, R., & Blais, C. (1985). Motor skill acquisition by individuals with Down syndrome. *American Journal of Mental Deficiency, 90,* 313-318.

Kerr, R., & Blais, C. (1987). Down syndrome and extended practice of a complex motor task. *American Journal of Mental Deficiency, 91,* 591-597.

Latash, M.L. (1992). Motor control in Down syndrome: The role of adaptation and practice. *Journal of Developmental and Physical Disabilities, 4,* 227-261.

Latash, M.L., Almeida, G.L., & Corcos, D.M. (1993). Preprogrammed reactions in individuals with Down syndrome: The effects of instruction and predictability of the perturbation. *Archives of Physical Medicine and Rehabilitation, 73,* 391-399.

Latash, M.L., & Anson, J.G. (1996). What are "normal movements" in atypical populations? *Behavioral and Brain Sciences, 19,* 55-68.

Latash, M.L., & Corcos, D.M. (1991). Kinetic and electromyographic characteristics of single-joint movements of individuals with Down syndrome. *American Journal on Mental Retardation, 96,* 189-201.

Latash, M.L., & Gottlieb, G.L. (1990). Compliant characteristics of single joints: Preservation of equifinality with phasic reactions. *Biological Cybernetics, 62,* 331-336.

Linkous, L.W., & Stutts, R.M. (1990). Passive tactile stimulation effects on the muscle tone of hypotonic, developmentally delayed young children. *Perceptual and Motor Skills, 71,* 951-954.

McIntire, M.S., Menolascino, F.J., & Wiley, J.H. (1965). Mongolism—Some clinical aspects. *American Journal of Mental Deficiency, 69,* 794-800.

Morris, A.F., Vaughan, S.E., & Vaccaro, P. (1982). Measurements of neuromuscular tone and strength in Down's syndrome children. *Journal of Mental Deficiency Research, 26,* 41-46.

Mustard, B.E., & Lee, R.G. (1987). Relationship between EMG patterns and kinematic properties for flexion movements at the human wrist. *Experimental Brain Research, 66,* 247-256. '

Newell, K.M. (1989). *Down's syndrome and motor control: Comments and notes.* Paper presented at the Motor Control in Down Syndrome Conference, Chicago, IL.

Perán, S., Gil, J.L., Ruiz, F., & Fernandez-Pastor, V. (1997). Development of physical response after athletics training in adolescents with Down's syndrome. *Scandinavian Journal of Medicine and Science in Sports, 7,* 283-288.

Pfann, K.D., Hoffman, D.S., Gottlieb, G.L., Strick, P.L., & Corcos, D.M. (1998). Common principles underlying the control of rapid, single degree-of-freedom movements at different joints. *Experimental Brain Research, 118,* 35-51.

Sainburg, R.L., Ghilardi, M.F., Poizner, H., & Ghez, C. (1995). Control of limb dynamics in normal subjects and patients without proprioception. *Journal of Neurophysiology, 73,* 820-835.

Seyfort, B., & Spreen, O. (1979). Two-plated tapping performance by Down's syndrome and non-Down's syndrome retardates. *Journal of Child Psychology and Psychiatry, 20,* 351-355.

Shumway-Cook, A., & Woollacott, M.J. (1985). Dynamics of postural control in the child with Down syndrome. *Physical Therapy, 65,* 1315-1322.

Wachholder, K., & Altenburger, H. (1926). BeitrSge zur Physiologie der willknrlichen Bewegung. X. Mitteilung. Einzelbewegungen. *Pflugers Archiv fur die gesamte physiologie des menschen unter der tiere, 214,* 642-661.

Wang, P.P. (1996). A neuropsychological profile of Down syndrome: Cognitive skills and brain morphology. *Mental Retardation and Developmental Disabilities, 2,* 102-108.

Wing, A., Keele, S., & Margolin, D. (1984). Motor disorder and the timing of repetitive movements. In J. Gibbon & L. Allan (Eds.), *Timing and time perception: Vol. 423.* New York: Annals of the New York Academy of Science.

Wisniewski, K.E., Miezejeski, C.M., & Hill, A.L. (1988). Neurological and psychological status of individuals with Down syndrome. In L. Nadel (Ed.), *The psychobiology of Down syndrome* (pp. 315-343). Cambridge, MA: MIT Press.

Author Note

The preparation of this chapter was supported in part by the Fundação de Amparo à Pesquisa do Estado de São Paulo (FAPESP), Brazil (grants 95/9608-1, 97/02770-3, 97/02771-0, and 97/02769-5); the National Institute of Neurological and Communicative Disorders and Stroke (grant R01-NS 28127); and the National Institute of Arthritis and Musculoskeletal and Skin Diseases (grant R01-AR 33189).

8

Attention and Cognitive-Skill Acquisition

Cynthia L. Dulaney
Department of Psychology
Xavier University

Phillip D. Tomporowski
Department of Kinesiology
University of Connecticut

Key words

attention ◆ cognitive skill ◆ automatic processing ◆ skill acquisition ◆ encoding ◆ inspection time ◆ controlled processing ◆ priming ◆ visual search ◆ flankers ◆ decision-making ◆ practice ◆ memory search ◆ reaction time ◆ speed-accuracy ◆ interference

Skill is characterized by performance involving accuracy and uniformity of execution that is goal directed. Interest in how skills develop can be traced back to ancient civilizations, and the topic of skill acquisition continues to intrigue modern scientists and educators. Perhaps the continued interest in skill development is fueled by observations of the dramatic changes in human performance that can take place as a function of training. Indeed, no other area of study provides such compelling evidence for the malleability and adaptability of human behavior as does the study of skilled performance.

Individuals differ in the manner in which they acquire skills. Some learn skills slowly and fail to attain the accuracy and uniformity of performance displayed by others. Mental retardation is a term employed to describe individuals who evidence slower rates of development and who are physically and mentally less skilled than their chronologically equivalent peers (Bruininks, 1974; Newell, 1985, 1997). One of the most formidable challenges facing researchers today is to explain the basis for intelligence-related differences in the acquisition of skills.

Motor and Cognitive Skills

Researchers have made clear distinctions between two different types of skills. Motor skills require voluntary body and/or limb movement to achieve a goal. Activities such as playing musical instruments, football, and swimming are motor skills. Cognitive skills do not involve muscular movement or motion to achieve a goal. Activities such as problem-solving and reading are cognitive skills (Magill, 1993). It is recognized, of course, that this distinction between types of skills is arbitrary, as skilled behavior reflects both motor and cognitive components. Nevertheless, the tradition of categorizing skill into two types has had a pronounced effect on the academic study of skill development. Presently, they are treated as two relatively separate domains of academic study. Researchers from one domain examine motor skills and place a secondary emphasis on cognitive processes, whereas researchers in the other domain examine cognitive skill and place secondary emphasis on motor movement (Proctor & Dutta, 1995; Stelmach & Hughes, 1983; Tomporowski, 1997).

The view that cognitive skills can be studied in a fashion analogous to motor skills can be traced to the work of Bartlett (1958), who proposed that mental skills, like motor skills, are acquired on the basis of information accumulated from experience and practice. His work laid the foundation for the application of the information-processing model to the study of cognitive-skill development (Proctor & Dutta, 1995). This model is characterized by multiple operators and processes that guide thought and behavior. A typical stage model of information processing defines roles for perceptual operators that involve scanning, searching, and detecting stimuli; decision operators that involve discrimination, identification, and categorization of stimuli; and response-selection operators that determine which of many possible responses to an ever-changing environment will be chosen and translated into action.

Traditionally, attentional processes are seen as the "controllers" of the components or operators of the information-processing system. Effortful attention has been conceptualized as processing that initiates the actions of individual operators without direct control over what is going on within the various operators. This form of attention provides individuals the means to respond to task demands in a flexible and strategic fashion. Indeed, skilled performance is often defined in terms of the manner in which actions are executed and timed in a serial fashion. One of the limiting factors in executing skills, however, is the extent to which limited attentional resources are allocated and utilized (Kahneman, 1973; Stelmach & Hughes, 1983; Wickens, 1984, 1987). Automatic attention has been conceptualized as processing that affects the efficiency of functions within individual mental operators. This form of attention provides individuals with the means to process information and execute behaviors rapidly without having to draw from a limited pool of attentional resources (Shiffrin & Schneider, 1977). Developing automatic processing is usually considered to be beneficial to an individual because it permits behaviors to be selected and executed with minimal attentional effort. Under ideal conditions, effortful and automatic attentional processes orchestrate the information-processing system so that it is in concert with environmental demands. The manner in which experience and practice modify attentional processes has been a topic of considerable debate and interest over the past few decades, and these discussions are directly relevant to understanding intelligence-related differences in learning and skill development.

Systematic practice on tasks is generally associated with several changes. First, practice typically leads to increases in the speed at which tasks are performed. The relation that exists between the number of practice trials an individual has and increases in his or her speed of performance has been shown to be similar across motor, psychomotor, and cognitive tasks (Newell & Rosenbloom, 1981). Second, practice typically results in a decrease in response variability and improvement in the accuracy of performance (e.g., Anderson & Fincham, 1994; Logan, 1988). Third, the completion of some processes becomes automatized with extensive practice (Shiffrin & Schneider, 1977). Indeed, one of the defining features of skill acquisition is that, as skill develops, some processes no longer require attentional effort and are completed automatically (Anderson, 1983; Fitts & Posner, 1967).

There has been a long-standing interest in improving the cognitive skills of individuals with mental retardation, and numerous educational-based programs that focus on cognitive-skill training have been developed. Unfortunately, the impact of these global training programs on participants' cognitive performance has been difficult to interpret (see Spitz, 1986, for a review). Laboratory-based experimental investigation of the components of information processing has provided researchers with an alternative strategy to isolate and study those factors that underlie intelligence-related differences in performance, as well as the effects of experience and training on performance. It has been suggested that the component-analyses approach can provide insight into intelligence-related differences in the manner in which stimuli are detected, organized, and evaluated, and the manner in which responses are selected and executed (Detterman et al., 1992; Maisto & Baumeister, 1984; Tomporowski & Tinsley, 1997). This approach has also been employed as a framework to examine how repeated experience and practice affects skill development in individuals with mental retardation (Carr, 1984).

Our overview of cognitive-skill acquisition in individuals with mental retardation is divided into two sections. First, we provide a selective review of studies in which researchers have isolated specific components of the information-processing system and have examined the effects of practice on the performance of individuals with and without mental retardation. Second, we link empirical research findings to the constructs of mental flexibility and rigidity and their relation to learning and performance.

The empirical studies we review are restricted to those in which researchers have examined how practice or training affects intelligence-related differences in encoding processes, decision processes, and response processes. The majority of the studies selected for review assess the performance of individuals without mental retardation and individuals with mild or moderate mental retardation. When possible, the performance of individuals with Down syndrome is compared and contrasted with the performance of individuals with mental retardation of unspecified etiology.

Encoding Processes

In this section we examine studies that evaluate the manner in which raw stimulus information is extracted from the environment and transformed into meaningful memory representations. Skilled motor and cognitive performance depends not only on the ability to scan complex environments and to identify and select for further processing specific bits of information that are relevant to the task at hand, but also the ability to filter out irrelevant bits of information that have the potential to interfere with performance. Attention has been implicated as the agent responsible for focusing awareness (Johnston & Dark, 1986) and for determining what information will be processed and what information will be filtered from processing (Broadbent, 1958). Numerous tasks have been used to evaluate intelligence-related differences in encoding (Puff, 1982). We examine four tasks that have been used to assess the effects of practice or experience on the encoding processes of individuals with and without mental retardation: the inspection-time task, the priming task, the visual-search task, and the flanker task.

Inspection-Time Tasks

These tasks are designed to provide indices of the time required of observers to extract and utilize environmental information. The inspection-time paradigm developed by Vickers (1970, 1979) and expanded by Nettelbeck and his colleagues (see Nettelbeck, 1985, and Nettelbeck & Wilson, 1997, for reviews) has been used extensively to assess intelligence-related differences in stimulus encoding (see

Kranzler & Jensen, 1989, for a review). The technique involves measuring individuals' ability to discriminate between two visual stimuli under conditions in which the stimulus presentation duration is varied systematically by means of a masking stimulus. Typically, it requires individuals with mental retardation to inspect stimuli about twice as long (approximately 250 ms) as it does individuals without mental retardation (approximately 100 ms) in order to extract the information necessary to make accurate discriminations (Nettelbeck, Evans, & Kirby, 1982).

The extent to which intelligence-related differences in inspection time might be ameliorated by practice was assessed by Nettelbeck et al. (1982). They contrasted inspection-time indices of adults with mild mental retardation (M IQ = 60) and adults without mental retardation at various points during approximately 800 practice trials. Practice resulted in concomitant decreases in encoding times for both IQ groups, and the inspection times of individuals with mental retardation continued to be about twice those of individuals without mental retardation.

Priming Tasks

These tasks provide measures of the extent to which experience prepares individuals to respond to successively presented stimulus events. In a typical priming paradigm, individuals are presented with visual information on one trial, followed by the presentation of the same or related information on subsequent trials. For example, Posner and Snyder (1975) presented individuals with pairs of letters, and individuals were to decide as quickly as possible whether the pair of letters matched. Each letter pair was preceded by the presentation of a related letter (a letter the same as one or both letters in the pair) or a neutral plus sign. Positive priming was evidenced by faster reaction times on letter matching when the letter pair was preceded by a related letter cue rather than a neutral cue. The faster reactions are presumably due to previous activation of a mental representation, such that activation of subsequent information is primed or facilitated.

Several investigators have examined whether this facilitation or positive priming occurs for individuals with mental retardation. Using a priming paradigm similar to the Posner and Snyder (1975) paradigm, Meador and Ellis (1987) examined positive priming in individuals without mental retardation, individuals with mental retardation due to brain injury (M IQ = 61), and individuals with mental retardation due to unknown etiology and with no evidence of brain injury (M IQ = 64). Following two sessions of practice on the priming task, individuals without mental retardation and both groups of individuals with mental retardation showed facilitative effects as a result of a positive prime. However, the priming effects occurred for individuals with mental retardation only if the prime preceded the letter pair by 500 ms, whereas the priming effects occurred for individuals without mental retardation when the prime preceded the letter pair by less than 300 ms. Thus, the benefits of the prime were slower to accumulate for individuals with mental retardation.

Using a different priming task developed by Tipper and Cranston (1985), Cha and Merrill (1994) and Merrill and Taube (1996) examined intelligence-related differences in positive priming and negative priming. Positive priming occurs when previous experience with stimuli facilitates performance, whereas negative priming occurs when previous experience with stimuli inhibits performance. Participants were presented with pairs of letters in which the target letter was presented in blue, and a distractor letter was presented in red. The participants' task was to identify the blue letter and ignore the red letter. In this procedure, positive priming should occur when the target letter identified on the previous trial (prime trial) is the same letter to be identified on the next trial (target trial). Positive priming is evidenced by faster responding on the target trial when it is preceded by the same letter relative to a neutral letter. In the negative priming trials, a previously ignored letter (e.g., B presented in red) becomes the target letter on the next trial (e.g., B presented in blue). In this case, negative priming is evidenced by slower responding on the target trial when the target item was ignored on the previous trial.

Both the Cha and Merrill (1994) and the Merrill and Taube (1996) studies found that the performance of individuals with mental retardation (M IQs = 64 and 62, respectively, for the two studies) was facilitated by positive primes. In fact, individuals with mental retardation showed greater positive priming effects than individuals without mental retardation. On negative priming trials, individuals without mental retardation showed negative priming, whereas individuals with mental retardation did not. Individuals without mental retardation responded more slowly to the target information if it was ignored on a previous trial. The slower responding by individuals without mental retardation is presumably due to their active inhibition of irrelevant information on previous trials. This inhibition, which develops as a result of past experience with the stimulus, is functional in that it reduces the potential for irrelevant information in the environment to distract the processing of relevant information. Individuals with mental retardation did not show negative priming, suggesting that they do not actively inhibit irrelevant information. This failure to inhibit irrelevant information results in a greater potential for distraction for individuals with mental retardation than for individuals without mental retardation.

Visual-Search and Detection Tasks

These tasks evaluate individuals' efficiency in allocating attention to one of several possible stimuli. In the typical visual-search task such as that developed by Schneider and Shiffrin (Schneider & Shiffrin, 1977; Shiffrin & Schneider, 1977), individuals are presented with a target set, which consists of the target items for which the individuals should search. Individuals are instructed to search a display for a target item, and the number of items in the display set is varied (e.g., from one to six items). Initially, the search time required to detect a target increases as the set size of items searched increases. With extensive practice, however, detection of targets occurs as quickly for a large search set as for a small search set. Extensive practice leads to the development of an automatic attentional response to targets, such that when a target is present, its presence visually "pops out" of the searched environment.

Merrill, Goodwyn, and Gooding (1996) examined the development of automatic visual search processes for members of a target category (e.g., animals; experiment 1). Individuals without mental retardation were able to automatize their detection of targets in the display after approximately 500 trials of practice, whereas individuals with mental retardation (M IQ = 63) required approximately 1,000 trials of practice. Merrill et al. also examined the development of automatic search processes for unfamiliar, anomalous shapes (experiment 2). Individuals without mental retardation were able to automatize their detection of targets after approximately 1,200 trials of practice, whereas individuals with mental retardation (M IQ = 65) required approximately 2,000 trials of practice. Thus, in both experiments, individuals with mental retardation required about twice as much training as individuals without mental retardation before performance was automatized. Furthermore, the time required of individuals with mental retardation to detect stimuli following approximately 2,000 trials of practice was roughly comparable to the time required of individuals without mental retardation prior to any practice.

Not only do individuals with mental retardation apparently require more training to automatize encoding processes than do individuals without mental retardation, there is evidence to suggest that the acquisition of encoding skills depends on the method of training that is employed. Merrill, Alexander, and Williams (1992) compared the development of automatic encoding processes by adults with and without mental retardation on tasks that provided either consistent or partial stimulus-response mapping conditions. Previous research (Schneider & Fisk, 1982) has shown that the development of automatic target detection is related to the consistency of stimulus-response pairing. In a search task, consistent mapping involves training in which a target item is never used as a distractor stimulus; partial mapping involves training in which a target item sometimes appears as a distractor item. Merrill et al. (1992) contrasted the performance of adults with mental retardation (M IQ = 61) and adults without mental retardation on tasks with 100% mapping consistency and 75% mapping consistency. Individuals without mental retardation developed an automatic attentional encoding response more quickly under the 100% condition than under the partial mapping condition. In contrast, individuals with mental retardation showed similar rates of performance for both mapping conditions. These results were interpreted to mean that individuals without mental retardation were detecting targets by automatically focusing their search for those items and, at the same time, inhibiting the processing of irrelevant or distractor information in the display. Therefore, their performance was hampered in the partial mapping condition when stimuli that were previously targets were to be ignored. Individuals with mental retardation, on the other hand, did not actively suppress irrelevant information, and, as a result, previously experienced distractor information had less of an effect on performance when presented as a target in the partial mapping condition. As in other studies conducted by Merrill and his colleagues, individuals with mental retardation required approximately twice as many practice trials to develop automatic encoding processes as did individuals without mental retardation.

Flanker Tasks

Flanker tasks assess the ability of individuals to narrow their focus of attention in the visual field as a function of the visual separation between target and distractor information. In a typical flanker task (e.g., Eriksen & Eriksen, 1974), target information (e.g., a letter) is presented in the center of the visual field, and this target information is flanked on both sides by distractor information. The distance of the distractor information from the target information is varied (e.g., .06° versus 1.03° of arc). Merrill and O'Dekirk (1994) compared the performance of individuals with and without mental retardation on a flanker task. Nontarget information was more of a distraction for individuals with mental retardation than for those without mental retardation, who evidenced distraction only when the nontarget information was very close to the target stimulus. Merrill and O'Dekirk inferred that individuals with mental retardation were not able to narrow their focus of attention as well as individuals without mental retardation. They suggest that individuals without mental retardation develop an attentional set that facilitates the focusing of attention, whereas individuals with mental retardation do not. Importantly, Merrill and O'Dekirk did not find any differences between individuals with mild, unspecified mental retardation (M IQ = 61) and individuals with Down syndrome (M IQ = 50) in the ability to narrow the focus of attention. It appears that individuals with mental retardation, regardless of etiology, have more difficulty narrowing their focus of attention than individuals without mental retardation.

Decision Processes

In this section we focus on those studies that examined intelligence-related differences in the manner in which decisions are made and how practice affects decision processes. Attentional processing has been implicated in this stage of processing as the agent or "executor" that controls and organizes information in short-term or working memory (Baddeley, 1986). Skilled cognitive performance is characterized by the efficiency in which knowledge derived from past experience that is stored in terms of declarative and procedural information is accessed and utilized in working memory (Ackerman & Kyllonen, 1991; Anderson, 1983). Several laboratory techniques have been developed to isolate working-memory processes. We examine two tasks that provide indices of the effects of practice and experience on the decision processes of adults with and without mental retardation: memory-search tasks and response-interference tasks.

Memory-Search Tasks

Memory-search tasks provide indices of the rate and accuracy with which individuals scan short-term or long-term memory storage. One method of assessing the mental processes that underlie scanning memory stores was developed by S. Sternberg

(1966). The procedure typically requires participants to first memorize a list of items (e.g., digits) that are referred to as members of the "positive set." Once these are learned, participants are presented a series of probe items and asked to indicate whether the probe is a member of the positive set by saying "yes" if it is and "no" if it is not. Positive set size is manipulated and participants' performance is evaluated by plotting mean reaction time to positive and/or negative probes as a function of the number of items in the positive set. The relation between reaction time and set size is usually linear, and the rate of memory scanning is typically expressed in terms of the angle of the slope of the item-recognition regression function.

A number of studies using a variety of methodological procedures have reported steeper slope values for persons with mental retardation than for persons without mental retardation, suggesting that individuals with mild mental retardation scan their short-term memory (Dugas & Kellas, 1974; Harris & Fleer, 1974; Maisto & Jerome, 1977; Mosley, 1985) and long-term memory (Merrill, 1985) more slowly than do individuals without mental retardation. Phillips and Nettelbeck (1984) addressed one possible explanation for intelligence-related differences in short-term memory-search performance. They hypothesized that intelligence-related differences were due to the lack of experience by individuals with mental retardation in performing demanding cognitive tasks. They compared the memory-scanning performance of adults with mild mental retardation (M MA = 11.2 years) to the performance of groups of individuals without mental retardation matched in chronological age and mental age. Participants were evaluated over seven testing sessions. Practice resulted in decreased variability in the reaction times of individuals with mental retardation, and the slopes of the regression function were significantly reduced. However, despite the improvement in memory-search speed, their regression slopes were consistently steeper than those of adults and children without mental retardation. Intelligence-related differences in performance remained even when persons with mental retardation participated in an additional 18 training sessions. Even with extended practice, participants evidenced greater variability in speed and accuracy performance across sessions than was observed in the control groups with less practice. Phillips and Nettelbeck hypothesized that the differences in performance that remained following practice were attributable to lapses in concentration or failure to allocate sufficient attentional resources to the tasks by individuals with mental retardation. Despite the continued intelligence-related differences in performance, Phillips and Nettelbeck emphasize that practice did, in fact, improve performance of memory-search tasks for individuals with mental retardation. Indeed, the absolute gain in performance achieved by persons with mental retardation was far greater than the gain achieved by participants without mental retardation.

Response-Interference Tasks

Response-interference tasks examine the manner in which a well-learned response pattern competes with or interferes with a less well-learned response pattern. A paradigm frequently used to assess this type of interference is the Stroop task (Stroop,

1935). In the Stroop task, color words are presented in incongruent ink colors (e.g., the word "RED" printed in blue ink). Individuals are instructed to ignore the word and to name the ink color as quickly as possible. This is a difficult task because activation of the word response is automatic and must be suppressed in order to name the ink color. This difficulty is referred to as the Stroop interference effect. Several studies have found that individuals with mental retardation exhibit a Stroop interference effect, which is an indication of an automatic reading response (Bergen & Mosley, 1994; Das, 1969, 1970; Ellis, Woodley-Zanthos, Dulaney, & Palmer, 1989).

Not only do individuals with mental retardation exhibit a Stroop interference effect, they exhibit a larger Stroop interference effect than individuals without mental retardation. It is unlikely that the larger Stroop interference effect for individuals with mental retardation is due to a more automatized reading response. Instead, it is likely that individuals with mental retardation have greater difficulty inhibiting or controlling a well-learned, automatic response. This explanation is consistent with a number of studies showing that individuals with mental retardation have deficits in controlled processes (e.g., Belmont, 1978; Bray, 1979; Brown, 1974, 1975; Butterfield & Belmont, 1977; Ellis, 1978).

Ellis and Dulaney (Dulaney & Ellis, 1994; Ellis & Dulaney, 1991; Ellis et al., 1989) have conducted a number of studies examining how control or inhibition of automatic processes can be altered with training. Individuals with and without mental retardation were given extensive practice on the Stroop task to determine whether practice would improve the ability to inhibit an automatic response. In one study (Ellis et al., 1989), individuals received over 2,200 practice trials on the Stroop task. Individuals with mental retardation (M IQ = 64) and without mental retardation improved on the task; however, the effects of training were similar for both groups such that differences in performance between the two groups at the beginning of training were similar at the end of training. The training-related improvement was hypothesized to be due to the development of a reading suppression response. Thus, improvements on the Stroop task were attributed to the efficiency with which individuals became more efficient at inhibiting an automatic reading response. All individuals who had acquired an automatic reading response had more difficulty reading after practice than before practice. However, individuals with mental retardation had more difficulty returning to reading following practice than did individuals without mental retardation. This finding suggests that individuals with mental retardation had greater difficulty controlling their newly acquired automatic process. These findings are important because they indicate that individuals with mental retardation can develop automatic processes, although they have more difficulty abandoning a newly acquired automatic process than do individuals without mental retardation.

Ellis and Dulaney (1991; experiment 1) further examined issues relevant to the development and control of automatic processes. They varied the amount of practice that individuals with mental retardation (M IQ = 65) and without mental retardation received on the Stroop task, with the number of practice trials varying from 560 to 4,480. As predicted, individuals with and without mental retardation showed greater improvement on the Stroop task as the number of practice trials increased. Furthermore, subjects' reading difficulty after practice increased as the number of practice trials increased. These findings suggest that the development of new automatic processes, specifically those designed to inhibit old automatic processes, will improve with practice. However, the difficulty in inhibiting these new automatic processes, when the task requires reinstating the old automatic process, will increase as a function of practice on the new task.

Ellis and Dulaney (1991; experiment 2) also examined the persistence of newly developed automatic processes. The magnitude of the reading suppression response was examined across three time periods: immediately following training, one month following training, and three months following training. The reading suppression response was not practiced between the initial training and the one- and three-month follow-up. The reading suppression response had dissipated for individuals without mental retardation by the one-month follow-up. However, the reading suppression response was still evident at the three-month follow-up for individuals with mental retardation (M IQ = 55). These findings indicated that individuals with mental retardation will maintain an automatic process over time, even without additional training. However, they maintain this automatic process even when it is no longer appropriate—in this case, when they were instructed to return to the task of reading.

Response Processes

The selection and execution of the "right" response at the "right" time often characterize cognitive skill. In the previous section we focused on those studies that examined intelligence-related differences in the manner in which decisions are made and how practice affects decision processes. In this section we focus on the processes involved in translating decision into action. It has been suggested that much of the improvement in skilled performance that develops from experience can be understood in terms of the effects of practice on response-selection and response-execution processes (Proctor & Dutta, 1995). We examine two tasks used to assess the effects of practice on the response processes of individuals with and without mental retardation: the reaction time task and the speed-accuracy task.

Reaction-Time Tasks

Laboratory methods that have been developed to isolate and assess participants' response processes are typically designed to reduce the impact of encoding processes and motoric action on performance. Reaction-time tasks usually employ stimuli that are readily discriminable and require simple motoric responses.

Nettelbeck and Brewer (1981) and Nettelbeck and Wilson (1997) reviewed studies that employed simple reaction-time and choice reaction-time tasks to assess intelligence-related differences in response processes. They reported that the reaction times of individuals with mental retardation, when compared to those of individuals without mental retardation, are generally slower, more variable, and more positively skewed because of infrequent, exceptionally long responses.

Hoover, Wade, and Newell (1981) performed two studies to determine the extent to which training would influence the reaction time and movement time of individuals with moderate and severe mental retardation. They determined that the effects of response feedback and praise on the reaction times of adults with mental retardation were task dependent. The reaction times of a group of individuals with mental retardation (M IQ = 45) who performed a simple keypress task decreased when performance was followed by praise and feedback; however, another group of individuals with mental retardation (M IQ = 41) who performed a relatively complex ballistic aiming task evidenced no improvement in reaction time as a function of training. These results were interpreted by Hoover et al. to mean that the improvement in the reaction times of individuals with mental retardation that accrues from training may be limited to tasks that do not require complex response requirements. However, given the level of intelligence of the participants in their study, this generalization may need to be qualified.

Speed-Accuracy Tasks

Nettelbeck (1985) and his colleagues (Nettelbeck & Brewer, 1981; Nettelbeck & Wilson, 1997) propose that intelligence-related differences in complex tasks can be explained in terms of less efficient use of response strategies by individuals with mental retardation, particularly when tasks involve speed-accuracy trade-off relationships. Brewer and Smith (1984, 1990) conducted a series of studies that examined the effects of practice on intelligence-related differences in speeded choice reaction-time performance. They employed a method assessing the relation between reaction time and response accuracy developed by Rabbitt (1981). He suggests that an individual's pattern of responding during complex reaction-time tasks is guided by information obtained from successive task trials. At the beginning of the task, a participant is unaware of the response speed that is necessary for accurate performance. This information is obtained through practice. Initially, the individual establishes a response criterion by responding progressively faster on successive trials until an error is made. The error results in an immediate slowing of response speed on the next few trials, and it modifies the individual's speed-accuracy function. The reduction in speed is temporary, however, as response speed increases over continued trials, until another error is made that, in turn, results in another modification of the speed-accuracy function. As the individual's optimal speed-accuracy function emerges, a reduction in the variance and skew of the reaction-time distribution is observed. It is hypothesized that examination of trial-to-trial changes in reaction times can reveal how individuals track or monitor their performance over repeated trials and how they stay within a restricted range or "band" of response-speed values.

Brewer and Smith (1984) assessed young adults with mild to moderate mental retardation (IQ range = 43-76) on a four-choice, reaction time task in which the level of difficulty was manipulated. Persons with and without mental retardation were given 2,000 trials of training, and their performance was assessed in terms of the number of errors associated with different reaction time levels. The error rates of persons with mental retardation were found to always be higher than the error rates of individuals without mental retardation. Further, individuals with mental retardation sometimes emitted extremely fast responses that were associated with high probabilities of error. Lastly, the band of response-speed values adopted by persons with mental retardation was much wider than those of persons without mental retardation, suggesting that performers with mental retardation were inefficient at adjusting their response functions on the basis of information made available from error trials. Individuals with mental retardation would, at times, continue to make errors over a number of successive trials without altering their response speed; further, when response speed was altered, the magnitude of the adjustments that were made was much greater than that evidenced in individuals without mental retardation.

Brewer and Smith (1990) conjectured that the inefficiency with which persons with mental retardation controlled their response speed during a complex choice task might be improved by means of training them to conform to response-regulation demands. They employed a procedure that placed a time constraint or "deadline" on responding and then provided extensive training to three individuals with mild mental retardation (IQ range 55-69). The training procedure did, in fact, reduce response variability and decrease the mean reaction times of individuals with mental retardation; however, these individuals continued to make significantly more response errors. Indeed, the response accuracy of participants with mental retardation did not change appreciably from initial levels of training even after 5,000 trials.

We have reviewed several aspects of information processing that play a role in skill acquisition and figure prominently in current models of skill development. Specifically, we focused on the effects of experience or training on attentional processes that are instrumental to encoding information, processing information, and selecting appropriate responses. Individuals with mental retardation showed improvements in the operation of basic components of information processing as a function of training or experience in nearly all of the studies we reviewed. However, individuals with mental retardation generally did not acquire the same level of performance as individuals without mental retardation.

Conclusions

Skilled action reflects the interaction among a multitude of component processes. A portion of the intelligence-related differences in the performance of both motor and cognitive skills can be explained in terms of the efficiency of the operations involved in stimulus encoding, decision-making, and response-selection processing. It is well documented that individuals with mental retardation have deficits in numerous aspects of information processing (Baumeister & Kellas, 1968; Bray, 1979; Ellis, 1978; Hagen & Huntsman, 1971; Merrill, 1990; Sperber & McCauley, 1984; Zeaman & House, 1979). We have examined the results of several laboratory-based studies that were designed to isolate, as much as possible, basic components of processing and to determine the effects of practice or experience on those processes. Despite the long-standing interest in improving the cognitive abilities of individuals with mental retardation, relatively few laboratory-based studies have been conducted that focus directly on the effects of practice on the operations of the components of information processing. Further, the available research has been performed almost exclusively with adults with familial mental retardation who are within the mild range of functioning; very few studies have been performed that assess the effects of practice on the cognitive skills of individuals with genetically linked disorders such as Down syndrome.

Despite the paucity of empirical studies, there is, we believe, sufficient evidence to show that systematic practice leads to improvements in the manner in which adults with mental retardation select and act on environmental information. Persons with mental retardation who were given task-specific practice demonstrated marked improvements in their ability to focus on, select, and encode relevant information from their environment. Their efficiency in detecting target information was facilitated with practice, and the execution of encoding processes became increasingly more automated with practice. Systematic training was also shown in several studies to lead to improved memory-search speed and the instantiation of memory processes that facilitate rapid-choice responding. Individuals with mental retardation also benefited from training directed at mental operations that are involved in the initiation and control of action.

The improvement of the efficiency of operations within the basic components of the information-processing system is viewed as critical to cognitive and motor skill acquisition. The automation of the execution of basic mental operations is expected to reduce the demands placed on working memory and, thereby, make attentional resources available for other aspects of a task that require controlled or strategic processing.

Practice and Resource Allocation

It appears that systematic practice can enhance the efficiency of processes that underlie cognitive skills of adults with mental retardation. However, our review also suggests that the changes that accrue as a function of practice differ between adults with and without mental retardation in at least two ways. First, individuals without mental retardation improve with fewer practice trials than do individuals with mental retardation. Second, even with extended practice, the performance of individuals with mental retardation continues to lag behind the performance of individuals without mental retardation. These two observations parallel those that have been explicated in reviews of intelligence-related differences in performance in complex learning tasks.

Regardless of whether information processing is conceived to occur in a series of discrete stages carried out in a serial fashion (Broadbent, 1958; Treisman, 1969) or as an interactive, dynamic system constrained by mental capacity or mental resources (Baddeley, 1986; Hasher & Zacks, 1979; Kahneman, 1973; Posner & Snyder, 1975; Wickens, 1984), a deficit in any aspect of processing may have cumulative effects on other aspects of processing. In a stage model, an early stage-processing deficit will cause performance to lag in subsequent stages of processing. In a resource model, inefficient processing of one task component will require more resources, thereby decreasing resources available for other information processing.

Consistent with the cognitive literature, there is neurophysiological evidence indicating that efficiency of brain activity is increased with practice (Haier, Siegel, McLachlan, et al., 1992). Within the nonretarded range of intelligence, individuals with higher IQs show the greatest gain in brain efficiency with practice (Haier, Siegel, Tang, Abel, & Buchsbaum, 1992). Furthermore, individuals with mental retardation and with Down syndrome have less efficient brain activity than individuals without mental retardation (Haier et al., 1995). These findings suggest that individuals with mild mental retardation and with Down syndrome are less efficient prior to practice, and they will benefit the least from practice in terms of increased efficiency. Regardless of the theoretical model used, it is clearly the case that cognitive skill involves multiple, interrelated mental processes and that deficits in any one of these processes can have a marked influence on performance.

A major issue we have addressed in our empirical review is whether practice can ameliorate some of these cognitive processing deficits in individuals with mental retardation. Although individuals with mental retardation achieve less gain from practice than do individuals without mental retardation, it appears that they still benefit from training to some degree. Research clearly shows that individuals with mental retardation can improve the efficiency of basic information processing through systematic practice (Dulaney & Ellis, 1994; Ellis & Dulaney, 1991; Ellis et al., 1989; Merrill et al., 1992; Merrill et al., 1996; Nettelbeck et al., 1982; Phillips & Nettelbeck, 1984).

Practice and Rigidity

Although systematic practice can increase the efficiency with which some processes related to skilled behavior are carried out, individuals with mental retardation may rigidly use those processes. Rigidity refers to less variable, or stereotyped, responding. Siegel (Siegel & Foshee, 1960; Smith & Siegel, 1986) proposed that individuals with mental retardation behave more rigidly because they are more distractible and, therefore, less likely to notice a change in the stimulus environment. This notion of rigidity is consistent with the priming research conducted by Merrill and his colleagues (e.g., Merrill & Taube, 1996). They show that individuals with mental retardation, like those without mental retardation, benefit from positive priming (e.g., experience facilitates the attention allocated to specific environmental stimuli). However, unlike individuals without mental retardation, those with mental retardation fail to inhibit irrelevant or distracting information and continue to allocate attention to that information that is not relevant to task performance.

The development of automatic processes, which are acquired by systematic practice, can also lead to rigid behavior in individuals with mental retardation. Once individuals with mental retardation develop an automatic process, however, these individuals have difficulty inhibiting the use of that automatic process even when it is no longer appropriate (Dulaney & Ellis, 1994; Ellis & Dulaney, 1991; Ellis et al., 1989). This type of persistence or rigidity also is seen in the performance of individuals without mental retardation, although to a lesser degree. Thus, there are sometimes persistent or rigid behaviors associated with skilled performance, even for individuals without mental retardation (Frensch & Sternberg, 1989; Reason & Mycielska, 1982), but especially for individuals with mental retardation (see Dulaney, 1998; Dulaney & Ellis, 1997, for a discussion).

Collectively, the work of Merrill and his colleagues as well as that of Dulaney and her colleagues points to the importance of examining the difficulty individuals with mental retardation have inhibiting irrelevant information, whether the inhibition deficit is related to distracting information in the stimulus environment or is related to attending to changes in the demands of a task. In either case, the end result is that individuals with mental retardation behave less flexibly than individuals without mental retardation. These findings are consistent with the theoretical position of Hasher and Zacks (1979), which explains individual differences in cognitive performance in terms of inhibitory deficits.

Beyond the domain of inhibitory processing, rigidity has been identified as one of the hallmark characteristics of individuals with mental retardation. Since the early 1900s, individuals with mental retardation have been characterized as being more perseverative, stereotyped, inflexible, and repetitive in their behaviors relative to individuals without mental retardation. There have been several theories attempting to explain this greater rigidity (Ellis et al., 1989; Goldstein, 1942; Kounin, 1941; Lewin, 1935; Siegel & Foshee, 1960; Werner, 1946, 1948; Zigler, 1962; Zigler & Balla, 1982), and the general finding in the empirical literature is that rigidity is greater in individuals who have lower intelligence. Increased rigidity has been explained in terms of both cognitive and motivational factors, depending on the nature of the task being performed (see Dulaney & Ellis, 1997, for a review).

The notion of rigidity is important because its converse, flexibility, is important in adapting to an ever-changing environment. In contrast to the rigidity that may evolve as a function of automatic processing, controlled processes are important because they allow individuals to flexibly allocate attention when confronted by novel or unpredictable situations, at least for individuals without mental retardation (Shiffrin & Schneider, 1977). However, deficits in controlled processing are cited frequently as a major contributor to performance deficits in many cognitive tasks for individuals with mental retardation (e.g., Belmont, 1978; Bray, 1979;

Brown, 1974, 1975; Butterfield & Belmont, 1977; Ellis, 1978). Because these individuals have deficits in controlled processing, their behavior is often less flexible and adaptive.

One aspect of controlled processing that may allow for increased flexible behavior is the selection of appropriate strategies for various tasks. Selection of the appropriate strategy is extremely important for individuals with mental retardation, as it can reduce the demands placed on their already limited attentional capacity. A number of studies have demonstrated that individuals with mental retardation have deficits in strategy use (see Bray & Turner, 1986; Brown, 1974). A number of studies have also examined the effects of training on the acquisition, maintenance, and transfer of strategies (Belmont, Butterfield, & Ferretti, 1982; Blackman & Lin, 1984; Borkowski & Cavanaugh, 1979; Campione & Brown, 1984; Campione, Brown, & Ferrara, 1982; Ferretti & Butterfield, 1992). The general finding is that individuals with mental retardation are able to learn appropriate strategies for some tasks with proper training. However, successful training effects are generally limited to simple tasks. Furthermore, the training effects rarely transfer to novel situations, even if the transfer situations are fairly similar to the trained situation (Campione et al., 1982). Thus, even when an appropriate strategy is learned, individuals with mental retardation rigidly apply that strategy in a new situation.

In conclusion, individuals with mental retardation can improve a number of components involved in skill acquisition with extensive practice. These practice effects generally lead to faster and more accurate performance. This finding is important because more efficient performance can reduce the demands placed on the limited attentional resources of these individuals. In spite of these practice effects, however, individuals with mental retardation will continue to appear more rigid and inflexible because they have difficulty noticing and adapting to novel or unpredictable situations.

Summary

Skilled behavior typically involves accurate and efficient execution of cognitive and motor processes. This chapter has focused on cognitive processes associated with skill acquisition in individuals with mental retardation. The empirical research indicates that, with extensive practice, individuals with mental retardation improve encoding, decision, and response processes associated with skill acquisition. However, individuals with mental retardation did not generally reach the same level of efficiency as individuals without mental retardation.

An important component of training is the development of automatic processes. One advantage of automatic processing is that it reduces the demands on limited attentional resources. Individuals with mental retardation are assumed to have more limited attentional resources than individuals without mental retardation. In this regard, it is especially beneficial for individuals with mental retardation to automatize some processes. However, there also are costs associated with automatic processing. Because these processes occur automatically, they are difficult to inhibit or stop. Inhibiting automatic processes is important when the demands of a task change and previous processing is no longer appropriate. In these situations, individuals with mental retardation will have more difficulty abandoning inappropriate responses. In addition, recognizing the difficulties associated with automatic processing for individuals with mental retardation, it is important to note that these individuals are more distractible than individuals without mental retardation. Therefore, training efforts geared toward facilitating attention to relevant information in the environment are beneficial.

In conclusion, the empirical evidence that has examined the effects of practice for cognitive-skill development in individuals with mental retardation can be viewed both optimistically and with some reservation. Clearly practice improves the efficiency of many of the components of the information-processing system. In some cases, the gains achieved by individuals with mental retardation as a function of practice are considerably greater than those achieved by individuals without mental retardation. However, their performance generally does not reach the level achieved by individuals without mental retardation, and they are likely to be more rigid in both their well-learned and their strategic behavior.

References

Ackerman, P.L., & Kyllonen, P.C. (1991). Trainee characteristics. In J.E. Morrison (Ed.), *Training for performance: Principles of applied human learning* (pp. 193-229). New York: Wiley.

Anderson, J.R. (1983). *The architecture of cognition.* Cambridge, MA: Harvard University Press.

Anderson, J.R., & Fincham, J.M. (1994). Acquisition of procedural skills from examples. *Journal of Experimental Psychology: Learning, Memory, and Cognition, 20,* 1322-1340.

Baddeley, A.D. (1986). *Working memory.* Oxford, England: Oxford University Press.

Bartlett, F. (1958). *Thinking: An experimental and social study.* New York: Basic Books.

Baumeister, A.A., & Kellas, G. (1968). Reaction time and mental retardation. In N.R. Ellis (Ed.), *International review of research in mental retardation: Vol. 3* (pp. 163-193). New York: Academic Press.

Belmont, J.M. (1978). Individual differences in memory: The case of normal and retarded development. In M.M. Gruneberg & P. Morris (Eds.), *Aspects of memory* (pp. 152-185). London: Methuen.

Belmont, J.M., Butterfield, E.C., & Ferretti, R.P. (1982). To secure transfer of training instruct self-management skills. In D.K. Detterman & R.J. Sternberg (Eds.), *How and how much can intelligence be increased* (pp. 147-154). Norwood, NJ: Ablex.

Bergen, A.E., & Mosley, J.L. (1994). Attention and attentional shift in individuals with and without mental retardation. *American Journal on Mental Retardation, 98,* 688-743.

Blackman, L.S., & Lin, A. (1984). Generalization training in the educable mentally retarded: Intelligence and its educability revisited. In P.H. Brooks, R. Sperber, &

C. McCauley (Eds.), *Learning and cognition in the mentally retarded* (pp. 169-193). Hillsdale, NJ: Erlbaum.

Borkowski, J.G., & Cavanaugh, J.C. (1979). Maintenance and generalization of skills and strategies by the mentally retarded. In N.R. Ellis (Ed.), *Handbook of mental deficiency, psychological theory and research* (2nd ed., pp. 569-618). Hillsdale, NJ: Erlbaum.

Bray, N.W. (1979). Strategy production in the retarded. In N.R. Ellis (Ed.), *Handbook of mental deficiency, psychological theory and research* (2nd ed., pp. 569-617). Hillsdale, NJ: Erlbaum.

Bray, N.W., & Turner, L.A. (1986). The rehearsal deficit hypothesis. In N.R. Ellis & N.W. Bray (Eds.), *International review of research in mental retardation: Vol. 14* (pp. 47-71). New York: Academic Press.

Brewer, N., & Smith, G.A. (1984). How normal and retarded individuals monitor and regulate speed and accuracy of responding in serial choice tasks. *Journal of Experimental Psychology: General, 113,* 71-93.

Brewer, N., & Smith, G.A. (1990). Processing speed and mental retardation: Deadline procedures indicate fixed and adjustable limitations. *Memory & Cognition, 18,* 443-450.

Broadbent, D.E. (1958). *Perception and communication.* London: Pergamon Press.

Brown, A.L. (1974). The role of strategic behavior in retardate memory. In N.R. Ellis (Ed.), *International review of research in mental retardation: Vol. 7* (pp. 55-111). New York: Academic Press.

Brown, A.L. (1975). The development of memory: Knowing, knowing about knowing, and knowing how to know. In H.W. Reese (Ed.), *Advances in child development and behavior: Vol. 10* (pp. 103-152). New York: Academic Press.

Bruininks, R.H. (1974). Physical and motor development of retarded persons. In N.R. Ellis (Ed.), *International review of research on mental retardation: Vol. 7* (pp. 209-261). New York: Academic Press.

Butterfield, E.C., & Belmont, J.M. (1977). Assessing and improving the executive control functions of mentally retarded people. In I. Bailer & M. Sternlicht (Eds.), *Psychological issues in mental retardation: Issues and approaches* (pp. 277-318). New York: Academic Press.

Campione, J.C., & Brown, A.L. (1984). Learning ability and transfer propensity as sources of individual differences in intelligence. In P.H. Brooks, R. Sperber, & C. McCauley (Eds.), *Learning and cognition in the mentally retarded* (pp. 265-293). Hillsdale, NJ: Erlbaum.

Campione, J.C., Brown, A.L., & Ferrara, R.A. (1982). Mental retardation and intelligence. In R.J. Sternberg (Ed.), *Handbook of human intelligence* (pp. 392-490). New York: Cambridge University Press.

Carr, T.H. (1984). Attention, skill, and intelligence: Some speculations on extreme individual differences in human performance. In P.H. Brooks, R. Sperber, & C. McCauley (Eds.), *Learning and cognition in the mentally retarded* (pp. 189-215). Hillsdale, NJ: Erlbaum.

Cha, K.H., & Merrill, E.C. (1994). Facilitation and inhibition effects in visual selective attention processes of individuals with and without mental retardation. *American Journal on Mental Retardation, 98,* 594-600.

Das, J.P. (1969). Development of verbal abilities in retarded and normal children as measured by Stroop test. *British Journal of Social and Clinical Psychology, 8,* 59-66.

Das, J.P. (1970). Changes in Stroop-test responses as a function of mental age. *British Journal of Social and Clinical Psychology, 9,* 68-73.

Detterman, D.K., Mayer, J.D., Caruso, D.R., Legree, P.J., Conners, F.A., & Taylor, R. (1992). Assessment of basic cognitive abilities in relation to cognitive deficits. *American Journal on Mental Retardation, 97,* 295-301.

Dugas, J.L., & Kellas, G. (1974). Encoding and retrieval processes in normal children and retarded adolescents. *Journal of Experimental Child Psychology, 17,* 177-185.

Dulaney, C.L. (1998). Automatic processing: Implications for job training of individuals with mental retardation. *Journal of Developmental and Physical Disabilities, 10,* 175-184.

Dulaney, C.L., & Ellis, N.R. (1994). Automatized responding and cognitive inertia in persons with mental retardation. *American Journal on Mental Retardation, 99,* 8-18.

Dulaney, C.L., & Ellis, N.R. (1997). Rigidity in the behavior of mentally retarded persons. In W.E. MacLean Jr. (Ed.), *Ellis' handbook of mental deficiency, psychological theory and research* (3rd ed., pp. 175-195). Mahwah, NJ: Erlbaum.

Ellis, N.R. (1978). Do the mentally retarded have poor memory? *Intelligence, 2,* 41-54.

Ellis, N.R., & Dulaney, C.L. (1991). Further evidence for cognitive inertia in persons with mental retardation. *American Journal on Mental Retardation, 95,* 613-621.

Ellis, N.R., Woodley-Zanthos, P., Dulaney, C.L., & Palmer, R.L. (1989). Automatic-effortful processing and cognitive inertia in persons with mental retardation. *American Journal on Mental Retardation, 93,* 412-423.

Eriksen, B.A., & Eriksen, C.W. (1974). Effects of noise letters upon the identification of a target letter in a nonsearch task. *Perception and Psychophysics, 16,* 143-149.

Ferretti, R.P., & Butterfield, E.C. (1992). Intelligence-related differences in the learning, maintenance, and transfer of problem-solving strategies. *Intelligence, 16,* 207-223.

Fitts, P., & Posner, M.I. (1967). *Human performance.* Belmont, CA: Brooks/Cole.

Frensch, P.A., & Sternberg, R.J. (1989). Expertise and intelligent thinking: When is it worse to know better? In R.J. Sternberg (Ed.), *Advances in the psychology of human intelligence: Vol. 5* (pp. 157-188). Hillsdale, NJ: Erlbaum.

Goldstein, K. (1942). Concerning rigidity. *Character and Personality, 11,* 209-226.

Hagen, J.W., & Huntsman, N. (1971). Selective attention in mental retardation. *Developmental Psychology, 5,* 151-160.

Haier, R.J., Chueh, D., Touchette, P., Lott, I., Buchsbaum, M.S., MacMillan, D., Sandman, C., LaCasse, L., & Sosa, E. (1995). Brain size and cerebral glucose metabolic rate in nonspecific mental retardation and Down syndrome. *Intelligence, 20,* 191-210.

Haier, R.J., Siegel, B., McLachlan, A., Soderling, E., Lottenberg, E., & Buchsbaum, M. (1992). Regional glucose metabolic changes after learning a complex visuospatial/motor task: A PET study. *Brain Research, 570,* 134-143.

Haier, R.J., Siegel, B., Tang, C., Abel, L., & Buchsbaum, M. (1992). Intelligence and changes in regional cerebral glucose rate following learning. *Intelligence, 16,* 415-426.

Harris, G.J., & Fleer, R.E. (1974). High speed memory scanning in mental retardates: Evidence for a central processing deficit. *Journal of Experimental Child Psychology, 17,* 452-459.

Hasher, L., & Zacks, R.T. (1979). Automatic and effortful processes in memory. *Journal of Experimental Psychology: General, 108,* 356-388.

Hoover, J.H., Wade, M.G., & Newell, K.M. (1981). Training moderately and severely mentally retarded adults to improve reaction and movement times. *American Journal on Mental Retardation, 85,* 389-395.

Johnston, W.A, & Dark, V.J. (1986). Selective attention. *Annual Review of Psychology, 37,* 43-75.

Kahneman, D. (1973). *Attention and effort.* Englewood Cliffs, NJ: Prentice-Hall.

Kounin, J.S. (1941). Experimental studies of rigidity: I. The measurement of rigidity in normal and feeble-minded persons. *Character and Personality, 9,* 251-272.

Kranzler, J.H., & Jensen, A.R. (1989). Inspection time and intelligence: A meta-analysis. *Intelligence, 13,* 329-347.

Lewin, K. (1935). *A dynamic theory of personality.* New York: McGraw-Hill.

Logan, G.D. (1988). Toward an instance theory of automatization. *Psychological Review, 95,* 492-527.

Magill, R.A. (1993). *Motor learning: Concepts and applications* (4th ed.). Madison, WI: Brown & Benchmark.

Maisto, A.A., & Baumeister, A.A. (1984). Dissection of component processes in rapid information processing tasks: Comparisons of retarded and nonretarded people. In P.H. Brooks, R. Sperber, & C. McCauley (Eds.), *Learning and cognition in the mentally retarded* (pp. 165-188). Hillsdale, NJ: Erlbaum.

Maisto, A.A., & Jerome, M.A. (1977). Encoding and high-speed memory scanning of retarded and nonretarded adolescents. *American Journal of Mental Deficiency, 82,* 282-286.

Meador, D.M., & Ellis, N.R. (1987). Automatic and effortful processing by mentally retarded and nonretarded persons. *American Journal of Mental Deficiency, 91,* 613-619.

Merrill, E.C. (1985). Differences in semantic processing speed of mentally retarded and nonretarded persons. *American Journal of Mental Deficiency, 90,* 71-80.

Merrill, E.C. (1990). Attentional resource allocation and mental retardation. *International Review of Research in Mental Retardation, 16,* 51-88.

Merrill, E.C., Alexander, S.L., & Williams, E.D. (1992). *The development of the automatic detection of category exemplars.* Paper presented at the 25th Gatlinburg Conference on Research and Theory in Mental Retardation and Developmental Disabilities, Gatlinburg, TN.

Merrill, E.C., Goodwyn, E.H., & Gooding, H.L. (1996). Mental retardation and the acquisition of automatic processing. *American Journal on Mental Retardation, 101,* 49-62.

Merrill, E.C., & O'Dekirk, J.M. (1994). Visual selective attention and mental retardation. *Cognitive Neuropsychology, 11,* 117-132.

Merrill, E.C., & Taube, M. (1996). Negative priming and mental retardation: The processing of distractor information. *American Journal on Mental Retardation, 101,* 63-71.

Mosley, J.L. (1985). High-speed memory-scanning task performance of mildly retarded and nonretarded individuals. *American Journal of Mental Deficiency, 90,* 81-89.

Nettelbeck, T. (1985). Inspection time and mild mental retardation. In N.R. Ellis & N.W. Bray (Eds.), *International review of research on mental retardation: Vol. 13* (pp. 109-141). New York: Academic Press.

Nettelbeck, T., & Brewer, N. (1981). Studies of mild mental retardation and timed performance. In N.R. Ellis (Ed.), *International review of research on mental retardation, Vol. 10* (pp. 61-106). New York: Academic Press.

Nettelbeck, T., Evans, G., & Kirby, N.H. (1982). Effects of practice on inspection time for mildly mentally retarded and nonretarded adults. *American Journal of Mental Deficiency, 87,* 103-107.

Nettelbeck, T., & Wilson, C. (1997). Speed of information processing and cognition. In W.E. MacLean Jr. (Ed.), *Ellis' handbook of mental deficiency, psychological theory and research* (3rd ed., pp. 245-274). Mahwah, NJ: Erlbaum.

Newell, K.M. (1985). Motor skill acquisition and mental retardation: Overview of traditional and current orientations. In J.E. Clark & J.H. Humphrey (Eds.), *Motor development: Vol. 1* (pp. 183-192). Princeton, NJ: Princeton Book.

Newell, K.M. (1997). Motor skills and mental retardation. In W.E. MacLean Jr. (Ed.), *Ellis' handbook of mental deficiency, psychological theory and research* (3rd ed., pp. 275-308). Mahwah, NJ: Erlbaum.

Newell, K., & Rosenbloom, P.S. (1981). Mechanisms of skill acquisition and the law of practice. In J.R. Anderson (Ed.), *Cognitive skills and their acquisition* (pp. 1-55). Hillsdale, NJ: Erlbaum.

Phillips, C.J., & Nettelbeck, T. (1984). Effects of practice on recognition memory of mildly retarded adults. *American Journal of Mental Deficiency, 88*, 678-697.

Posner, J.I., & Snyder, C.R.R. (1975). Facilitation and inhibition in the processing of signals. In P.M.A. Rabbitt & S. Dornic (Eds.), *Attention and performance: Vol. 5* (pp. 669-682). New York: Academic Press.

Proctor, R.W., & Dutta, A. (1995). *Skill acquisition and human performance.* Thousand Oaks, CA: Sage.

Puff, R.C. (Ed.). (1982). *Handbook of research methods in human memory and cognition.* New York: Academic Press.

Rabbitt, P.M.A. (1981). Sequential reactions. In D.H. Holding (Ed.), *Human skills* (pp. 153-175). London: Wiley.

Reason, J., & Mycielska, K. (1982). *Absent minded? The psychology of mental lapses and everyday errors.* Englewood Cliffs, NJ: Prentice-Hall.

Schneider, W., & Fisk, A.D. (1982). Degree of consistent training: Improvements in search performance and automatic process development. *Perception & Psychophysics, 31*, 160-168.

Schneider, W., & Shiffrin, R.M. (1977). Controlled and automatic human information processing: I. Detection, search, and attention. *Psychological Review, 84*, 1-55.

Shiffrin, R.M., & Schneider, W. (1977). Controlled and automatic human information processing: II. Perceptual learning, automatic attending, and a general theory. *Psychological Review, 84*, 127-190.

Siegel, P.S., & Foshee, J.G. (1960). Molar variability in the mentally defective. *Journal of Abnormal and Social Psychology, 61*, 141-143.

Smith, S.A., & Siegel, P.S. (1986). Molar variability and the mentally retarded. *International Review of Research in Mental Retardation, 14*, 73-104.

Sperber, R.D., & McCauley, C. (1984). Semantic processing efficiency in the mentally retarded. In P. Brooks, R. Sperber, & C. McCauley (Eds.), *Learning and cognition in the mentally retarded* (pp. 141-163). Hillsdale, NJ: Erlbaum.

Spitz, H.H. (1986). *The raising of intelligence: A selected history of attempts to raise retarded intelligence.* Hillsdale, NJ: Erlbaum.

Stelmach, G.E., & Hughes, B.G. (1983). Does motor skill automation require a theory of attention? In R.A. Magill (Ed.), *Memory and control of action* (pp. 67-92). New York: North-Holland.

Sternberg, S. (1966). High-speed scanning in human memory. *Science, 153*, 652-654.

Stroop, J.R. (1935). Studies of interference in serial and verbal reactions. *Journal of Experimental Psychology, 18*, 643-662.

Tipper, S.P., & Cranston, M. (1985). Selective attention and priming: Inhibitory and facilitory effects of ignored primes. *Quarterly Journal of Experimental Psychology, 37A*, 571-611.

Tomporowski, P. (1997). The effects of physical and mental training on the mental abilities of older adults. *Journal of Aging and Physical Activity, 5*, 9-26.

Tomporowski, P.D., & Tinsley, V. (1997). Attention in mentally retarded persons. In W.E. MacLean Jr. (Ed.), *Ellis' handbook of mental deficiency, psychological theory and research* (3rd ed., pp. 219-244). Mahwah, NJ: Erlbaum.

Treisman, A.M. (1969). Strategies and models of selective attention. *Psychological Review, 76*, 282-299.

Vickers, D. (1970). Evidence for an accumulator model of psychophysical discrimination. *Ergonomics, 13*, 37-58.

Vickers, D. (1979). *Decision process in visual perception.* London: Academic Press.

Werner, H. (1946). Abnormal and subnormal rigidity. *Journal of Abnormal and Social Psychology, 41*, 15-24.

Werner, H. (1948). The concept of rigidity: A critical evaluation. *Psychological Review, 53*, 43-53.

Wickens, C.D. (1984). Processing resources in attention. In R. Parasuraman & D. Davies (Eds.), *Varieties of attention* (pp. 63-102). New York: Academic Press.

Wickens, C.D. (1987). Attention. In P.A. Hancock (Ed.), *Human factors psychology* (pp. 29-79). New York: North-Holland.

Zeaman, D., & House, B.J. (1979). A review of attention theory. In N.R. Ellis (Ed.), *Handbook of mental deficiency, psychological theory and research* (2nd ed., pp. 63-120). Hillsdale, NJ: Erlbaum.

Zigler, E. (1962). Rigidity in the feebleminded. In E. Trapp & P. Himmelstein (Eds.), *Readings on the exceptional child* (pp. 141-162). New York: Appleton-Century-Crofts.

Zigler, E., & Balla, D. (1982). Rigidity—A resilient concept. In E. Zigler & D. Balla (Eds.), *Mental retardation: The developmental-difference controversy* (pp. 61-82). Hillsdale, NJ: Erlbaum.

9

<u>CHAPTER</u>

Motor Coordination in Down Syndrome: The Role of Adaptive Changes

Mark L. Latash

Department of Kinesiology
Pennsylvania State University

Key words

adaptive change ◆ coordination ◆ clumsiness ◆ motor redundancy ◆ movement patterns ◆ synergies ◆ cerebellum ◆ practice ◆ neural plasticity

Problems with motor coordination are just a fraction of all the challenges that persons with Down syndrome (DS) may face during their lifetime. However, poor motor coordination is arguably the most frequently encountered problem in everyday life. The problem presents itself virtually every minute, when one picks up and manipulates objects, navigates through familiar and less familiar environments, and communicates with other people.

A wide spectrum of motor abilities can be seen in persons with DS. Within this chapter, I will address problems with motor coordination in persons whose movements are not grossly different from those of the general population. However, even these mildly different movement patterns look apparently suboptimal to an external observer. They may be classified as "clumsy." There is no good definition for "clumsiness"; in lay terms, it means the opposite of good coordination. For the purposes of this chapter, let us define clumsy movements as those for which movement patterns differ, and are less effective, in achieving apparent motor goals than patterns seen in the general population. I am going to argue, however, that this understanding of clumsiness relies heavily on an accepted definition of "apparent motor goals." One of the main points of this chapter is that differences in motor goals can lead to the generation of movements that may look clumsy to an observer who is naive to the movement goals of the actor's central nervous system.

To understand issues related to motor coordination, one needs first to understand what motor coordination is and what its origins are.

Main Problems of Coordination of Natural Movements

First, we should acknowledge that the problem of motor coordination during the natural movements of persons from the general population is still without an answer. Actually, the situation is even worse, because the question itself has never been properly formulated. However, there is a spectrum of issues that is viewed as crucial for progress toward understanding the coordination of voluntary human movements:

- *The problem of motor redundancy* (for reviews, see Bernstein, 1967; Latash, 1996; Turvey, 1990). This problem can also be viewed as a problem of choice: At each level of analysis of the system for movement production, there are many possible solutions, only one of which is selected each time a movement is generated. It is unknown how the choice is made.

- *The problem of central variables* (for reviews, see Berkinblit, Feldman, & Fukson, 1986; Feldman & Levin, 1995; Latash, 1993; Stein, 1982). When the central nervous system plans and executes a movement, it probably formulates motor commands in an internal language that is likely different from the language of movement variables typically measured in motor control or biomechanics laboratories. The "words" and "rules of grammar" of this language are unknown.

- *The problem of coordinate systems* (for reviews, see Flanders, Tillery, & Soechting, 1992; Latash, 1993; McIntyre, Stratta, & Lacquaniti, 1997). This problem is related to the previous one. However, it also asks questions with respect to the external coordinate systems in which movements can be planned. For example, movement may be planned in the external Cartesian space or in the space of joint angles, with respect to the person's eyes or with respect to his or her shoulder (e.g., when an object is manipulated by an arm).

- *The problem of stability of movement patterns* (for reviews, see Kelso, 1995; Schöner & Kelso, 1988). We perform movements in an environment that can present unexpected challenges such as changing forces, changing target locations, and so on. We would definitely like our movements to be successful despite all these potentially complicating factors. In such conditions, stability of movement patterns becomes an important issue that may, in many cases, be crucial in defining the actual motor patterns generated by a person.

- *The problem of mapping solutions onto neurophysiological structures* (for reviews, see Georgopoulos, 1986; Houk, Buckingham, & Barto, 1996). Imagine that we have correctly formulated answers to all four problems above. Still, one would not be satisfied until the relations between these answers and the actual neural structures within the human body are understood. Obviously, this issue is particularly important for clinical studies and studies of movements in atypical persons.

Within this chapter, I will primarily address issues of motor redundancy and mapping solutions onto neurophysiological structures, assuming that there are no major differences between persons with and without DS with respect to central variables (this is likely to be true) and to coordinate systems (this assumption is much more questionable). There are probably differences between the stability properties of movement patterns generated by persons with Down syndrome and those of the motor patterns in the general population. The dynamical systems approach has been particularly successful in dealing with problems of stability of motor patterns. However, its application to understanding movement in atypical populations has been limited (for nice exceptions, see Wagenaar & Van Emmerik, 1996, and other papers in the same issue of *Human Movement Science*).

The Problem of Motor Redundancy

Humans are confronted with problems of choice virtually every minute: Which apples to choose from a huge bin containing hundreds of seemingly identical fruits. Which roads to take on your way to visit relatives. How to choose an apartment. How to choose a school for a child. How to choose a spouse.

Obviously, in some cases (like choosing apples in a supermarket, see the left side of figure 9.1), we do not much care about the outcome of the choice, as long as it does not lead to apparently poor results. Hence, we allow uncontrolled factors ("noise") to make the choice for us. It is likely that, if the same problem is presented several times, the solutions will be different during different attempts at solving it. Finding an apartment involves making a more responsible decision, and we are unlikely to rely on pure chance. Choosing a school or a spouse (see the right side of figure 9.1) are such important decisions that we would like to completely eliminate the possible effects of "noise" and find the optimal, unique solution. Depending on how much we care about the outcome of a decision-making process, we may use an optimization algorithm to a greater or lesser degree, and allow chance or noise to do the rest of the job.

Recurrent problems are encountered by the central nervous system each time it generates a voluntary movement. The human motor system is notoriously redundant. This means that its design imposes only weak constraints on possible solutions for motor problems. For example, if the reader puts his or her right finger on this line, he or she can easily move all the joints of the arm (in particular, wrist, elbow, and shoulder) without losing contact with the page. This means that pointing at a target may be performed with many (actually, an infinite number of) arm configurations. However, each time, a unique solution is selected somehow by the central nervous system. How does it do it?

At a different level, if a person wishes to generate a force of, say, 10 N with the palm against a stop, a number of muscles may contribute to generate force. Some muscles may act together in the direction of the required force. Other muscles may oppose the action of the first group. This opposing action may not be meaningless; it may actually contribute to stability of the arm configuration, which, as we have already mentioned earlier, is an important issue of motor coordination. In the simplest case, illustrated in figure 9.2, three flexor muscles are generating force in the required direction, and three extensors are in opposition to them. How much force will each muscle produce? It is obvious that this problem does not have a unique solution. It is similar to solving one equation with six unknowns.

Such problems are frequently addressed as ill-posed questions. They cannot be solved without additional constraints on the system. However, before trying to understand how such problems may be solved by the human central nervous system, the first question to ask is: "Does the central nervous system actually solve all these problems?" They look suspiciously similar to picking 6 apples from a bin containing 100 identical fruits, as illustrated in the left part of figure 9.1. I suggest that, in certain cases, the central nervous system may not be solving these problems but rather limiting areas where possible solutions can be found. Then, "noise" comes into play and picks an apple from the bin. As a result, the problem turns out to be formulated differently: "Which rules are used by the central nervous system to restrict possible solutions for problems involving choice?" Such rules may be called *coordinative*. They are somewhat similar to the rules of grammar: There is always an infinite number of possible word combinations that can be used to express a certain meaning. However, some of them obey the rules of grammar while others do not. Ideally, only the grammatical solutions would be selected each time a phrase is constructed, even though the number of possible grammatical solutions may be considerable.

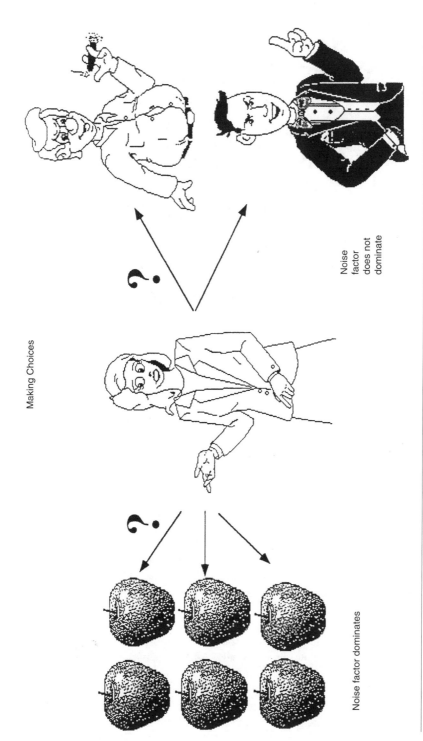

Making Choices

Noise factor does not dominate

Noise factor dominates

Figure 9.1 An illustration of two cases of making a choice.

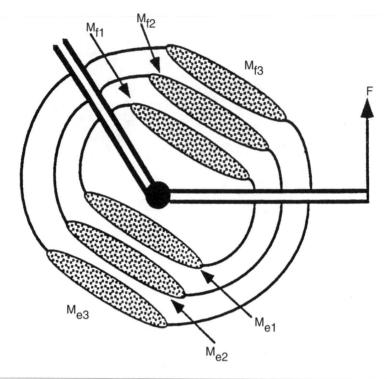

Figure 9.2 An illustration of the redundancy problem at the single-joint level. M_{f1} = first muscle flexor; M_{f2} = second muscle flexor; M_{f3} = third muscle flexor; M_{e1} = first muscle extensor; M_{e2} = second muscle extensor; M_{e3} = third muscle extensor; F = force.

Structural Units and Synergies

N. Bernstein (1947, 1967) suggested the notion of synergy as a biological means of limiting choice of coordinations during voluntary movements. Later, this line of thinking was advanced by Gelfand and Tsetlin (1966) who introduced the idea of a structural unit as a task-specific organization of elements. Synergies have been viewed as purposes of structural units, while actual behaviors emerge based on a synergy and possible changes in external conditions of movement execution. Structural units can be introduced for systems of different complexity; for example, an organism, a subsystem within an organism, or a group of organisms can each be viewed as a structural unit. Each structural unit is supposed to include several elements and be controlled by a hierarchically higher system (figure 9.3).

There are several advantages to using structural units to control large ensembles of elements. First, the controller does not need to specify what each element of a structural unit needs to do; rather, it sets a general common goal and modulates relations among the elements. One may view it as a hierarchical system that functions

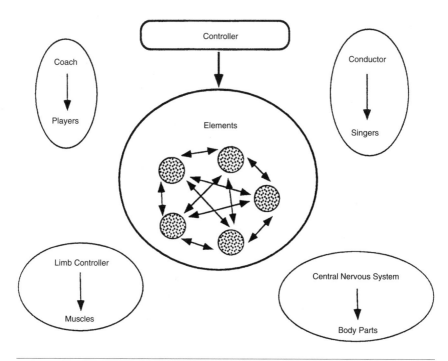

Figure 9.3   An illustration of a structural unit organization (center) with a few examples.

based on a nonauthoritarian principle in which elements are free to behave within certain constraints as long as the ultimate goal is met. For example, the players on a football team may be viewed as a structural unit controlled by the coach. The coach does not specify, prior to each play, exactly what each player should do. Rather, the coach sets a general pattern for the play and an objective. Note that unpredictable actions by the players of the opposing team make it impossible to set an exact pattern for each and every player. After the instruction of the coach is received, the play proceeds without further changes in the "control signal" from the coach.

Gelfand and Tsetlin (1966) introduced a *principle of minimal interaction* as the main coordinative principle applicable to all biological structural units. According to this principle, all elements behave like high school students whose major purpose is to attract as little attention from the teacher as possible. The principle of minimal interaction may be formulated at two levels:

- *Global:* The effect of changes in the output of each element on the common, functionally defined outcome tends to be minimized by the output of other elements.

- *Local:* The functional outcome of each element on its own state tends to be minimally dependent on the output of other elements and external conditions.

Imagine a large chorus. The conductor tells the baritones, "Listen to the level of sound. It should be exactly 10 decibels." This instruction unites the baritones into a structural unit. If one singer begins to sing less loudly or falls ill and quits, other singers will hear a general decrease in the level of sound and start to sing a bit louder, so that the level of sound will be kept at 10 dB, and the conductor will not need to interfere. This is an illustration of the first, global formulation of the principle of minimal interaction. On the other hand, all the singers are different. Some of them have very strong voices and like to sing very loudly, while others may have weaker voices. According to the local principle, the "loud ones" will sing more loudly compared to their friends, independent of the overall level of sound requested by the conductor. In other words, each element may have its own preference of behavior within a structural unit, and it will follow its preferred pattern as long as it is compatible with the overall functional goal. Note that the instruction by the conductor to the chorus did not specify exactly how loudly each baritone should sing. It allowed each singer to have a degree of personal freedom as long as the ultimate goal was reached. Had the conductor selected a nonbiological way of organizing the chorus and told each singer exactly how loudly to sing, the chorus would not be able to maintain the required level of sound if one singer became tired and decided to stop singing.

This example illustrates the main principles and also the main advantages of structural units. One of the major advantages is stability of solutions in the presence of unexpected and unpredictable external events (perturbations), which occur frequently in everyday life. A relative disadvantage is the unavoidable variability in performance of such units because they are based on the detection of errors by elements and corrections of those errors. Such things apparently take time, so that the actual output of a structural unit will always be slightly imperfect, varying about an ultimate goal.

In voluntary movements, structural units are frequently viewed as sets of individual joints (with their muscles and corresponding segmental spinal machinery) united by a goal commonly formulated in terms of movement of the "most important point" on the body or on the limb. Commonly, this "working point" is the end point of the limb: for example, the hand or fingertips when grasping or manipulating an object, or the tip of a foot when kicking a football. During voluntary movements, structural units rarely (and possibly, never) work alone. Because of the mechanical connections among all the joints within the body, a movement of a joint leads to perturbing forces acting on other joints that may not necessarily be explicitly involved in the task at hand (for a review, see Massion, 1992). For example, when a person picks up a briefcase, the weight of the briefcase creates perturbing forces acting on the body, which can, in principle, ruin the fragile postural equilibrium. In such a case, an adjustment in a structural unit assuring a postural synergy needs to take place. Thus, coordination of a number of structural units becomes a problem of its own.

The relation of structural units to anatomical or neurophysiological structures is unknown. However, there is a conspicuous brain structure that has fascinated researchers for literally thousands of years and whose function remains largely unknown. This structure has recently attracted attention as a potential site playing a central role in the formation of structural units and synergies. This structure is the cerebellum.

The Cerebellum

Ancient Greeks thought that the human soul resided in the cerebellum, the second largest structure of the brain. This view sounds rather "unscientific" to a 20th-century researcher, mostly because of the use of the poorly defined notion of "soul." However, the cerebellum (figure 9.4), which until recently was considered only with respect to motor functions, has attracted increasing attention as a potential partici-pant in purely mental, perceptual, and intellectual functions (for a review, see Thach, 1996). The new appreciation of the importance of the cerebellum, a "middleman" for the brain (Bloedel, 1992), for numerous functions of the human organism makes the ideas of ancient Greeks sound acceptable and perhaps appealing.

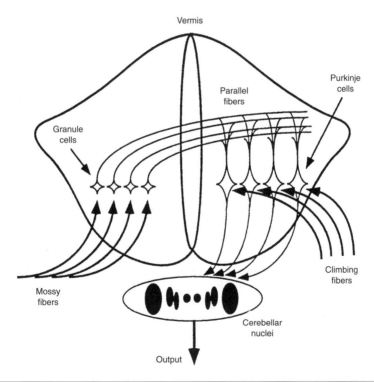

Figure 9.4   An illustration of major connections in the cerebellum. One major input (mossy fibers) leads to excitation of granule cells whose axons form the parallel fiber system. The other major input (climbing fibers) has strong projections on the main output neurons, Purkinje cells. The output is mediated by cerebellar nuclei.

The cerebellum consists of two hemispheres: a vermis (the phylogenetically oldest part) and several pairs of nuclei that serve as targets for cerebellar outputs and transfer information to other parts of the central nervous system (figure 9.4). The cerebellum contains more neurons than the rest of the central nervous system. The internal "wiring" of the cerebellum creates an impression of a very regular and rather simple design. Only five types of neurons exist in the cerebellum, and only one type of neuron, Purkinje cells, serves to provide its output. There are two major inputs to the cerebellum. The first carries information from various sources, including the spinal cord and brain stem structures. The fibers of this pathway are called mossy fibers. The mossy fibers make connections with small neurons (granule cells) whose output fibers (axons) run parallel to the cerebellar surface. Each Purkinje cell receives numerous inputs from these parallel fibers. The second input to the cerebellum is organized very differently. It originates from a well-defined structure, the inferior olive, and carries both sensory information about the state of peripheral organs and a reflection of motor commands generated at the spinal cord level (for a review, see Arshavsky, Gelfand, & Orlovsky, 1986). The input from the inferior olive is very powerful; these fibers (called the climbing fibers) make strong connections with individual Purkinje cells, so that a Purkinje cell can be forced to fire in response to a neural impulse in only one climbing fiber. The apparent simplicity and regularity of internal design have made the cerebellum a favorite structure for a variety of formal models. A number of hypotheses have been suggested with respect to cerebellar function:

- The cerebellum is a timing device. Apparently, relative timing of components is an important feature of virtually any action.

- The cerebellum is a memory device. In particular, it plays a central role in motor learning. This view is based on the demonstrated ability of connections among neurons in the cerebellum to show long-lasting changes under certain combinations of stimuli.

- The cerebellum is a predictive device. Given delays in the conduction of neural impulses within the human body, a motor command is always implemented some time after it was generated. Therefore, the organ issuing a command should be able to predict a future state of the peripheral organs and the environment at the time the command reaches the intended target organ.

- The cerebellum has been assumed to play a central role in the formation of coordinated commands to several muscles, joints, or limbs that assure a certain function. Such combinations of commands have been commonly associated with synergies. This view has been elaborated by a number of researchers, in particular by Houk and colleagues (Houk et al., 1996) who developed an elaborate model of synergy production by a cooperation of a number of brain structures including the cerebellum, the cortex of the large brain hemispheres, and the red nucleus, among others. Within this model, synergies have been associated with ensembles of Purkinje cells firing simultaneously.

• More recently, there has been an increasing awareness of the importance of the cerebellum for nonmotor functions. In particular, the cerebellum has been assumed to play important roles in mental activities such as language, cognition, and so on.

The cerebellum is the only structure within the central nervous system that has been reported to be different in persons with DS as compared to the general population. In particular, the weight of the cerebellum has been reported to be lower in people with DS (Bellugi, Bihrle, Jernigan, Trauner, & Doherty, 1990; Crome & Stern, 1967; Molnar, 1978). There have also been reports of changes in the cerebellum in other groups of atypical persons (Berntson & Torello, 1982; Keele & Ivry, 1990) whose movements also may be viewed as "clumsy." These observations, taken together with the mentioned involvement of the cerebellum in synergy organization and a variety of nonmotor functions, suggest that the cerebellum may indeed play a major role in the organization of elements into function-, task-, or purpose-specific ensembles. If muscles, joints, or limbs are the elements, then this suggestion is equivalent to the hypothesis that the cerebellum plays a major role in the organization of motor synergies. However, elements can also be associated with ideas. Consequently, purely mental performance can be expected to suffer from a cerebellar dysfunction. If elements are associated with persons, the cerebellum can be expected to play a crucial role in establishing interpersonal skills. Within this general scheme, one would expect the reported correlation of autism and cerebellar abnormalities. Keeping in mind the hypothesized role of the cerebellum in motor (and, perhaps, nonmotor) synergies, we now turn to a discussion of the differences in movement patterns in persons with DS as compared to so-called control subjects.

Movement Patterns in Down Syndrome

As mentioned earlier, there is no good definition for "clumsiness." Nevertheless, "clumsiness" seems to be the most frequent word used to describe the differences in movements of persons with DS. Researchers who study persons with DS report a number of movement features that may contribute to an impression of clumsiness. Other specific features, however, do not allow such a straightforward interpretation and sometimes look even puzzling.

Differences in motor performance can be seen in babies with DS starting from the first months of life. Generally, children with DS reach the milestones of motor development in the same order as children without DS but do so at later chronological ages (Carr, 1970; Fishler, 1975; Fishler, Share, & Koch, 1964; Kopp, 1979; Haley, 1986; Molnar, 1978). Slowness is probably the best known feature of voluntary movements in DS. Persons with DS typically take more time to initiate a response to a stimulus (longer reaction time; for a review, see Anson, 1992) and more time to complete a motor task (longer movement time; for a review, see Latash, 1992).

Patterns of muscle activation characterized by higher levels of co-contraction—that is, simultaneous activation of muscles acting in opposite directions (so-called antagonist muscles)—are another conspicuous feature of movements of persons with DS. Increased co-contraction has been described during simple voluntary movements performed about a joint (Aruin, Almeida, & Latash, 1996), during semiautomatic corrections of joint position in response to an unexpected mechanical perturbation, so-called preprogrammed reactions (Latash, Almeida, & Corcos, 1993), and during adjustments in control signals to muscles controlling limb or whole-body posture in anticipation of a perturbation (Aruin & Almeida, 1996). The prevalence of co-contraction patterns of muscle activation in such a variety of automatic, semiautomatic, and voluntary movements suggests that this is not an accidental, meaningless feature. It is particularly puzzling when one compares co-contraction patterns, commonly associated with an increase in joint apparent stiffness, with the reported hypotonia of persons with DS (Morris, Vaughan, & Vaccaro, 1982; Rarick, Dobbins, & Broadhead, 1976). Hypotonia is a poorly defined term for an impression of low resistance of joints to external motion—that is, low apparent stiffness. The relation between hypotonia (low apparent stiffness) and co-contraction (high apparent stiffness) remains poorly understood.

There are two other features of movements of persons with DS that do not appear compatible. These are the high variability of movement profiles and the high degree of accuracy in reaching the target. Pronounced variability of movement patterns (including those of kinematics, dynamics, and patterns of electrical muscle activation) has been reported for virtually all groups demonstrating atypical movements (Corcos, 1991; Elliott & Weeks, 1990; Shumway-Cook & Woollacott, 1985), ranging from patients with an injury to the central nervous system (e.g., spinal cord or brain injury), to patients with systemic disorders (e.g., multiple sclerosis), to patients with dysfunction of certain anatomical formations (e.g., Parkinson's disease), to persons without any clear neurological abnormality (e.g., schizophrenia). The ubiquitous nature of increased motor variability suggests that if any of the many hypothetical components participating in the generation of coordinated voluntary movements is malfunctioning, movement patterns are not going to be as smooth and reproducible. This is likely to lead to higher indices of motor variability as measured within a series of trials on the same task.

On the other hand, however, persons with DS have been reported to be highly or even exceptionally accurate in reaching the target despite highly variable motor patterns (Almeida, Corcos, & Latash, 1994; Kerr & Blais, 1985). To gain better understanding of all these controversies and inconsistencies, one needs to take a closer look at the effects of practice at a rather simple motor task on movement patterns in persons with DS.

Practice Effects

Practice can lead to improvement in motor performance as a result of two distinct factors. The first may be broadly defined as comprehension of the task. It includes not only understanding the explicit goal or instruction but also the relations between movements and the actions of mechanical attachments to the limb (if a tool of some kind is involved) or of an image on a monitor screen (if movements are performed in a "virtual reality" laboratory environment). Such comprehension is acquired through observation and active exploration. This first factor also involves creating confidence in the safety of the system and of the person. The second factor is what is usually implied by "practice," especially when relatively simple motor tasks are considered. It involves refinement of motor commands that may include not only commands to muscles directly involved in the explicit task but also to other muscles with a less obvious role, sometimes related to such task components as body or limb posture.

Motor control studies involving simple motor tasks performed by control subjects usually include a small number of familiarization trials for which the apparent goal is to minimize the possible influence of the first factor—that is, to make sure that the subject understands the task and feels confident in the experimental setup. These initial trials are usually quite erratic and are often discarded from future analyses. After a few such trials, the subject reports that he or she is ready to perform the task, and the "actual experiment" begins.

Persons with DS may require much more time for the kind of exploration necessary to understand the task and to build the confidence in the environment. Another important factor that is likely to slow down the process of improvement in motor performance is the higher safety margin, typical for persons with DS (Cole, Abbs, & Turner, 1988; Henderson, Morris, & Frith, 1981). Apparently, these persons are more inclined to "play it safe" in laboratory experiments. Together, these factors highlight the importance of a friendly, quiet laboratory atmosphere, constant encouragement by the experimenter, and the avoidance of mental and physical fatigue for optimization of performance in persons with DS. According to this view, persons with DS have greater room for improvement as compared to control subjects. Thus, the challenge for an experimenter, therapist, or parent is to create conditions in which the aforementioned restrictions can be lifted and, as a result, performance can be optimized.

In relatively simple motor tasks that involve movement of a single joint from a starting position to a target, subjects with DS show considerably higher movement times and lower indices of movement velocity compared to control subjects. They are also likely to demonstrate a mixture of smooth fast movements and slow ones, with irregular trajectories (figure 9.5). Muscle activation patterns may also show both the typical, phasic patterns observed in well-trained control subjects (for a review, see Gottlieb, Corcos, & Agarwal, 1989) or a sequence of irregular bursts of activation in the muscles controlling the joint (as in the solid traces in figure 9.5). Surprisingly, this mixture of "good" and "bad" trials is associated with high accuracy in attaining the final position, even before practice. Obviously, subjects with DS view the accuracy requirements of the task as much more important than the speed requirements. This trading of speed for accuracy may be viewed as a trademark of movements of these individuals, probably because, in their everyday lives, accuracy is much more important than speed for avoiding complete failure (or even hurting

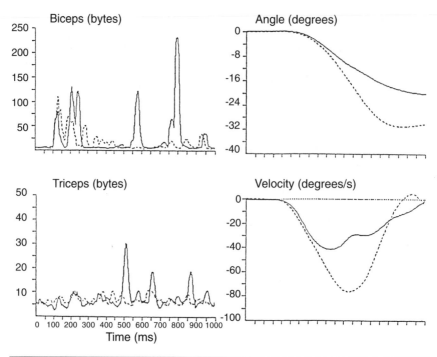

Figure 9.5 An illustration of two trials at a fast elbow-flexion movement by a person with DS. Note the smooth trajectory in one trial (dotted traces), and the "bumpy" velocity trace and multiple electromyographic (EMG) bursts in the biceps and triceps during the other trial (solid traces). Scales are in degrees, degrees/s, and ms. EMG scales are in bytes.

Reprinted, by permission, from M.L. Latash and D.M. Corcos, 1991, "Kinematic and electromyographic characteristics of single-joint movements of individuals with Down Syndrome," *American Journal on Mental Retardation* 96(2): 189-201.

themselves). For example, it is much better to pour hot tea into a cup slowly and carefully than to do it fast and risk scalding oneself. One may assume that persons with DS view many everyday tasks as risky or potentially dangerous, and this attitude is reflected in their performance in laboratory tests.

After a few days of intense training with constant encouragement, subjects with DS show a dramatic improvement in indices of velocity (figure 9.6 top panel); this relative improvement is much higher than that demonstrated by control subjects after a comparable amount of practice (figure 9.6 bottom panel). The original difference between the performances of subjects with and without DS all but disappears. Interestingly, the improvement in movement velocity by persons with DS is not associated with a deterioration in the accuracy of their performance. They continue to be very accurate in reaching the required final position, but become much more confident, and the "bad" trials disappear altogether.

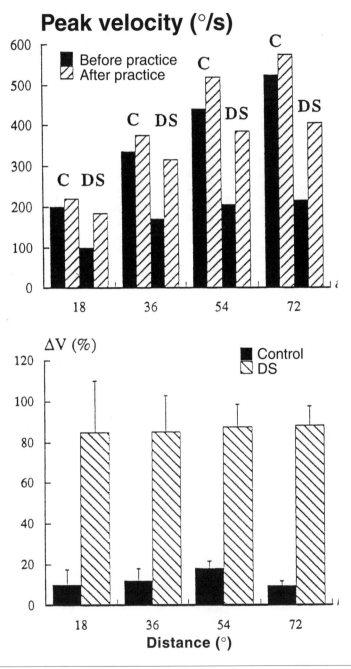

Figure 9.6 Indices of improvement in peak velocity after a prolonged practice of movements over 54° in a control group (C) and in a group of subjects with DS (DS). Note the dramatic improvement in the DS group, particularly obvious in the lower panel.

If subjects with DS practice movements from a fixed initial position to a fixed target, the improvement in their performance is seen not only for the practiced task but also for other tasks that may start from a different position and/or require stopping at a different position (note the similar magnitudes of improvement in the peak velocity for different distances illustrated in figure 9.6). This transfer of learning to other versions of the task carries another optimistic message. Namely, extensive practice may be viewed as a tool for potential improvement of motor performance not only at the practiced task but at other tasks similar to it in certain aspects. Unfortunately, it is unknown just how general the effects of transfer in persons with DS might be. There may be a safety catch: When a person with DS improves his or her performance in a standard test performed in a friendly laboratory environment, improvement at similar tests within the same laboratory may not mean that performance at functionally important tasks will be improved as well. It is quite possible that on stepping out of the laboratory into the real world, the individual quickly returns to the reliable, safe motor patterns developed during the lifetime. In order to avoid this safety catch, one needs to design practice that is targeted at deeper processes within the central nervous system, rather than merely facilitate performance at a particular laboratory test.

Adaptive Changes in the Central Nervous System

We have already discussed problems of choice that challenge the central nervous system virtually every moment of life. One commonly analyzed example is the problem of motor redundancy, also known as Bernstein's problem (Bernstein, 1967; Latash, 1996). Motor redundancy may be viewed as a nuisance, a source of complicated computational problems that the central nervous system needs to solve. Alternatively, it may be considered a source of flexibility and adaptability that allows humans to switch to alternative, atypical motor coordination strategies with respect to everyday motor tasks. In each particular case of movement generation, actual motor patterns emerge based on principles that are presently unknown to us and that are likely to be common across the general population.

Persons differ from one another in the relative strength of their muscles, dimensions and weight of their body and its parts, lifestyle, traditions, and many other factors that affect movement patterns during everyday activity. However, despite all these differences, there are certain features common to most of the movements of most people. These preferred patterns of motor coordination are apparently selected from available options by the central nervous system based on a set of criteria. Although we do not know the criteria used by the central nervous system to make such selections, we may assume that these criteria exist and that they are common for all persons who belong to the general population (and do not have highly specialized motor skills). Let us use the term "CNS priorities" for this hypothetical set of rules that makes possible choice among movement patterns by the central nervous system.

According to this definition, voluntary movements of all "control subjects" are generated based on the same set of CNS priorities that are applicable across tasks and conditions. However, there are subgroups of apparently healthy persons whose movement patterns may differ dramatically from one another. For example, walking patterns of a ballet dancer and of a top sumo wrestler may show differences not smaller than those between walking patterns of an "average control subject" and of a person with Parkinson's disease or with a prosthetic leg. We may assume, therefore, that CNS priorities are not immutable and can be modified as a result of practice. If so, changes to these sets of rules may also be expected under conditions of long-lasting changes in structures or processes participating in the production of voluntary movements. The feature that is likely to play a central role in the hypothesized changes in CNS priorities is called *neural plasticity*.

Plasticity is one of the most exciting and poorly understood features of the central nervous system. If one studies projections of certain groups of neurons onto other groups of neurons, "maps" can be seen that demonstrate high stability and are reproducible across the general population. Corresponding pictures of distorted human bodies (homunculi) have been drawn on virtually all major brain structures and reproduced in numerous textbooks. Recent studies have shown, however, that most if not all of these maps are flexible and able to demonstrate a quick and major reorganization following a significant change in patterns of incoming signals. Such map modifications have been reported after specialized training or immobilization of effectors, after stroke, and after amputation (Fuhr et al., 1992; Jenkins, Merzenich, & Recanzone, 1990; Kew et al., 1994; Merzenich et al., 1984). Neuronal mechanisms of plasticity have been studied in such brain structures as the hippocampus and the cerebellum and are assumed to participate in processes underlying memory, in particular motor memory (for a review, see Crepel, Hemart, Jaillard, & Daniel, 1996; Linden, 1996). This amazing ability of the central nervous system to "rewire itself" is likely to contribute to adaptive changes in motor coordination.

For example, a person after a leg amputation needs to cope with the altered biomechanics of the walking apparatus and the altered organization of spinal reflexes, as well as altered projections of both sensory signals to brain structures and motor signals from brain structures to neurons in the spinal cord (for a review, see Latash & Anson, 1996). It would be unrealistic to expect such a person to demonstrate the same patterns of motor coordination during walking as those demonstrated by unimpaired people. After sufficient practice, many persons with a prosthetic leg elaborate walking patterns that allow them to navigate successfully through the environment. These new walking patterns may be viewed as optimal with respect to their functional goals—that is, being able to walk over large distances without getting tired or hurt. However, these patterns may look clumsy to an external observer unaware of their origin.

Similarly, a person with a neurological disorder (e.g., Parkinson's disease, stroke, or multiple sclerosis) may also be expected to elaborate atypical patterns of motor coordination (for a review, see Latash & Anson, 1996). If one takes into account the actual state of the central structures participating in movement production, these atypical patterns may be viewed as optimal with respect to a certain group of motor tasks that this person considers important. These atypical motor patterns can hardly be viewed as "wrong" or "pathological," because they have been elaborated by the person's central nervous system based on its actual state and functional goals.

Changes in coordination patterns may also be expected in cases when there are no obvious changes in the effector apparatus or in the central neural structures. For example, patients with schizophrenia demonstrate characteristic movements that allow experienced neurologists and psychiatrists to suspect schizophrenia following only a few seconds of observation. One may assume that altered perception of the world and of one's place in it may lead to the elaboration of atypical movement patterns that are optimal within the fictitious world of the patient but look clumsy or unusual to an external observer.

Let us now return to motor coordination in persons with DS. We may suspect that these persons, too, perceive certain aspects of the external world differently from their peers without DS. In particular, the reported mental retardation of persons with DS may be expected to require of those persons more time to solve relatively simple problems that face all human beings in everyday life. Further, remember that the cerebellum is the only brain structure that shows signs of impairment in DS. According to our earlier analysis, the cerebellum is likely to play a major role in the formation of synergies, both motor and nonmotor. Therefore, one may conclude that the formation of synergies presents more serious problems to persons with DS than to other people.

Synergies are assumed to be the main biological mechanism of controlling a large number of elements with relatively few command signals. In particular, they are supposed to simplify control of numerous muscles and joints involved even in rather simple movements of the human body. If this mechanism is malfunctioning, the everyday motor repertoire, which people from the general population take for granted and perform without any visible effort, may start to pose major problems affecting such automatic movements as walking, standing, or reaching for an object.

It is common for everyday motor tasks to require a person to make a decision and perform a movement under time pressure. Such tasks are likely to be viewed by persons with DS as challenging while their peers may view them as trivial. For example, it is not uncommon for humans to misjudge external forces: the weight of an object, the distance to an object, the height of a step, and numerous other factors. These errors in judgment require urgent corrections to avoid failure in the task at hand. Any movement correction needs to be quick and proper; otherwise, it can be useless or even aggravate the effects of an original error rather than alleviate them. An impaired ability to generate quick, appropriate corrective actions may be critical to a person who considers routine, everyday tasks, such as picking up objects or walking over an unknown terrain, as challenging and even potentially dangerous.

This may be the main reason that persons with DS generate patterns of motor coordination that look clumsy. If such a person expects perturbations during a movement, this person is likely to

- take more time before generating a movement;
- move more carefully and slowly; and
- try to make movement patterns stable against possible perturbations.

These expectations fit well the described increase in reaction time, in movement time, and in muscle co-contraction that are typical of movements of persons with Down syndrome (figure 9.7). The present analysis brings us to the following conclusion:

> Everyday life has taught persons with Down syndrome to be careful and accurate. They have learned that speed is not as vital as personal safety and ultimate success in the task at hand. Hence, these persons are willing to trade speed and elegance of movements for safety and reliability.

This conclusion suggests that the described features of movement of persons with DS need not be considered "wrong" or "pathological," because they are likely to represent consequences of adaptive processes within the central nervous system, which is "aware" of its power and limitations and tries to optimize motor performance in functionally important tasks. Optimization of performance of everyday

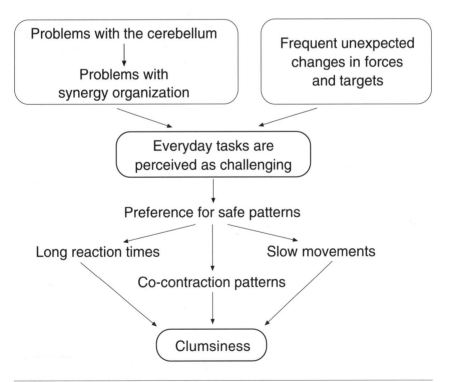

Figure 9.7   A hypothetical scheme of the origins of "clumsiness" in Down syndrome.

movements, in particular making sure that failure is avoided in important task components (e.g., not losing balance and falling down), may be incompatible with optimization of performance in laboratory tests that do not carry functional significance. There seems to be a safety catch. Is there a way of overcoming it? And should one even try to optimize what has already been optimized by a person's central nervous system?

Possible Routes to Optimization of Special Physical Education Programs

There are two general approaches to movement rehabilitation. The first advocates bringing movement patterns as close to "normal" as possible. Along these lines, for example, patients with Parkinson's disease are trained to walk taking larger steps rather than using their typical shuffling gait (Morris, Iansek, Summers, & Matyas, 1995). The second approach assumes that functionally optimal movement patterns may well be different in persons with a neurological or other chronic disorder as compared to unimpaired persons. According to this view, shuffling gait in patients with Parkinson's disease may be optimal in a sense that it minimizes the transient torques acting on the body during walking and therefore presents a smaller challenge to the impaired system of postural control. Patients with Parkinson's disease are physically able and can be encouraged to take larger steps in a friendly and predictable laboratory environment. However, taking such steps in the much less predictable street may not be wise.

According to these two views, different aspects in the role of a therapist or a parent can be emphasized:

- teaching a person who demonstrates atypical, clumsy movements "correct movement patterns," or
- providing assisting tools and directing adaptive processes so as to optimize functionally important behaviors.

A number of factors can lead us to question the former approach. First, there is no general definition for a "correct movement pattern." "Correctness" and "normality" are commonly used misnomers that do not help us understand biological phenomena and are usually misleading. Second, our knowledge of the processes of motor coordination is so limited and fragmented that it would be extremely presumptuous to even try to formulate general rules for how people should and should not move. Third, external motor patterns are consequences of complex interactions among many subsystems within the body and also external factors acting on the body. Therefore, even if an atypical person generates the same control patterns within the central nervous system, external patterns of movements are likely to be different from those seen in the general population.

There are potential complications within the second approach as well. For example, if the central nervous system of a person with DS is allowed to find optimal motor patterns on its own, without any external help, it may settle down in a local optimum with respect to a function. Further exploration may be stopped due to such factors as fatigue (or even pain), avoidance of potential risk, and lack of abilities to predict long-term effects of different motor strategies. Consequently, such a person will never discover that there may be a much better solution beyond a nearby ridge. Thus, an important role of a therapist is to encourage continual exploration, including exercise through discomfort, even if it leads to temporary deterioration of function. On the one hand, the central nervous system has the advantage of "knowing" more about its actual state and about the available control means and strategies. On the other hand, the therapist knows more about possible long-term effects of chosen strategies and what goals may ultimately be achievable.

Initial studies examining the effects of prolonged practice in persons with DS have provided optimistic results demonstrating that considerable improvement can occur even in simple tasks. Remember that the differences between typical motor performance indices in control subjects and in subjects with DS increase with an increase in task complexity. Therefore, one might expect an even larger capacity for improvement in more complex, functionally significant tasks. However, there are two issues to consider. First, it remains to be demonstrated that similar improvement in motor performance can be observed as a result of practice at more natural, multijoint tasks. Second, it is possible that any improvement may be limited to particular groups of tasks used during practice and may not be transferred to other tasks, in particular to functionally important everyday activities. What good is a dramatic improvement in the performance of a specialized laboratory test if it is applicable only to a very narrow range of similar tasks?

The aforementioned safety catch is likely to prevent persons with DS from exploring different means and different motor coordination opportunities to solve everyday motor tasks. However, it seems that this exploration is the only way to let the central nervous system discover new and better solutions that can be used to solve everyday motor problems.

Conclusions

Two major strategies are offered as potential solutions to these motor problems. The first is to try to avoid the emergence and fixation of safe motor stereotypes. The second is to try to encourage exploration of alternative solutions if safe patterns have already been established.

Given the first strategy, early intervention seems to be the most promising and powerful tool. The earlier a baby with DS is encouraged to explore different motor solutions, the higher is the probability that this exploratory activity will enable the baby's central nervous system to discover more challenging but also more efficient general rules of motor coordinations (sets of CNS priorities).

Consistent practice seems to be effective for improvement of the performance of motor task in persons with DS. However, if exploration of alternative solutions is to be encouraged, practice tasks need to be designed accordingly. For example, practice with an element of unpredictability in task parameters (such as the action of unexpected perturbing forces or unexpected changes in goals) may be effective in encouraging persons with DS to explore different solutions and find better optima. Our limited laboratory experience suggests also that, irrespective of the complexity of the task, it should remain fun, promote interest and competitiveness, and never turn into boring, tedious repetition.

Summary

It is possible that new and emerging technologies, such as virtual environments, will help provide persons with DS and therapists practically unlimited opportunity for exploratory behaviors without the adverse effects of pain or temporary deterioration of function. Virtual reality could also be used to simulate environments with unexpectedly changing goals, external forces, and so on. However, to realize these goals one needs to be able to represent important variables in virtual environments and also provide realistic sensory feedback, such as about "external forces" and "target locations." As we have already discussed, the question of which variables are important is not trivial. In everyday behavior, people are likely to try to optimize complex functions consisting of a number of components related to ultimate success in the task at hand, including lack of negative interference with other tasks, comfort, and even aesthetics. Formal representation of these components is likely to represent a major problem. On the other hand, to develop adequate sensory corrections, the central nervous system needs to experience a variety of sensations that emerge during repetitions of a motor task under varying conditions. So, until virtual reality can simulate adequate sensations, its usefulness in the elaboration of sensory corrections is likely to be limited. Our present knowledge of sensory-motor integration is insufficient to suggest which components of sensation are necessary and sufficient. Thus, a number of hidden obstacles remain on the way to optimization of special education programs using virtual environments.

Although there may be no definitive answers to many of the questions posed here, I would like to emphasize the optimistic messages of this overview:

- Practice does lead to a dramatic improvement of motor performance of persons with DS.
- The room for improvement seems to be larger in DS than in the general population.

- Progress in neurophysiology and technology is likely to improve our understanding of "clumsy movements" in DS and help optimize special education programs.

References

Almeida, G.L., Corcos, D.M., & Latash, M.L. (1994). Practice and transfer effects during fast single joint elbow movements in individuals with Down syndrome. *Physical Therapy, 74,* 1000-1016.

Anson, J.G. (1992). Neuromotor control and Down syndrome. In J.J. Summers (Ed.), *Approaches to the study of motor control and learning* (pp. 387-412). Amsterdam: North-Holland.

Arshavsky, Y.I., Gelfand, I.M., & Orlovsky, G.N. (1986). *Cerebellum and rhythmical movements.* Berlin: Springer-Verlag.

Aruin, A.S., & Almeida, G.L. (1996). A coactivation strategy in anticipatory postural adjustments in persons with Down syndrome. *Motor Control, 1,* 178-191.

Aruin, A.S., Almeida, G.L., & Latash, M.L. (1996). Organization of a simple two-joint synergy in individuals with Down syndrome. *American Journal of Mental Retardation, 101,* 256-268.

Bellugi, U., Bihrle, A., Jernigan, T., Trauner, D., & Doherty, S. (1990). Neuropsychological, neurological, and neuroanatomical profile of Williams syndrome. *American Journal of Medical Genetics, 6* (Suppl.), 115-125.

Berkinblit, M.B., Feldman, A.G., & Fukson, O.I. (1986). Adaptability of innate motor patterns and motor control mechanisms. *Behavioral and Brain Sciences, 9,* 585-638.

Bernstein, N.A. (1947). *On the construction of movements.* Moscow: State Medical Publishing House.

Bernstein, N.A. (1967). *The co-ordination and regulation of movements.* Oxford: Pergamon Press.

Berntson, G.G., & Torello, M.W. (1982). The paleocerebellum and the integration of behavioral function. *Physiological Psychology, 10,* 2-12.

Bloedel, J.R. (1992). Functional heterogeneity with structural homogeneity: How does the cerebellum operate? *Behavioral and Brain Sciences, 15,* 666-678.

Carr, J. (1970). Mental and motor development in young mongol children. *Journal of Mental Deficiency Research, 14,* 205-218.

Cole, K.J., Abbs, J.H., & Turner, G.S. (1988). Deficits in the production of grip force in Down Syndrome. *Developmental Medicine and Child Neurology, 30,* 752-758.

Corcos, D.M. (1991). Strategies underlying the control of disordered movement. *Physical Therapy, 71,* 36-49.

Crepel, F., Hemart, N., Jaillard, D., & Daniel, H. (1996). Cellular mechanisms of long-term depression in the cerebellum. *Behavioral and Brain Sciences, 19,* 347-353.

Crome, L.C., & Stern, J. (1967). *Pathology of mental retardation.* London: Churchill.

Elliott, D., & Weeks, D.J. (1990). Cerebral specialization and the control of oral and limb movements for individuals with Down's syndrome. *Journal of Motor Behavior, 22,* 6-18.

Feldman, A.G., & Levin, M.F. (1995). The origin and use of positional frames of reference in motor control. *Behavioral and Brain Sciences, 18,* 723-804.

Fishler, K. (1975). Mental development in mosaic Down syndrome as compared with trisomy 21. In R. Koch & F. de la Cruz (Eds.), *Down syndrome (mongolism): Research, prevention, and management* (pp. 87-98). New York: Brunner/Mazel.

Fishler, K., Share, J., & Koch, R. (1964). Adaptation of Gesell development scales for the evaluation of development in children with Down syndrome (mongolism). *American Journal of Mental Deficiency, 68,* 642-646.

Flanders, M., Tillery, S.I.H., & Soechting, J.F. (1992). Early stages in a sensorimotor transformation. *Behavioral and Brain Sciences, 15,* 309-362.

Fuhr, P., Cohen, L.G., Dang, N., Findley, T.W., Haghighi, S., Oro, J., & Hallett, M. (1992). Physiological analysis of motor reorganization following lower limb amputation. *Electroencephalography and Clinical Neurophysiology, 85,* 53-60.

Gelfand, I.M., & Tsetlin, M.L. (1971). On mathematical modeling of the mechanisms of the central nervous system. In I.M. Gelfand, V.S. Gurfinkel, S.V. Fomin, & M.L. Tsetlin (Eds.), *Models of the structural-functional organization of certain biological systems* (pp. 9-26). Cambridge, MA: MIT Press. (Original work published 1966; Moscow: Nauka.)

Georgopoulos, A.P. (1986). On reaching. *Annual Review of Neuroscience, 9,* 147-170.

Gottlieb, G.L., Corcos, D.M., & Agarwal, G.C. (1989). Strategies for the control of voluntary movements with one mechanical degree of freedom. *Behavioral and Brain Sciences, 12,* 189-250.

Haley, S.M. (1986). Postural reactions in infants with Down syndrome. Relationship to motor milestone development and age. *Physical Therapy, 66,* 17-22.

Henderson, S.E., Morris, J., & Frith, V. (1981). The motor deficit in Down's syndrome children: A problem of timing? *Journal of Child Psychology and Psychiatry, 22,* 233-245.

Houk, J.C., Buckingham, J.T., & Barto, A.G. (1996). Models of the cerebellum and motor learning. *Behavioral and Brain Sciences, 19,* 368-383.

Jenkins, W.M., Merzenich, M.M., & Recanzone, G. (1990). Neocortical representation dynamics in adult primates: Implications for neuropsychology. *Neuropsychologia, 28,* 573-584.

Keele, S.W., & Ivry, R. (1990). Does the cerebellum provide a common computation for diverse tasks? A timing hypothesis. *Annals of the New York Academy of Sciences, 608,* 179-211.

Kelso, J.A.S. (1995). *Dynamic patterns: The self-organization of brain and behavior.* Cambridge, MA: MIT Press.

Kerr, R., & Blais, C. (1985). Motor skill acquisition by individuals with Down Syndrome. *American Journal of Mental Deficiency, 90,* 313-318.

Kew, J.J.M., Ridding, M.C., Rothwell, J.C., Passingham, R.E., Leigh, P.N., Sooriakumaran, S., Frackowiak, R.S.J., & Brooks, D.J. (1994). Reorganization of cortical blood flow and transcranial magnetic stimulation maps in human subjects after upper limb amputation. *Journal of Neurophysiology, 72,* 2517-2524.

Kopp, C.B. (1979). Perspectives on infant motor development. In M.H. Bornstein & W. Kessen (Eds.), *Psychological development from infancy: Image to intention* (pp. 9-35). Hillsdale, NJ: Erlbaum.

Latash, M.L. (1992). Motor control in Down syndrome: The role of adaptation and practice. *Journal of Developmental and Physical Disability, 4,* 227-261.

Latash, M.L. (1993). *Control of human movement.* Champaign, IL: Human Kinetics.

Latash, M.L. (1996). How does our brain make its choices? In M.L. Latash & M.T. Turvey (Eds.), *Dexterity and its development* (pp. 277-304). Mahwah, NJ: Erlbaum.

Latash, M.L., Almeida, G.L., & Corcos, D.M. (1993). Pre-programmed reactions in individuals with Down syndrome: The effects of instruction and predictability of the perturbation. *Archives of Physical Medicine and Rehabilitation, 73*, 391-399.

Latash, M.L., & Anson, J.G. (1996). What are normal movements in atypical populations? *Behavioral and Brain Sciences, 19*, 55-106.

Latash, M.L., & Corcos, D.M. (1991). Kinematic and electromyographic characteristics of single-joint movements of individuals with Down Syndrome. *American Journal of Mental Retardation, 96*, 189-201.

Linden, D.J. (1996). Cerebellar long-term depression as investigated in a cell culture preparation. *Behavioral and Brain Sciences, 19*, 339-346.

Massion, J. (1992). Movement, posture and equilibrium: Interaction and coordination. *Progress in Neurobiology, 38*, 35-56.

McIntyre, J., Stratta, F., & Lacquaniti, F. (1997). Viewer-centered frame of reference for pointing to memorized targets in three-dimensional space. *Journal of Neurophysiology, 78*, 1601-1618.

Merzenich, M.M., Nelson, R.J., Stryker, M.S., Cynader, M.S., Schoppman, A., & Zook, J.M. (1984). Somatosensory cortical map changes following digit amputation in adult monkeys. *Journal of Comparative Neurology, 224*, 591-605.

Molnar, G.E. (1978). Analysis of motor disorder in retarded infants and young children. *American Journal of Mental Deficiency, 83*, 213-222.

Morris, A.F., Vaughan, S.E., & Vaccaro, P. (1982). Measurements of neuromuscular tone and strength in Down's syndrome children. *Journal of Mental Deficiency Research, 26*, 41-46.

Morris, M.E., Iansek, R., Summers, J.J., & Matyas, T.A. (1995). Motor control considerations for the rehabilitation of gait in Parkinson's disease. In D.J. Glencross & J.P. Piek (Eds.), *Motor control and sensory motor integration: Issues and directions* (pp. 61-96). Amsterdam: North-Holland.

Rarick, G.L., Dobbins, D.A., & Broadhead, G.G. (1976). *The motor domain and its correlates in educated handicapped children.* Englewood Cliffs, NJ: Prentice-Hall.

Schöner, G., & Kelso, J.A.S. (1988). Dynamic pattern generation in behavioral and neural systems. *Science, 239*, 1513-1520.

Shumway-Cook, A., & Woollacott, M.H. (1985). Dynamics of postural control in the child with Down Syndrome. *Physical Therapy, 65*, 1315-1322.

Stein, R.B. (1982). What muscle variable(s) does the nervous system control in limb movements? *Behavioral and Brain Sciences, 5*, 535-577.

Thach, W.T. (1996). On the specific role of the cerebellum in motor learning and cognition: Clues from PET activation and lesion studies in man. *Behavioral and Brain Sciences, 19*, 411-431.

Turvey, M.T. (1990). Coordination. *American Psychologist, 45*, 938-953.

Wagenaar, R.C., & Van Emmerik, R.E.A. (1996). Dynamics of movement disorders. *Human Movement Science, 15*, 161-176.

Author Note

The preparation of this chapter was supported in part by an NIH grant, NS-35032. The author would like to thank all the persons with Down syndrome who participated in his studies and their parents for their exceptional patience and cooperation.

10

Motor Development in Down Syndrome: A Longitudinal Perspective

Anne Jobling

Schonell Special Education Research Centre
University of Queensland

Mark Mon-Williams

Department of Human Movement Studies
University of Queensland
and School of Psychology
University of St. Andrews

Key words

motor development ◆ intervention ◆ balance ◆ reaction time ◆ fine motor skills ◆ speed ◆ coordination ◆ strength ◆ dexterity ◆ agility

The progressive monitoring of age-related changes in skilled movement provides a developmental perspective of motor development. Longitudinal monitoring is especially important for children with Down syndrome (DS), as extant studies offer only limited information about the progressive attainment of movement skill. A catalog of charted attainment may show individual patterns of change for some movement skills but stability for other motor behavior. As new skills are built on previously acquired proficiency, it is vital that we understand individual patterns of change and stability in the development of motor ability.

There are a reasonable number of studies that have documented changes in motor performance as children without developmental problems progress to "higher levels of proficiency" (Gallahue, 1989; Payne & Isaacs, 1991). In contrast, there is only limited knowledge about the motor development of individuals with intellectual disabilities (Henderson, 1985; Newell, 1985). Those studies that do exist suggest that children with intellectual disabilities demonstrate a low level of proficiency in their motor performance (Bruininks, 1974; Rarick, Dobbins, & Broadhead, 1976). Rarick et al.'s study provided a cross-sectional analysis of the motor proficiency of children with mild to moderate levels of intellectual disability in two age groupings: 6 to 9 years and 10 to 13 years. This extensive study found that the children with intellectual disabilities showed poorer performance than their peers in muscular strength and power, balance, flexibility, and gross and fine motor coordination. These researchers also noted a significantly greater range of individual differences in motor proficiency among the children with intellectual disabilities.

Developmental Progress of Infants and Young Children With Down Syndrome

A number of studies have investigated age-related changes in the motor development of infants and young children with DS. In infancy, these studies are frequently related to motor milestones such as sitting and walking. Data have generally been collected using clinical measurements and observations and a range of standardized assessment tools, including the Griffith Scales (Griffith, 1970), the Gesell Scales (Gesell & Amatruda, 1941), and the Bayley Scales of Infant Development (Bayley, 1969), the latter being the most frequently used. It is widely thought that the attainment of motor milestones is delayed in infants with DS even following intervention (Eipper & Azen, 1978; Fishler, Share, & Koch, 1964; Ramsay & Piper, 1980; Schneider & Brannen, 1984). There is, however, considerable variability in the rate at which those with DS attain motor milestones (LaVeck & Brehm, 1978; Sayers, Cowden, Newton, Warren, & Eason, 1996), and Carr (1975) has suggested that the level of variability is greater than that observed in normally developing children. In addition, some studies have highlighted infants with DS who have reached motor milestones within the expected normative period (Berry, Andrews, & Gunn, 1980; Berry, Gunn, & Andrews, 1984; Share, Koch, Webb, & Graliker, 1964).

The delays observed in the motor development of infants with DS have been compared with the progression of mental milestones (Eipper & Azen, 1978; Harris, 1981; LaVeck & LaVeck, 1977; Ramsay & Piper, 1980; Rauh et al., 1991; Schneider & Brannen, 1984). These studies have indicated that mental development seems to increase with age in DS, while there appears to be a co-occurrent deceleration of the infants' motor development. The decrease in motor development, however, appears to be particularly associated with the degree of hypotonia observed, especially prior to walking (Carr, 1975; Harris, 1981). It has been suggested that gender differences exist, with girls' movement skills being superior to those of boys in the early years (Connolly, Morgan, & Russell, 1984; Connolly, Morgan, Russell, & Richardson, 1980; LaVeck & LaVeck, 1977), but a number of studies have not found gender differences (e.g., Eipper & Azen, 1978; Harris, 1983; Neser, Molteno, & Knight, 1989; Ramsay & Piper, 1980; Sharav & Shlomo, 1986).

The developmental sequence of motor milestones has also been of interest to researchers: that is, is the pattern and/or sequence of the slower motor development the same as that for typically developing infants? This question has generally been addressed using either the Bayley Scales of Infant Development (Bayley, 1969) or the Uzgiris-Hunt Scales (Uzgiris & Hunt, 1975). Several studies have reported that the motor development of the infants with DS paralleled that of the assessment scales, with hypotonia again being a factor that altered the normality of this pattern (Champion, 1987; Cicchetti & Sroufe, 1976; Harris, 1983). Dunst (1988) reported that infants with DS made transitional progress through the Uzgiris-Hunt sequences of development, albeit at a much slower rate than normally developing infants. An observational study has also reported the normal sequence of motor development, although variability was again evident (MacLean, Ellis, Galbreath, Halpern, & Baumeister, 1991). Further evidence for a pattern of normal developmental sequences been obtained by an examination of the pass/fail pattern of tasks in assessment profiles. Dyer, Gunn, Raugh, and Berry (1990) and Rauh et al. (1991) analyzed the age at which 707 infants with DS passed or failed the Bayley Scales of Infant Development (BSID) test items. The results indicated that the developmental path broadly reflected the BSID scale. It was reported, however, that motor items that required aspects of strength and balance (such as standing and walking) developed more slowly than other motor behavior and that the infants with DS showed a far higher degree of variability. In summary, researchers have found the normal sequencing of motor development in infants with DS, although the pattern of development is slower and the variability higher.

Intervention Programs

One important issue in longitudinal studies that explore the progressive attainment of motor skills is the impact of intervention. The benefits available from maintaining a continued program of intervention in young children with DS have been demonstrated by Connolly and colleagues, who have suggested that therapy programs accelerate motor gains in children with DS (Connolly et al., 1980; Connolly et al., 1984).

This notion was supported by Lydic (1980) who stressed that intervention needed to be tailored individually to each child. It has been suggested that parental participation is an important aspect of programming (Connolly et al., 1980; Dmitriev, 1971; Reed, Pueschel, Schnell, & Cronk, 1980; Sanz-Aparicio & Menendez-Balana, 1992; Share & French, 1982). It should be noted, however, that although improvements may occur in the motor development of children with DS, motor proficiency still falls below an acceptable level following intervention (e.g., Fewell & Oelwein, 1991).

Environments

Prior to the 1970s, most data regarding the motor progress of infants and children with DS had been obtained from those in institutional environments. Since then, however, longitudinal studies by Carr (1975) and Berry et al. (Berry et al., 1980; Berry et al., 1984) have begun to compare children who have lived at home with their parents since birth with information available from those children who have lived in an institution. Carr (1975) reported that by 36 months, the home-reared children with DS had passed twice as many items related to walking as those children from institutional environments. Accelerated progress was also reported by Berry et al. (Berry et al., 1980; Berry et al., 1984), with two girls and one boy walking within the accepted time frame for normally developing children. These results not only indicated the wide range in motor milestone achievements of infants with DS, but confirmed reports (Centerwall & Centerwall, 1960; Donoghue, Kirman, Bullmore, Laban, & Abbas, 1970) that young children with DS raised at home are likely to walk earlier than those placed in institutions.

Summary

Research studies and program reports have demonstrated that infants and young children with DS have a range of delays in the attainment of motor milestones. On the other hand, the motor development of young children with DS appears to progress through a similar sequence to that observed in normally developing children. The influence of the home environment and specific early intervention appear to be important for continual progress and the amelioration of delays in motor development. It is difficult to draw definitive conclusions, however, due to differences across studies that have typically used small samples of children over large age ranges.

Developmental Progress Into the School-Age Years

A number of studies have explored how young children with DS progress into the school years. Consideration has been given to the rate at which the children's motor skills progress to higher levels of complexity and proficiency (Connolly et al., 1984; Connolly & Michael, 1986; Connolly, Morgan, Russell, & Fulliton, 1993; Shea,

1987). Studies have also compared the patterns and sequences of motor development in children with and without developmental problems (Henderson, Morris, & Frith, 1981; Messerly, 1981; O'Brien & Hayes, 1989).

Shea (1987) reported a significant relation between motor performance and hypotonia in the early years but found that this correlation weakened as the children grew older. The children studied by Shea demonstrated a low level of proficiency in tasks involving balance and strength such as ball playing and locomotion (run, hop, and jump). Connolly and colleagues (1980, 1984, 1986) used the Bruininks Oseretsky Test of Motor Proficiency (Bruininks, 1978) to evaluate performance over time and reported that children with DS had particular difficulties with tasks involving balance, run-agility, visual-motor control, and response speed. In contrast, more proficient performance was seen in tasks that required upper-limb coordination and strength. In a follow-up assessment, Connolly et al. (1993) reported that running speed, balance, and reaction time continued to be problem areas for some of the children. Table 10.1 summarizes the data collected by Connolly et al. (1993).

The fine motor skills of school-aged children have been a neglected aspect of DS motor research (but see Hogg & Moss, 1983, and Moss & Hogg, 1983). This is cause for concern, especially given the fact that the demonstration of educational achievement relies predominantly on handwriting and typing. These classroom skills were explored by Ziviani and Elkins (1993) in a preliminary study of children (mean age 10.75 years) who were involved with the longitudinal study at the University of Queensland (Crombie, 1994; Jobling & Gunn, 1995). Ziviani and Elkins provided some qualitative clinical observations and interview information on the children's

Table 10.1 Overview of the BOTMP Results

	Connolly et al. (1984) n = 15	Connolly & Michael (1986) n = 12	Connolly et al. (1993) n = 10
Mean CA	8.90	9.60	16.30
Mean IQ	52.40	54.50	40.10
Subtest 1	< 4.17	4.17*	5.42
Subtest 2	4.00	4.33*	4.92
Subtest 3	5.17	5.17*	5.92
Subtest 4	5.92	5.92*	7.42
Subtest 5	5.92	5.92*	6.67
Subtest 6	< 4.17	< 4.17*	4.92
Subtest 7	4.42	4.42*	5.92
Subtest 8	5.42	5.42*	6.42

*Median scores
Data from Connolly & Michael, 1986, and Connolly et al., 1984, 1993.

handwriting and keyboard skills. There was variability across the general performance of the children as well as in specific aspects of the writing task such as legibility and speed. It is interesting to note that the authors reported that both the motoric actions and keyboard knowledge were lacking in the children with DS, suggesting that intervention for such skills needs to be directed toward both the motor and the cognitive domain.

Youn and Youn (1991) reported that a specific manual perceptual educational program produced positive short-term results in children with DS. Dyer (1994) has reported motor performance benefits in 10 children with DS (mean age 13.7 years) after a 13-week motor skills and fitness program.

Two Australian Studies

Little information exists on the progress of motor proficiency through adolescence in DS even though motor development must be considered a lifelong process (Burns & Gunn, 1993). Two recent studies have attempted to explore motor proficiency through adolescence in DS. These studies followed a group of children with DS through the ages of 10 to 16 years (Jobling & Gunn, 1995). The children ($n = 105$) lived in Brisbane, Australia, with their families (Berry et al., 1980; Berry et al., 1984). It has been argued that these children are highly representative (constituting nearly 90%) of the 10- to 16-year-olds with DS living in Brisbane (Bailey, Gunn, Tovey, & Jobling, 1989; Crombie, 1994). Most of the group attended early intervention programs and all had access to school physical education programs. The cytogenetic status was primarily trisomy 21.

Over a period of 10 years, data were collected continually using the Stanford-Binet Intelligence Scale (Terman & Merrill, 1972), height and weight measures, a family environment scale (Moos & Moos, 1986), and school physical education program details. The data that this chapter will focus on were collected using the Bruininks Oseretsky Test of Motor Proficiency (BOTMP) with clinical notes. The BOTMP provides point scores for the subtests, and these scores can be converted into age-equivalent scores. These scores indicate the chronological age at which the observed level of performance would normally be attained. The BOTMP consists of eight subtests (each of which contain a number of different tasks or items) designed to explore the following areas of motor performance:

1. Running speed and agility
2. Balance
3. Bilateral coordination
4. Strength
5. Upper-limb coordination
6. Response speed
7. Visual-motor control
8. Upper-limb speed and dexterity

Subtest 1 measures the speed at which children can run 13.7 m, pick up an object, and return to the start. Subtest 2 explores performance on a number of balance items, such as standing on one leg with eyes open and with eyes closed. Subtest 3 consists of items that require different limbs to be temporally coordinated (e.g., synchronized tapping of the finger and the foot on the same side and the opposite side of the body). Subtest 4 measures performance on some tasks that require strength (e.g., sit-ups and push-ups). Subtest 5 has items that explore ball skill and manual dexterity (e.g., finger opposition). Subtest 6 provides a measure of reaction time to a simple stimulus. Subtests 7 and 8 both test performance on a number of tasks requiring manual control. The tasks in subtest 7 involve cutting, drawing, and copying, but allow the children to complete the task in their own time. The tasks in subtest 8 generally need a sequence of manual movements (e.g., posting coins through a slot) and require the task to be completed in a particular time (i.e., temporal constraints exist). It should be noted that the allocation of a task to a specific subtest is somewhat arbitrary within the BOTMP. For example, the item "Drawing a line through a straight path with preferred hand" is placed within subtest 7 (visual-motor control), whereas "Drawing vertical lines with preferred hand" is placed within subtest 8 (upper-limb speed and dexterity). Furthermore, the subtests are designed to provide a global measure of performance so that the number of tasks (items) varies between the subtests.

The various subtests of the BOTMP have been designed to explore specific areas of movement. It should be noted, however, that despite the titles attached to the subtests, they do not yield information on any underlying control deficits. For example, the visual-motor control subtest uses a number of tasks that require eye-hand coordination (e.g., cutting out a shape). Poor performance on such a task does not allow us to ascribe the failure to a deficit in visual-motor control per se. Suggesting that such dysfunction exists is merely to propose a diffuse hypothesis as to the nature of eye-hand coordination. Even if we accepted the validity of a specific process, understanding why a particular task causes difficulty hinges on finding a definitive and exclusive test of that process. The purpose of the BOTMP is not, therefore, to discover the underlying causes of reduced movement performance but rather to time-stamp the children's motor skill acquisition in terms of their current performance with reference to chronological norms. Assessments of this type are essential to monitor stability and change within a research population and supplement more specific research measures or direct appraisals of a specific intervention. There is thus considerable appeal in using a single movement battery test across a research population over time.

The aim of the first study was to (1) document the parameters of the developmental trajectories (changes over time) for motor proficiency; (2) provide a profile of the strengths and weaknesses of the children with DS; and (3) explore the influence of specific characteristics of the individual children on movement performance. The second study was carried out to explore further the performance of the children on tasks that required postural balance. The studies were designed to explore the development of movement skill from middle childhood into adolescence (Jobling & Gunn, 1995).

Study 1

In study 1, the assessments were considered in both a cross-sectional and longitudinal design. Various factors (including illness, school attendances, residential moves, and death) made it difficult to assess all the study children at every age level.

In the first part of study 1, 205 assessments (119 boys and 86 girls) were grouped into four restricted age groups with mean ages of 10 years 7 months, 12 years 7 months, 14 years 6 months, and 16 years 6 months, respectively (see table 10.2). Assessments that fell at ages outside these group ranges were not used. There was only one assessment of each child in each age group. In the second part of study 1, all available assessments (263) were used within a cluster analysis. In the third part of study 1, analyses were carried out on longitudinal data from 29 children who had been assessed at three different stages (10.5, 12.5, and 16.5 years). The relation among mental age, chronological age, and motor performance was further explored using a group of 81 children with a restricted age range (11.5 to 15.25 years) from

Table 10.2 Chronological Age and IQ Scores for Each Age Group in Study 1

	Chronological age (years)	IQ
Age group 1 (n = 53; 31 boys and 22 girls)		
Range	10.17-10.75	35-68
Mean	10.55	48
Median	10.58	48
SD	0.14	8
Age group 2 (n = 63; 35 boys and 28 girls)		
Range	12.17-12.83	30-62
Mean	12.56	46
Median	12.58	46
SD	0.13	8
Age group 3 (n = 38; 22 boys and 16 girls)		
Range	14.08-14.75	32-59
Mean	14.51	43
Median	14.50	42
SD	0.14	7
Age group 4 (n = 51; 31 boys and 20 girls)		
Range	16.0-17.17	28-52
Mean	16.53	39
Median	16.50	38
SD	0.26	6

the original sample (*n* = 105). The second study used 58 children from the original sample.

Point scores were used in the statistical analyses because both age-equivalent and standard scores were at base level for many children on several of the subtests. Median scores were used to represent age-equivalent group scores rather than means.

Parameters of Developmental Trajectories. Changes in the children's age-equivalent scores (AE) over time are presented in table 10.3 and figure 10.1.

Table 10.3 Age-Equivalent BOTMP Scores for Subsets Across Four Age Groups: Study 1

Subtest	Age 10.5 (*n* = 53)	Age 12.5 (*n* = 63)	Age 14.5 (*n* = 38)	Age 16.5 (*n* = 51)
Running speed and agility				
Median	5.92	5.92	5.92	8.92
Range	<4.17-8.92	<4.17-15.92	<4.17-15.92	<4.17-15.92
Balance				
Median	<4.17	4.17	4.17	4.17
Range	<4.17-5.42	<4.17-5.17	<4.17-6.92	<4.17-8.17
Bilateral coordination				
Median	4.42	5.42	5.67	5.92
Range	<4.17-6.92	<4.17-7.42	<4.17-10.42	<4.17-7.42
Strength				
Median	5.17	5.31	5.67	6.17
Range	4.17-8.92	<4.17-9.42	<4.17-15.42	<4.17-15.42
Upper-limb coordination				
Median	5.67	6.67	6.92	7.42
Range	<4.17-7.67	<4.17-10.42	<4.17-12.67	<4.17-14.42
Response speed				
Median	4.17	4.92	4.92	5.67
Range	<4.17-6.92	<4.17-9.92	<4.17-7.92	<4.17-11.67
Visual-motor control				
Median	4.92	5.42	6.42	6.92
Range	4.17-10.17	<4.17-12.92	<4.17-15.92	<4.17-15.92
Upper-limb speed and dexterity				
Median	5.67	6.17	6.67	6.67
Range	<4.17-6.92	<4.17-8.92	<4.17-7.92	<4.17-10.17

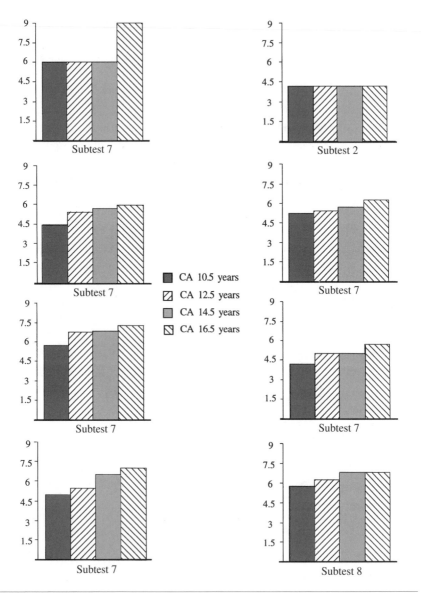

Figure 10.1 Results from study 1. The data (expressed in age-equivalent scores) for the four age groups are shown for each of the eight BOTMP subtests.

A statistically reliable progression in task performance with chronological age over the duration of the study was found for each subtest. On the other hand, this increase was not uniform across the ages 10.5 to 16.5 years. A reliable increase in performance level on the bilateral coordination, upper-limb coordination, response speed, and upper-limb speed and dexterity was found only when the scores at 10.5 years of age were compared with those at 12.5 years. The other four subtests showed a reliable age effect only between the scores found at 10.5 years and the scores recorded at the 14.5- and 16.5-year levels.

A multiple-regression analysis was carried out to explore whether performance level was predicted by chronological age, mental age, or both. It was found that performance was best predicted by mental age, with chronological age adding reliability only to the prediction of point scores in the upper-limb coordination and upper-limb speed and dexterity subtests. The effect of chronological age in these subtests was found to be due to an improvement in performance between the 10.5- and 12.5-year age levels.

The data from the subtests of the BOTMP showed a wide range in the level of motor proficiency found among children at the same age level. It was also found that the children showed a wide variability on how they performed across the different subtests. These wide variations have been previously reported for children with DS (Anwar, 1981; Hayes & Gunn, 1991; LaVeck & LaVeck, 1977). The data demonstrated individual patterns of change in the participants' motor development and supported Wishart's (1991) statement that "Down syndrome has no uniform impact on developmental progress" (p. 81).

Profiles of Strengths and Weaknesses.   A cluster analysis was used to discover whether the children showed different strengths and weaknesses on the subtests. All available BOTMP assessments (n = 263; 145 boys and 118 girls) were used. The analyses revealed two groups who showed reliably different age-equivalent scores for running speed and agility ($F(1, 259) = 358.4, p < .001$), balance ($F(1, 259) = 41.91$, $p < .001$), and visual-motor control ($F(1, 261) = 64.48, p < .001$). Figure 10.2 illustrates the differences between two children: one who fell into the first cluster (left column) and one who fell into the second cluster (right column).

The first cluster with 183 assessments (117 boys and 66 girls) had a higher score for running speed and agility and a lower score for balance and visual-motor control when compared with the second cluster of 80 assessments (28 boys and 52 girls). A χ^2 test showed that there were reliably more girls than boys in the second cluster (χ^2 = 17.69, $p < .001$). It should be noted that despite the differences between the groups, both clusters showed poor scores on the balance subtest. Most participants tended to stay in one cluster across assessments, and changes in cluster membership could often be explained by clinical observations. For example, one girl with scores in cluster 2 for four assessments from 10 to 16 years had her hips pinned at the age of 10. Another girl who had been in cluster 1 had been scoring highly for running speed and agility but suffered a stroke that affected her mobility and fell into the second cluster two years later.

Across the study, balance emerged as the most characteristic area of weakness, though at the youngest age group bilateral coordination and response speed also caused difficulties. Although significantly delayed in balance, the children and adolescents could attain reasonable levels of proficiency on running speed and agility,

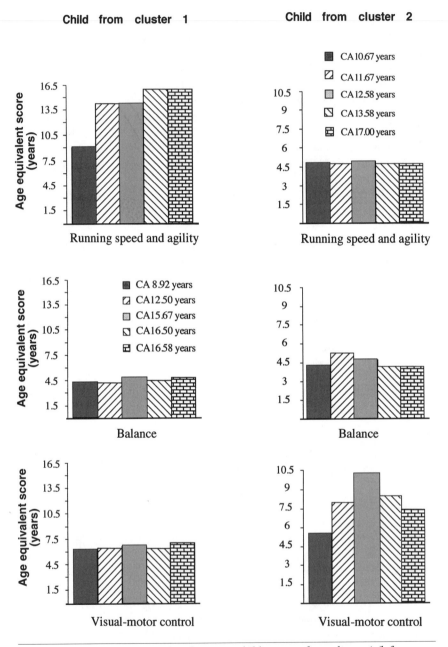

Figure 10.2 Representative data from two children, one from cluster 1 (left column) and one from cluster 2 (right column). Reliable differences between the groups were found for the three illustrated subtests. Cluster 1 showed reliably superior performance on running speed and agility but reliably lower performance on balance and visual-motor control.

236

upper-limb coordination (especially boys), and visual-motor control (especially girls). Several children in each age group scored at or above their chronological age on these subtests by 16 years. Figure 10.3 illustrates the subtest scores for a 16-year-old boy who showed good performance on the running speed and agility subtest.

An examination of the participants' performance on individual items within each of the BOTMP subtests indicated which types of tasks caused the most problems for individuals with DS. The majority of items within the response speed subtest and items within other subtests that required a response related to an external event (such as subtest 5, item 6: "Touching a swinging ball with preferred hand") were difficult for both the younger children and the adolescents. The study participants seemed to find it almost impossible to respond to the speed of the stimulus event together with the spatial requirements of touching the ball. At chronological age 16.5 years (mean mental age 5.38), the children's median age-equivalent score for response speed was only 5.67 years, and only 10 children (7 boys and 3 girls) scored above zero on item 6 of the upper-limb coordination subtest. Similar observations have been made by Frith and Frith (1974) and Henderson et al. (1981).

Certain individual tasks caused special difficulties for the children. The items "Touching thumb to fingertips with eyes closed" and "Pivoting thumb and index finger" in subtests 3 and 5, respectively, caused the participants particular problems. The participants generally performed poorly on tasks that involved asymmetrical activities or on tasks that required complex sequences of a somewhat contrived nature. Examples include "Tapping with foot and finger on opposite side synchro-nized," "Jumping in place with leg and arm on opposite side synchronized," and "Jumping up and touching heels with hands." These difficulties are consistent with the general idea that the movement responses of people with DS are less lateralized (Elliott, 1990).

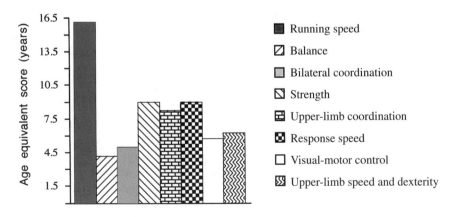

Figure 10.3 Illustrative movement profile of a 16.5-year-old child who showed a chronological age-appropriate level of performance for running speed and agility but performed at a level below chronological age for all other subtests.

In comparison to the other strength subtest items, the children and adolescents demonstrated a significant lack of proficiency on knee push-ups (item 3a) or full push-ups (item 3b). Only five boys could maintain the body position required for item 3b.

Child Characteristics. As differences in gender and mental age were present in the composition of the four age groups, longitudinal data were used to examine within-child characteristics. Children assessed at 10.5 years, 12.5 years, and 16.5 years were used (n = 29 children [16 boys and 13 girls] = 87 pairs of BOTMP and Stanford-Binet assessments). These children had been assessed at three of the age levels analyzed in the previous section: 10.5 years, 12.5 years, and 16.5 years. There were no reliable gender differences regarding chronological age or IQ at any of these three age levels. A multivariate analysis of variance with subtest point scores as repeated measures, age level, and gender as factors and mental age as a covariate revealed reliable main effects for gender ($F(1, 79)$ = 14.67, $p < .001$), age level ($F(2, 79)$ = 8.74, $p < .001$), and mental age ($F(1, 79)$ = 105.43, $p < .001$), but no reliable interaction between gender and age level was observed. Follow-up univariate analysis with mental age as the covariate showed that gender effects were significant for three subtests. These were running speed and agility ($F(1, 79)$ = 13.74, $p < .001$), strength ($F(1, 79)$ = 10.13, $p < .005$), and upper-limb coordination ($F(1, 80)$ = 15.29, $p < .001$). Males achieved higher scores than females on all three subtests. The effect of chronological age level was significant for only two subtests: upper-limb coordination ($F(2, 80)$ = 10.24, $p < .001$) and upper-limb speed and dexterity ($F(2, 80)$ = 10.45, $p < .001$). On the other hand, mental age had a significant effect ($p < .001$) on all subtests. Further analyses showed that the chronological age effect was reliable when the two subtests were compared at the 10.5- and 12.5-year levels but not when the subtest scores at 12.5 years were compared with those at 16.5 years. Observational notes made at the time of assessment showed that 12 adolescents (5 boys and 7 girls) had varying degrees of lower-limb abnormalities, particularly hallux abduct valgus, while 14 (5 boys and 9 girls) showed postural problems and gait abnormalities such as in-toeing, slumping forward, head hanging, and shuffling foot movements.

The body mass index (BMI) data revealed that 15 adolescents (8 boys and 7 girls) showed evidence of creeping obesity, with a BMI > 25 by 16 years, with two adolescents (1 boy) reaching the medically significant range BMI > 33. In contrast, one boy lost weight to achieve the desirable level (BMI 22-24 at 16 years) from a BMI score > 25 at 14.5 years. For the total group of children, BMI scores increased across all the age groups of the study, but there was no relation between BMI and BOTMP age-equivalent scores. Specific examination of 21 adolescents (11 boys) who had a BMI > 25 in age group 4 suggested that there was no reliable relation between BOTMP age-equivalent scores and BMI. The mean BMI was higher for girls than boys.

As this analysis of 29 children showed some reliable relations between gender and mental age, the relation was investigated further with a larger sample of children. Only assessments that were undertaken within 10 months of a Stanford-Binet assessment were considered, and the chronological age range was restricted so that the effect of age on the scores was minimized. There were 81 children (44 boys and 37 girls) in this sample (age 11.50 to 15.25 years, mean = 12.68 years; SD = .74 years). Mental-age scores were 2.87 to 7.17 years (mean = 4.86 years, SD = 1.07 years). A multivariate analysis of variance with subtest point scores as repeated measures, gender as an independent variable, and mental age as the covariate showed a significant effect for mental age ($F(1, 78)$ = 66.08; p < .001). Mental age made a significant contribution (p < .001) to all subtest scores. Figure 10.3 (page 237) shows a movement profile for a 16.5-year-old child who demonstrated an age-appropriate level of performance for running speed and agility despite showing reduced performance on all of the other subtests. Follow-up univariate analysis showed a significant gender effect for two subtests, running speed and agility ($F(1, 78)$ = 15.48; p < .001) and strength ($F(1, 78)$ = 17.96; p < .001), with boys scoring higher than girls. Regression equations that included gender, mental age, and chronological age as predictors and a subtest point score as the criterion confirmed that chronological age did not reliably add to the prediction of point scores over this narrowed age range. It was also found that neither the activity participation scores from the Family Environment Scale (Moos & Moos, 1986) nor the BMI scores calculated from height/ weight measures contributed significantly to the regression equations.

Because of the strong predictive relation between mental age and subtest point scores, the possibility that the age-equivalent scores would be close to mental age was investigated. Wilcoxon Signed Ranks testing revealed reliable differences between mental age and age-equivalent scores for all subtests except response speed. Mental age was reliably higher than the age-equivalent score for balance but reliably lower than the age-equivalent scores for the remaining six subtests (figure 10.4).

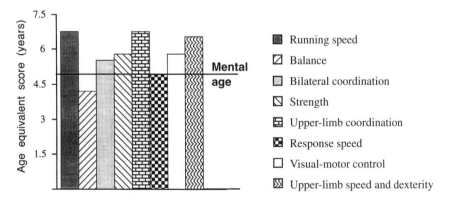

Figure 10.4   Age-equivalent scores on the BOTMP for 81 children with DS. The median mental age is indicated on the graph. The only subtest performance predicted by mental age was response speed. The children showed better performance than expected from mental age on all other subtests, apart from balance where the age-equivalent score was lower than mental age.

Study 2

One of the major conclusions from the first study was that the children with DS demonstrated the most significant and enduring problems with their attainment of balance proficiency. The balancing skill of the children from 10 years to adolescence seemed to plateau at a low level of proficiency (i.e., median age-equivalent score < 4.5 years). From the performance data, there was no evidence of a series of spurts and plateaus in balance development as suggested for normally developing children (Winnick, 1979) nor of any transitional phase during which balance was refined (Woollacott & Shumway-Cook, 1986, 1989). Balancing is a complex activity, and although Shumway-Cook and Woollacott (1985) consider that children with DS can progress with practice, the children in the current study showed persistent difficulties in mastering this skill (especially when comparisons were made with other aspects of the children's motor performance). As balance is integral to skilled behavior, this level of proficiency is of concern as it further handicaps individuals with DS in motor tasks.

The nature of the BOTMP balance tasks has been criticized (Burton & Davis, 1992); so it was decided to further investigate the poor balance evidenced by the children. Study 2 was designed to discover whether the results of the first study were an artifact of the BOTMP items or whether other variables (age, sex, BMI, and mental age) contributed to balance performance. In order to validate the balance data, another movement battery was used. The test employed was the Henderson revision of the Test of Motor Impairment (the TOMI-H, Henderson, 1984). The test explores four different types of movement skill in separate sections: manual dexterity, static balance, dynamic balance, and ball skill. Each section consists of two parts, with each part scoring between 0 and 2 in half-point increments. A score of 0 indicates that the task was successfully carried out in the designated time period, whereas a score of 2 means that the performance of the task did not meet the required standard (either the task was not carried out correctly or was not completed in the necessary time). The total score is then compared with normalized scores for the age group. The test battery provides different tasks for four age groups: 5-6 years (age band 1), 7-8 years (age band 2), 9-10 years (age band 3), and over 11 years old (age band 4). Children are never tested at a level above their chronological age, but if a child fails, testing may be continued at a lower level until a baseline is met. The test also includes a checklist to allow the tester to make concurrent qualitative observations on the manner in which the task was carried out.

The participants in the second study were 58 children and adolescents (31 boys and 27 girls) who had all participated in study 1 and had attained independent walking between the ages of 13 to 60 months. Details of the participants' chronological ages and language ages are provided in table 10.4. An assessment protocol was developed that included the eight balance tasks of the BOTMP, nine balance tasks from the TOMI-H, the Peabody Picture Vocabulary Test-Revised (PPVT-R) (Dunne & Dunn, 1981), BMI scores, and a parental report on bicycle riding. Age bands 1, 2, and 3 TOMI-H items were chosen, as they provided tasks suitable for

Table 10.4   Chronological Age and Receptive-Language Age for Children: Study 2

	Chronological age (years)	Receptive-language age (years)
Range	12.17-20.50	2.42-10.33
Mean	15.67	5.78
Median	15.42	5.67
SD	2.36	1.71

the age groups explored in study 1. Checklists provided with the TOMI-H enabled the assessor to note the qualitative aspects of the child's performance.

Data were collected during a visit to the Schonell Research Centre, University of Queensland. The results of the assessments were examined in three cross-sectional groups to match the ages of study 1. The results from study 2 confirmed the data on balance from study 1. Balance is a persistent difficulty in the development of motor proficiency for children with DS. The balance tasks used in study 2 clearly indicate that if the children lacked proficiency on the balance tasks in the BOTMP, they were likely to perform poorly on the TOMI-H tasks and have difficulty riding a bicycle.

Gender, age of walking, BMI, and PPVT-R scores were considered possible variables in the children's performance of balance tasks. Across all the items in the protocol, there were no reliable gender differences, and BMI did not make a significant additional contribution to predicting balance scores. The PPVT-R receptive-language scores were reliably related to the performance scores on both sets of balance tasks. We would suggest, however, that the poor performance was not due to the children failing to understand the instructions. It was found that only those children whose receptive language fell below 3.75 years had difficulties comprehending the balance tasks; the others clearly understood the nature of the task (as witnessed by their attempts to carry out the task) but failed to demonstrate the necessary level of skill.

Perhaps the most informative aspect of study 2 was provided by the concurrent checklists supplied with the TOMI-H tasks. It appeared that the children in study 2 did not know or understand which aspect of their performance needed correcting or alternatively how to modify their movements to maintain stability. The movements they made were either inappropriate (too fast or too many) or too limited (just stumbled forward). On static balance tasks (e.g., standing on one leg), the children seemed unsure whether to use none, few, or many compensatory movements in order to maintain balance. In dynamic balance tasks (e.g., jumping, hopping, etc.) the children had difficulty controlling their forward momentum, and the children tended to move too fast to terminate a movement over which they were losing control.

Conclusions

The results of these studies agree with the conclusions of other authors who have suggested that individuals with DS demonstrate specific areas of movement impairment (Connolly et al., 1984; Connolly et al., 1993; Connolly & Michael, 1986; Dyer, Gunn, Rauh, and Berry, 1990; Henderson, 1985) and confirmed that motor proficiency continues to develop, albeit slowly. On the other hand, it is difficult to compare the current results with other studies due to age differences (Connolly et al., 1993), differences in the size and origin of the sample (Connolly et al., 1984; Connolly et al., 1993; Connolly & Michael, 1986), and the different instruments used (Henderson et al., 1981; Messerly, 1981; Shea, 1987). We would suggest, however, that the results reported here are more representative of adolescents with DS than previous work. In contrast to previous work, it was found that the motor proficiency of the school-aged children with DS did not fit into concise developmental categories as suggested by Reid and Block (1996), nor did performance remain at "the lower end of the developmental scale" (Reid & Block, 1996, p. 321). Some children progressed rapidly at first and then development seemed to slow, while others were slow starters who progressed more quickly at later ages. This underlines the necessity to provide instruction in schools that is both continuing and pays attention to the quality of movement as it relates to the proficient performance of motor skill.

The results clearly indicate that improvements can be observed when the level of motor performance at 10.5 years of age is compared with performance at 16.5 years. On the other hand, the results suggest that gains in motor performance do not gradually increase with age. Performance either plateaus following an observed improvement between the measures taken at 10.5 and 12.5 years of age or shows an improvement only when the measures at 10.5 years are compared with those at 14.5 years (i.e., no improvement occurs between either the measurements taken at 10.5 and 12.5 years or the measurements taken at 14.5 and 16.5 years). This may suggest that although the children continued to grow and physically mature, the relevant skills for motor development were not being acquired or consolidated. It is possible that the observed changes in movement proficiency occurred when the participants had access to a learning environment that focused on the development of motor skills. It was noted from the school program data that after 13 years of age, the focus of the school physical education programs shifted from skill development to recreational participation. We would suggest that the motor skills shown by the 16-year-old children with DS may be considered as just beginning to provide a stable platform on which other skills could be built. Therefore, we would argue that it is important for intervention programs to continue instruction in movement skill past the adolescent years and into adulthood.

The results of the present study indicate that improvements in performance are best predicted by changes in mental age rather than chronological age. On the other hand, motor performance was not dictated by mental age—on most tasks the children's motor performance was higher than that predicted by mental age (figure 10.4). The two exceptions were the children's response time, which was predicted by mental age, and the children's balance performance, which was lower than that expected from mental age. One common feature of the movement performance observed in children with DS is the variability across and within children (e.g., Carr, 1975). Heterogeneity across the participants was evident in the present study, with some children performing reasonably well on some items. Despite the disparities in relative abilities, motor control difficulties made several tasks extremely difficult for even the most proficient performers. The predominant problem areas across the group were response speed, tasks involving bilateral coordination, and especially tasks requiring postural balance. The second study demonstrated that these difficulties with balance were not due to the nature of the tasks adopted within the movement test battery but are a consistent feature of movement control in DS.

Performances across the children were represented by two cluster profiles, with gender differences occurring between cluster membership. The reasons for the appearance of these clusters is not clear. For example, why were reliable differences found on the visual-motor control subtest but not the upper-limb speed and dexterity subtest when both of these explore aspects of manual control? It is also not clear why one group of children should show a higher level of performance on running speed and agility together with a lower performance on balance tasks. One possible (tentative) interpretation is that as a group the boys had a higher level of general fitness but lacked control, as indexed by their balance and visual-motor control performance levels. Moreover, gender differences in manual control might have been masked by those tasks that placed additional (temporal) constraints on performance (i.e., a floor effect occurs in the upper-limb speed and dexterity subtest). If this interpretation is correct, then the higher level of fitness observed in the boys may be occurring because the boys with DS are more likely to engage in physical activity. If this is the case, then it reflects a similar picture of participation in physical activity to that found with normally developing girls and boys in Australia (Dyer, 1989). In other words, stereotypic patterns of boys and girls participating in physical activity (Oldenhove, 1989) may contribute to gender differences occurring in the fitness levels of children with DS in Australia. One optimistic aspect of the current study was the fact that some of the children with DS could perform well on the running speed and agility subtest. This finding suggests that it should be possible to combat the creeping obesity that is known to occur in DS with programs that encourage participation in physical activity. Low muscle tone in individuals with DS has been shown to improve with age (Morris et al., 1982) and to respond positively to specific interventions designed to improve muscle strength (Connolly et al., 1984; Dyer, 1994; Sayer et al., 1996; Weber, 1987). A gradual trend toward obesity was found within the present study, but the relation of BMI to motor development was not as clearly defined as suggested by some authors (e.g., Block, 1991) and contributed little to explain the development of motor proficiency.

Summary

In summary, it is worth asking why the children with DS performed so poorly on the movement tasks. Henderson et al. (1981) and Elliott (1985) have suggested that sustaining continuous movement in a task sequence is difficult for those with DS, as each part of the sequence is treated as a separate activity. This hypothesis could explain the children's poor performance on some of the tasks explored within the current study. The slow establishment of arm and/or leg dominance in the participants (with preference not generally established till after 12.5 years) may also have contributed to the reduced skill levels. It is impossible, however, to deduce the nature of the underlying movement deficits on the basis of the observed performance. The use of a general movement battery provides a useful frame of reference but is limiting as a research tool. Once the periodic status of the children's general performance has been assessed, the goal of research should be to go beyond this level of appraisal and establish why the child's performance is deficient or appraise what aspects of control have contributed to an improvement in performance. We would suggest, however, that the data reported within this chapter paint a comprehensive picture of motor development through adolescence in DS and thus provide a useful starting point for future research. The challenge is to now discover the reasons for the reduced motor performance, so effective strategies may be designed to ameliorate the movement problems associated with DS.

References

Anwar, F. (1981). Motor function in Down's syndrome. *International Review of Research in Mental Retardation, 10*, 107-138.

Bailey, N., Gunn, P., Tovey, C., & Jobling, A. (1989). Screening the vision of special school children with Down syndrome. *Australia and New Zealand Journal of Developmental Disabilities, 15*, 49-55.

Bayley, N. (1969). *The Bayley Scales of Infant Development (BSID)*. New York: Psychological Corporation.

Berry, P., Andrews, R.J., & Gunn, V.P. (1980). *The early development of Down's syndrome infants. Final report to National Health and Medical Research Council*. St. Lucia: Fred and Eleanor Schonell Educational Research Centre.

Berry, P., Gunn, V.P., & Andrews, R.J. (1984). Development of Down's syndrome children from birth to five years. *Perspectives and Progress in Mental Retardation, 1*, 167-177.

Block, M.E. (1991). Motor development in children with Down syndrome: A review of the literature. *Adapted Physical Activity Quarterly, 8*, 179-209.

Bruininks, R.H. (1974). Physical and motor development of retarded persons. In N.R. Ellis (Ed.), *International review of research in mental retardation: Vol. 7* (pp. 209-261). New York: Academic Press.

Bruininks, R.H. (1978). *Bruininks-Oseretsky Test of Motor Proficiency*. Minneapolis: American Guidance Service.

Burns, Y., & Gunn, P. (Eds.) (1993). *Down syndrome: Moving through life*. London: Chapman & Hall.

Burton, A.W., & Davis, W.E. (1992). Assessing balance in adapted physical education: Fundamental concepts and applications. *Adapted Physical Activity Quarterly, 9,* 14-46.

Carr, J. (1975). *Young children with Down's syndrome.* London: Butterworth.

Centerwall, S.A., & Centerwall, W.R. (1960). A study of children with mongolism reared in the home compared to those reared away from home. *Pediatrics, 25,* 678-685.

Champion, P. (1987). An investigation of the sensorimotor development of Down's syndrome infants involved in an ecologically based early intervention program: A longitudinal study. *British Journal of Mental Subnormality, 33,* 88-99.

Cicchetti, D., & Sroufe, L. (1976). The relationship between affective and cognitive development in Down syndrome infants. *Child Development, 47,* 920-929.

Connolly, B., & Michael, B.T. (1986). Performance of retarded children, with and without Down syndrome, on the Bruininks-Oseretsky Test of Motor Proficiency. *Physical Therapy, 66,* 344-348.

Connolly, B.H., Morgan, S., & Russell, F.F. (1984). Evaluation of children with Down syndrome who participated in an early intervention program: Second follow-up. *Physical Therapy, 64,* 1515-1519.

Connolly, B.H., Morgan, S.B., Russell, F.F., & Fulliton, W.L. (1993). A longitudinal study of children with Down syndrome who experienced early intervention programming. *Physical Therapy, 73,* 170-179.

Connolly, B., Morgan, S., Russell, F.F., & Richardson, B. (1980). Early intervention with Down syndrome children: Follow-up report. *Physical Therapy, 60,* 1405-1408.

Crombie, M. (1994). *Development of adolescents with Down syndrome: Does early intervention have a long term effect?* Unpublished doctoral dissertation, University of Queensland, Brisbane.

Dmitriev, V. (1971). Exercises for infants birth to six months. *Sharing Our Caring, 1,* 25-29.

Donoghue, E.C., Kirman, B.H., Bullmore, G.H.L., Laban, D., & Abbas, K.A. (1970). Some factors affecting age of walking in a mentally retarded population. *Developmental Medicine and Child Neurology, 12,* 781-792.

Dunn, L.M., & Dunn, L.M. (1981). *Peabody Picture Vocabulary Test-Revised (PPVT-R).* Minneapolis: American Guidance Services.

Dunst, C.J. (1988). Stage transitioning in the sensorimotor development of Down syndrome infants. *Journal of Mental Deficiency Research, 32,* 405-410.

Dyer, K. (Ed.) (1989). *Sportwomen towards 2000.* Richmond, South Australia: Hyde Park Press.

Dyer, S., Gunn, P., Rauh, H., & Berry, P. (1990). Motor development in Down's syndrome children: An analysis of the motor scale of the Bayley Scale of Infant Development. In A. Vermeer (Ed.), *Motor development, adapted physical activity and mental retardation: Vol. 30. Medicine and sport science* (pp. 7-20). Basel, Switzerland: Karger.

Dyer, S.M. (1994). Physiological effects of a 13 week physical fitness program on Down syndrome subjects. *Pediatric Exercise Science, 6,* 88-100.

Eipper, D.S., & Azen, S.P. (1978). A comparison of two developmental instruments in evaluating children with Down syndrome. *Physical Therapy, 58,* 1066-1069.

Elliott, D. (1985). Manual asymmetries in the performance of sequential movement by adolescents and adults with Down syndrome. *American Journal of Mental Deficiency, 90,* 90-97.

Elliott, D. (1990). Movement control and Down's syndrome: A neuropsychological approach. In G. Reid (Ed.), *Problems in movement control* (pp. 201-216). Amsterdam: North-Holland.

Fewell, R.R., & Oelwein, P.L. (1991). Effective early intervention: Results from the model preschool program for children with Down syndrome and other developmental delays. *Topics in Early Childhood Special Education, 11,* 56-68.

Fishler, K., Share, J., & Koch, R. (1964). Adaptation of Gesell Developmental Scales for evaluation of development in children with Down's syndrome. *American Journal of Mental Deficiency, 68,* 642-646.

Frith, V., & Frith, C.D. (1974). Specific motor disabilities in Down's syndrome. *Journal of Child Psychology and Psychiatry, 15,* 293-301.

Gallahue, D.L. (1989). *Understanding motor development in infants, children and adults.* Indianapolis: Benchmark Press.

Gesell, A., & Amatruda, C. (1941). *Developmental diagnosis.* New York: Hoeber.

Griffith, R. (1970). *The abilities of young children.* High Wycombe, UK: The Test Agency.

Harris, S.R. (1981). Relationship of mental and motor development in Down's syndrome infants. *Physical and Occupational Therapy in Pediatrics, 1,* 13-18.

Harris, S.R. (1983). Comparative performance levels of female and male infants with Down syndrome. *Physical and Occupational Therapy in Pediatrics, 3,* 15-21.

Hayes, A., & Gunn, P. (1991). Developmental assumptions about Down syndrome and the myth of uniformity. In C. Denholm (Ed.), *Adolescents with Down syndrome: International perspectives on research and programme development* (pp. 73-81). Victoria, BC: University of Victoria.

Henderson, S.E. (1984). The Henderson Revision of the Test of Motor Impairment. *British Journal of Physical Education, 15,* 72-75.

Henderson, S.E. (1985). Motor skill development. In D. Lane & B. Stratford (Eds.), *Current approaches to Down's syndrome* (pp. 187-218). London: Holt, Rinehart & Winston.

Henderson, S.E., Morris, J., & Frith, V. (1981). The motor deficit in Down's syndrome children: A problem of timing? *Journal of Child Psychology and Psychiatry, 22,* 233-245.

Hogg, J., & Moss, S.C. (1983). Prehensile development in Down's syndrome and non-handicapped preschool children. *British Journal of Developmental Psychology, 1,* 189-204.

Jobling, A., & Gunn, P. (1995). The motor proficiency of children and adolescents with Down syndrome. In M. Hebbelink & R.J. Shephard (Series Eds.) and A. Vermeer & W.E. Davis (Vol. Eds.), *Medicine and sport science: Vol. 40. Physical and motor development in mental retardation* (pp. 181-190). Basel, Switzerland: Karger AG.

LaVeck, B., & Brehm, S.S. (1978). Individual variability among children with Down's syndrome. *Mental Retardation, 16,* 135-137.

LaVeck, B., & LaVeck, G.D. (1977). Sex differences in development among children with Down syndrome. *Journal of Pediatrics, 91,* 767-769.

Lydic, J.S. (1980). Assisting the motor development of the child with Down syndrome. *Sharing Our Caring, 10,* 3-6.

MacLean, W.E., Ellis, D.N., Galbreath, H.N., Halpern, L.F., & Baumeister, A.A. (1991). Rhythmic motor behavior of preambulatory motor impaired Down syndrome and nondisabled children: A comparative analysis. *Journal of Abnormal Child Psychology, 19,* 319-330.

Messerly, D.L. (1981). A comparison of Down's syndrome and moderately retarded children on selected gross motor skills and body somatotyping. *Dissertation Abstracts International, 42,* 2022A.

Moss, S.C., & Hogg, J. (1983). The development and integration of fine motor sequences in 12-18 month old children: A test of the modular theory of motor skill acquisition. *Genetic Psychology, 107,* 145-187.

Moos, R.H., & Moos, B.S. (1986). *Family Environment Scale* (2nd ed.). Palo Alto, CA: Consulting Psychologists Press.

Morris A. F., Vaughan, S.E., & Vaccaro, P. (1982). Measurement of neuromuscular tone and strength in Down's syndrome children. *Journal of Mental Deficiency Research, 26,* 41-46.

Neser, P.S.J., Molteno, C.D, & Knight, G.J. (1989). Evaluation of preschool children with Down's syndrome in Cape Town using the Griffiths Scales of Mental Development. *Child: Care, Health and Development, 15,* 217-226.

Newell, K.M. (1985). Motor skill acquisition and mental retardation: Overview of traditional and current orientations. In J.E. Clark & J.H. Humphrey (Eds.), *Motor development: Current Research: Vol. 1* (pp. 183-205). Princeton: Princeton Book.

O'Brien, C., & Hayes, A. (1989). Motor development in early childhood of clumsy, intellectual delayed and Down syndrome children: Guidelines for adapted motor activity programs. *ACHPER Journal, 124,* 15-18.

Oldenhove, H. (1989). Turning on the turned off girl. In K. Dyer (Ed.), *Sportswomen towards 2000* (pp. 175-182). Richmond, South Australia: Hyde Park Press.

Payne, V.G., & Isaacs, L.D. (1991). *Human motor development: A lifespan approach.* Mountain View, CA: Mayfield.

Ramsay, M., & Piper, M.C. (1980). A comparison of two developmental scales in evaluating infants with Down syndrome. *Early Human Development, 4,* 89-95.

Rarick, G., Dobbins, D.A., & Broadhead, G.O. (1976). *The motor domain and its correlates in educationally handicapped children.* Englewood Cliffs, NJ: Prentice-Hall.

Rauh, H., Rudinger, G., Bowman, T., Berry, P., Gunn, P., & Hayes, A. (1991). The development of Down syndrome children. In M. Lamb & H. Keller (Eds.), *Infant development: Perspectives from German speaking countries* (pp. 329-355). Hillsdale, NJ: Erlbaum.

Reed, R.B., Pueschel, S.M., Schnell, R.R., & Cronk, C.E. (1980). Interrelationships of biological, environmental and competency variables in young children with Down syndrome. *Applied Research in Mental Retardation, 1,* 161-174.

Reid, G., & Block, M.E. (1996). Motor development and physical education. In B. Stratford & P. Gunn (Eds.), *New approaches to Down syndrome* (pp. 309-340). London: Cassell.

Sanz-Aparicio, M.T., & Menendez-Balana, F.J. (1992). Vicarious learning of parents and early motor acquisition of Down's syndrome. *Early Child Development and Care, 83,* 27-31.

Sayers, L.K., Cowden, J.E., Newton, M., Warren, B., & Eason, B. (1996). Qualitative analysis of a pediatric strength intervention on the developmental stepping movement of infants with Down syndrome. *Adapted Physical Activity Quarterly, 13,* 247-268.

Schneider, J.W., & Brannen, E.A. (1984). A comparison of two developmental evaluation tools used to assess children with Down's syndrome. *Physical and Occupational Therapy in Pediatrics, 4,* 19-29.

Sharav, T., & Shlomo, L. (1986). Stimulation of infants with Down syndrome: Longterm effects. *Mental Retardation, 21,* 81-86.

Share, J., & French, R. (1982). *Motor development of Down syndrome children: Birth to six years.* Jack Share, Sherman Oaks, CA 91423, USA.

Share, J., Koch, R., Webb, A., & Graliker, B. (1964). The longitudinal development of infants and young children with Down syndrome. *American Journal of Mental Deficiency, 68,* 685-692.

Shea, A.M. (1987). *Motor development in Down syndrome*. Unpublished doctoral dissertation, Harvard University, Cambridge.

Shumway-Cook, A., & Woollacott, M.H. (1985). Dynamics of postural control in the child with Down syndrome. *Physical Therapy, 65*, 1315-1322.

Terman, L.M., & Merrill, M.A. (1972). *Stanford-Binet Intelligence Scale: Manual for third revision, Form L-M*. Boston: Houghton Mifflin.

Uzgiris, I.C., & Hunt, J. (1975). *Assessment in infancy*. Chicago: University of Illinois Press.

Weber, R.C. (1987). Weight training for adolescents with Down's syndrome. *Down's Syndrome Association Papers*, p. 6.

Winnick, J.P. (1979). *Early movement experiences and development: Habilitation and remediation*. Toronto: W.B. Saunders.

Wishart, J. (1991). Motivational deficits and the relation to learning difficulties in young children with Down's syndrome. In J. Watson (Ed.), *Innovatory practice and severe learning difficulties* (pp. 80-100). Edinburgh: Moray House.

Woollacott, M.H., & Shumway-Cook, A. (1986). The development of the postural and voluntary motor control systems in Down's syndrome children. In M.G. Wade (Ed.), *Motor skill acquisition of the mentally handicapped: Issues in research and training* (pp. 45-71). Amsterdam: Elsevier Science.

Youn, G., & Youn, S. (1991). Influence of training and performance IQ on the psychomotor skill of Down syndrome persons. *Perceptual and Motor Skills, 73*, 1191-1194.

Ziviani, J., & Elkins, J. (1993). Fine motor skills in the classroom. In Y. Burns & P. Gunn (Eds.), *Down syndrome: Moving through life* (pp. 135-150). London: Chapman & Hall.

Author Note

Anne Jobling would like to thank the Down Syndrome Research Program (Schonell Special Education Research Centre, The University of Queensland), especially Dr. Pat Gunn and the participating children and their families. Preparation of this manuscript was partly supported by a grant to the authors from the National Health and Medical Research Council, Australia.

Current Research Strategies in the Investigation of Perceptual-Motor Behavior in Down Syndrome

As in any area of research, investigators are guided, but also constrained, by their theoretical assumptions and by the methods and technology associated with their scientific paradigm. In this section of the volume, we present four chapters that take different theoretical, as well as methodological, approaches to understanding perceptual-motor behavior in children and adults with Down syndrome. These approaches are expected to have increasing impact as we move into the new millennium.

In chapter 11, Geert Savelsbergh, John van der Kamp, Annick Ledebt, and Tjasa Planinsek put forward a research paradigm to examine the coupling between perception and action in persons with Down syndrome from an ecological psychology framework. The approach holds that the emergence of perceptual-motor behavior is subject to the mutual constraints of the task goal, environmental conditions, and performer characteristics.

In chapter 12, Michael Wade, Richard Van Emmerik, and Thomas Kernozek suggest that the ubiquitous periodic signatures that are replete not only in perceptual-motor behavior but in both the biology and social behavior of individuals without Down syndrome appear to some degree diminished, or absent, in persons with the syndrome. These authors present an approach and research strategy to understanding movement problems in Down syndrome in which aperiodicities are signature features of the syndrome.

In chapter 13, Matthew Heath, Digby Elliott, Daniel Weeks, and Romeo Chua provide an overview of their research program extending over the past decade. The chapter centers around the current status of their neuropsychological model of cerebral function and its implications for understanding performance, learning, and brain-behavior relations in persons with Down syndrome.

Finally, chapter 14 by Giuseppe Chiarenza and Paolo Stagi presents the neurophysiological aspects of perceptual-motor development in children with Down syndrome. Through the examination of skilled perceptual-motor behavior and associated movement-related brain macropotentials, the authors promote the utility of electrophysiological measures for further understanding of perceptual-motor behavior in children with Down syndrome.

11

CHAPTER

Information-Movement Coupling in Children With Down Syndrome

Geert Savelsbergh, John van der Kamp, and Annick Ledebt

Institute for Fundamental and Clinical Human Movement Sciences
Vrije University, Amsterdam

Tjasa Planinsek

University of Ljubljana

Key words

catching ◆ affordances ◆ constraints ◆ information ◆ optic array ◆
grasping ◆ Tau ◆ binocular vision ◆ optic flow ◆ postural control ◆
coupling ◆ visual perception ◆ ecological psychology

Recently, the study of motor development has become a major testing ground for examining the developmental implications of several new theoretical approaches, including the ecological approach to perception and action. Applying the central concepts of such new perspectives to the study of infancy and childhood and the associated rapid changes in perception and action leads to a deeper understanding of movement development. In addition, the study of infancy and childhood also serves to further refine many of the concepts stemming from these approaches. This mutuality is to a large extent responsible for current major interest in motor development (Gibson, 1987; Savelsbergh, 1993; Thelen & Smith, 1994).

Down syndrome (DS) presents a unique etiology that affects both cognitive and physical development. Children with DS show an extra chromosome number 21, a condition referred to as trisomy 21. Although considerable inter-individual variability exists, general characteristics can be discerned (Block, 1991; Henderson, 1985). For instance, nearly half the children with DS have congenital cardiac abnormalities, which are detrimental to their growth and fitness. In addition, individuals with DS often suffer from skeletal problems, the most significant of which is atlantoaxial instability. A third characteristic is hypotonia, which results in an increase in the range of motion of the joints. Hypotonia is probably linked with delays in motor development and the occurrence of abnormal movement patterns. The exact cause of hypotonia is still unknown. Davis (Davis & Kelso, 1982; Davis & Sinning, 1987) has suggested that hypotonia may actually be a manifestation of problems in the control of muscle stiffness and recruitment.

Moreover, children with DS often exhibit significant perceptual problems. Auditory problems, often in association with ophthalmologic disorders such as cataracts, strabismus, and nystagmus, and visual (Courage, Adams, Reyno, & Kwa, 1994) and tactual impairments have been reported. However, as Stratford (1980) argued, sometimes the apparent visual-perceptual problems in children with DS are actually due to deficits in the ability to physically perform the required tasks. Knights, Atkinson, and Hyman (1967) found that only a small proportion of children with DS were able to perform successfully on tactual and kinesthetic discrimination tasks (e.g., to discriminate among objects by texture, size, and weight while blindfolded), although the inclusion of visual input improved tactual performance in these children.

In sum, children with DS show both motor and perceptual impairments that may influence the development and learning of various fundamental and complex actions. These influences have been widely reported over the years, but unfortunately, not many findings have addressed the functional coupling of information and movement. Such a functional coupling is precisely the cornerstone of Gibson's (1979) ecological approach to visual perception (i.e., the direct perception approach). Gibson emphasized the role of optical information in the coordination and control of action. A perception-action cycle was proposed in which optical information guides the movement, and the movement, in turn, generates information. In other words, action-relevant information (the kinematic optical flow field) is used to control and coordinate actions (the dynamics of motion) (see figure 11.1). Therefore, from an ecological approach, one of the important issues concerns the nature of the information used in the control and coordination of action. Insight into the (changing) sources of information involved in the regulation of action will enhance the understanding of developmental perceptual-motor processes.

Specifically, it is our conviction that the theory of direct perception offers insights into (a) what is learned over the course of development, (b) what learning depends on, and (c) how learning occurs.

The goal of this chapter is to show how concepts from the direct perception perspective can assist in assessing the functional coupling of information and movement in children with Down syndrome. In order to achieve this goal, the concepts of affordance, constraint, and information will be introduced briefly. Subsequently, the information regulating prehension, interceptive timing, and postural control in children with DS will be discussed. Finally, the chapter will conclude with some discussion of the issues that should be addressed in future research involving children with DS.

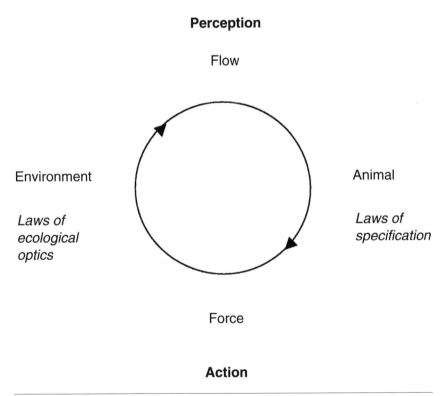

Figure 11.1   The coupling of perception and action.

The Functional Coupling of Information and Movement: Affordances, Constraints, and Information

The key concept in Gibson's (1979) approach is *affordance*. An affordance is the possibility for action of an organism in a particular environment in relation to the actor's own action system. This implies the use of a body-scaled, not an absolute, metric (e.g., meters, kilograms, etc.) for perceiving. Body scaling means that the movement pattern is determined by the ratio between a metric of the action space and a metric of the actor (body dimension). For a human climbing stairs, for instance, the coordination pattern is specified by the ratio between the tread height (action space) and the actor's leg length (metric of the actor) (Warren, 1984). In more general terms, perceiving and acting are guided by body-scaled ratios, which should be similar over individual differences in body dimensions. Henceforth, developmental changes in body dimensions due to physical growth should not affect the perception of affordances. That is, during development children should remain tuned to similar body-scaled ratios without the need for new learning or reorganization of the action system (Pufall & Dunbar, 1992; van der Kamp, Savelsbergh, & Davis, 1998). This should also be the case for children with DS. In the next section we will discuss grasping patterns of children with DS in relation to body scaling.

As in the body scaling example, movement patterns emerge from the relation between different *constraints*. Newell (1986) proposed three categories of constraints on the coordination of motor behavior: organismic (e.g., the central nervous system), task (e.g., accuracy demands), and environmental (e.g., size of an object). These different constraints do not operate in isolation, and their interaction leads to a task-specific organization of the coordination pattern. Thus, from this point of view, coordination patterns do not uniquely originate from the central nervous system, as argued by the traditional neuro-maturational theories. Rather, coordination patterns emerge from the relation between the three categories of constraints. Development, therefore, can be considered the changing interaction between constraints. Savelsbergh and van der Kamp (1994) examined the effect of body orientation to gravity on infants' early reaching and grasping behavior. Two groups, 12- to 19-week-old and 20- to 27-week-old infants, were seated in three positions, vertical (90° from horizontal), recline (60°), and supine (0°), and shown nine balls on a blackboard. Both the number and duration of reaches of the 12- to 19-week-olds in the vertical position were equal to that of 20- to 27-week-old infants. The younger infants, however, showed fewer and shorter reaches in the supine and recline orientations. It was concluded that the development of reaching does not just reflect maturation of the central nervous system but is due to a changing interaction between organismic (e.g., arm strength) and environmental (e.g., gravity) constraints.

The human actor needs to be able to detect *information* about objects, places, and events to adjust his or her movements to the environment (i.e., the actor needs to be sensitive to environmental constraints). Gibson argued that objects, places, and events in the environment are meaningfully perceived without the need for cognitive mediation. Hence, Gibson's ecological approach to visual perception is often referred to as direct perception: objects, events, and places are unambiguously specified by the change and persistence of optical patterns in the optic array, the pattern of light coming from all directions of the environment to a point of observation. Hence, perception of objects, events, and places involves the detection of the information in the optic array. During development, the child learns to pick up and attune to the appropriate information instead of learning to interpret discrete static stimuli and construct meaningful perception out of it. Therefore, when the infant or child learns to (actively) pick up or detect the information, he or she perceives events. This concept of information is closely related to the concept of affordances because information specifies affordances.

The optic array contains a wealth of information about not only the layout of the environment but also the organism's own movement. Experiments show that a functional coupling exists between information and movement. These functional relations between information that constrains movement and movement that generates information are consistent with, but not reducible to, the natural laws of physics. Warren (1990; see also Kugler & Turvey, 1987) describes these relations as follows (see figure 11.1, page 253):

Law of ecological optics: Flow = f (Force)

Law of control: Force = g (Flow)

The important issue is to discern the specific laws for different classes of action and, with respect to development, how infants and children with or without DS learn to couple information and movement.

Research Strategy

The theory of direct perception offers insights into developmental perceptual-motor processes. Namely, one should determine (a) what is learned over the course of development, (b) what learning depends on, and (c) how learning occurs (Gibson, 1987; Savelsbergh, Wimmers, van der Kamp, & Davids, in press).

First, with respect to what is learned, infants and children must learn to detect affordances, that is, to perceive the action possibilities the environment affords. In this respect, learning to move and coordinate action involves learning to select the appropriate information sources.

Such learning depends on, among other things, the available action capabilities of the infant. These action capabilities may change as a function of the maturation of the central nervous system, the sensitivity for certain information sources, the growth of body dimensions, and the ability to couple information and movements.

This brings us to the third point. From a direct perception perspective, it is the active and directed exploration of the environment with their own action systems through which infants learn to detect affordances, pick up relevant information, and couple that information to movements. The challenge is to denote these three aspects in a developing system.

The following research strategy results:

1. In order to discover the information regulating the action, various constraints should be manipulated.
2. The functional relation between information and movement should be examined. In other words, how is a particular source of information used in the control and coordination of motor behavior?

In the following sections, we illustrate the first of these strategic steps with respect to children with Down syndrome.

Grasping: Size as a Constraint

Grasping is an extremely important act that usually involves a one- or two-handed movement but also can be accomplished using other body parts. It has been a focus of much empirical work by motor control researchers (Cole & Abbs, 1986; Savelsbergh, Steenbergen, & van der Kamp, 1996) as well as developmental psychologists (Castner, 1932; Connolly, 1973; Savelsbergh, Von Hofsten, & Jonsson, 1997).

Traditionally, qualitative descriptions of grip configurations have been used to study the development of grasping (e.g., Connolly & Elliott, 1972; Gesell, 1928). Similar to studies in posture and locomotion, grip configurations were reported to occur in regular and orderly sequences. Thus, just after birth, grasping patterns are regarded as primitive reflex movements that progress from crude power (whole hand) grasps to grasps involving precise index finger-thumb opposition. The latter are regarded as representative of "mature" patterns (Connolly, 1973). The progression to adult grips is usually explained in maturational or cognitive terms. Maturation theory argues that as the nervous system matures, new brain structures make novel movement patterns possible. In the cognitive approach, movement patterns are prescriptive schemas or motor programs that are executed to achieve a task goal. Novel acts are built up from "chunks of previously learned actions which are incorporated as wholes, and subsequently adapted to fit the new situation" (Moss & Hogg, 1981, p. 39). The maturation and cognitive approaches both differ radically from an ecological perspective. The latter holds that movement patterns emerge spontaneously from mutual constraints imposed by the task goal, environmental conditions (e.g., object size), and performer characteristics (Davis & Van Emmerik, 1994; Newell, 1986; van der Kamp et al., in press). For instance, Newell, Scully, McDonald, and Baillargeon (1989) examined the grasping behavior of 4- to 8-month-old infants, who were presented with four objects of different diameters. Although 1,023 possible combinations of the 10 fingers could be used, Newell and coworkers found that the grasping behavior could be classified primarily by five grips. It was concluded that the relation between hand size and object size constrains the grip configuration. Several studies have replicated and extended these findings to older age groups (Newell, Scully, Tenenbaum, & Hardiman, 1989; Savelsbergh & van der Kamp, in press; van der Kamp et al., in press).

van der Kamp et al. (in press) found evidence that, during childhood, grasping is body scaled and thus remains invariant during development. Children who were 5, 7, and 9 years old were required to grasp and lift 14 cardboard cubes of different sizes (ranging from 2.2 to 16.2 cm in diameter). The percentage of one-handed grasps for each cube was recorded. The findings showed that older children exhibited more one-handed grasps. Moreover, for older children, larger cubes were still predominantly taken with one hand. However, when grasping behavior of the cubes was scaled to hand size rather than age, the shift from one- to two-handed grasps occurred at a similar cube-size/hand-span ratio for all three age groups. Thus, the differences in prehension disappeared when hand size was taken into account (cf. Newell, Scully, McDonald, & Baillargeon, 1989, and Newell, Scully, Tenenbaum, & Hardiman, 1989). It can be concluded that, in nonhandicapped children, grasping pattern is body scaled.

In spite of the importance of grasping tasks in daily living, relatively few studies have analyzed the grasping patterns of children with DS. An exception is the work of Hogg and Moss (1983; Moss & Hogg, 1981). These authors followed the traditional cognitive approach. Children with DS and age-matched controls (age range of 15 to 44 months) both demonstrated an increasing use of precision grips instead of power grips. However, the oldest children with DS did not advance to the same level of precision grip as the nonhandicapped participants. Unfortunately, the hand-object size ratios were not taken into account, although it is well known that shorter fingers contribute to smaller hand size for persons with DS (Chumlea, Malina, Rarick, & Seefeldt, 1979).

Savelsbergh, van der Kamp, and Davis (1998; cf. van der Kamp et al., in press) examined the functional coupling of object size and hand size. The use of body-scaled information was assessed by deriving the dimensionless ratio between hand size and object size. Children 4 to 11 years old with DS were required to grasp a cube presented by the experimenter seated opposite to the participant. A set of 14 cardboard cubes ranging in size from 2.2 to 16.2 cm in 1 cm steps was used. All boxes were easy to lift and weight differences were negligible. After the subject closed his or her eyes, the box was placed in a marked position in front of the subject. Upon opening the eyes, the subject had to lift and place the box on a spot indicated by an "X." The distance to be covered was about 30 cm. The 14 cubes were presented four times.

As anticipated, the hand size of children with DS was indeed smaller than the hand size of their nonhandicapped peers (NH) matched for age. The children with DS used a one-handed grasping pattern less frequently than the NH children (39 and 55%; figure 11.2a). However, a comparison of the dimensionless ratio between object size and hand size at the point at which the children shifted from one- to two-handed grasping showed no significant difference (figure 11.2b). This is taken as evidence for the use of body-scaled information for both nonhandicapped children and children with DS. These findings support the hallmark of the ecological approach to movement coordination. Specifically, they illustrate the existence of a functional coupling between perception and movement. This explanation contrasts the traditional cognitive explanation given by Hogg and Moss (1983; Moss & Hogg, 1981). These authors suggested that children with DS did not advance to the same

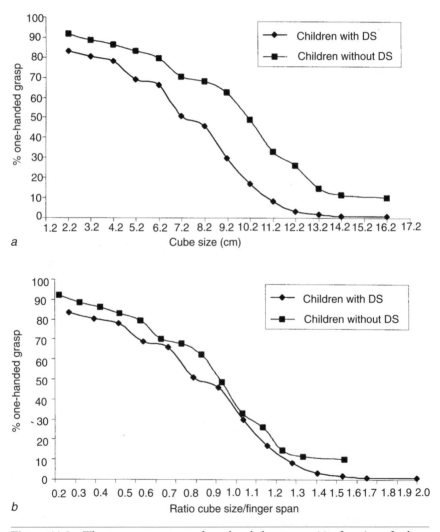

Figure 11.2   The mean percentage of one-handed grasps as (*a*) a function of cube size and (*b*) a function of cube-size/finger-span ratio for the DS and NH groups.

level of grip development as their nonhandicapped peers as a result of cognitive delay. Our findings, however, indicate that body scaling should be taken into account in studies examining the development of motor behavior.

Future research should consider not only the shift from one- to two-handed grasping, but also include differences in grip configurations (e.g., pincer grip, etc.) in order to determine whether these differences are due to an immature grip in children with DS or related to anthropometric differences.

Catching

The ability to catch a ball enables participation in a wide range of play, sport, and leisure activities and hence has the potential to provide numerous physical and social benefits. However, catching is no simple act. It is a multisegmental action involving both a reaching and grasping component. High-speed film analysis by Alderson, Sully, and Sully (1974) demonstrated a gross spatial orientation of the catching hand some 200 ms prior to the catch, followed by a fine orientation some 50 ms later. A grasp and hold action starting some 32-50 ms before the completion of the catch concludes the action. For a ball speed of 10 m/s, Alderson et al. (1974) found that accuracy in timing the closure of the hand is constrained to 40-50 ms. Closing the hand too early results in the ball deflecting off the fingers, while closing too late results in the ball bouncing off the palm of the hands.

Like other interceptive actions, catching requires information not only about where and when to catch the ball, but also about the movement of the hand and body in relation to the ball. Different perceptual systems (e.g., visual, proprioceptive) are involved in the detection of the required information. Prior studies have shown that a number of variables influence catching performance. For instance, viewing time, vision of the hand, the diameter of the ball, the direction of approach, and ball velocity all appear to be important variables. The relative importance of some of these factors depends on age or experience. In this section, we will focus exclusively on the visual regulation of the temporal aspect of the catch. First, some general findings of catching in adults will be discussed. Second, an experiment involving children with DS will be reported.

Visual Information Sources in Catching

Alderson et al. (1974) showed that even for closing the hand, a reactive grasp is insufficient to catch a ball successfully. In other words, catching a ball involves anticipatory behavior. A study conducted by Von Hofsten (1983) showed that infants were already able to predict the future location of a moving object. Eight-month-old babies demonstrate considerable catching competence when presented with objects traveling in a horizontal arc at 60 cm/s. Indeed, some were able to catch objects moving at 90 and 120 cm/s. Even 18-week-olds were able to catch objects moving at 30 cm/s. Thus, the infants appeared to perceive whether a catch was possible or not. When the object was approaching at a high velocity, no catching attempt was made. In other words, from 5 months onward, signs of anticipatory behavior in catching can be discerned. What visual information sources are involved in regulating the temporal characteristics of anticipatory acts such as catching?

Tau. Schiff, Caviness, and Gibson (1962) demonstrated that an optically expanding shadow on a white screen resulted in defensive reactions in various animal species. Bower, Broughton, and Moore (1970a, 1970b) reported that 10-day-old babies already show avoidance when a solid object gives rise to optical expansion (the "looming" effect) (cf. Ball & Tronick, 1971; Yonas et al., 1977).

It was Lee (1976, 1980) who proposed that the pattern of optical expansion generated by approaching objects contained predictive temporal information. Specifically, in the case of constant approach velocity, the inverse of the relative rate of optical expansion of an object approaching an observer exactly specifies the time remaining before the ball will reach the eye. This optical variable was denoted Tau. Time-to-contact is specified directly and therefore can be perceived without perceiving distance and speed separately (Schiff & Detweiler, 1979). A number of experiments have demonstrated the contribution of Tau in controlling the temporal properties of one-handed catching (Savelsbergh, Whiting, & Bootsma, 1991; Savelsbergh, Whiting, Pijpers, & Santvoord, 1993). In the study by Savelsbergh et al. (1991), a direct manipulation of the optical pattern was carried out. Researchers used two luminescent balls of constant size and a luminescent ball that changed its diameter during flight. Changing the ball diameter during flight perturbed the relative rate of optical expansion during approach such that a longer time before contact was specified. The results of two experiments (binocular and monocular vision) show that the moment of the maximal closing velocity of the hand occurred later for the deflating ball than for the balls of constant size.

Thus, Tau appears to be a likely candidate for the timing of the opening and closing of the hand in ball catching. As the ball approaches, its image on the retina expands, and the inverse of the relative rate of dilation directly specifies time-to-contact, which can be used to determine when to initiate the grasp. More recent experiments, however, have shown that Tau is not the only candidate.

Binocular Sources of Information. Judge and Bradford (1988) examined the effects of manipulating disparity and/or convergence on one-handed catching performance. Subjects, who had their interocular separation artificially increased by wearing a telestereoscope, showed a deterioration in catching performance. Bennett, van der Kamp, Savelsbergh, and Davids (in press) and van der Kamp, Bennett, Savelsbergh, and Davids (in press) have recently replicated these effects of the telestereoscope with a more refined analysis, examining not only outcome measures but also anticipatory timing. They found that subjects started to close their hands too early when disparity and/or convergence was increased (i.e., when wearing the telestereoscope). Consistent with these findings are the observations of van der Kamp, Savelsbergh, and Smeets (1997), who examined the effects of ball diameter on the timing of the catch. Subjects were required to catch balls of four different diameters (i.e., 4, 6, 8, and 10 cm) under both monocular and binocular viewing conditions. The experiment was conducted in a completely dark room and only the luminous balls were visible. In the monocular condition, subjects opened and closed their hands later as a function of ball size: the smaller the ball, the closer to ball-hand contact the hand was opened and closed. In the binocular condition, no differences in the timing pattern were found as a function of ball diameter. These findings suggest that different sources of information regulate the timing of a one-handed catch under binocular and monocular viewing. Further, the findings also suggest that it is not exclusively Tau that controls interceptive timing. Moreover, other studies suggest that degrading information from the environmental surroundings increases the amount of temporal catching errors (e.g., Rosengren, Pick, & Von Hofsten, 1988; Savelsbergh & Whiting, 1988; cf. van der Kamp et al., 1997).

In sum, dependent on the task constraints, adults show different timing patterns, suggesting the contribution of different or compound information sources in the guidance of the one-handed catch. Do children with DS show the same timing patterns under similar conditions?

Children With Down Syndrome and Catching

Not much is known about catching in children with DS. O'Brien and Hayes (1995) argued that children with DS have problems with interceptive action. However, from their global performance measures, it remains unclear whether poor performance is due to spatial or temporal errors, or both. Moreover, it also remains difficult to determine whether the problem has a perceptual (e.g., different sources of information involved) or motor origin (e.g., they are more clumsy or just slow).

Although previous studies have indicated that children with DS may have deficiencies in controlling the timing and spatial parameters of a movement (Henderson, 1985), little is known about deficiencies for tasks that require timing and anticipation. However, two experiments are of special interest in this respect. Frith and Frith (1974) and Henderson, Morris, and Frith (1981) required children with DS to perform a task under temporal constraints.

In the Frith and Frith (1974) experiment, children performed two simple motor tasks: tracking and finger-tapping. There were two major differences in the performance of the children with DS compared to nonhandicapped and autistic children. First, the children with DS failed to show an improvement in tracking, whereas nonhandicapped and autistic children did show a marked improvement. Secondly, children with DS tapped more slowly. Hence, the authors argued that DS is associated with specific difficulties in using feed-forward motor programs (i.e., planning and producing movement without feedback) and that children with DS may therefore be dependent on simple feedback processes to perform motor tasks.

Henderson et al. (1981) were also interested in the regulation of the temporal aspects of catching.

> The young child may make the correct sequence of movements and may be in the right place but be too late to successfully catch it. There are two possible reasons for his failure to arrive in position at the correct time. First, he may be unable to make the perceptual judgments necessary to plan the correct sequence of movement. Alternatively, he may know when he should arrive but be unable to make the required movement fast enough. This problem of timing, whatever its sources, is common in many children with movement difficulties. The specific problem in the programming of movements apparently shown by the children with Down syndrome may only reside in this timing component, but not in the spatial component. This hypothesis would allow us to explain the sometimes-contradictory findings relating to movement control in children with Down syndrome. (Henderson et al., 1981, p. 234)

Thus, according to Henderson et al. (1981), children with DS have no more difficulty than their peers who are also developmentally delayed when success depends on the accurate performance of a particular movement pattern, provided the task is free of time demands. However, when the child is required to complete a sequence of movement in a prescribed time, or time a movement to coincide with external events, difficulty will become evident. Henderson et al. (1981) sought to find a task that would allow the examination of responses to a highly predictable input over a reasonable period of time. Catching a ball, where failure is so obvious, was considered unsuitable. Thus Henderson et al. (1981) investigated the tracking performance of 10-year-old mildly mentally retarded children with and without DS, as well as a group of 5- and 6-year-old children without mental retardation. Each child performed two tracking tasks (a sinusoidal track and an accelerating track) and two subsidiary drawing tasks (drawing from memory). The tracking task was introduced as a driving game in which the participant would drive a vehicle of their choice along the "road." The children used a pencil to trace a curvy path on a slowly moving piece of paper and were tested on their ability to anticipate changes in the path of the road by copying the movement. In the subsidiary freehand drawing tasks, subjects were tested on how they reproduced the paths they had been tracing with the pencil.

Henderson et al. (1981) operationalized timing as the temporal accuracy with which the peaks of the sinusoidal track were copied (i.e., were the peaks reached too early, just in time, or too late?). A second measure was simply the total amount of time the subject remained in contact with the sinusoidal track. In order to hit the peaks exactly, it is necessary to slow down when approaching the turn, subsequently change the direction of movement, and speed up again on the sides. The nonhandicapped children had no difficulty following the path with a pencil. The mentally handicapped children without DS did not perform as well in this task as the nonhandicapped children, but they were better than the children with DS. Henderson et al. (1981) concluded that problems associated with anticipatory movement tasks (such as catching) are due to temporal rather than spatial errors.

However, such a generalization between tasks may be hazardous. The available information for the tracking and catching tasks is quite different. Hence, it is highly probable that different functional information movement couplings are involved. For instance, it has been argued that the pattern of optical expansion generated by the approaching ball (e.g., Tau) guides the temporal properties of the catch (e.g., Savelsbergh et al., 1991). In the tracking task used by Henderson et al. (1981), no optical expansion information is available. It is unclear what information the children used to perform the sinusoidal track.

Kerr and Blais (1985) showed that although children with DS have problems in tasks involving coincidence timing, they could improve their performances with training. In their study, children with DS, mentally handicapped children without DS, and nonhandicapped children performed a subject-paced, pursuit-tracking task. The main finding was that children with DS did not respond to directional probability in the same manner as the other children. This difference in strategy also was reflected in their greater emphasis on accuracy rather than speed. These effects were consistent across the subjects with DS despite the large inter-subject variability. Sugden and Keogh (1990) argued that the central-processing limitation specifically related to memory might be associated with the inability of children with DS to utilize accumulated knowledge in anticipatory tasks.

In sum, tracking tasks seem to suggest that the poor performance in catching by children with DS is due to deficiencies in the timing of movement patterns. However, because the information available in the two tasks differs dramatically, this conclusion might be misleading. In addition, it remains unclear whether the poor performance was due to the use of other sources of information or whether impaired movements cause problems. For instance, perhaps the most consistent finding in the literature on mental retardation is that mentally handicapped individuals perform more slowly than their nonhandicapped peers (Block, 1991; Henderson, 1985). Indeed, the bulk of the evidence seems to suggest that individuals with DS perform even more slowly than other participants of the same mental age. Berkson (1960) was one of the first authors to report systematic differences in reaction times of persons with DS. Using a series of tasks of increasing difficulty, he found that the participants with DS were not only slower but also fell more and more behind as the task became increasingly complex. Henderson (1985), in reviewing simple and choice reaction-time experiments, confirmed this early finding. She concluded that children with DS have longer premotor reaction times. Moreover, once initiated, the actual movement is often observed to be slower in children with DS.

A Catching Experiment

The review so far shows that it remains unclear whether the poor performance in one-handed catching (O'Brien & Hayes, 1995) is due to spatial errors, temporal errors (Henderson et al., 1981), or both. This issue can partly be resolved by projecting the ball on a fixed spatial trajectory (e.g., Savelsbergh et al., 1991; van der Kamp et al., 1997). In such a situation, catching failures are exclusively attributable to temporal errors. Planinsek (1996) used this approach to examine whether the poor performance of children with DS was due to different temporal judgments. However, if differences in timing could be discerned, the issue remains whether these differences have a perceptual origin (i.e., other information sources), a motor origin (i.e., slowness of movement), or whether it is the coupling between the two that results in the impaired performance.

The procedure of the experiment of Planinsek (1996) was similar to the one used by van der Kamp et al. (1997) with adults. Children with and without DS, aged 5 to 12 years, were required to catch luminous balls projected by the Ball Transport Apparatus. Three different ball diameters were used, ranging from 3 to 7 cm, depending on the size of the hand. The child was seated in a chair with a fixed hand position, which ensured that the hand was in the path of the ball. Consequently the balls always hit the hand, and only temporal judgments were required for the child to catch the ball.

Two cameras were used to record the position of light-emitting diodes (LED) attached on the wrist and tips of the thumb and the index finger. The position profiles of the LEDs were used to determine the moment of opening and closing of the hand and the moment of completion of the catch.

All three balls were presented five times in binocular light, monocular dark, and binocular dark conditions. The first binocular light trials were considered practice trials. During the dark monocular and binocular conditions, only the ball was visible. In the monocular condition, children wore a special eye patch (a "pirate patch") to cover the left eye. Most subjects understood the task; however, four children with DS caught the balls only in the light binocular condition and thus were excluded from analysis. One child with and one child without DS caught only nine balls in each viewing.

The findings showed that children with DS missed more balls than the other children (figure 11.3). Specifically, children with DS missed an average 29% of the balls, while children without DS missed only an average 7% of the balls. With respect to the temporal characteristics of catching, the children in the DS group tended to complete the catch later than the control participants. Figure 11.4a represents the average of the moment of completion of the catch of all trials for each subject. The estimated time window is also indicated. Catching the ball outside the time window results in a failure. It is clear that there is a tendency for children with DS to delay completion of the catch, resulting in more misses. Thus, when the standard deviations are taken into account, the time region (i.e., average plus or minus 2 SD; figure 11.4b) within which children with DS caught the balls falls more often outside the time window. Only one child with DS closed his hand early. These observations are confirmed by a Mann-Whitney rank order test, which was found to be significant ($U = 19$, $p < .05$).

In conclusion, the results of Planinsek (1996) reveal that children with DS tend to miss more than nonhandicapped children. In other words, children with DS are less successful in a motor performance involving temporal constraints than their unimpaired peers. Given that only temporal judgments were required, it can be

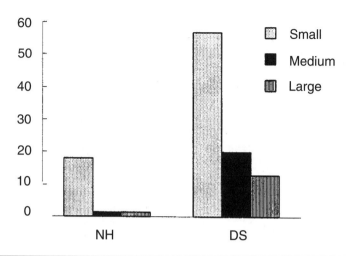

Figure 11.3   The percentage of misses for children with Down syndrome (DS) and nonhandicapped children (NH).

concluded that the less-successful catching performance associated with DS is at least partly due to a different timing pattern (i.e., completing the catch too late). However, there were no group differences in anticipatory timing; that is, the moment of opening and closing the hand in children with DS was similar to that of their nonhandicapped counterparts. This suggests that the children with DS either used different sources of information during the closure of the hand or, alternatively, closed their hands more slowly.

A related goal of the Planinsek (1996) study was to identify the visual information sources involved in the timing of the catch in children with DS. Do children with DS use different information sources than their nonhandicapped peers? The findings of the Planinsek (1996) study show that both the children with and without DS made more catching mistakes with the small balls under the monocular condition in comparison with the binocular condition (figure 11.5a). The movement kinematics showed that this effect was due to a delay in hand closure (i.e., time of maximal aperture; figure 11.5b) and completion of the catch (figure 11.5c) for the smaller balls. The hand was closed later when catching smaller balls in the monocular condition but not in the binocular viewing condition. These findings are similar to those found for adults (van der Kamp et al., 1997).

These effects were apparent for both groups and indicate that the children with DS use the same visual information as the control subjects and adults. The fact that the specific effects were different for the two viewing conditions suggests that the exact nature of information sources used in the two situations differs. Moreover, because ball diameter influenced the timing of the catch in the monocular condition, it can be concluded that it is not solely Tau that is used to control the catch. The Tau margin specifying time-to-contact is similar for different ball diameters.

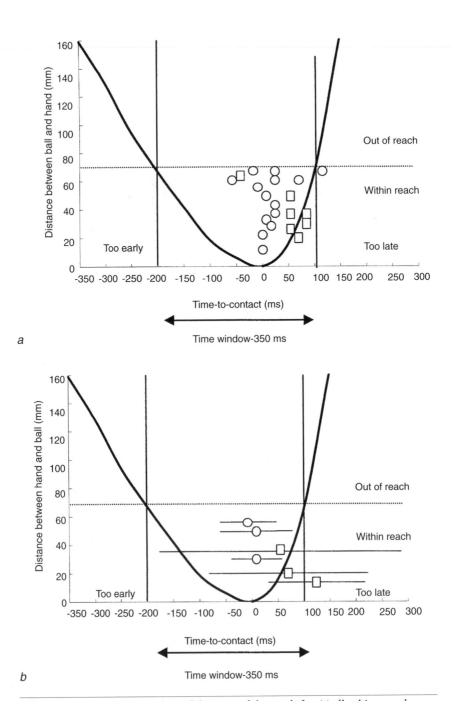

Figure 11.4 The time window of the time of the catch for (*a*) all subjects and (*b*) for some subjects with the standard deviations. Squares represent children with DS, and circles represent children without DS.

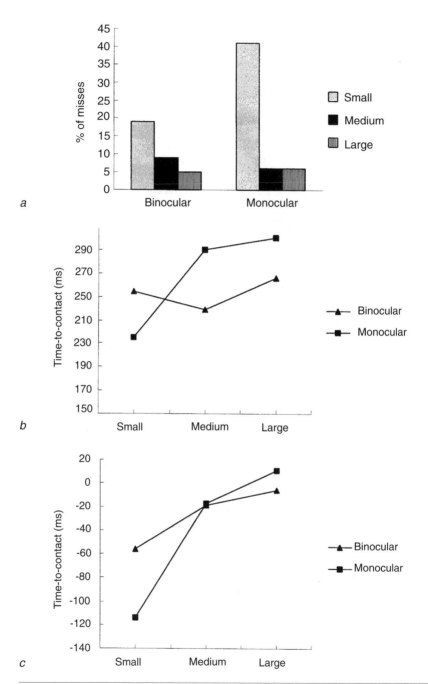

Figure 11.5 The effect of the visual manipulations for (*a*) the percentage of misses, (*b*) the time of hand closure, and (*c*) the time of completion of the catch as a function of DS and NH children. Minus signs indicate time before contact.

In conclusion, the difference in catching performance is at least partly due to delayed completion of the catch. The visual manipulations, however, did not result in differences between children with and without DS. It appears that the children with DS and the nonhandicapped children used the same information sources in the regulation of the catch. This indicates that the timing deficiency is probably due to a slowness of movement. Though no differences were found in anticipatory timing, one could argue that if the children with DS could learn to start their movements earlier (giving them more time), catching (timing) performance might improve.

Posture and Optic Flow Information

The perceptual-motor coupling involved in postural control implies the integration of different sensory information sources. In fact, information about the environment and the position of the body in space as well as the relative position of body segments is needed in order to keep balance during standing and locomotion. This information is provided not only by vision, but also by the vestibular and proprioceptive systems. Nevertheless, the study of perceptual control of posture, especially in children, is dominated by research investigating postural compensations to optic flow.

The optic flow field affords a wealth of information about the layout of the environment and the organism's movement. Many studies have shown a functional relation between optic flow and posture. One of the first experiments that examined the effect of visual information on posture made use of what has become known as the "moving-room" paradigm. This is a room that can be moved above a stable floor (Lee & Lishman, 1974; Lishman & Lee, 1973). When the room is moved, subjects experience self-motion when they stand or sit. This results in falls (with very young children) and oscillations of the body with the motion of the room. Thus, Lee and coworkers showed that vision has a proprioceptive function in maintaining postural stability.

A moving room-like paradigm has also been used with 3-day-old infants who were supported by a specially constructed baby seat with two air bags positioned at the head level to measure the head pressure variation (Jouen, 1988). Jouen perturbed the peripheral optic flow pattern by simulating backward and forward movement with different acceleration and deceleration values. He found a significant difference in head pressure between motion and nonmotion, indicating that infants were sensitive to optic flow information. Butterworth and coworkers (Butterworth & Hick, 1977; Pope, 1984) elicited compensatory head movements—movements opposite to the room movements—in 2- to 5-month-olds. More recently, Bertenthal and coworkers (Bertenthal, Rose, & Bai, 1997) showed coupling between optic flow pattern and motor behavior in children 5 to 9 months of age.

To our knowledge, only one study analyzed the behavior of children with DS in the moving-room situation (Butterworth & Cicchetti, 1978). The participants were infants with and without DS divided in different groups matched according to their experience in independent sitting or in standing without support. The postural reactions to the moving room were scored according to the rating scale developed by Lee and Aronson (1974), who categorized the visible reactions as sways, staggers, or falls. The standing results indicated that although infants with DS responded as often as the control infants, the amplitude of their response was different. In fact, falls were more frequent in infants with DS than in children without DS. This finding is in apparent contradiction with the results involving sitting where infants with DS had no visible, or only small, postural reactions. In contrast, the young sitters in the control groups were destabilized. Thus, when standing, infants with DS who have just learned to stand compensate more than nonhandicapped infants do. When sitting, infants with DS are less responsive to optic flow. The results also revealed a decline in response occurrence with postural experience. The number of falls declined after more than 3 months of standing experience in nonhandicapped infants and after 7 to 12 months of experience in infants with DS. Infants who had recently learned to stand without support were more destabilized by the experimentally induced discrepancy between visual and vestibular information than were the infants with more experience in standing. Usually, this developmental trend is taken to indicate that the importance of vision in the control of balance decreases as infants gain experience in motor control. However, recent studies using the same paradigm with more precise measurements of posture (i.e., displacements of the center of pressure) have led to a different conclusion. Bertenthal (Bertenthal et al., 1997; Boker, Schreiber, Pompe, & Bertenthal, in press) reported that for sitting, 5- to 9-month-old infants showed a significant developmental change in the dependency (measured by cross-correlations) between the position of the moving room and the fore-aft displacement of the center of pressure. During this period, postural oscillations became more and more linked to the oscillations of the room. Therefore, it is the strength of the coupling of postural oscillations to visual stimuli, rather than the magnitude of the sway, that provides the researcher knowledge about the influence of vision on postural control. The conclusion from these studies is that with increasing age or experience with a specific posture, postural control becomes more strongly linked to optic flow information in a way that ensures an increase in postural stability. It may be that this specific perceptual-motor coupling is an important factor for maintaining balance in different posturo-locomotor actions such as crawling and walking.

The classic interpretation would be that, after onset of independent standing, infants with DS remain dependent on visual information for a longer period of time than nonhandicapped infants. An alternative interpretation, however, might be that the delayed decline of falls seen in infants with DS is a consequence of the lack of general postural control (i.e., insufficient muscle strength and coordination). This would be in accordance with the common finding that children with DS show delays in motor development (e.g., O'Brien & Hayes, 1995). Unfortunately, in the study by Butterworth and Cicchetti (1978), the behavioral classification from the postural reactions does not provide sufficient detail about the prolonged duration of falls in children with DS. There is clearly a lack of experimental work concerning the strength of visual-postural coupling in children with DS.

Nevertheless, another study that analyzed the dynamics of postural control in children with DS provides interesting results concerning their ability to cope with discrepant sensory information in postural control (Shumway-Cook & Woollacott, 1985a). The experimental paradigm used by Shumway-Cook and Woollacott is different from the moving room. The standing position is not perturbed by movement of the visual surroundings but is directly challenged by movement of the support base (i.e., a movable platform). In this paradigm, one of the experimental conditions consists of rotations of the platform that are in direct proportion to the magnitude of the anterioposterior sway motion of the subject. For example, if the subject oscillates forward, the platform also rotates forward at the same time about an axis collinear with the ankle joint. The device ensures a fixed ankle joint angle and therefore reduces the orientational information from the ankle. The result is an intersensory conflict between, on the one hand, the ankle propriocepsis indicating stability and, on the other hand, the visual and vestibular information indicating body sway. Shumway-Cook and Woollacott analyzed the muscular coordination of the legs with surface electromyograms in children with and without DS aged from 15 months to 6 years. The results showed an interesting paradox in the responses of the children with DS: myotatic reflexes at normal latencies were present, with delays in long latency postural responses that often led to increased body sway and loss of balance. According to the authors, this supports the suggestion of Davis and Kelso (1982) that muscle stiffness and motoneuron pool excitability are comparable to those of normal children. Hence, Shumway-Cook and Woollacott (1985a) concluded that the responses of children with DS could not be attributed to pathology of the stretch reflex mechanism but rather are likely due to problems in the organizational processes underlying the resolution of multimodal sensory conflict. To determine whether the problems concern absence or delayed processes, this kind of experiment needs to be extended to older children with DS, given that a resolution of multimodal sensory conflict is normally reached between 7 and 10 years of age (Forssberg & Nashner, 1982; Shumway-Cook & Woollacott, 1985b).

Conclusions

It is our position that by examining the functional coupling between information and movement in children with DS, we can gain insight into important developmental perceptual-motor processes, including (a) what is learned over the course of development, (b) what this learning depends on, and (c) how it occurs. For example, one learns to move and coordinate actions by coupling the movements to the appropriate information sources. This coupling is expressed by the concept of affordances and depends not only on the maturation of the central nervous system, but also on the sensitivity for certain information sources. For example, grasping depends on the ratio between hand size and object size. In more general terms, the coupling depends on the action capabilities of the child under that certain set of constraints. These constraints may be different for children with DS. However, in discovering these constraints, one can gain insight into how the developmental process occurs—for example, by a coupling of optic flow information and posture, or binocular information and closing the hand in catching. From the perspective advocated in this chapter, children with DS should be encouraged to actively explore the environment. Through such exploration, these children will detect affordances, pick up the relevant information, and learn to couple the information to their movements.

Summary

Children with DS have perceptual-motor impairments that influence the development and learning of various fundamental and complex skills. The literature has documented many of these, but, unfortunately, not many findings are provided regarding the functional coupling of information and movement. This chapter examined such a functional coupling from an ecological approach to visual perception (Gibson, 1979). The role of optical information, such as object size, Tau, and optic flow, in the coordination and control of actions such as grasping, catching, and posture was reviewed. We concluded that by actively exploring the environment, children with DS can detect affordances, pick up the relevant information, and learn to couple the information to their movements.

References

Alderson, G.J.K., Sully, D.L., & Sully, H.G. (1974). An operational analysis of a one handed catching task using high speed photography. *Journal of Motor Behavior, 6,* 217-226.

Ball, W., & Tronick, E. (1971). Infant responses to impending collision: Optical and real. *Science, 171,* 812-820.

Bennett, S.J., van der Kamp, J., Savelsbergh, G.J.P., & Davids, K. (in press). Timing a one-handed catch: I. Effects of telestereoscopic viewing. *Experimental Brain Research.*

Berkson, G. (1960). An analysis of reaction time in normal and mentally deficient young men. *Journal of Mental Deficiency Research, 4,* 51-77.

Bertenthal, B.I., Rose, J., & Bai, D.L. (1997). Perception-action coupling in the development of visual posture. *Journal of Experimental Psychology: Human Perception and Performance, 23,* 1631-1643.

Block, M.E. (1991). Motor development in children with Down's Syndrome: A review of literature. *Adapted Physical Activity Quarterly, 8,* 175-209.

Boker, S.V., Schreiber, T., Pompe, B., & Bertenthal, B.I. (in press). Nonlinear analysis of perceptual-motor coupling in the development of postural control. In H. Kanz, J. Kurths, & G. Mayer-Kress (Eds.), *Nonlinear techniques in physiological time series analysis.* Berlin: Springer-Verlag.

Bower, T.G.R., Broughton, J.M., & Moore, M.K. (1970a). The coordination of visual and tactile input in infants. *Perception & Psychophysics, 8,* 51-53.

Bower, T.G.R., Broughton, J.M., & Moore, M.K. (1970b). Demonstration of intention in the reaching behaviour of neonate humans. *Nature, 228,* 679-681.

Butterworth, G., & Cicchetti, D. (1978). Visual calibration of posture in normal and motor retarded Down's syndrome infants. *Perception, 7,* 513-525.

Butterworth, G., & Hick, L. (1977). Visual proprioception and postural stability in infancy: A developmental study. *Perception, 5,* 255-263.

Castner, B.M. (1932). The development of fine prehension in infancy. *Genetic Psychology Monographs, 12,* 105-193.

Chumlea, W.C., Malina, R.M., Rarick, G.L., & Seefeldt, V.D. (1979). Growth of short bones of the hand in children with Down's syndrome. *Journal of Mental Deficiency Research, 23,* 137-150.

Cole, K.J., & Abbs, J.H. (1986). Coordination of three-joint digit movements for rapid finger-thumb grasp. *Journal of Neurophysiology, 55,* 1395-1406.

Connolly, K.J. (1973). Factors influencing the learning of manual skills by young children. In R.A. Hinde & J.S. Hinde (Eds.), *Constraints on learning* (pp. 337-365). London: Academic Press.

Connolly, K., & Elliott, J. (1972). The evolution and ontogeny of hand function. In N. Blurton Jones (Ed.), *Ethological studies of child behaviour* (pp. 337-365). London: Cambridge University Press.

Courage, M.L., Adams, R.J., Reyno, S., & Kwa, P.-G. (1994). Visual acuity in infants and children with Down syndrome. *Developmental Medicine and Child Neurology, 36,* 586-593.

Davis, W.E., & Kelso, J.A.S. (1982). Analysis of "invariant characteristics" in the motor control of Down syndrome and normal subjects. *Journal of Motor Behavior, 14,* 194-212.

Davis, W.E., & Sinning, W.E. (1987). Muscle stiffness in Down syndrome and other mentally handicapped subjects: A research note. *Journal of Motor Behavior, 19,* 130-144.

Davis, W.E., & Van Emmerik, R.E.A. (1994). An ecological task analysis approach for understanding motor development in mental retardation. Research paradigm and questions. In A. Vermeer & W.E. Davis (Eds.), *Physical and motor development in persons with mental retardation* (pp. 1-32). Basel, Switzerland: Karger.

Forssberg, H., & Nashner, L.M. (1982). Ontogenetic development of postural control in man: Adaptation to altered support and visual conditions during stance. *The Journal of Neuroscience, 2,* 545-552.

Frith, U., & Frith, C.D. (1974). Specific motor disabilities in Down syndrome. *Journal of Child Psychology and Psychiatry, 15,* 293-301.

Gesell, A. (1928). Maturation and infant behaviour pattern. *Psychological Review, 36,* 307-319.

Gibson, E.J. (1987). Introduction essay: What does infant perception tell us about theories of perception? *Journal of Experimental Psychology: Human Perception and Performance, 13,* 515-523.

Gibson, J.J. (1979). *The ecological approach to visual perception.* Boston: Houghton Mifflin.

Henderson, S.E. (1985). Motor skill development. In D. Lane & B. Stratford (Eds.), *Current approaches to Down syndrome* (pp. 187-218). London: Holt, Rinehart & Winston.

Henderson, S.E., Morris, J., & Frith, U. (1981). The motor deficit in Down's syndrome children: A problem of timing? *Journal of Child Psychology and Psychiatry, 22,* 233-245.

Hogg, J., & Moss, S.C. (1983). Prehensile development in Down's syndrome and nonhandicapped preschool children. *British Journal of Developmental Psychology, 1*, 8-17.

Jouen, F. (1988). Visual-proprioceptive control of posture in newborn infants. In B. Amblard, A. Berthoz, & F. Clarac (Eds.), *Posture and gait: Development, adaptation and modulation* (pp. 13-22). Amsterdam: Elsevier Science.

Judge, S.J., & Bradford, C.M. (1988). Adaptation to telestereoscopic viewing measured by one-handed ball-catching performance. *Perception, 17*, 783-802.

Kerr, R., & Blais, C. (1985). Motor skill acquisition by individuals with Down syndrome. *American Journal of Mental Deficiency, 90*, 313-318.

Knights, R.M., Atkinson, B.R., & Hyman, J.A. (1967). Tactual discrimination and motor skills in mongoloid and non-mongoloid retardates and normal children. *American Journal of Mental Deficiency, 71*, 894-900.

Kugler, P.N., & Turvey, M.T. (1987). *Information, natural law, and the self-assembly of rhythmic movements*. Hillsdale, NJ: Erlbaum.

Lee, D.N. (1976). A theory of visual control of braking base on information about time to contact. *Perception, 5*, 437-459.

Lee, D.N. (1980). Visuo-motor coordination in space-time. In G.E. Stelmach & J. Requin (Eds.), *Tutorials in motor behavior* (pp. 281-293). Amsterdam: North-Holland.

Lee, D.N., & Aronson, E. (1974). Visual proprioceptive control of standing in human infants. *Perception & Psychophysics, 15*, 529-532.

Lee, D.N., & Lishman, J.R. (1974). Visual proprioceptive control of stance. *Journal of Human Movement Studies, 1*, 87-95.

Lishman, J.R., & Lee, D.N. (1973). The autonomy of visual kinaesthesis. *Perception, 2*, 287-294.

Moss, S.C., & Hogg, J. (1981). Development of hand function in mentally handicapped and nonhandicapped preschool children. In P. Mittler (Ed.), *Frontiers of knowledge in mental retardation: Vol. 1. Social, educational, and behavioural aspects* (pp. 35-44). Baltimore: University Park Press.

Newell, K.M. (1986). Constraints on the development of coordination. In M. Wade & H.T.A. Whiting (Eds.), *Motor development in children: Aspects of coordination and control* (pp. 341-360). Dordrecht: Martinus Nijhoff.

Newell, K.M., Scully, D.M., McDonald, P.V., & Baillargeon, R. (1989). Task constraints and infant grip configurations. *Developmental Psychobiology, 22*, 817-832.

Newell, K.M., Scully, D.M., Tenenbaum, F., & Hardiman, S. (1989). Body-scale and the development of prehension. *Developmental Psychobiology, 22*, 1-13.

O'Brien, C., & Hayes, A. (1995). *Normal and impaired motor development theory into practice*. San Diego: Chapman and Hall.

Planinsek, T. (1996). *The control of timing among children with Down Syndrome*. Unpublished master's thesis, Catholic University, Leuven, Belgium.

Pope, M. (1984). *Visual proprioception in input postural development*. Unpublished doctoral dissertation, University of Southampton.

Pufall, P.B., & Dunbar, C. (1992). Perceiving whether or not the world affords stepping onto and over: A developmental study. *Ecological Psychology, 4*, 17-38.

Rosengren, K.S., Pick, H.L., & Von Hofsten, C. (1988). Role of visual information in ball catching. *Journal of Motor Behavior, 20*, 150-164.

Savelsbergh, G.J.P. (1993). *The development of coordination in infancy*. Amsterdam: Elsevier Science.

Savelsbergh, G.J.P., Steenbergen, B., & van der Kamp, J. (1996). The role of fragility information in the guidance of the precision grip. *Human Movement Science, 15,* 115-127.

Savelsbergh, G.J.P., & van der Kamp, J. (in press). The influence of the de-stabilization of the head orientation on infants prehension. *Journal of Human Movement Studies.*

Savelsbergh, G.J.P., & van der Kamp, J. (1994). The effect of body orientation to gravity on early infant reaching. *Journal of Experimental Child Psychology, 58,* 510-528.

Savelsbergh, G.J.P., van der Kamp, J., & Davis, W.E. (1998). *A body-scaled ratio as a control parameter for grasping in children with Down syndrome.* Unpublished manuscript.

Savelsbergh, G.J.P., Von Hofsten, C., & Jonsson, B. (1997). The coupling of head, reach and grasp movement in nine months old infant prehension. *Scandinavian Journal of Psychology, 38,* 325-335.

Savelsbergh, G.J.P., & Whiting, H.T.A. (1988). The effects of skill level, external frame of reference and environmental changes on one handed catching. *Ergonomics, 31,* 1655-1663.

Savelsbergh, G.J.P., Whiting, H.T.A., & Bootsma, R.J. (1991). 'Grasping' Tau. *Journal of Experimental Psychology: Human Perception and Performance, 19,* 315-322.

Savelsbergh, G.J.P., Whiting, H.T.A., Pijpers, J.R., & Santvoord, A.M.M. (1993). The visual guidance of catching. *Experimental Brain Research , 93,* 146-156.

Savelsbergh, G.J.P., Wimmers, R.H., van der Kamp, J., & Davids, K. (in press). The development of movement control and coordination. In A. Kalverboer, M. Genta, & B. Hopkins (Eds.), *Current issues in developmental neuropsychology.* Dordecht: Kluwer Academic Press.

Schiff, W., Caviness, J.A., & Gibson, J.J. (1962). Persistent fear responses in rhesus monkeys to the optical stimulus of 'looming'. *Science, 136,* 982-983.

Schiff, W., & Detweiler, M.L. (1979). Information used in judging impending collision. *Perception, 8,* 647-658.

Shumway-Cook, A., & Woollacott, M.H. (1985a). Dynamics of postural control in the child with Down syndrome. *Physical Therapy, 65,* 1315-1322.

Shumway-Cook, A., & Woollacott, M.H. (1985b). The growth of stability: Postural control from a developmental perspective. *Journal of Motor Behavior, 17,* 131-147.

Stratford, B. (1980). Perception and perceptual-motor processes in children with Down's syndrome. *Journal of Psychology, 104,* 139-145.

Sugden, D.A., & Keogh, J.F. (1990). *Problems in movement skill development.* Columbia: University of South Carolina Press.

Thelen, E., & Smith, L.B. (1994). *A dynamic systems approach to the development of cognition and action.* Cambridge, MA: MIT Press.

van der Kamp, J., Bennett, S.J., Savelsbergh, G.J.P., & Davids, K. (in press). Timing a one-handed catch: II. Adaptation to telestereoscopic viewing. *Experimental Brain Research.*

van der Kamp, J., Savelsbergh, G.J.P., & Davis, W.E. (1998). Body-scaled ratio as control parameter for prehension in 5 to 9 year old children. *Developmental Psychobiology, 33,* 351-361.

van der Kamp, J., Savelsbergh, G.J.P., & Smeets, J. (1997). Multiple information sources in interceptive timing. *Human Movement Science, 16,* 787-822.

Von Hofsten, C. (1983). Catching skills in infancy. *Journal of Experimental Psychology: Human Perception and Performance, 9,* 75-85.

Warren, W.H. (1984). Perceiving affordances: Visual guidance of stair climbing. *Journal of Experimental Psychology: Human Perception and Performance, 10,* 683-703.

Warren W.H. (1990). The perception-action coupling. In H. Bloch & B.I. Bertenthal (Eds.), *Sensory-motor organizations and development in infancy and early childhood* (pp. 23-37). Dordecht: Kluwer Academic Publishers.

Yonas, A., Bechtold, A.G., Frankel, D., Gordon, R.F., McRobert, G., Norcia, A., & Sternfels, S. (1977). Development of sensitivity to information for impending collision. *Perception & Psychophysics, 21*, 97-104.

12
CHAPTER

Atypical Dynamics of Motor Behavior in Down Syndrome

Michael G. Wade

School of Kinesiology and Leisure Studies
University of Minnesota

Richard Van Emmerik

University of Massachusetts

Thomas W. Kernozek

University of Wisconsin—LaCrosse

Key words

dynamics ◆ periodicity ◆ patterned behavior ◆ coordination ◆ self-organization ◆ homeostasis ◆ attractors ◆ coupling ◆ direct perception ◆ locomotion ◆ posture ◆ phenotype ◆ somatotype ◆ motion sickness ◆ control

Studies of motor behavior, whether focused on contemporary issues of coordination and control or on the more traditional approaches of motor learning and performance, demonstrate the ubiquity of peoples' ability to display temporal accuracy and to exhibit rhythmicity in skilled activity. Over a wide range of motor behavior, individuals exhibit appropriate temporal order in coordinating the necessary muscles and joints involved in the intended task. All living systems exhibit "rhythmicity" in their activities regardless of their loci; at multiple levels of analysis, animals exhibit periodic behaviors in their living habits. The origins of the universe itself and its ongoing evolution may well be conceived in the context of periodic phase. Predicting the future of the universe is difficult, as we are unable to accurately pinpoint our present location on this hypothetical evolutionary cycle. The more immediate concerns about global warming and reports of a rise in the earth's core temperature suggest that global warming may well be a representation of a periodic phenomenon, the frequency domain of which is presently unknown. Seasonal and daily periodicity notwithstanding, humans exhibit a variety of periodic activity (sometimes referred to as biorhythms; Wade, 1970). Our daily living patterns are driven in part by diurnal and circadian rhythms, and at the glandular and cellular level, there are a variety of periodicities evident in both the excretion and metabolism of our biochemistry, insulin being one of the better-known cases. In addition to periodicities evident in our biology, similar periodic phenomena, one may assume, are exhibited in human social behavior. The popular misconception about "biorhythms" notwithstanding, many aspects of our ongoing social behavior reflect a regularity that suggests that the peaks and valleys of our behavioral states are evidence of this periodicity.

Periodicity as Patterned Behavior

The 17th-century philosophers Descartes and Locke influenced much of 20th-century scientific inquiry, including both the behavioral and biological sciences. The Russian physiologist Nicolai Bernstein, whose work was first published in English in 1967, remarked that the richly varied coordination movements exhibited by people and animals possessed a simplicity of control despite the enormous complexity of the nervous system involved and the environment in which all of this activity took place. It appeared that this *simplicity* was derivable from low-dimensional informative structures; and the paradox faced by scientists interested in explaining coordination is in the lawful restrictions on the behavioral degrees of freedom as a basis for the infinite number of qualitative distinctions among coordination patterns. Periodicity or rhythmicity has long been recognized as characteristic of both living systems and the living universe itself. The philosophy of Descartes and Locke that promoted the separation of body and mind (dualism) argued for either an exogenous or an endogenous referent that controls or generates the periodic profile evident in living systems. This view influenced not only research on coordination, but also most of the sciences of modern psychology, biology, and neuroscience. The notion of an internal referent or comparator, which either imposes order or controls action, has been the hallmark of much of the research on human and animal behavior over the past 50 years.

The study of complex systems in physical biology and its application to research on the coordination and control of human movement offer a very different paradigmatic view of how action and motor skills might be organized and executed. The study of complex systems that applies the mathematics of nonlinear dynamics and thermodynamics suggests that the many and varied elements that make up the universe exhibit a capacity to self-organize in response to state changes. More importantly, the same ideas may apply equally well to patterns of behavior and not only to molecules and cells. Kelso (1988), in referring to the term "complexity," noted the following in regard to the emergence of complex behavioral patterns:

> From our point of view . . . the mapping of complex patterns of behavior onto lower-dimensional laws may be even more crucial as we consider those "typically biological" features of physical systems—their ability to perceive, coordinate actions, memorize, learn, and anticipate—including intentional and linguistic aspects. (Kelso, 1988, p. 4)

The idea that coordination arises via the system self-organizing rather than being a slave to a central executive is appealing because it offers an opportunity to resolve what is now commonly referred to as "Bernstein's Problem." Coordination (i.e., the bringing of parts into proper relations) is a very complex problem of organization. The human body consists of approximately 10^2 joints, 10^3 muscles, and 10^{14} cells. How all the degrees of freedom for any human action are coordinated is an insurmountable problem viewed from a computational perspective. Over the past 25 years, considerable research effort has been directed toward explaining the coordination and control of movement. Generally, the approach has been to assume an intelligent executive (the "ghost in the machine") that must get smarter as the magnitude of the coordination problem grows. The alternative approach, influenced by the study of complex systems, assumes that coordination is influenced by the properties of nonlinear systems. Thus, to provide a description of the principles that underlie coordination, research has focused on examining low-dimensional regularities that have lawful properties and low-dimensional informative structures (optic and haptic invariants; Turvey, 1990).

Solving problems of coordination in intact normal systems is daunting enough, but seeking an account of *atypical* motor behavior of persons with developmental disabilities is even more difficult. Descriptive information on atypical development in the standard terminology both of psychology and movement science is well known (e.g., slower rates of learning in acquiring task skills, higher levels of variability in performance, little or no strategic development, slower reaction time, etc.). Scientists have only begun attempting to describe the capacity of the atypical individual to exhibit self-organizing behaviors relative to problems of control and coordination. Standard descriptive accounts usually point to neurological damage of one kind or another, and inferences are then made regarding an impaired capacity to "compute" acceptable solutions to the problems posed by movement skills that require coordination and control (cf. Keele & Ivry, 1990; Williams, Woollacott, & Ivry, 1992). An alternative approach is to determine whether or not the low-dimensional regularities that account for the capacity to self-organize in intact living systems are present in atypical populations. Complexity has been described as "at the edge of order and chaos" (Waldrop, 1993). This approach (i.e., searching for dynamic patterns in complex systems) attempts to account for atypical motor behavior by examining the action system's capacity (we believe most likely *incapacity*) to exhibit these kinds of rhythmic stabilities. Those individuals who exhibit via pathology a disability, disease, or genetic abnormality may be grounded in their inability to exhibit self-organization. This hypothesis needs to be tested and, if found reliable, offers a strong clinical tool for the early detection of atypical development, both motor and, more generally, intellectual.

How the Inability to Self-Organize Might Show Itself: What's the Signature?

Coordinated activity represents patterned behavior; thus, any activity that exhibits a rhythmic or periodic pattern of behavior over time may well be key in the study of coordination. A methodology that seeks to detect the presence of rhythm or periodicity in coordinated activity is a good place to begin. While evidence of periodicity is commonplace in living systems, it is important first to review the theorizing, or at least the hypothesizing, before reviewing the available empirical support, and then suggest a direction for future research.

Standard accounts of periodic behavior look to exogenous mechanisms such as the sun and the moon (diurnal and circadian rhythms; cf. Klietman, 1963) and endogenous mechanisms, which govern or control our temporal mechanisms (Michon, 1967). In 1929, the British physiologist W.B. Cannon proposed his theory of "homeostasis" as a regulatory mechanism of the physiological system of humans (Cannon, 1929). Cannon's ideas had their roots in the earlier writings of the French scientist Claude Bernard (ca. 1888), whose notion of a "milieu internale" proposed that for living systems, a physiological regulatory mechanism sought to maintain the normal state of the organism in equilibrium. Any increase in physiological activity required that homeostasis be disturbed to "get things done." Activity having ceased, the system "works" to restore itself to a level of equilibrium. For example, a person running to catch a bus produces an increase in heart rate in order to supply the muscles with the necessary oxygenated blood. Having successfully caught and boarded the bus, our passenger (now seated) recovers from the energy expended. Having restored the system, the heart returns to its usual resting (basal) level. Cannon (1929) argued that this was characteristic of how the many subsystems in the body maintain the physiological system's state of equilibrium. The homeostatic system may be regarded as part of the overall periodic phenomena of living systems, because when homeostasis is disturbed, the regulatory mechanism that seeks to return to equilibrium works against any outside demands. This conflict can produce periodic behavior. When physiological stasis finds itself in competition with an epistemic system (Berlyne, 1960), the living organism is stimulated to seek information and interaction with the environment. The physiological system is required to provide the energy necessary to pursue this interaction. Periodicity thus can be a resultant property when an epistemic (information-seeking) behavioral system that exhibits high levels of exploratory activity is in conflict with a homeostatic physiological regulatory mechanism requirement. Such an interaction necessitates that depleted energy (e.g., O_2 debt) be restored before further activity is possible. We have demonstrated that these work/rest ratios emerge from such system conflicts in the free play of young children (Wade, 1970; Wade & Ellis, 1971; Wade, Ellis, & Bohrer, 1973) and are absent in the play activity of atypical individuals (Wade, 1973).

The notion that living systems can self-organize may characterize diurnal and circadian cycles as emergent self-organizing phenomena that reflect the dynamic interaction between the animal (person) and the environment (sun and moon). Homeostasis may be a dynamic "mechanism" that reflects a self-organizing capacity, which emerges at an optimal level of stasis. Resting HR becomes a point of stability or "attractor," which, other things being equal, supports an optimal level of self-regulation. Perturbations introduced into this environment have a destabilizing effect, which, if sufficiently powerful, produce fluctuations or instabilities in the system, which, if sufficiently intense, produce a change from one level of organization to another. Thus, the system reorganizes at some new point of stability. For example, basal metabolic rate (BMR) may either go up or down as a function of such things as regular physical exercise. The central point is to recognize that periodicities, which are presumed to be controlled by some kind of "biological clock," may in fact be the attractors, and the stability points emerge as a function of a living system being required to live, work, and behave under a particular set of environmental constraints. In a similar fashion, BMR may also be a stability point, which reflects our activity level, our nutrition, and possibly our genetic predisposition. Anytime the scalar values of these properties change (i.e., the introduction of a program of physical activity), these increased values produce a change in BMR, which is an emergent property and the stability point for the system based on its new physiological capacity. There are many examples in living systems of a capacity to show regularity in behavior. We see it not only in the everyday requirements of locomotion and gait, but also in the regularity of our speech patterns and in our nutritional, digestive, and reproductive systems. The question we may ask, then, is does an individual whose development is delayed, either because of genetic abnormality or possibly disease, produce atypical or degraded periodicity in their movement behaviors?

Ecological psychology argues that periodicity of a different kind is demonstrated in the interplay between perception and action. Central to this ecological view proposed by James Gibson (1979) is the notion that our perceptual systems rely on the activity of the organism in discovering and interacting with and within its environment, such that perception and action become equal partners in the life course of living systems. The coordination and control exhibited by the organism in interacting successfully with environmental demands are reflected in the periodic nature of living systems. Our earlier work demonstrated periodicities in the play activity of children; in a similar fashion, the dynamics of perception/action coupling, via ambient arrays from perceptual flow fields, may reflect our capacity to directly perceive information from the environment. A good example of this is the optical flow field generated by moving an enclosure backward or forward about a subject. Such movement specifies motion of self (ego-motion) to the subject. Just as periodicity emerges from the proposed epistemic system of the organism (Berlyne, 1960), which resonates on the physiological regulatory mechanisms to produce work/rest cycles in the organism, so do the dynamic properties of perception/action coupling of a living system demonstrate periodicity, as motion specified from the environment couples to the movement of the perceiving individual.

Stability

Kugler and Turvey (1987) have demonstrated that intact living systems exhibit preferred rates (tempos) and thus behave as stable attractors. The degrees to which perturbations can be tolerated are usually a function of the stability of the attractor space. This is hypothetically illustrated in figure 12.1.

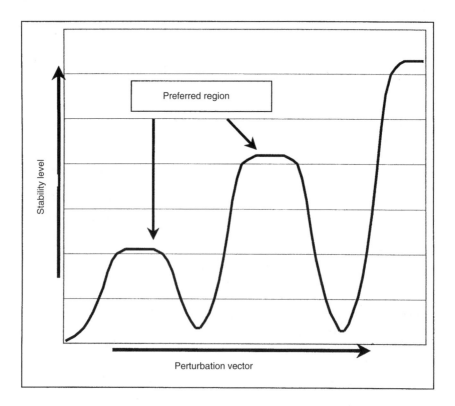

Figure 12.1 Hypothetical relationship between the level of stability and the strength of the perturbation.

The illustration in figure 12.1 is a hypothetical representation of both the level of stability, represented on the ordinate by the tolerance limits (expressed as a variability score), and the scalar value of the perturbation (abscissa). Thus the system is more stable when the stability factor has high variability to a specific level of perturbation. In figure 12.1, the preferred rates as "attractors" represent optimal or near-optimal levels of self-organization under a given set of constraints (task-performer-environment). The actor couples perception of mass and/or range of motion with the attractor point (rate or cycle) that is optimal (i.e., its most efficient rate). Further, the "attractor" remains stable and shows tolerance to perturbation across a set range (variability is large).

The dynamic properties of perception/action coupling demonstrated in children (Bertenthal & Bai, 1989; Lee & Aronson, 1974) and in adults (Stoffregen, 1985) represent another form of periodic behavior. The correlation between the oscillation rate of the moving room and the sway motion of an individual in that room is high ($r = .7$; Stoffregen, 1985) and reliable. This oscillatory coupling is above postural threshold (0.1–0.3 Hz), and presumably the stability of this relation will be relatively constant across a range of values above threshold but below a breakdown point (chaos). A similar example might be a group of runners or joggers who couple to a preferred rate of stride cadence. This "preferred" jogging rate may not be representative of any single person in the group, but represents a preferred rate or attractor about which fluctuations represented by each individual runner can be tolerated.

Our work with Down syndrome (DS) assumes the general hypothesis that a periodicity principle operates as an attractor that is present in normally functioning individuals. We seek to determine in populations of individuals with DS if such atypical behavior exhibits different periodic characteristics or levels of tolerance before breakdown. Down syndrome is an especially useful case study because the condition presents clinically both motor deficits and mental retardation (MR) as well as a high concentration of several other anomalies (Shapiro, 1983). Before addressing specifically the issue of a periodic behavior in motor activity, a review of some of the clinical aspects of DS as well as some of the physical and behavioral constraints on coordination and control in this population is in order.

Clinical Studies

The study of DS has undergone a lengthy and focused investigation since it was first described clinically by Langdon Down in 1866. Since that time its genetic anomalies have been identified, and a range of both genetic and clinical abnormalities occurring in the syndrome have been reported and recorded. Psychology has studied DS as a special case of mental retardation, and movement scientists have recorded both the skill level and the motor deficits associated with its clinical description. From the perspective of both psychology and kinesiology, persons with DS usually require more trials to learn a task to criterion, show greater variability in performance, and characteristically show poor ability to generate strategies to solve either verbal or motor tasks or to generalize learning strategies acquired in tasks that are similar (Campione & Brown, 1977).

Over the usual range of what is diagnosed as a mentally handicapping condition, individuals with DS fall into the midrange category and have been described as educationally and mentally handicapped (EMH) as defined by standard IQ scores, somewhere in the range of 45 to 75. Typically their motor abilities reflect a slower reaction time (RT) and movement time (MT), an increase in performance variability (Berkson, 1960a, 1960b, 1960c), and a diminished capacity to deal with increased information loads (Wade, Newell, & Wallace, 1978) but with some ability to pre-program responses under conditions where temporal order is maintained (Hoover, Wade, & Newell, 1981). These research efforts represent part of a strong empirical record of the documented limitations of persons with DS, but do not provide a principled account of the underlying deficits. Perception clearly plays a key role in all movement activity requiring control and coordination, but until recently the focus of perception research has been more on *how* perception might work rather than the nature of the information available.

Over the past three decades, cognitive psychology has produced several models of how the perceptual system "works," with the majority employing a computer analogy of one form or another. While the results of this work have been useful, they have not focused on *what* is perceived and thus ignore a whole array of other interesting questions that focus more on the nature of the information available to the perceiver. Past researchers who studied perception always assumed that the information entering the "system" was in need of translation to "make sense" of the input so that an appropriate response could be generated by the central nervous system. This assumption now is being questioned from an epistemological view and in terms of the empirical analysis and protocols used.

Gibson (1979) proposed that "the perceiver" is directly sensitive to the information available in the environment and, further, that this information is not only directly perceived but rich in content. Gibson's proposal reduces dramatically the need for a complex "in the head" perceptual mediator that is both computational and inferential. While for some this notion remains unacceptable, those who have pursued direct perception are producing a growing body of empirical evidence supporting Gibson's view. It is in the vein of direct perception that we present our preliminary ideas to account for the motor deficits associated with DS and quite possibly to extend this argument to the more general problems of motor deficits and mental retardation.

As part of its inferential effort, early research on DS alluded to a limitation in the individual's capacity to process certain levels of information (Olson, 1971), the development of poor strategic behavior (i.e., mediational or production strategies as suggested by Brown, 1978), and problems of structure versus control processes in the human memory model proposed by Atkinson and Shiffrin (1968). We also contributed to this database (Wade et al., 1978; Wade, Hoover, & Newell, 1984) and philosophical view.

An ecological account of coordination in normal individuals would read more in the following terms: (1) normal human organisms are both complex and essentially nonlinear, but meet the thermodynamic requirements of self-organization; (2) the many degrees of freedom are organized functionally by the formation of *collectives*; and (3) complex systems reflect preferred, but not obligatory, movement patterns. Dynamic attractors are either stable or unstable depending on the environmental demands and stability of the system, and nonlinear phase shifts from one attractor state to another occur as a function of changes in the control parameters to which the system is sensitive. Kugler et al. (1980) and Thelen and Ulrich (1991) have promoted this viewpoint both theoretically and empirically.

In normally functioning systems, the component subsystems are seen to cooperate to allow new behaviors to emerge. Knowing a priori the motor deficits of mentally handicapped persons with and without DS, we would seek, from an ecological viewpoint, to determine the following characteristics of movement behavior:

- the presence or absence of preferred rates of movement patterns;
- the capacity of persons with DS to exhibit perception/action coupling in specific contexts (e.g., sensitivity to optical flow that specifies motion of self or oscillatory optical flow to which the subject couples his or her motion); and
- the sensitivity of perceptual mechanisms in individuals with DS to environmentally available information.

These "dynamical" properties known to be present in normal individuals may be degraded or differentially arrayed in individuals with DS.

Ulrich and Ulrich (1992) employed a dynamical systems analysis to better understand motor delay in Down syndrome. Their work was an extension of the work of Esther Thelen (1979) and sought to determine whether or not the emergence of typical motor behaviors such as crawling and walking (which are delayed in DS) may be a function of a difference in the organizing capacity of the coordination system that permits the emergence of such behaviors. Ulrich and Ulrich (1992) argued that the process by which the new behaviors emerge is the same as in normal individuals regardless of where on the development rate continuum the infant resides. They opined that the process by which these early locomotor skills are acquired should not be affected by differences in anatomical or neurophysiological mechanisms, the environmental context, or the task. They argued that *rate* of change may be the issue in that the behaviors emerge to fit a task while the details of the patterns may vary considerably. They focused their research on factors related to the emergence of walking and reported data that they claim relates dynamical systems principles to the motor development of infants with Down syndrome. Their data demonstrated that infants with DS were able to produce highly coordinated and consistently alternating stepping patterns many months before they were able to walk. Eleven-month-old infants with DS produced a significant number of alternating steps when supported upright with their feet resting on the belt of a motorized treadmill. Ulrich and Ulrich (1992) argued that the neurosubstrates are not causing the delay, but that insufficient development of other equally important elements, such as muscle strength and postural control, mask the ability of DS infants to demonstrate stepping patterns in a normal context. This is the first such work reported on subjects with DS, and it supports the idea of both examining atypical behavior from a dynamical systems perspective and evaluating the capacity of such individuals to exhibit a level of self-organization in their motor behavior.

Our earlier work on this problem (Wade, 1973, 1990) suggested that sensitivity to information specifying common preferred attractor states might not be present in populations of individuals with mentally handicapping conditions. We reported a lack of periodic behavior in the free play of subjects with mental handicaps (Wade, 1973). More recently this notion was further supported on a small group of subjects ($n = 6$) who recorded minimal postural motion of the center of pressure measured by standard Stabilographic procedures (Wade, 1990). This was in direct contrast to a group of subjects without handicaps who exhibited reliable periodicities in free play (Wade, Ellis, & Bohrer, 1973) and who appeared sensitive to optical flow perturbations that specified motion of self as the subject stood upright (Wade, 1990).

Questions regarding the sensitivity of the perceptual systems of individuals with DS are further complicated by the notion that the homeostatic system of a person with DS is devoid of what Shapiro (1983) terms "developmental and physiological buffers" to develop the standard phenotype that emerges from normal genetic formation. Shapiro (1983) has suggested that one of the emerging general problems of individuals with DS is that, via a disturbed homeostatic system, the genetic abnormality produces an abnormal phenotype. This also is manifested motorically and kinematically in an atypical somatotype. Thus from a general perspective, we would expect persons with DS to exhibit atypical behaviors in a variety of domains where perceptual sensitivity is critical to coordination and control. We present a preliminary empirical foray into this problem area by presenting data on two separate but related aspects of this problem: (1) the sensitivity of subjects with DS to optical flow generated by a moving-room protocol, and (2) a survey of the incidence of motion sickness in individuals with DS compared with the general population.

As with any issue that relates perceptual abilities to coordination and control, there are other developmental and biomechanical characteristics of individuals with DS to provide a contextual backdrop to issues relating to perception and action. A brief review of these issues is presented.

Locomotion and Posture

Griffiths (1976) reported that 25% of children with DS are able to walk at 2 years of age, with the mean age being 30 months. They also exhibit considerable variability in the attainment of individual walking. Comparing percentile graphs of children with DS to those of other children, the curve for individuals with DS shifts markedly to the right, with a lesser slope indicating a slower rate of skill attainment. However, the overall shape of the curve was similar to the control group. Ulrich, Ulrich, and Collier (1992) reported that alternate stepping patterns are observed at 11 months of age. This indicates that the neural networks appear to be established, and that other factors are inhibiting locomotion. Just as the attainment of walking has shown considerable variability, so has the range of the walking skills of children with DS. Parker and Bronks (1980) studied 7-year-old children with DS and found that walking patterns were similar to newly independent walkers rather than to the mature patterns seen in adults. One of the characteristics of these walking patterns was a shuffling gait pattern (Eichstaedt & Kalakian, 1987). Parker and Bronks (1980) reported that a lack of plantar flexion of the ankle accompanied by reduction of hip extension resulted in a lack of propulsion and thus a stepping or shuffling-type gait pattern. Another characteristic often seen is a consistent toeing out (Lydic & Steele, 1979; Parker & Bronks, 1980). Mahan, Diamond, and Brown (1983) found the amount of toeing out to be 16° of abduction. They hypothesized that this may provide a wider base of support to reduce lateral motion and so facilitate postural stability. Indeed, Share and French (1982) noted that overall balance was poor in DS children, necessitating a wider base of support. Eichstaedt and Kalakian (1987) suggested that the excessive toeing out was perhaps a result of years of incorrect gait rather than congenital effects. They suggested that obesity also might be a factor, predisposing individuals with DS to toeing out while placing excessive stress on the longitudinal arch.

Share and French (1982) reported that individuals with DS begin to run without falling by about 36 months of age. This reflects a considerable delay in locomotor skill attainment, since a normal child usually can run without falling by 24 months. The DS individual shows similar patterns with running as with walking: running patterns are typically of shuffling type, and toeing out and a lack of propulsion during toeoff are often present during running.

Somatotype and Physical Constraints in Typical Physical Activity

Individuals with DS have a myriad of factors thought to inhibit their locomotor skills. Factors that can influence their ability to locomote are their hypotonic muscles and a ligamentous laxity, which contribute to joint hypermobility (Livingstone & Hirst, 1986), delayed appearance of postural responses (Butterworth & Cichetti, 1978; Shumway-Cook & Woollacott, 1985a, 1985b), obesity (Chumlea & Cronk, 1982; Cronk, Chumlea, & Roche, 1985), and less active exploration of their environment (Beeghly, Weiss-Perry, & Cichetti, 1989). Hypotonia is thought to decrease with age (Griffiths, 1976), and Eichstaedt and Kalakian (1987) have suggested that hypotonia might be reduced if intervention such as manipulation and strength training was provided to the young individual with DS as a therapeutic intervention.

Ligamentous laxity may be a precursor to the many orthopedic problems of the lower extremities associated with DS. Most common problems consist of metatarsus primus varus, resulting in a wide space between the first and second toes; patellar instability with the prevalence of subluxation or dislocation; severe flat feet (pes planus); and excessive external rotation of the femur (Diamond, Lynne, & Sigman, 1981; Dugdale & Renshaw, 1986; Scheffler, 1973). These orthopedic problems can inhibit the DS individual's ability and desire to participate in physical activity and exercise programs, especially those that require weight bearing such as walking or running.

Children with DS are frequently overweight and in fact often become obese after age 5 (Mahan et al., 1983). Eichstaedt and Kalakian (1987) reported that individuals with DS are prone to obesity because of the early termination of their growth period at about 16 years of age. With this cessation in growth, the individual's metabolic rate slows, requiring less caloric intake. Pueschel and Rynders (1982) reported that obesity results from excessive caloric intake, decreased physical activity, and inadequate caloric expenditure. Because of the many orthopedic problems, alternative exercises should be prescribed in place of walking and running. Eichstaedt and Kalakian (1987) suggest riding a stationary bike and swimming as alternative exercise. With alternative forms of exercise and proper diet, problems with obesity may be reduced as the individual ages.

Atlantoaxial dislocation condition (ADC) is another pathology that can inhibit participation in certain physical activities. This condition, consisting of displacement of space between the C1 and C2 vertebrae, produces excessive movement of the neck, potentially endangering the spinal cord. Individuals with ADC should not participate in activities in which a radical hyperflexion or hyperextension of the neck might occur.

Because of the earlier termination of the growth period, individuals with DS typically are much shorter than the average individual; the average height for adult males with DS is 5 ft and for adult females is 4 ft 7 in. (Eichstaedt & Kalakian, 1987).

The individual with DS has many characteristics that tend to hamper his or her interaction with the environment. Thus, activities need to be geared to the individual needs of the person. Specific training protocols are required if any benefits are to occur. Exercise programs should be provided as a means of secondary prevention of conditions such as obesity (Brooks-Bertram, 1986). Individuals with DS also require adequate footwear and good orthopedic care. The goal is to encourage self-care and self-maintenance of individuals toward more independent living environments while encouraging as active a lifestyle as possible.

Coordination and Control

The motor behavior of DS is perplexing because much of the research already reported in the literature has failed to detect specific abnormalities in the mechanisms of motor control. Davis and Sinning (1987) reported only small differences between nonhandicapped persons and subjects with DS in reproducing target locations when acting against force. More recently, data from a study by Latash, Almeida, and Corcos (1992) reported no abnormalities in motor control mechanisms other than high variability in the performance of some subjects. Once again, the overall picture for subjects with DS is arguably no different from that of many other mentally handicapped groups in that mean performance usually requires more trials to reach criterion and performance variability is usually greater.

For an individual with a developmental disability, the capacity to "couple" or "phase-lock" to an attractor is diminished. Our earlier research (Wade et al., 1973) used spectral analysis to parse continuous heart rate data of children's free play to detect evidence of periodic behavior in play groups of young male and female children. A replication of that study (Wade, 1973) using subjects with MR showed a lack of periodic behavior in that sample. The pioneering work of Lee and his coworkers (Lee & Aronson, 1974; Lee & Lishman, 1975) demonstrated that young infants are sensitive to visual proprioceptive control posture. In a similar study of children with DS, Butterworth and Cichetti (1978) reported essentially the same results as the Lee and Aronson (1974) study. The Butterworth and Cichetti (1978) work reported some minor differences between groups of children with and without DS. In a standing position, children with DS were more influenced by optical flow than children without DS; in a sitting position, children with DS seemed less or equally influenced. There is question about the measurement procedures used in both their work and Lee's experiments. Neither Lee and his coworkers nor Butterworth and Cichetti used direct measurement posturography; thus the sensitivity of their measurement techniques might be questioned. Further, when comparing children with and without DS in both upright and sitting modes, Butterworth and Cichetti (1978) reported equivocal findings and resorted to a rather eclectic set of inferences to explain their results. Bertenthal (1989) reported that young standing infants can couple their motion to the oscillatory motion of a moving room.

Somatotype and Phenotype

Shapiro (1983) addressed the problem of DS in a more global fashion based on genetic characteristics. Shapiro begins with a principled account of the genetic abnormalities of DS and goes on to argue in this and in a more recent paper (Shapiro, 1992) that the disruption of the evolved genetic balance in DS decreases the developmental and physiological buffering against genetic and environmentally based forces exhibited in essentially four categories of abnormality: (1) decreased developmental homeostasis (i.e., an increase in the variability of metric traits); (2) amplification of the instability of developmental pathways, which ultimately produced a deviant phenotype; (3) reduced precision of homeostatic controls (i.e., the ability to show adaptation or habituation); and (4) increased general morbidity (Shapiro, 1983, pp. 246-247).

Shapiro opined that the chromosomal imbalance produced in trisomy 21 produces a disruption of evolved genetic balance, which in turn produces decreased developmental physiological buffering resulting in decreased developmental and physiological homeostasis. This generates an abnormal phenotype and a narrowing of the somatotypical index when compared to the distribution of somatotypical indices across the normal population (Sheldon, 1954). Thus, abnormal genetic origin of trisomy 21 produces an *atypical phenotype* and, from the resulting *somatotype*, constrains the potential in the motor domain of the individual with DS. Shapiro notes the following:

> The standard phenotype therefore depends on a coordinated, balanced species gene pool that is the result of an evolutionary history of that species. The species gene pool provides not only raw information for specific traits, but also provides buffering systems so that gene derived traits can withstand the ever present genetic and environmental forces that occur throughout an organism's existence. (Shapiro, 1983, p. 245)

What Shapiro (1983) regards as a disruption of homeostasis is vested in the genetic abnormality of DS. Where we might disagree is on the notion that the homeostatic mechanism is an *internal referent* that controls the physiological system, rather than an *attractor* that functions more as an optimal or preferred point of equilibrium. At this point the issue is moot, but of more importance is that Shapiro's observations provide a window to better view the problem of DS beyond purely descriptive clinical information. It might also be the case that aberrant genetics limits the system's capacity to self-organize and produce stable attractor states, what Shapiro (1983) labels as a disrupted homeostatic system.

Our research has focused on this issue of preferred rates or attractor states, which is a signature of motor behavior that is essentially self-organizing. With respect to individuals diagnosed with DS, the question is whether or not as a group they share similar or different dynamic behavior as it relates to their capacity to coordinate and control skilled activity. Empirically we have investigated the response of individuals with DS to perturbations of visual information in the form of a designated optical flow field. Our earlier work (Wade, 1990) compared changes in center of pressure (CP) in persons who are mentally handicapped (MH) with those in nonhandicapped individuals. The results suggested reduced levels of response of CP motion in MH subjects generated by an optical flow field. In a second study, we compared older adults to younger adults (all nonhandicapped) and found that older subjects had higher levels of postural motion in response to global optical flow (Wade, Lindquist, Taylor, & Treat-Jacobson, 1995).

A separate but related aspect of coordination and control is the issue of motion sickness outside of the traditional view that motion sickness is produced by conflict between two or more of the perceptual systems (eyes and vestibular). In two reviews, Stoffregen and Riccio (1991a, 1991b) questioned the traditional perceptual conflict theory of motion sickness (1991a) and proposed an ecological theory that had prolonged postural instability as its foundation.

In the following sections, we report preliminary data from two studies. The first study examines the responses of subjects with DS to a visual perturbation using optical flow. The second study reports the results of a preliminary study in which we surveyed 250 families in the metropolitan Minneapolis/St. Paul community to determine reported levels of motion sickness in young adults with DS.

Optical Flow and the Control of Posture

Even during the so-called quiet stance, our bodies continually move. These sway patterns have been observed through force-platform assessments. Such assessments of degree of body sway often are used as an index of postural stability. Several studies have indicated differences in amount of sway in both anterioposterior (AP) and mediolateral (ML) directions by measuring the variability (standard deviation) of the center of foot pressure or of the shear forces on the platform. In healthy subjects, there is typically more sway in AP direction than in ML direction (Van Emmerik,

Sprague, & Newell, 1993). However, previous studies have reported that individuals with developmental disabilities (e.g., those diagnosed with tardive dyskinesia) show an increase in the degree of ML sway compared to healthy control subjects (Van Emmerik et al., 1993). The same observations also have been seen in Parkinson's disease patients (Mitchell, Collins, DeLuca, Burrows, & Lipsitz, 1995). In these populations, it is possible that the increase in ML sway is a direct manifestation of the disease, and there are suggestions in the literature that the increase in ML sway is a predictor of postural instability (Maki, Holliday, & Topper, 1994).

In a recent study, we sought to determine the level of postural response to optical perturbations in individuals with DS. The majority of studies on postural control have challenged balance via mechanical perturbation to the feet (Horak, Henry, & Shumway-Cook, 1997). This research has provided insights into the different motor strategies that subjects use to counteract these perturbations. Our approach is different.

In the present project, we examined differences in postural strategies to imposed perturbations between healthy children and children with DS, not via mechanical perturbations but by visually challenging posture through the moving-room paradigm (e.g., Lishman & Lee, 1973). Systematic motion of a moving room (in which the walls can move independently of the floor) has been shown to induce sway or even result in loss of balance in children. This sway emerges as the visual system apparently overrides other sensory sources in tricking the subject into a perception of self-motion. As such, the moving-room paradigm has been used to assess visual dependency or sensitivity to imposed visual flow. In previous research by Butterworth and Cichetti (1978), infants with DS showed larger postural responses to imposed visual flow in the moving room than did healthy controls. Shumway-Cook and Woollacott (1985a) also reported increased responses in younger children with DS under conditions in which somatosensory and visual systems provide conflicting information.

The Butterworth and Cichetti (1978) and Shumway-Cook and Woollacott (1985a) studies investigated DS infants and children below the age of 6 years. Several studies (e.g., Shumway-Cook & Woollacott, 1985b) have shown that in healthy children significant changes occur in the postural control system between 6 and 7 years of age. These changes result in reduced postural sway during quiet stance conditions and a reduced reliance on visual information. To investigate whether similar changes occur in children with DS, we examined older children of average 10 years of age.

Methods

In this study, we investigated whether or not children with DS respond differently to imposed visual perturbations than control children. We examined an older age group than previously studied, given significant age-related changes in healthy children at 6-7 years of age. Response patterns were evaluated in terms of magnitude of postural sway. Additional comparisons included sway direction (anterioposterior versus mediolateral) and response strategies.

Participants. The total participant population consisted of 26 children. There were children with DS with an average age of 10.62 years and a standard deviation of 3.28 years. The healthy participant group consisted of subjects with an average age of 11.31 years and standard deviation of 4.23 years.

Apparatus. Ground reaction forces and moments were collected with a custom-built force platform. Force-platform measurements yielded the forces and moments in the vertical, mediolateral, and anterioposterior directions. Accelerations of the trunk and head were recorded with uniaxial accelerometers. The anterioposterior motion of the hip was assessed through an accelerometer distally attached at the level of the lumbar spine. The mediolateral motion of the hip was obtained through an accelerometer attached at the level of the greater trochanter, but horizontally aligned with the lumbar spine accelerometer. The head accelerometers were attached at the level of the frontal bone (anterioposterior sway) and the parietal bone (mediolateral sway). All accelerometers were attached with elastic bands. The accelerometer signals were amplified through a transducer-coupler.

Visual perturbations were applied through a moving room (c.f. Lee & Aronson, 1974). The room was 250 cm high, 150 cm wide, and 300 cm long. The side walls and front walls could be moved independently or together. The movement of the room was recorded through a potentiometer attached to a cable.

Procedures. Subjects were asked to stand as quietly as possible following a signal from the experimenter. The following experimental manipulations were performed: (1) baseline condition with eyes open and stationary room; (2) moving-room manipulations with three different conditions: entire room (front and sides together), front wall only (inducing foveal flow), and side walls only (inducing peripheral flow); and (3) a second baseline condition with eyes open and stationary room. In the present paper, no analysis of the different room conditions is presented. Data from the moving-room conditions were averaged.

The moving-room manipulations were repeated three times each. The room movement lasted for 2 s and was performed over a distance of 40 cm. No oscillatory movements of the room were imposed. Data were collected for a duration of 60 s. After every 15 s, a perturbation of the room was performed under one of the conditions above. For the present analysis the stability of postural sway was assessed over a 2.5 s period interval. For the perturbation trials, this interval was obtained by taking the first 0.5 s before the perturbation to the 2 s following the onset of the room perturbation.

Data Analysis. The following dependent measures were obtained:

1. Standard deviation of ground reaction forces in AP and ML directions.

2. Standard deviation of accelerometer data in AP and ML directions for the hip.

3. Standard deviation of accelerometer data in AP and ML directions for the head.

Statistical Analysis.   Data were analyzed with a repeated measures analysis of variance (ANOVA). The main factors were *group* (control versus DS), *perturbation* (baseline versus movement of room), body *location* (head versus hip), and sway *direction* (anterioposterior versus mediolateral).

Results

The experiment showed larger postural responses to imposed visual flow in children with DS. These results are consistent with earlier findings (e.g., Butterworth & Cichetti, 1978, and Shumway-Cook & Woollacott, 1985a) on younger children 1-6 years old. The present results demonstrate that these differences remain in older children.

Reactive Forces at Feet.   Figure 12.2 depicts the changes in standard deviation in shear forces at the force platform between the first baseline and all moving-room conditions combined. The overall group effect approached conventional levels of significance ($F(1, 24) = 4.10$, $p = .0542$), indicating that the degree of sway is larger in the DS group than in the control group. There was, however, a significant interaction between *group* and *perturbation* condition: in the DS group, there was an increase in sway from baseline to room perturbation, but this was not the case for the control group ($F(1, 24) = 6.74$, $p < .05$).

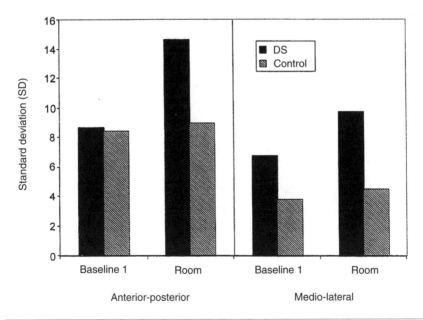

Figure 12.2   Comparison of quiet stance (baseline 1) with moving-room conditions for the standard deviation of the reactive forces at the feet (force platform). The moving-room conditions are averaged across all types of flow induced (whole room, peripheral, foveal) as well as across all three trials in each condition.

In both groups and room conditions, the degree of sway was larger in the AP than in the ML direction. Similar results were obtained from comparing baseline 2 with moving-room conditions.

Accelerations at Hip and Head.   Figures 12.3 and 12.4 depict the changes in standard deviation of acceleration at the hip and head, respectively. There is again a significant group effect ($F(1, 15) = 4.55, p < .05$). Subjects with DS had overall larger sway (higher standard deviation) than control subjects, and this was observed both at the head and at the hip. A significant interaction effect between group and perturbation condition was observed ($F(4, 60) = 8.94, p < .001$). There is more sway in the moving-room conditions as compared to the stationary baseline conditions, but this is the case for only the DS group. This was observed for both the hip and the head.

There was also a significant difference between head and hip sway ($F(1, 15) = 13.02, p < .01$). Overall there was more sway at the head than at the hip. In addition, there was a significant interaction between direction of sway and body location ($F(1, 15) = 5.00, p < .05$). At the head, there is more AP than ML sway, whereas at the hip there is no difference in sway direction (see figures 12.3 and 12.4).

An important observation was the stability in postural sway between preperturbation baseline 1 and postperturbation baseline 2. No significant differences between these baselines were observed ($p > .05$) (see figures 12.3 and 12.4).

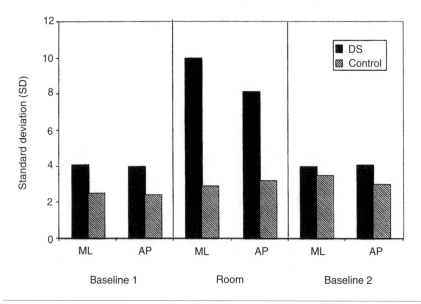

Figure 12.3   Comparison of quiet stance (at baseline 1 and baseline 2) with moving-room conditions for the standard deviation of the accelerations at the hip. The moving-room conditions are averaged across all types of flow induced (whole room, peripheral, foveal) as well as across all three trials in each condition. AP = anterioposterior direction; ML = mediolateral direction; room = all moving-room conditions averaged.

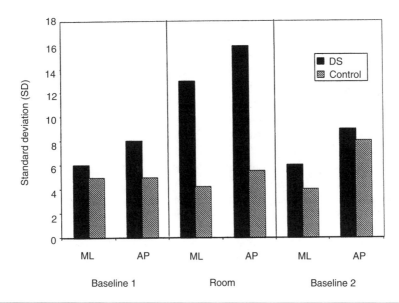

Figure 12.4   Comparison of quiet stance (at baseline 1 and baseline 2) with moving-room conditions for the standard deviation of the accelerations at the head. The moving-room conditions are averaged across all types of flow induced (whole room, peripheral, foveal) as well as across all three trials in each condition. AP = anterioposterior direction; ML = mediolateral direction; room = all moving-room conditions averaged.

Discussion

The data presented demonstrate changes in postural responses in children with Down syndrome to visual-field perturbations. Overall, children with DS showed a much stronger level of response to movement of the room, and this was observed for the reactive forces at the feet as well as hip and head acceleration. The pattern of response in different body parts, however, was preserved.

A major finding from the present experiment is that children with DS in the investigated age range (average 10 years) show larger responses to imposed optic flow than control subjects. These data are consistent with Butterworth and Cichetti's (1978) results on younger children with DS. They observed that during standing, children (infants) with DS showed larger postural responses to imposed visual flow than healthy control children. This was not observed during sitting conditions, in which the children with DS showed equal or even less response to imposed optic flow. The current results thus suggest that larger responses to visual-field motion also exist in older children with DS. This suggests that in contrast to children without DS, children with DS do not exhibit the same postural changes between the ages of 6 and 7 years. As mentioned earlier, in children without DS, adultlike responses in postural sway patterns emerge around 7 years of age (see Shumway-Cook & Woollacott, 1985b).

One could argue that these responses might not be directly related to the dependency of the postural system on the visual system (or sensitivity to visual flow), but that these children are perhaps more curious about what is happening in their surroundings (e.g., the movement of the room). In future experiments, we hope to distinguish between these possibilities by inducing visual oscillations that are *below* perceptual threshold. These oscillations are not consciously perceived by the subject but do lead to increased body sway. This manipulation will allow us to distinguish between these two different possibilities and enhances our knowledge of changes in sensitivity to visual flow in children with DS.

Different postural response strategies, such as correcting primarily from the ankle or the hip (e.g., Horak et al., 1997) have been demonstrated in mechanical perturbation experiments. In the present experiment we examined possible differences in response strategies in DS under induced visual flow. Overall larger responses to visual-field motion were observed in the head as compared to the hip. The anterioposterior response in the head was larger than the response in mediolateral direction, but this was not the case for the hip. This pattern of response was observed both in children with and without DS.

Motion Sickness

A recent paper by Stoffregen and Riccio (1991; see also Riccio & Stoffregen 1991) critically reviewed the century-old view of motion sickness as sensory conflict. They proposed a theory of motion sickness (MS) based on the notion that MS is caused by prolonged postural instability. They argue that rapid adaptation to postural instability will stop the development of motion sickness and quickly reduce or eliminate symptoms. If the animal detects the instability and fails to respond, is unable to respond, or changes its behavior, motion sickness will result. Because animals are exquisitely sensitive to postural instabilities, they can avoid the symptoms of motion sickness by making such rapid adaptations. The inability to adaptively respond often causes motion sickness in humans (e.g., an individual "caught" on a carnival ride and unable to stop the ride immediately will often experience the symptoms of motion sickness). In a similar vein, a long sea voyage where the subject has little control over the ocean swell can produce a similar outcome. Thus for the normal system, motion sickness is the result of a failure to adapt after detecting the postural instabilities. Very little is known about the incidence of reported motion sickness in individuals with DS. Clearly, sensitivity to perceptual information and the rapidity with which the individual adapts to changes in postural instability play a role in avoiding motion-induced sickness. Therefore, we sought a preliminary determination of the incidence of motion sickness in individuals with DS.

In order to derive preliminary information, we developed a motion sickness questionnaire, which was distributed to 250 families who cooperated in this project via an organization known as the Twin Cities DS Association (TCDSA). The questionnaire asked for the age and sex of the family member with DS and the incidence of motion sickness, including symptoms, frequency, recency, and the situation where the symptoms appeared. The number of surveys distributed was 248, of which we had a 96% return. Seventeen of the questionnaires that were returned indicated that there were no members in the family with DS. These were discarded, leaving a usable sample of 221 (89%). Of the usable sample of 221, 128 were male, 193 were female, the mean age was 8 years, and the standard deviation was 10.6 years. Of this group, 4.5% of families reported an incidence of motion sickness (10 individuals). Furthermore, of these 10 individuals, 8 reported that the symptoms had occurred only once or twice throughout their lives. With only 10 families in the 221 usable questionnaires, the 4.5% reporting an incidence of motion sickness is extremely low compared to the normal population. In the normal population, the susceptibility to motion sickness is extremely high between the ages of 2 and 12 years and stays high through the college years before beginning to drop off toward the fifth decade. For comparison purposes, we obtained a sample of college males, average age 22 years, who had completed a motion sickness questionnaire from the Essex Corporation. The percentage of occurrence in this group was 85%. By way of comparison, the scores of the DS group and the normal group of college males are presented in figure 12.5.

Clearly, the incidence of motion sickness in the DS group is much lower than that of the normal population. In addition, no gender differences were present among the individuals with DS screened, with 4.7% males and 4.3% females of the total sample of 10 individuals reporting motion sickness. Some reported data (Reason, 1978) suggest that females experience motion sickness more frequently than males in the normal population; this does not appear to be the case with our DS sample.

These preliminary data should be interpreted with caution. It may be that the parents and family members of the individuals with DS may not have been aware of the symptoms of motion sickness, and the subjects with DS themselves may not have been able to report or verbalize such symptoms. It is also possible that the parents and friends of persons with DS may have avoided situations that would provoke the

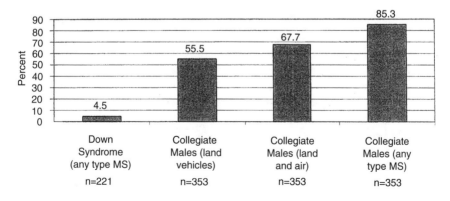

Figure 12.5   Incidence of motion sickness (MS) among collegiate males and individuals with Down syndrome.

production of the nauseogenic symptoms of motion sickness, as a protection for the individuals concerned. Again it must be remembered that the range over which low-frequency vibration events can be tolerated is wide, and atypical sensitivity to such frequencies may be constrained for individuals with DS.

Conclusions

An important element that underpins the dynamical systems perspective of coordination and control is the existence of attractor states or preferred regions in which the individual's functional coordinative behavior is shown to be stable (see figure 12.1, page 282). Thus, a first hypothesis for accounting for both the hypersensitivity to optical flow and the low incidence of motion sickness may be that such attractor states or preferred regions of functional stability are absent in such individuals. Thus we would expect individuals with Down syndrome to be sensitive to optical flow field perturbations irrespective of the frequency domain in which they occur. The absence of a preferred attractor state would mitigate producing the kind of prolonged postural instability that might result in motion sickness. Recent work by Stoffregen and Smart (1998) suggests that individuals uniformly report feelings of motion sickness as a moving room oscillates at frequencies within the range of normal upright posture (approximately 2-3 Hz).

A second reason for both the high level of sensitivity to optical flow perturbations and possibly the low incidence of motion sickness may focus on the attentional state of individuals with DS. Recall that Shapiro (1983) in his review talked about the lack of habituation to such things as a flicker-fusion test and other responses that show minimal habituation. Weak attentional states to environmental stimulation can reduce the cumulative effects of prolonged instabilities that cause motion sickness (Stoffregen & Riccio, 1991b). Research on the postural responses to optical flow perturbations in samples of normally functioning individuals indicates it is usually the initial trial that produces the largest magnitude of response, with subsequent trials showing a dampening of the postural response as the individual focuses attention to what is *really* happening (i.e., the individual is not moving, but the room *is* moving). It seems this is not the case for the person with DS, who senses ego-motion at every occurrence and does not recognize over several trials the true state of affairs. In a similar vein, failure to pay specific attention to the specific frequency domain of a carnival ride, which can produce a rapid nauseogenic effect in many normally functioning individuals, is essentially benign to an individual with DS because their attentional state is not sufficiently focused (coupled) to a specific frequency domain. This clearly begs the question: under what circumstances might one induce motion sickness in individuals with DS, and what type of experimental strategies will it require?

It might be that in both cases (the moving-room protocol and motion sickness) individuals with DS need to fix their gaze on a particular target. In the moving-room protocol, the subject would focus on a light or a mark in the room, and the experimenter would need to continually prompt the individual with DS to watch that target. A second strategy would be to determine whether or not the frequency domain for upright posture for DS is outside the normal 2-3 Hz frequency range that is found for other individuals. In fact, it may be the case that individuals with DS simply do not attempt to stabilize their motor system in response to optical flow or similar inputs. This would explain the lack of accommodation to sway motion and a reported low incidence of motion sickness. Individuals with DS may unconsciously tolerate the instabilities produced by such perturbations. The lack of such a response minimizes the nauseogenic effect and shows increased sensitivity to optical flow. This "relaxed" musculoskeletal state certainly is congruent with the known hypotonia and ADC. Thus, we may be observing and recording in individuals with DS both an anatomic and biobehavioral failure to "tune" either the musculoskeletal apparatus or the behavioral/cognitive system.

Summary

Our data demonstrate striking differences between the high occurrence of motion sickness in the population at large, approximately 85%, and the low incidence reported from our sample of 221 participants with DS. In the questionnaire data completed by the 221 families, there was an opportunity to record whether any preventative strategies were used; no such responses were obvious. Thus, an explanation as to why individuals with DS are less susceptible to motion sickness remains. Our initial thinking was that a lowered sensitivity threshold to optical flow and possibly other forms of visual perturbation may result in a low incidence of motion sickness in individuals with DS. In fact, our sample group of young participants with DS formally tested in situations where optical flow was the perturbation showed enhanced levels of sensitivity to such perturbations rather than reduced levels. Thus, our initial working hypothesis of reduced sensitivity accounting for a reduced incidence of motion sickness clearly is not supported. Sensitivity to optical flow in postural stabilography and the low levels of motion sickness suggest that individuals with DS may not exhibit preferred regions of stability in terms of postural or other domains of coordination and control. Past research may well be reflected in a DS individual's inability to effectively "search" the perceptual-motor space to detect such preferred regions. Thus, we return to the old problem of mental retardation, with individuals exhibiting poor strategic behavior, high performance variability, and an inability to generalize strategic behavior acquired in one context to another.

Dynamical systems interpretation of these observed motor deficits offers interesting opportunities to further investigate motor behavior of individuals with DS. Traditional issues of attention deficit now can be coupled to the dynamics of coordination and control as they might relate to performance of motor skills.

References

Atkinson, R.C., & Shiffrin, R.M. (1968). Human memory: A proposed system and its control processes. In K.W. & J.T. Spence (Eds.), *The psychology of learning and motivation: Vol. 2* (pp. 189-195). New York: Academic Press.

Beeghly, M., Weiss-Perry, B., & Cichetti, D. (1989). Structural and affective dimensions of play development in young children with Down syndrome. *International Journal of Behavior Development, 12*, 257-277.

Berkson, G. (1960a). An analysis of reaction time in normal and mentally deficient young men: I. Duration threshold experiment. *Journal of Mental Deficiency Research, 4*, 51-58.

Berkson, G. (1960b). An analysis of reaction time in normal and mentally deficient young men: II. Variations of complexity in reaction time tasks. *Journal of Mental Deficiency Research, 4*, 59-67.

Berkson, G. (1960c). An analysis of reaction time in normal and mentally deficient young men: III. Variation of stimulus and of response complexity. *Journal of Mental Deficiency Research, 4*, 99-77.

Berlyne, D.E. (1960). *Conflict, arousal and curiosity.* New York: McGraw-Hill.

Bernstein, N.A. (1967). *The coordination and regulation of movement.* New York: Pergamon Press.

Bertenthal, B.I., & Bai, D.L. (1989). Infant's sensitivity to optical flow for controlling posture. *Developmental Psychology, 25*, 936-945.

Brooks-Bertram, P. (1986, Spring). Health education and mental retardation. *Mental Retardation*, 67-69.

Brown, A.L. (1978). Knowing when, where and how to remember: A problem of metacognition. In R. Glaser (Ed.), *Advances in instruction and psychology* (pp. 68-89). Hillsdale, NJ: Erlbaum.

Butterworth, G., & Cichetti, D. (1978). Visual calibration of posture in normal and motor retarded Down syndrome infants. *Perception, 7*, 513-525.

Campione, J.C., & Brown, A.L. (1977). Memory and motor sensory development in educable retarded children. In R.V. Kail Jr. & J.W. Hagen (Eds.), *Perspectives on the development of memory and cognition* (p. 378) Hillsdale, NJ: Erlbaum.

Cannon, W.B. (1929). Organization and physiological homeostasis. *Physiological Review, 9*, 379-431.

Chumlea, W.C., & Cronk, C.E. (1982). Overweight among children with Trisomy 21. *Journal of Mental Deficiency Research, 25*, 275-279.

Cronk, C., Chumlea, W.C., & Roche, A.F. (1985). Assessment of overweight children with Trisomy 21. *American Journal of Mental Deficiency, 89*, 433-436.

Davis, W.E., & Sinning, W.E. (1987). Muscle stiffness in Down syndrome and other mentally handicapped subjects: A research note. *Journal of Motor Behavior, 19*, 130-144.

Diamond, L.S., Lynne, D., & Sigman, B. (1981). Orthopaedic disorders in patients with Down syndrome. *Orthopaedic Clinics of North America, 21*, 57-71.

Dugdale, T.W., & Renshaw, T.S. (1986). Instability of the patellofemoral joint in Down syndrome. *The Journal of Bone and Joint Surgery, 68-A*, 405-413.

Eichstaedt, C.B., & Kalakian, L.H. (1987). *Developmental/adapted physical education: Making ability count* (2nd ed.). New York: Macmillan.

Gibson, J.J. (1979). *The ecological approach to visual perception.* Boston: Houghton Mifflin.

Griffiths, M.I. (1976). Development of children with Down syndrome. *Physiotherapy, 62*, 11-24.

Hoover, J.H., Wade, M.G., & Newell, K.M. (1981). The trainability of reaction time and movement time in moderately mentally handicapped workers. *American Journal of Mental Deficiency, 85*, 389-395.

Horak, F.B., Henry, S.M., & Shumway-Cook, A. (1997). Postural perturbations: New insights for treatment of balance disorders. *Physical Therapy, 77*, 517-533.

Keele, S.W., & Ivry, R. (1990). Does the cerebellum provide a common computation for diverse tasks? A time hypothesis. *Annals of the New York Academy of Sciences, 608*, 179-211.

Kelso, J.A.S. (1988). Introductory remarks: Dynamic patterns. In J.A.S. Kelso, A.J. Mandel, & M.F. Schlesinger (Eds.), *Dynamic patterns in complex systems* (pp. 221-230). Singapore World Scientific Congress.

Kleitman, N. (1963). *Sleep and wakefulness.* Chicago: University of Chicago Press.

Kugler, P.N., Kelso, J.A.S., & Turvey, M.T. (1980). On the concept of coordinated structures as dissipated: I. Theoretical lines of convergence. In G.E. Stelmach & J. Requin (Eds.), *Tutorials in motor behavior* (pp. 3-47). New York: North-Holland.

Kugler, P.N., & Turvey, M.T. (1987). *Information, natural law and self-assembly of rhythmic movement.* Hillsdale, NJ: Erlbaum.

Latash, M.L., Almeida, G.L., & Corcos, D.M. (1992). Preprogrammed reactions in individuals with Down syndrome: The effects of instruction and predictability of the perturbation. *Archives of Physical Medical Rehabilitation, 73*, 178-186.

Lee, D.N., & Aronson, E. (1974). Visual proprioceptive of standing in human infants. *Perception and Psychophysics, 15*, 529-532.

Lee, D.N., & Lishman, J.R. (1975). Visual proprioceptive control of stance. *Journal of Human Movement Studies, 1*, 87-95.

Lishman, J.R., & Lee, D.N. (1973). The autonomy of visual kinaesthesis. *Perception, 2*, 287-294.

Livingstone, B., & Hirst, P. (1986). Orthopaedic disorders in school children with Down's syndrome with special reference to the incidence of joint laxity. *Clinical Orthopaedics and Related Research, 207*, 74-76.

Lydic, J.S., & Steele, C. (1979). Assessment of the quality of sitting and gait patterns in children with Down syndrome. *Physical Therapy, 59*, 1489-1494.

Mahan, K.T., Diamond, E., & Brown, D. (1983). Podiatric profile of the Down's syndrome individual. *Journal of the American Podiatry Association, 73*, 173-179.

Maki, B.E., Holliday, P.J., & Topper, A.K. (1994). A prospective study of postural balance and risk of falling in an ambulatory and independent elderly population. *Journal of Gerontology, 49*, M72-M84.

Michon, J.A. (1967). *Timing monograph.* Amsterdam: North-Holland.

Mitchell, S.L., Collins, J.J., De Luca, C.J., Burrows, A., & Lipsitz, L.A. (1995). Open-loop and closed-loop postural control mechanism in Parkinson's disease: Increased mediolateral activity during quiet standing. *Neuroscience Letters, 197*, 133-136.

Olson, D.R. (1971). Information processing limitation of mentally retarded children. *American Journal of Mental Deficiency, 75*, 478-486.

Parker, A.W., & Bronks, R. (1980). Gait of children with Down syndrome. *Archives of Physical Medicine and Rehabilitation, 61*, 345-350.

Pueschel, S.M., & Rynders, J.E. (Eds.). (1982). *Down syndrome advances in biomedicine and the behavioral sciences.* Cambridge, MA: The Ware Press.

Reason, J.T. (1978). Motion sickness adaptation: A neuron mismatch model. *Journal of the Royal Society of Medicine, 71*, 819-829.

Riccio, G.E., & Stoffregen, T.A. (1991). An ecological theory of motion sickness and postural stability. *Ecological Psychology, 3*, 195-240.

Scheffler, N.M. (1973). Down's syndrome and clinical findings related to the foot. *Journal of the American Podiatry Association, 63*, 18-20.

Shapiro, B.L. (1983). Down syndrome—A disruption of homeostasis. *American Journal of Medical Genetics, 14*, 241-269.

Shapiro, B.L. (May 1992). Development of human autosomalaneuploid phenotypes (with an emphasis on Down's syndrome). *Acta Zoological. Fennica, 191*, 95-103.

Share, J., & French, R. (1982). *Motor development of Down syndrome children: Birth to 6 years.* Sherman Oaks, CA: J.B. Share.

Sheldon, W.H. (1954). *Atlas of man.* New York: Gramercy.

Shumway-Cook, A., & Woollacott, M.H. (1985a). Dynamics of postural control in the child with Down syndrome. *Physical Therapy, 65*, 1315-1322.

Shumway-Cook, A., & Woollacott, M.H. (1985b). The growth of stability: Postural control from a developmental perspective. *Journal of Motor Behavior, 17*, 131-147.

Stoffregen, T.A. (1985). Flow structure versus retinal location in the optical control of stance. *Journal of Experimental Psychology: Human Perception and Performance, 11*, 554-565.

Stoffregen, T.A., & Riccio, G.E. (1991). An ecological critique of the sensory conflict theory of motion sickness. *Ecological Psychology, 3*, 159-194.

Stoffregen, T.A., & Smart, L.J. (1998). Postural instability precedes motion sickness. *Brain Research Bulletin, 47*, 437-448.

Stollberger, A. (1965). *Biological rhythm research.* Amsterdam: Elsevier.

Thelen, E. (1979). Rhythmical stereotippers in normal human infants. *Animal Behavior, 27*, 699-715.

Thelen, E., & Ulrich, B. (1991). Hidden skills: A dynamic systems analysis of treadmill stepping during the first year. *Monographs of the Society for Research in Child Development, 56* (1, Serial No. 223).

Turvey, M.T. (1990). Coordination. *American Psychologist, 45*, 938-953.

Ulrich, B.D., & Ulrich, D.A. (1992). Dynamic systems approach to understanding motor delay in infants with Down syndrome. In G.J.P. Savelsbergh (Ed.), *The development of coordination in infancy* (pp. 445-459). Amsterdam: North-Holland.

Ulrich, B.D., Ulrich, D.A., & Collier, D.H. (1992). Alternating stepping patterns: Hidden abilities in 11-month-old infants with Down syndrome. *Developmental Medicine and Child Neurology, 34*, 233-239.

Van Emmerik, R.E.A., Sprague R.L., & Newell, K.M. (1993). Quantification of postural sway profiles in tardive dyskinesia. *Movement Disorders, 8*, 305-314.

Wade, M.G. (1970). *Biorhythms in children during free play.* Unpublished doctoral dissertation, University of Illinois, Champaign-Urbana.

Wade, M.G. (1973). Biorhythms and activity level of institutionalized mentally retarded persons diagnosed hyperactive. *American Journal of Mental Deficiency, 78*, 262-267.

Wade, M.G. (1990). Impact of optical flow on postural control in normal and mentally handicapped persons. In A. Vermeer (Ed.), Motor development adapted physical activity and mental retardation. *Medicine and Sports Science: Vol. 30* (pp. 21-29). Basel, Switzerland: Karger.

Wade, M.G., & Ellis, M.J. (1971). Measurement of free range activity in children as modified by social and environmental complexity. *American Journal of Clinical Nutrition, 24*, 1457-1460.

Wade, M.G., Ellis, M.J, & Bohrer, R.E. (1973). Biorhythms in the activity of children during free play. *Journal of the Experimental Analysis of Behavior, 20*, 155-162.

Wade, M.G., Hoover, J.H., & Newell, K.M. (1984). Training and trainability of motor skills: Performance of mentally retarded persons. In J. Hogg & P. Mittler (Eds.), *Aspects of competence in severely mentally handicapped people: Vol. 2* (pp. 175-203). London: Wiley.

Wade, M.G., Lindquist, R., Taylor, J.R., & Treat-Jacobson, D. (1995). Flow structure and retinal location in the optical control of posture in elderly adults. *Journal of Gerontology: Psychological Sciences, 50B*(1), 51-58.

Wade, M.G., Newell, K.M., & Wallace, S.A. (1978). Decision time and movement time as a function of response complexity in retarded persons. *American Journal of Mental Deficiency, 83*, 135-144.

Waldrop, M.M. (1993). *Complexity: The emerging science at the edge of order and chaos.* London: Penguin.

Williams, H.G., Woollacott, M.H., & Ivry R. (1992). Timing and motor control in clumsy children. *Journal of Motor Behavior, 24*, 165-172.

A Functional-Systems Approach to Movement Pathology in Persons With Down Syndrome

Matthew Heath
University of Waterloo

Digby Elliott
McMaster University

Daniel J. Weeks
Simon Fraser University

Romeo Chua
University of British Columbia

Key words

handedness ◆ lateralization ◆ dichotic listening ◆ speech
perception ◆ speech production ◆ lateral asymmetries ◆ haptic
processing ◆ oral movements ◆ speech errors

Much of what is known about brain-behavior relations comes from clinical studies involving patients who have sustained localized damage to the cerebral cortex following stroke or head injury. From the late 1800s, it has been clear that speech and language disruption occur much more frequently as a result of left-hemisphere damage than right-hemisphere damage. This is particularly true for right-handed individuals.

Handedness and Language Lateralization

Because right-handers make up approximately 90% of the general population, many models of cerebral specialization adopt a biological codetermination of handedness and speech and language lateralization. For example, Kimura (1979) proposed that both handedness and language lateralization are related to the superiority of one cerebral hemisphere, usually the left, in sequencing complex movements (i.e., speech movements, finger and limb movements). The primary problem with this view of cerebral specialization is that it has difficulty accounting for the lateralization of language in left-handed individuals. Specifically, although there is a greater incidence of bilateral or right-hemispheric specialization for language in left-handers than right-handers, the majority of left-handers exhibit the same pattern of cerebral organization for language as right-handers; that is, they have language lateralized to the left hemisphere.

The current most popular genetic account of handedness and language lateralization holds that there is a single allele (RS+) that leads to both right-handedness and left-hemisphere specialization for speech and language (Annett, 1985; McManus & Bryden, 1992; cf. Coren, 1996). In this model, the presence of a second allele (RS−) results in the independent and random determination of handedness and language lateralization. Given that at least some proportion of left-handedness and/ or atypical language lateralization may be due to prenatal or perinatal pathology, this model does a good job explaining the proportions of left- and right-handers with left- and right-hemisphere speech within the general population.

Our initial interest in cerebral lateralization in persons with Down syndrome (DS) came from findings that indicated that this group may exhibit a quite different pattern of cerebral organization. The first studies to examine cerebral specialization for language in persons with DS employed a noninvasive speech perception procedure termed dichotic listening.

The dichotic listening technique involves the simultaneous presentation of word or letter pairs to the right and left ears via headphones. Following a brief series of presentations, the participant is asked to report all the sounds he or she heard (free recall) or the sounds presented to either the right or the left ear (selective listening). A substantial body of literature indicates that, regardless of the specific procedure, most children and adults are able to report a greater number of right-ear than left-ear sounds (see Bryden, 1982, for a review). Because the major auditory pathways are crossed, this right-ear advantage for the perception of speech sounds is consistent with left-hemisphere specialization for speech and language function in the vast majority of the general population.

The dichotic listening studies involving persons with DS indicated that these individuals performed quite differently on tests of dichotic listening. Specifically, the majority of the research indicates that participants with DS display a left-ear superiority for speech perception. In a 1994 meta-analysis of the 17 published studies to that point, we found that the left-ear superiority for dichotic listening in children and adults with DS exists relative to both age-matched control participants with or without intellectual handicaps as well as to a theoretical ear difference of zero (Elliott, Weeks, & Chua, 1994). This left-ear precedence for the perception of speech sounds in persons with DS suggests that, for this group, the right cerebral hemisphere may play a primary role in speech and language function.

Given current genetic models of cerebral specialization and handedness (e.g., Annett, 1985), the dichotic work discussed above suggests that the trisomy 21 karyotype may be associated with a distinct pattern of brain organization in persons with DS. Also drawing heavily on the early dichotic listening work, Hartley (1982, 1986) and Pipe (1988) have proposed that children and adults with DS may have a reversed pattern of cerebral specialization. Moreover, it has been suggested that this atypical brain organization may be, at least in part, responsible for some of the specific information-processing difficulties exhibited by these individuals, especially in the areas of language comprehension and production.

Although the dichotic listening work points toward a reversed pattern of cerebral specialization for speech perception, other studies examining lateral asymmetries in persons with DS indicate that a model of reversed cerebral specialization is not tenable. For example, studies examining hand preference and asymmetries in hand performance reveal that while persons with DS are more likely to exhibit left-hand or mixed-hand preference than the norm, estimates of right-hand preference range from 75 to 85% in this group (e.g., Batheja & McManus, 1985; Elliott et al., 1994; Murphy, 1962; Pickersgill & Pank, 1970). Moreover, like the majority of the population, persons with DS typically exhibit right-hand performance asymmetries on unimanual tasks such as rapid finger-tapping (Elliott, 1985; Elliott, Weeks, & Jones, 1986) and finger-sequencing (Edwards & Elliott, 1989). In general, this pattern of hand asymmetry is thought to reflect the superiority of the contralateral (left) cerebral hemisphere in the specification and timing of muscular forces. Together, these performance data along with the preference studies indicate that like most of the general population, the majority of persons with DS are left-hemisphere specialized for the organization and control of movement.

In table 13.1, we report the proportions of hand preference and ear advantage (dichotic listening) for 28 adolescents and young adults with DS for which we have both sets of information (from both Elliott & Weeks, 1993a, and Heath, Smith, & Elliott, 1998). While this certainly does not represent a random selection of persons with DS, all volunteers were accepted without reference to handedness. Exclusion from the studies was based only on pure tone audiometry criteria (e.g., hearing loss in one or both ears) and an understanding of the task requirements. The proportions in this group of young adults with DS are vastly different from those in the general population predicted by the Annett (1985) or McManus (1985) models of handedness and cerebral lateralization ($\chi^2(3) = 174.9, p < .001$; see table 13.1). These theoretical proportions were calculated assuming a 90% occurrence of right-handedness in the general population.

Thus, it would seem that DS is associated with a very different pattern of brain organization than would be predicted by any of the neurobehavioral models developed to explain the relation between handedness and the lateralization of language (see Bryden, Bulman-Fleming, & MacDonald, 1996, and Coren, 1996, for reviews). It was our hope (and our continuing belief) that the study of brain-behavior relations in this group would lead both to a better understanding of perceptual-motor and cognitive performance in DS and to a more general awareness of how the specialization of cerebral function develops in the general population.

Table 13.1 Participants With DS With a Particular Ear Advantage and Hand Preference*

	Ear advantage	HAND PREFERENCE Right	Left
Down syndrome			
	Right	.21	.04
	Left	.54	.21
Annett's model			
	Right	.85	.05
	Left	.05	.05

* Compared to the proportions predicted by Annett's model.

Cerebral Specialization for Haptic and Visual Processing

Although there were enough published dichotic listening studies involving persons with DS to conduct a meta-analysis in 1994, almost no research had been done using other noninvasive neuropsychological paradigms. This motivated us to examine cerebral specialization for spatial processing as well as language processing in other modalities.

While most people, including persons with DS, are able to perform tasks such as finger-tapping and finger-sequencing better with the right hand than the left hand, there are several tasks for which right-handed people typically exhibit a *left-hand advantage.* For example, most of us are better able to match nonsense shapes (Witelson, 1974) and make tactile judgments of orientation and position (Benton, Varney, & Hamsher, 1978; Roy & MacKenzie, 1978) with the left hand than the right hand. This asymmetry is usually attributed to the left hand having direct access via sensory and motor pathways to the right cerebral hemisphere, which is specialized for holistic/spatial processing.

Following a procedure developed by Sandra Witelson (1974), we had adults with and without DS bimanually manipulate pairs of rubber nonsense shapes before attempting to match the right- and left-hand shapes to a visual display (Elliott, Pollock, Chua, & Weeks, 1995). Participants with and without DS exhibited the same pattern of hand performance, with right-handed participants exhibiting no lateral advantage and left-handed participants demonstrating left-hand superiority.

In a second study, we had control subjects and young adults with DS haptically manipulate pairs of shapes that corresponded to letters (Weeks, Chua, Elliott, Lyons, & Pollock, 1995). Here we expected control subjects to exhibit a right-hand/left-hemisphere advantage because of the language-based nature of the task. Interestingly, while non-DS participants failed to display a lateral advantage, participants with DS performed better on shapes they manipulated with their left hand. This finding is consistent with the dichotic listening work that suggests that persons with DS are right-hemisphere specialized for receptive-language function. However, it could also be the case that poor receptive-language function in persons with DS forces them to rely on spatial discrimination to identify the letter shapes.

As well as the tactile-matching studies, we developed a technique for examining asymmetries in visual processing in persons with DS (Elliott et al., 1995). We had participants use their index fingers to move a mouse on a graphics tablet in order to move a cursor on a computer monitor from a home position at the bottom of the screen to a small target in the center of the screen. The cursor's arrival at the target position initiated the very brief presentation of stimuli in either the right or left visual field that subjects were required to identify. In this type of situation, participants typically exhibited a right visual-field advantage for the identification of linguistic stimuli and a left visual-field advantage when stimulus identification required some sort of spatial judgment. These lateral advantages are assumed to reflect the specialization of the contralateral cerebral hemisphere for language-based and spatial processing, respectively. Our interest was whether participants with DS would demonstrate a similar pattern of lateral advantage.

For a dot-enumeration task, which is assumed to involve spatial processing (Kimura, 1966), participants with and without DS displayed a left visual-field advantage (Elliott et al., 1995). This suggests that, like the majority of the general population, persons with DS are right-hemisphere specialized for spatial processing. The results of a second study involving linguistic material (columns of letters) were less clear cut (Weeks et al., 1995). Here we obtained a slight left-field/right-hemisphere advantage for participants with DS but no field difference for control subjects. Again, this pattern of finding is consistent with the idea that persons with DS are right-hemisphere specialized for receptive-language function.

Cerebral Specialization for Speech Production

While most of the early work on cerebral specialization and DS was concerned with speech perception (e.g., dichotic listening) and manual motor control (e.g., performance differences between the hands), almost no work was designed to examine cerebral specialization for speech *production*. In our initial study (Elliott, Edwards, Weeks, Lindley, & Carnahan, 1987), we employed a dual-task paradigm originally developed by Kinsbourne and Cook (1971; see also Kinsbourne & Hicks, 1978). Young adults with and without DS were required to finger-tap as fast as possible with the left and the right index fingers. They performed the finger-tapping task both alone and while speaking aloud (e.g., sound-shadowing a series of high frequency words presented via headphones). In the dual-task situation, the concurrent speech typically interferes with right-hand but not left-hand performance. This is thought to occur due to within-hemisphere interference between the left-hemisphere control centers for speech production and right-hand motor control. Although the participants with DS exhibited greater dual-task interference overall, like the control subjects, right-hand performance was disrupted more by speech production than was left-hand performance. Several years later, Piccirilli, D'Alessandro, Mazzi, Sciarma, and Testa (1991) replicated this finding. Together, these two studies and the manual asymmetry work indicate that while persons with DS may be right-hemisphere specialized for speech perception, the left hemisphere appears to play the major role in the production of speech and other oral and manual movements.

Although the dual-task studies provide a reasonable starting point, we have recently had some doubts about the utility of the paradigm for isolating speech and language lateralization from motor control in general. Specifically, Heath, Elliott, Roy, and Veeneman (1999) have suggested that the pattern of interference may be better explained by a shared praxis system within the left hemisphere that limits the ability of the information processing system to perform a manual and oral-motor task simultaneously. In such a model, it is the limited capacity of the praxis system that hinders concurrent performance of the right hand. In order to extend the results of the dual-task paradigm, we (Heath & Elliott, 1999) have employed a direct method of identifying the cerebral hemisphere dominant for speech production in persons with DS. It involves measuring mouth asymmetries during speech production.

The mouth-asymmetry methodology is another noninvasive neuropsychological technique used to determine the cerebral hemisphere dominant for speech and language (Graves, Goodglass, & Landis, 1982). Graves and colleagues (Cadalbert, Landis, Regard, & Graves, 1994; Graves, 1983; Graves & Landis, 1985; Graves et al., 1982) have examined a wide variety of speech tasks, including propositional speech, automatic speech, visual-picture description, and singing. They have found that the right side of the mouth opens wider than the left side of the mouth during spontaneous speech, while tasks such as visual-picture description requiring mediation from the right hemisphere lessens the degree of right-mouth asymmetry during speech. More recently, Wolf and Goodale (1987) have developed more sensitive measurement techniques to quantify the magnitude of mouth asymmetry. Their results have indicated that the right side of the mouth not only opens wider but also sooner and at a greater rate than that of the left when participants produce speech and/or make other oral movements.

Graves and colleagues were the first to suggest that the right-mouth asymmetry is reflective of the left-hemisphere dominance for speech and language (e.g., Graves, 1983; Graves et al., 1982). Specifically, the right-mouth asymmetry has been attributed to the neuromuscular innervation on the right side of the mouth and its direct access to the systems responsible for speech production within the left hemisphere. Indeed, Van Gelder and Van Gelder (1990) have indicated that because the facial nerve lies below the level of the pyramidal decussation, the right side of the face has direct access to innervatory patterns programmed by speech-production systems within the left hemisphere, thereby facilitating the right side of the mouth during speech.

We employed the mouth-asymmetry methodology and the data-reduction procedure advanced by Wolf and Goodale (1987) to examine the cerebral specialization for speech production in right-handed individuals with DS and a group of nonhandicapped participants matched for gender and chronological age. Based on our previous research, it was anticipated that persons with DS would exhibit a pattern of right-mouth asymmetry consistent with left-hemisphere dominance for speech production. Participants were videotaped while producing bilabial syllables (e.g., /ma/) in three different experimental conditions: single, repeated, and sequential. In the single conditions, participants were instructed to produce a target syllable once (e.g., /ma/). In the repeated condition, participants were required to repeat the target syllable 10 times at a rate of 1 syllable per second (e.g., /ma//ma//ma//ma/). During the sequential trials, participants were required to produce a string of syllables (e.g., /ma//ba//pi// ma//ba//pi//ma//ba//pi/). Prior to each trial in all conditions, the experimenter demonstrated the target syllable to be produced and the rate of production. Later the videotaped performance was analyzed using a stable frame-by-frame digitizing technique (see also Wolf & Goodale, 1987) to examine the extent of horizontal and vertical lip displacement on the left and right sides of the face.

Consistent with our dual-task findings, our participants with DS exhibited a right-mouth advantage for the production of speech. Specifically, persons with DS exhibited a right-mouth asymmetry during speech initiation. These results were consistent with the initial aperture in the nonhandicapped participant group. Support for the validity of the mouth-asymmetry methodology stems from our results, indicating that despite a smaller overall aperture of the mouth, a right-mouth asymmetry for speech production was evident for persons with DS. These data indicate that mouth asymmetry is not an artifact related to the magnitude of mouth displacement but reflects an underlying innervatory process that facilitates a right-mouth displacement during speech production.

In addition to the raw displacement values, asymmetry values $(R - L/R + L)$ were also calculated to determine if the degree of asymmetry differed between people in the DS and nonhandicapped groups. Although one might anticipate that the degree of asymmetry for persons with DS would be less than that of nonhandicapped participants, our results indicated that there was no difference in the degree of asymmetry between the two groups. In fact, the degree of lateralization was slightly greater in the DS group (0.06) than in the control group (0.05). These results indicate that the side and degree of lateralization for speech production are similar for persons with and without DS. They are also consistent with dual-task findings (e.g., Elliott, Edwards, et al., 1987), and indicate that atypical cerebral specialization in persons with DS involves only speech perception and not speech production.

The Biological-Dissociation Model

Rather than exhibiting reversed cerebral specialization for all functions (see Hartley, 1986, and Pipe, 1988), young adults with DS exhibit *atypical* right-hemisphere specialization for speech perception in combination with *typical* left-hemisphere specialization for the organization and control of movement, including speech movements. As in the general population, the right hemisphere of persons with DS seems to play the primary role in decisions related to the evaluation of spatial relations in personal and extrapersonal space.

Based primarily on the anomalous right-hemisphere specialization for speech perception, we have developed a neurobehavioral model of brain organization in persons with DS to help us explain some of the specific information-processing difficulties experienced by these people as well as to guide our research (Elliott, Weeks, & Elliott, 1987). The model is depicted in figure 13.1. Its main feature is the dissociation or separation of right-hemisphere speech perception from left-hemisphere movement production in persons with DS.

Our model holds that persons with DS will have particular difficulty performing tasks that involve both the perception of speech and the organization of complex movement (see Chua, Weeks, & Elliott, 1996). Within the model, this is attributable to the biological dissociation of speech perception and movement organization functions that are typically subserved by the same cerebral hemisphere. This is

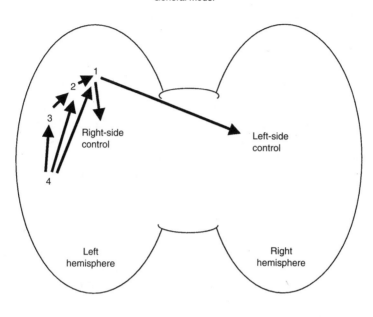

Figure 13.1 A model of functional cerebral organization in the general population and in persons with Down syndrome: 1. Movement executive; 2. praxis control; 3. speech production; 4. speech perception.

because the "separation of speech perception and movement production systems leads to a breakdown in communication, presumably because interhemispheric transmission between these systems results in the partial loss of information" (Elliott & Weeks, 1993a, p. 104).

Our model is not only consistent with a number of cognitive and psychometric studies comparing persons with DS to other mentally challenged individuals, but it has also been able to predict both within- and between-group differences in performance on a number of verbal-motor tasks. For example, we have shown that persons with DS have greater difficulty performing single and sequential oral and manual movements on the basis of *verbal direction* than do other individuals of a similar mental age. Young adults with DS demonstrate no such handicap, however, when they are *visually directed* to perform the same movements (Elliott & Weeks, 1990; Elliott, Weeks, & Gray, 1990). The "verbal-motor problem" experienced by persons with DS becomes more severe as the number of movement elements is increased (Elliott et al., 1990). Compared with visual demonstration, when persons with DS are verbally cued about the sequence requirements, they provide movements in the wrong order, substitute more incorrect responses, and simply fail to complete a movement sequence more often (Elliott et al., 1990). These specific problems are not related to a verbal memory difficulty but rather to the inability to sequence movement on the basis of verbal instruction.

Within a group of adults with DS, the individuals with the strongest dissociation between speech perception and movement organization (e.g., strongest right-hemisphere dichotic listening scores) also show the greatest verbal-motor performance difficulties (Elliott & Weeks, 1993a). Interestingly, these individuals also exhibit problems on tasks such as the Raven's Matrices, which have been shown to depend on right-hemisphere function. Perhaps the development of right-hemisphere speech perception carries with it an added cost: the reduction in neural resources that are available for spatial decision-making.

Finally, we also have demonstrated that persons with DS have greater difficulty learning a new motor task on the basis of verbal instruction than other individuals of a similar mental age (Elliott, Gray, & Weeks, 1991). At least part of this problem appears to be the result of difficulty in using verbal cues to rapidly structure a motor program (LeClair & Elliott, 1995). This work suggests that persons with DS will benefit more from an instructional strategy that emphasizes the visual as opposed to the verbal communication of information. Motor learning studies in which instructional modality as well as knowledge of results and performance are manipulated are needed to put this hypothesis to an empirical test.

Speech Errors and the Dissociation of Speech Perception and Movement (Speech) Production

Until recently our research has focused on the visual versus verbal control of limb movements. However, the examination of speech-production errors also has ramifications for our model of cerebral organization. In addition to allowing the determination of the cerebral specialization for speech production, the mouth-asymmetry paradigm allowed the assessment of verbal-fluency errors made during the sequential-speech condition. Stimulated by the high proportion of errors committed by persons with DS and the relative simplicity of the sequential-speech condition, we attempted to determine the type of verbal errors committed by our participants with DS. Using an error-notation system adapted from Square-Storer, Qualizza, and Roy (1989), we recorded the number of incorrect responses in the sequential-speech condition (50%). Analysis of these responses revealed three major types of errors: (a) substitution errors (46%)—intrusion of a consonant or vowel that preceded or followed the target syllable; (b) mispronunciation errors (29%)—inappropriate production of the target syllable (e.g., /mom/ instead of /ma/); and (c) pausing errors (19%)—situation in which the experimenter had to initiate a second prompt if the participant had not begun the speech task within 3 s of the initial prompt. Repetition (5%) and timing (1%) errors accounted for only a small percentage of the total number of errors (Heath, 1997).

The high proportion of verbal errors and the types of errors made by participants with DS are consistent with our limb sequencing data. That is, compared to control participants, subjects with DS had difficulty transforming an experimenter-generated verbal production of the speech sequence into a set of oral-movement commands. Once again this finding is compatible with our biological-dissociation model, which predicts that persons with DS will have difficulty with any task that involves both speech perception and the production of complex movement.

Devenny and colleagues (Devenny & Silverman, 1990; Devenny, Silverman, Balgley, Wall, & Sidtis, 1990) have suggested that the verbal-fluency problems associated with DS are related to a breakdown of the neural organization of speech at the consonant level. Certainly the functional dissociation principle combined with the ideas of Devenny and colleagues explains the high proportion of substitution errors. Participants were given verbal instructions concerning the syllable-production task. Thus, sound-substitution errors reflect an impaired ability to perceive (right hemisphere) and translate the acoustic pattern into an accurate motor output (left hemisphere). According to our model, the interhemispheric transmission of information probably resulted in a partial loss of information, which limits the ability of movement-production systems to construct the commands necessary for the production of the appropriate oral movements required on that trial.

Although the verbal errors could reflect an impairment at the linguistic-processing level, it is doubtful that the errors were a result of intelligence or language ability per se, given the simplicity of the task and the ability of our participants to generate spontaneous speech. Given that the mental age of participants with DS used in our study was 7.3 years, we believe that the biological-dissociation model provides a useful framework for understanding why verbal errors were made in the context of that investigation. Further investigation may be better able to extend this hypothesis by examining the relation between individual dichotic-listening scores and the type and extent of the verbal error. Based on the biological-dissociation model, the production of speech from verbal instructions would be more impaired in persons with speech perception strongly lateralized to the right hemisphere.

Future Directions

There are three types of studies we plan to complete over the next several years. First, because our model is based almost exclusively on behavioral data, we intend to employ some of the latest brain-imaging techniques to verify the brain-behavior relations that we have identified using noninvasive neuropsychological paradigms. This work is being developed by the group at Simon Fraser University.

In our current behavioral work, we are looking more closely at verbal-motor difficulties in persons with DS by having participants produce single and sequential limb movements in situations in which competing instructions are simultaneously presented to the right and left ears. This combination of the dichotic-listening and movement-sequencing procedures will provide a strong test of our model of brain organization for receptive language and motor control in persons with DS.

From a practical point of view, our most important work is concerned with the implications of atypical cerebral organization for the learning of new motor skills. In this work, we will examine the effectiveness of various instruction modes (i.e., visual, verbal, both) for the long-term retention and transfer of novel motor skills. Within the population of persons with DS, we will attempt to determine if any combination of laterality indices is able to predict skill acquisition.

Conclusions

With respect to cerebral specialization in general, we have found that persons with DS do not exhibit a simple reversed pattern of laterality as suggested by investigators who used only dichotic-listening procedures (Hartley, 1986; Pipe, 1988). While there appears to be greater variability in the lateralization of function in persons with DS than in the general population, there are also several predictable patterns that make this group unique. Specifically, most adolescents and young adults with DS exhibit right-hemisphere specialization for speech perception (Elliott et al., 1994) and perhaps other receptive-language functions, while at the same time they are dependent on left-hemisphere neural systems for the organization and control of movement (Chua et al., 1996), including the oral movements necessary for fluent speech (Heath & Elliott, 1999). Like most of the general population, the majority of persons with DS appear to be right-hemisphere specialized for spatial processing, although there is some evidence to suggest that specialization for this function may be compromised by atypical receptive-language lateralization.

With respect to the relation between cerebral specialization in persons with DS and performance, we have demonstrated that, compared with individuals of a similar mental age, persons with DS have particular difficulty with tasks that involve both the perception of speech and the organization and control of simple limb and oral movements (Elliott et al., 1990; Elliott & Weeks, 1990). In what can best be characterized as a disconnection model (e.g., Geschwind, 1965), we have suggested that these specific information-processing difficulties may be due to the separation of functional systems (e.g., receptive language and motor control) that are normally subserved by the same (left) cerebral hemisphere (Elliott & Weeks, 1993b).

Summary

Our research to date has focused on two issues. First, we have attempted to describe the pattern of cerebral specialization in persons with DS for language and spatial processing as well as motor control. In this work, we have employed a number of noninvasive neurobehavioral paradigms. Our second research concern has been related to the impact of atypical cerebral specialization in persons with DS on their ability to successfully perform various perceptual-motor and simple cognitive tasks. In that research, we have compared persons with DS to other individuals of a similar mental and/or chronological age, and we also have examined performance differences and their neural correlates within samples of persons with DS.

While a number of studies provide support for our model, there is still much work to be done, particularly with respect to the implications of our model for learning.

References

Annett, M. (1985). *Left, right, hand and brain: The right shift theory.* Hillsdale, NJ: Erlbaum.

Batheja, M., & McManus, I.C. (1985). Handedness in the mentally handicapped. *Developmental Medicine and Child Neurology, 27,* 63-68.

Benton, A.L., Varney, N.R., & Hamsher, K.D. (1978). Lateral differences in tactile directional perception. *Neuropsychologia, 16,* 109-114.

Bryden, M.P. (1982). *Laterality: Functional asymmetry in the intact brain.* New York: Academic Press.

Bryden, M.P., Bulman-Fleming, M.B., & MacDonald, V. (1996). The measurement of handedness and its relation to neuropsychological issues. In D. Elliott & E. A. Roy (Eds.), *Manual asymmetries in motor performance* (pp. 57-81). Boca Raton, FL: CRC Press.

Cadalbert, A., Landis, T., Regard, M., & Graves, R. (1994). Singing with and without words: Hemispheric asymmetries in motor control. *Journal of Clinical and Experimental Neuropsychology, 16,* 664-670.

Chua, R., Weeks, D.J., & Elliott, D. (1996). A functional systems approach to understanding verbal-motor integration in individuals with Down syndrome. *Down Syndrome: Research and Practice, 4,* 25-36.

Coren, S. (1996). Pathological causes and consequences of left-handedness. In D. Elliott & E. A. Roy (Eds.), *Manual asymmetries in motor performance* (pp. 83-98). Boca Raton, FL: CRC Press.

Devenny, D.A., & Silverman, W. (1990). Speech dysfluency and manual specialization in Down's syndrome. *Journal of Mental Deficiency Research, 34,* 253-260.

Devenny, D.A., Silverman, W., Balgley, H., Wall, M.J., & Sidtis, J.J. (1990). Specific motor abilities associated with speech fluency in Down's syndrome. *Journal of Mental Deficiency Research, 34,* 437-443.

Edwards, J.M., & Elliott, D. (1989). Asymmetries in intermanual transfer of training and motor overflow in adults with Down's syndrome and nonhandicapped children. *Journal of Clinical and Experimental Neuropsychology, 11,* 959-966.

Elliott, D. (1985). Manual asymmetries in the performance of sequential movement by adolescents and adults with Down syndrome. *American Journal of Mental Deficiency, 90,* 90-97.

Elliott, D., & Chua, R. (1996). Manual asymmetries in goal-directed movement. In D. Elliott & E. A. Roy (Eds.), *Manual asymmetries in motor performance* (pp. 143-158). Boca Raton, FL: CRC Press.

Elliott, D., Edwards, J.M., Weeks, D.J., Lindley, S., & Carnahan, H. (1987). Cerebral specialization in young adults with Down syndrome. *American Journal of Mental Deficiency, 91,* 480-485.

Elliott, D., Gray, S., & Weeks, D.J. (1991). Verbal cuing and motor skill acquisition for adults with Down's syndrome. *Adapted Physical Activity Quarterly, 8,* 210-220.

Elliott, D., Pollock, B.J., Chua, R., & Weeks, D.J. (1995). Cerebral specialization in adults with Down syndrome. *American Journal on Mental Retardation, 99,* 605-615.

Elliott, D., & Weeks, D.J. (1990). Cerebral specialization and the control of oral and limb movements for individuals with Down's syndrome. *Journal of Motor Behavior, 22,* 6-18.

Elliott, D., & Weeks, D.J. (1993a). Cerebral specialization for speech perception and movement organization in adults with Down's syndrome. *Cortex, 29,* 103-113.

Elliott, D., & Weeks, D.J. (1993b). A functional systems approach to movement difficulties associated with Down syndrome. *Adapted Physical Activity Quarterly, 10,* 312-323.

Elliott, D., Weeks, D.J., & Chua, R. (1994). Anomalous cerebral lateralization and Down syndrome. *Brain and Cognition, 26,* 191-195.

Elliott, D., Weeks, D.J., & Elliott, C.L. (1987). Cerebral specialization in individuals with Down's syndrome. *American Journal on Mental Retardation, 92,* 263-271.

Elliott, D., Weeks, D.J., & Gray, S. (1990). Manual and oral praxis in adults with Down's syndrome. *Neuropsychologia, 28,* 1307-1315.

Elliott, D., Weeks, D.J., & Jones, R. (1986). Lateral asymmetries in finger-tapping by adolescents and young adults with Down syndrome. *American Journal of Mental Deficiency, 90,* 472-475.

Geschwind, N. (1965). Disconnexion syndromes in animals and man. *Brain, 88,* 585-644.

Graves, R. (1983). Mouth asymmetry, dichotic ear advantage and tachistoscopic visual field advantage as measures of language lateralization. *Neuropsychologia, 21,* 641-649.

Graves, R., Goodglass, H., & Landis, T. (1982). Mouth asymmetry during spontaneous speech. *Neuropsychologia, 20,* 371-381.

Graves, R., & Landis, T. (1985). Hemispheric control of speech expression in aphasia. *Archives of Neurology, 42,* 249-251.

Hartley, X.Y. (1982). Receptive language processing of Down's syndrome children. *Journal of Mental Deficiency Research, 26*, 263-269.

Hartley, X.Y. (1986). A summary of recent research into the development of children with Down's syndrome. *Journal of Mental Deficiency Research, 30*, 1-14.

Heath, M. (1997). *Cerebral specialization for speech and complex oral movements in persons with Down syndrome.* Unpublished master's thesis, McMaster University, Hamilton, Ontario.

Heath, M., & Elliott, D. (1999). Cerebral specialization for speech production in persons with Down syndrome. *Brain and Language, 69*, 193-211.

Heath, M., Elliott, D., Roy, E.A., & Veeneman, D. (1999). Performance of the manual and oral-motor system using the dua-task paradigm. *Brain and Cognition, 40*, 147-150.

Heath, M., Smith, K., & Elliott, D. (1998). [Cerebral specialization for speech perception in Down syndrome]. Unpublished raw data.

Kimura, D. (1966). Dual functional asymmetry of the brain in visual perception. *Neuropsychologia, 29*, 877-888.

Kimura, D. (1979). Neuromotor mechanisms in the evolution of human communication. In H.D. Steklis & M.J. Raleigh (Eds.), *Neurobiology of social communication in primates: An evolutionary perspective* (pp. 197-219). New York: Academic Press.

Kinsbourne, M., & Cook, J. (1971). Generalized and lateralized effects of concurrent verbalization on a unimanual skill. *Quarterly Journal of Experimental Psychology, 23*, 341-345.

Kinsbourne, M., & Hicks, R.E. (1978). Functional cerebral space: A model for overflow, transfer and interference effects in human performance. In J. Requin (Ed.), *Attention and performance VII* (pp. 345-362). New York: Academic Press.

LeClair, D.A., & Elliott, D. (1995). Movement preparation and the costs and benefits associated with advance information for adults with Down syndrome. *Adapted Physical Activity Quarterly, 12*, 239-249.

McManus, C.I. (1985). Handedness, language dominance and aphasia: A genetic model. *Psychological Medicine* (Monograph Suppl. 8).

McManus, C.I., & Bryden, M.P. (1992). The genetics of handedness and cerebral lateralization. In I. Rapin & S.J. Segalowitz (Eds.), *Handbook of neuropsychology: Vol. 6* (pp. 115-144). Amsterdam: Elsevier.

Murphy, M.M. (1962). Hand preferences of three diagnostic groups of severely deficient males. *Perceptual and Motor Skills, 14*, 508.

Piccirilli, M., D'Alessandro, P., Mazzi, P., Sciarma, T., & Testa, A. (1991). Cerebral organization for language in Down's syndrome patients. *Cortex, 27*, 41-47.

Pickersgill, M.J., & Pank, C. (1970). Relation of age and Mongolism to lateral preferences in severely subnormal subjects. *Nature, 228*, 1342-1344.

Pipe, M.E. (1988). Atypical laterality and retardation. *Psychological Bulletin, 104*, 343-349.

Roy, E.A., & MacKenzie, C.L. (1978). Handedness effects in kinesthetic spatial location judgements. *Cortex, 14*, 250-258.

Square-Storer, P.A., Qualizza, L., & Roy, E.A. (1989). Isolated and sequenced oral motor posture production under different input modalities by left hemisphere damaged adults. *Cortex, 25*, 371-386.

Van Gelder, R.S., & Van Gelder, L. (1990). Facial expression and speech: Neuroanatomical considerations. *International Journal of Psychology, 25*, 141-155.

Weeks, D.J., Chua, R., Elliott, D., Lyons, J., & Pollock, B.J. (1995). Cerebral specialization for receptive language in individuals with Down syndrome. *Australian Journal of Psychology, 47*, 137-140.

Weeks, D.J., & Elliott, D. (1992). Atypical cerebral dominance in Down syndrome. *Bulletin of the Psychonomic Society, 30,* 23-25.

Witelson, S.F. (1974). Hemispheric specialization for linguistic and nonlinguistic tactual perception using a dichotomous stimulation technique. *Cortex, 10,* 3-17.

Wolf, M., & Goodale, M. (1987). Oral asymmetries during verbal and non-verbal movements of the mouth. *Neuropsychologia, 25,* 375-396.

Author Note

We would like to acknowledge the support of the Scottish Rite Charitable Foundation, the British Columbia Health Research Foundation, and the Natural Sciences and Engineering Research Council of Canada.

14

Neurophysiological Correlates of Perceptual-Motor Behavior in Down Syndrome

Giuseppe A. Chiarenza and Paolo Stagi

Child and Adolescent Neuropsychiatry Department
Azienda Ospedaliera "G. Salvini" Rho Hospital

Key words

brain characteristics ◆ evoked potentials ◆ Alzheimer's disease ◆ EEG ◆ aging ◆ conduction time ◆ plasticity ◆ habituation ◆ contingent negative variation ◆ skilled performance ◆ movement-related potentials ◆ EMG ◆ movement preparation

Down syndrome (DS) represents the most common genetic cause of mental retardation (1.6 per 1,000 born alive). In addition to its social impact, the peculiar genetic and neuropathological findings make this disorder an object of research with regard to mental retardation and its impact on learning. In 95% of the cases, the syndrome is due to a nondisjunction of maternal chromosomes during meiosis. The observation of a few patients with a partial duplication of 21q and features suggestive of DS has allowed the mapping of a critical region of 21q22.3 that, if triplicated, results in the phenotypic characteristics of the syndrome (Delabar et al. 1993).

Macroscopic neuropathological findings peculiar to DS are brain size and weight reduction; shorter fronto-occipital diameter; and smaller frontal lobes, brain stem, and cerebellum. The cortical structure appears to be simplified, with the main sulci less deep and the secondary ones fewer. Moreover, the gyri are wider and the cortex is thinner (Colon, 1972). These macroscopic characteristics are due to a structural organization at the microscopic level consisting of (a) poor myelination or dysmyelination of nervous fibers, particularly of arcuate fibers that connect primary sensory cortex with association areas (Benda, 1969); (b) a severe neuronal loss, including an apparently selective loss of cholinergic neurons of the Meynert's nucleus; and (c) abnormalities in the dendritic formation process (Balazs & Brooksbank, 1985; Ball & Nuttal, 1980; Colon, 1972; Ohara, 1972). The formation of dendritic spines seems to be normal throughout the gestation and then drastically decreases during the postnatal period. This process, which can be attributed to an early growth standstill (Takashima, Becker, Armstrong, & Chan, 1981), explains the reduced number of dendritic spines in adults (Balazs & Brooksbank, 1985).

Most histopathological microscope investigations deal with the relation between early onset of mental deficiency in DS and dementia in Alzheimer's disease. These two conditions present similar histopathological patterns characterized by cerebral atrophy and by the occurrence of senile plaques, neurofibrillar bodies, and granulovacuolar degeneration (Balazs & Brooksbank, 1985; Ball & Nuttal, 1980; Crapper, Dalton, Skopitz, Scott, & Hachinski, 1975). In subjects with a normal karyotype, the occurrence of senile plaques and neurofibrillar bodies has been found to increase with age and to correlate positively with the degree of intellective decay. In contrast, it is not certain at all whether in DS the early occurrence and the rapid increase of such changes are associated with early mental deterioration (Ropper & Williams, 1980). The detection of clinical signs of mental deterioration in persons with DS is very difficult, given that mental retardation is in itself a clinical characteristic of the syndrome. In fact, it has been shown that the most significant age-correlated clinical signs in persons with DS are much more subtle and selective, and concern the short-term memorization of visual stimuli as well as the occurrence of frontal inhibitory release reflexes (Crapper et al., 1975; Ropper & Williams, 1980). So it seems that dementia and neuropathological alterations in DS dissociate: the high density of such abnormalities in itself is not sufficient to explain the sporadic appearance of a demential pattern in elderly individuals with DS.

Investigations aiming to show the early occurrence of biochemical, cerebral, and noncerebral reactions typical of the normal aging process have been carried out with individuals with DS. Abnormalities in the metabolism of nucleic acids and particularly of free oxygen radicals have been detected. A basic enzyme in the metabolism of free oxygen radicals is superoxide dismutase, codified by chromosome 21. The activity of this enzyme is increased by 50% in the red blood cells of persons with DS (Balazs & Brooksbank, 1985). An increased production of peroxides with consequent lipoperoxidation of biological membrane lipids would alter the fluidity of the double lipidic layer, causing a biochemical and functional disorganization in biological membranes.

Neurophysiological measurements of peripheral and central nervous system conduction parameters support the evidence of aging in DS. In fact, conventional nerve conduction studies reveal evidence of peripheral nerve dysfunction consistent with axonal degeneration. Upper-limb somatosensory-evoked potentials are delayed compared with age-matched controls in both young and older age groups of persons with DS. Lower-limb somatosensory-evoked potentials are also delayed when correction for height is made; furthermore the "central conduction time" is prolonged in young and older groups. These results suggest that both peripheral and central nervous system functions are impaired in DS, and the pattern of change is similar to that found with aging in normal individuals (Mackenzie, Creasy, & Huang, 1983).

It seems likely that in DS the formation of both biochemically and functionally anomalous cellular membranes takes place at an early ontogenetic stage. However, neither the increased production of intracellular free radicals nor the loss of membrane fluidity is peculiar to DS. In fact, both events occur in the normal aging process (Hansford, 1983). But in DS they occur earlier and more clearly, being present even during the initial postnatal period (Balazs & Brooksbank, 1985).

Biochemical investigations also provide information about the involvement of various receptor systems, at both central and peripheral levels. In particular, in DS as well as in Alzheimer's disease, the cholinergic system is certainly involved, as indicated both by the decrease in the cortical choline acetyltransferase activity and by the neuronal depauperation of Meynert's nucleus (considered to be the origin of most cholinergic projections toward the neurocortex). However, since the decrease in cortical choline acetyltransferase activity far exceeds the neuronal loss of the basal Meynert's nucleus, the subcortical damage is likely to be secondary to a primary cortical damage (Perry et al., 1985). Histochemical investigations carried out on subjects affected by Alzheimer's disease suggest that just the senile plaques might be the site of damage of cholinergic nerve endings (Kitt, Price, & Struble, 1984; Price et al., 1982). The remarkable sensitivity of subjects affected by DS to the peripheral effects of atropine, a selective blocker of the muscarine receptor, points to a generalized anomaly of the cholinergic transmitter system (Harris & Goodman, 1968).

The dopaminergic neurons of the substantia nigra projecting toward the basal ganglia and those of the ventral tegmentum area projecting toward the frontal and limbic cortex also appear seriously affected, probably by secondary reverse degeneration from a primitive cortical damage (Mann, Yates, & Marcyniuk, 1987). The low serotonin blood concentration in patients with DS and the reduced plasmatic activity of dopamine-β-hydroxylase may be peripheral signs of a change in the catecholaminergic metabolism (Wetterberg, Gustavson, Backstrom, Ross, & Froden, 1972). In addition to neuroanatomical and biochemical studies, investigations have been carried out by recording cerebral electrical activity. It has been shown that the diffuse neuronal loss, the senile plaques, and the neurofibrillar degeneration may bring about a change in synaptic transmission in which the involved neurons would lose the ability to produce postsynaptic potentials (Crapper et al., 1975).

Despite the neuropathological findings, visual analysis of the electroencephalogram does not show specific signs of DS. Ellingson and Peters (1980) found significant retardation in the maturation of brain electrical activity in infants with trisomy 21, which was correlated with delayed early behavioral development, but not with the presence of conventional signs of EEG abnormality. EEG studies on cerebral aging in persons with DS have demonstrated that from the fourth to the sixth decades of life, 75% of these subjects have a normal EEG, while the rest show a diffuse but nonspecific slowing of cortical electrical activity (Ellingson, Eisen, & Ottersberg, 1973). Moreover, there are not many EEG characteristics that specifically correlate with any form of mental retardation (Bigum, Dustman, & Beck, 1970). More recently, spectral analysis of digitized EEG of individuals with DS aged 6 months to 5 years has been examined. The analysis revealed a significant increase in absolute power, especially theta power, while the absolute alpha power was less markedly increased or even decreased. The most significant differences, however, were observed when calculating the relative alpha power. Children with DS showed a reduced relative alpha power at the age of 6 months, with the reduction becoming even more prominent with increasing age (Schmid, Sadowsky, Weinmann, Tirsch, & Poppl, 1985). Despite the absence of pathognomic EEG patterns characterizing the brain in DS, studies of the early and late components of sensory-evoked potentials (EPs) and event-related potentials (ERPs) or cognitive potentials have yielded consistently abnormal findings. Clearly, at the neurofunctional level, such patients are unique in that they differ substantially from both normal subjects and subjects affected by other forms of mental retardation. Furthermore, the studies of sensory- and cognitive-evoked potentials allow cognitive components of mental deficiency to be distinguished from the merely perceptive ones.

Somatosensory-evoked potentials (SEPs) following median and posterior tibial nerve stimulation have been shown to have greater amplitudes, resulting in a wider scalp distribution for all components in DS (Kakigi & Shibasaki, 1993). Moreover, middle-latency SEPs were shorter in latency in patients with DS than in the controls (Kakigi & Shibasaki, 1991). However, the differences between persons with DS and aged controls (over 65 years) were much smaller than those between persons with DS and age-matched controls. Therefore, it was concluded that the generator sources and generating mechanisms of SEPs in DS are not different from those of non-DS controls. However, SEP potentials in DS are remarkably enhanced, resulting in a wider distribution, probably due to accelerated aging in persons with DS (Kakigi & Shibasaki, 1993).

Brain stem auditory-evoked potentials (BAEPs) reflect the brain stem function at the pontomesencephalic level. Comparing BAEPs from DS and normal control subjects, waves II, III, and the IV-V complex show shorter latencies in the former for monoaural (Ferri et al., 1986; Gigli, Ferri, Musumeci, Tomassetti, & Bergonzi, 1984;

Gliddon, Galbraith, & Busk, 1975) and binaural stimulation (Squires, Aine, Buchwald, Norman, & Galbraith, 1980). An age-related shortening of the I-V interpeak interval found in individuals with DS was interpreted as being a result of changes in central inhibitory/excitatory mechanisms. Some authors have also related the reduction in the brain stem conduction time to the shorter brain stem length, measured as inion-C7 distance, and to its perpendicular insertion in the brain (Squires et al., 1980), identified in anatomopathological studies (Benda, 1969; Burger & Vogel, 1973). In contrast, other authors have related the reduction to the degree of mental retardation (Ferri et al., 1986) or to a generalized abnormality of the nerve conduction speed also present at the peripheral level (Scott, Petit, Becker, & Edwards, 1981).

The most consistent and significant finding concerning sensory EPs in DS is the greater amplitude and the longer latency of late components, as compared with findings both from normal subjects and those affected by other forms of mental retardation. This particular aspect emerges with all types of EPs (Dustman & Callner, 1979; Galbraith, Gliddon, & Busk, 1970; Gliddon et al., 1975; Straumanis, Shagass, & Overton, 1973), irrespective of age and with reduced intra- and inter-individual variability (Bigum et al., 1970). On this basis, it has been assumed that the increase in the amplitude of EPs in DS is due to a failure of cerebral inhibitory processes. This inhibitory deficit, which lowers the neuronal threshold of discharge, might cause an increase in amplitude of cortical-evoked responses through a neurophysiological disinhibition mechanism. The inhibitory failure is probably due to the reduced activity of the reticulothalamic sensory gating system, resulting in absent or abnormal inhibition of the sensory stimuli afferent to the cortex. In fact, the experimental block of the nonspecific thalamocortical system produces an increase in the amplitude of visual and auditory EPs (Skinner & Lindsley, 1971). In support of the assumption that reduced activity of the reticulothalamic sensory gating system occurs, there are some investigations showing that subjects affected by DS do not present the phenomenon of "habituation" in cerebral EPs (Schafer & Peeke, 1982).

The lack of age-related changes of evoked responses in DS further suggests that the development of central inhibitory processes stops very early. This harmonizes with the hypothesis that the rate of cortical development in DS quickly decreases after the first months of life (Barnet & Lodge, 1967).

The ERPs associated with DS have shown that the main differences do not concern the components N1-P1, but rather the components N2-P3, which have a longer latency and a lower amplitude in DS (Karrer & Ivins, 1976b; Lincoln, Courchesne, Kilman, & Galambos, 1986; Squires, Galbraith, & Aine, 1979). Therefore, ERP differences between individuals with DS and control subjects cannot be attributed to a different sensory perception, because latencies and amplitudes of the component N1 do not differ in the two groups. The appearance of P3 is usually related to the recognition of an external event. The increase in P3 latency would represent a greater slowness, in persons with DS, of the processes of stimulus recognition and response selection. Furthermore, the P3 amplitude is influenced by dimensions such as subjective probability, stimulus meaning, and the proportion of information lost during transmission due to equivocation or inattention (Johnson, 1986). The lower amplitude of P3 in DS could reflect a failure in one of these dimensions and in the processes of memory and formation of expectancy patterns (Squires et al., 1979). This assumption is confirmed by studies carried out on the Contingent Negative Variation (CNV). In subjects affected by mental retardation and in a control group, there were no significant differences in amplitudes, but differences were seen in latency and CNV rise time recorded at Cz, both of which were prolonged in the mentally retarded subjects (Karrer & Ivins, 1976a, 1976b). Individuals with DS take more time to develop the CNV, which then tends to increase during the test. As the CNV is considered an "expectancy" potential that can reflect both an orientation process following a warning stimulus and the expectancy and/or preparation for the motor response after an imperative stimulus, this behavior could indicate the inability to evaluate and utilize correctly the time succession of external events in programming a perceptual-motor act. From a behavioral point of view, this results in an increase in reaction times, which are steadily and markedly longer than those of control subjects.

As we have seen, EPs and ERPs allow, respectively, the evaluation of sensory functions and of basic neuropsychological mechanisms, such as attention, memory, and so on. On the other hand, more complex perceptual-motor abilities in persons with DS have been studied only from a behavioral point of view by means of neuropsychological tests.

Until now there have been few controlled investigations of the electrical cerebral activity of subjects with severe mental deficiency in relation to perceptual-motor tasks involving programming a temporal sequence of self-paced and goal-directed actions. The method to evaluate these processes consists in the study of motor performances, electromyographic activity, and movement-related macropotentials.

Researchers have demonstrated that when a subject is engaged in a skilled perceptual-motor task in order to achieve a preset goal and receives real-time information about the quality of his or her performance, a characteristic sequence of brain macropotential can be recorded from the scalp, both in adults (Papakostopoulos, 1978a) and in children (Chiarenza, Papakostopoulos, Guareschi-Cazzullo, Giordana, & Giammari Aldè, 1983). The electrical brain activity accompanying the performance of such tasks is defined as movement-related brain macropotentials (MRBMs). Through observation of the myographic and electrical brain activity, one can distinguish four periods: premotor, sensory-motor, motor completion, and postmotor (Papakostopoulos, 1978b). Figure 14.1 shows a detailed diagram of the sequence of the electrical brain events that accompany task execution.

The premotor period is characterized by basic tonic muscular activity and the presence on the scalp of a phasic negative potential lasting 800 to 1,200 ms: the Bereitschaftspotential (BP) (Kornhuber & Deecke, 1965), or readiness potential (Vaughan, Costa, & Ritter, 1968), which is absent during passive movements. Its amplitude increases progressively with age, being absent in children under 6 years of age and reaching adult values at adolescence (Chiarenza, 1986a). Moreover, it is proportional to the complexity of the task both in adults (Papakostopoulos, 1978b) and children (Chiarenza, Papakostopoulos, Guareschi-Cazzullo, & Giordana, 1980). It is mainly recorded in the frontal and central regions. The BP is believed to reflect the processes of organization and selection of the strategy needed to carry out the

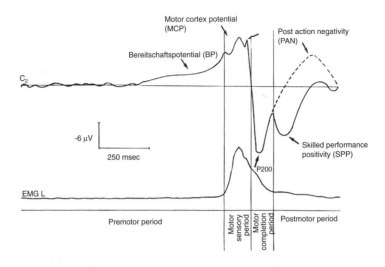

Figure 14.1 Schematic diagram of movement-related brain macropotentials and rectified electromyographic activity related to the skilled task.

Adapted, by permission, from G.A. Chiarenza, 1993, "Movement-related brain macropotentials of persons with Down Syndrome during skilled performance," *American Journal on Mental Retardation* 97(4): 449-467.

task, and has been proposed as an electrophysiological index of cerebral efficiency during the premotor period.

The sensory-motor period begins at the onset of phasic electromyographic activity and lasts about 200 ms. It is during this period that behavior is manifested. It coincides with the appearance on the scalp of the motor-cortex potential, followed by a negative potential with a latency of 100 ms. The motor-cortex potential (mcp) is a negative potential that follows the BP; it is absent during passive movements, present in simple voluntary motor actions, and increases in amplitude during ballistic and sustained motor actions (Grunewald, Grunewald-Zuberbier, Homberg, & Netz, 1979; Papakostopoulos, 1978a). Scalp and cortical recordings have shown that the motor-cortex potential is mainly present in the precentral and central regions and absent from the parietal regions (Papakostopoulos, 1980; Papakostopoulos & Crow, 1984). The motor-cortex potential is proposed as an index of response-generated reafferent activity from the muscle, skin, and tendon receptors (Papakostopoulos, Cooper, & Crow, 1975). It is present in children and adults, its amplitude decreasing with senescence (Papakostopoulos & Banerji, 1980). The N100 is a negative potential with a latency of 100 ms that follows the motor-cortex potential and represents the response evoked by the appearance of the oscilloscope trace and is normally inhibited in the frontal and postcentral areas during movement.

The motor completion period is characterized by the completion of the electromyographic phasic activity and the presence of a positive potential with a latency of 200 ms, defined as P200, that follows N100 with a latency of about 200 ms from the beginning of the light stimulus (Vaughan et al., 1968). This potential is present during passive and active movements, both simple and complex, and is believed to be one of the components of the reafferent somatosensory potentials on the basis of its developmental course (Chiarenza et al., 1983).

The postmotor period is characterized by the electromyographic tonic activity similar to the premotor period, by the appearance on the scalp of a positive potential with a latency of about 450 ms, called skilled performance positivity (SPP) (Papakostopoulos, 1978a, 1980), and by a slow negative potential defined as postaction negativity (PAN), with a latency of about 600 ms (Chiarenza et al., 1983). The SPP has a higher amplitude in the parietal regions and appears in the frontocentral regions when a child is approximately 9 years old (Chiarenza, 1986b). Scalp and cortical recordings have shown that SPP is present only when the subject can evaluate the result of his or her performance (Papakostopoulos, 1980; Papakostopoulos, Stamler, & Newton, 1986). This potential is independent of the motor action and the presence of any exteroceptive stimulation; it coincides with the subject's awareness of success or failure in the performance (Chiarenza, 1986b; Papakostopoulos, 1980).

The PAN has a specific spatial distribution, mainly recorded in the frontocentral regions, and decreases in amplitude with age, disappearing around the 10th year (Chiarenza et al., 1983). Like the SPP, PAN is independent of the motor act and seems to be related to analysis and evaluation strategies different from those generating SPP (Chiarenza et al., 1984). The presence of these positive and negative potentials following the performance of a skilled action has been confirmed by other authors each time a voluntary goal-directed motor task is employed (Elbert, Lutzenberger, Rockstroch, & Birbaumer, 1986; Foit, Grozinger, & Kornhuber, 1982; Grunewald et al., 1979; Knapp, Schmid, Ganglberger, & Haider, 1980; Netz, Homberg, Grunewald-Zuberbier, & Grunewald, 1984; Taylor, 1978; Weinberg, 1980).

Materials and Methods

The present study was designed to compare the performances and the MRBMs of a group of young adults with DS and two control groups, one with the same chronological age (CA) and the other with the same mental age (MA), in order to evaluate the perceptual-motor and cognitive processes related to the selection and evaluation of operative strategies during the execution of a skilled task.

Participants

Participants were nine right-handed males with DS, aged 18 to 25 years (average 23.10), with a mean IQ of 63 on the Wechsler Intelligence Scale (WISC), a mean mental age of 10.6 years on the Terman-Merrill Scale, and a mean age of 10.2 years on the Psychosocial Development Scale. In addition, two control groups were tested. The mental age-matched group consisted of nine normal children, with a mean age of 10 years and a mean IQ of 123.3 on the WISC. The chronological age-matched group consisted of nine young adults of normal intelligence, with a mean age of 25.9 years. None of the subjects had visual or auditory deficiencies or severe neurological abnormalities.

Procedure

The Skilled Perceptual-Motor Task. The subject sat in an armchair 70 cm in front of an oscilloscope in a lighted and electrically shielded room and held a joystick-type push button in each hand. The excursion of the button was 5 mm. The task consisted in starting a sweep of the oscilloscope trace with the left thumb and stopping it in a predetermined area of the oscilloscope by pushing the other button with the right thumb. The sweep velocity was 1 mm per ms and the target area corresponded to a time interval between 40 and 60 ms.

After a verbal explanation of the task, to ensure that all subjects understood the verbal instructions, the experimenter conducted a few trials, and the subjects had to indicate the performance results. So that all subjects started from the same training level, they were allowed a short practice period. None of the subjects had previous experience with this or related experimental tasks.

The recording procedure was initiated only after all subjects were able to stop the oscilloscope sweep at least twice in the 40 to 60 ms interval. This practice was also necessary to enable the subjects to become familiar with controlling eye movements or blinking during the execution of the task and to keep an interval of 7 to 20 seconds between any two attempts. The subjects were also asked to remain relaxed during the task and to avoid muscular preparatory movements before pressing.

EEG Recording. Silver chloride electrodes were fixed to the scalp with collodion in the prefrontal (FPz), frontal (Fz), central (Cz), right precentral (RPC), left precentral (LPC), and parietal (Pz) regions. Each electrode was referred bilaterally to the mastoids. The surface EMG was recorded from the flexor muscles on the right and left forearms. The impedance of the electrodes was less than 3 KΩ. The EEG was amplified with Physio Amp Marazza preamplifiers. Time constant and low-pass filters (6 dB/octave) were set at 8.0 seconds and 700 Hz for the EEG and 0.03 seconds and 700 Hz for the EMG, respectively.

The EEGs and EMGs were stored on FM magnetic tape (Racal Store 14; bandwidth: 0-625 Hz) for off-line analysis, which was controlled by a PDP-11/23 computer system interfaced with a MINC data-collection system. The analysis started with sampling for each channel, a square wave of ±25 µV for calibration and equalization procedures. During the off-line analysis, reception of the trigger pulse obtained from an electric pulse generated at the press of the left-hand button started the acquisition for each channel of 1,600 points at a frequency of 500 Hz for 3.2 s. Of the points, 1,100 preceded the trigger and 500 followed it. The first 500 points were averaged to give a baseline from which the amplitude of the various potentials was measured. All values were normalized to the calibration detected and stored on disc.

Data Analyses

Performance. The time interval between the two button presses was measured and defined as *performance time.* The distance from the target area was also measured and defined as the *performance shift.* The number of performances in the target interval was measured and defined as *target performance.* The number of performances shorter than 40 ms and longer than 60 ms was also counted and defined as *incorrect performance.*

Movement-Related Brain Macropotentials. For every subject, 4 blocks of 25 sequential trials free of muscular artifacts, blinking, or eye movements were measured and averaged. In addition, to ensure that any differences in movement-related brain macropotentials between the three groups were not due to a jitter effect (latency shift) related to performance variability or to an increased number of incorrect performances in the DS group, performance during the skilled perceptual-motor task was grouped according to performance time. This resulted in nine time intervals (interval 1: 0 to 20 ms; interval 2: 21 to 39 ms; interval 3: 40 to 60 ms; interval 4: 61 to 80 ms; interval 5: 81 to 100 ms; interval 6: 101 to 125 ms; interval 7: 126 to 150 ms; interval 8: 151 to 200 ms; interval 9: >200 ms). Subsequently, the MRBMs were averaged.

Electromyograms and Movement-Related Brain Macropotentials Measurements. The mean amplitude before movement, the peak amplitude during movement, and the rise time of the rectified surface EMG from the left and right forearms were calculated. The MRBMs were measured as follows. The area of the BP was measured from BP onset to the point corresponding to the EMG onset. Then the mean BP amplitudes and MCP were computed for 200 ms periods, the BP immediately preceding the left-EMG onset, and the MCP immediately following it. The MCP value was measured as the difference between the BP and MCP values measured from the baseline. The latency of the MCP peak was measured with respect to the EMG onset. The amplitudes of N100 and P200 were measured from the baseline, and their latencies were calculated from the trigger. The mean amplitude of SPP was taken as the average value from the baseline over 200 ms centered around the main positive peak in the latency band between 350 and 700 ms. The SPP latency was measured from the trigger. For each parameter of the performances and MRBMs of the three groups, tolerance intervals were calculated at 95%, $p < .05$, and 99%, $p < .01$, and compared in pairs (the DS group was compared once with the MA control group and once with the CA control group, and the two control groups were also compared to each other).

Results

The participants with DS required a longer training period to learn the correct sequence of bimanual movements than did the control groups.

Performance

The mean performance time value was 179 ms for participants with DS, 63 ms for the MA control group, and 58 ms for the CA control group. The target performance rate was 13.82% in participants with DS, 26.00% in the MA control group, and 32.00% in the CA control group. The subjects with DS were also less accurate, their performance shift being 134 ms, whereas that of the children was 19 ms and that of the normal adults 14 ms. All these differences were significant according to the student's t-test ($p < .01$). The CA control group showed a higher target performance rate than the MA control group ($p < .05$) and was also more accurate ($p < .01$) (table 14.1). Moreover the subjects with DS showed a higher rate of performances above 60 ms (58.10%) than either the MA control group (47.50%) ($p < .01$) or the CA control group (39.80%) ($p < .01$). The difference was also significant between the two control groups ($p < 0.05$). For the subjects with DS, 32.30% of performances were above 200 ms, versus 0.25% in the adults and 0.22% in the children (see figure 14.2).

Table 14.1 Performance of Subjects With Down Syndrome and Two Control Groups (Means and SD)

In this table, the superscript a or b indicates a significant correlation between the subjects with Down syndrome and the control group in question. The asterisks indicate a significant difference between the two control groups.

Block		PERFORMANCE TIME (MS)		PERFORMANCE SHIFT (MS)		TARGET PERFORMANCE (%)	
		M	SD	M	SD	M	SD
I	A	70.30[b]	45.90	22.01[b]	38.86	31.11[b]	46.39
	C	67.54[b]	37.87	22.31[b]	26.59	22.22[a]	41.66
	D	260.76	278.98	214.14	268.30	12.00	32.58
II	A	56.21[b]	27.67	12.93[b]	17.13	32.44[b]	46.92
	C	64.32[b]	53.35	21.28[b*]	45.67	23.11[a]	42.24
	D	161.41	224.54	117.48	215.79	13.71	34.49
III	A	51.20[b]	22.64	9.84[b]	11.81	34.22[a]	47.55
	C	59.40[b]	45.35	16.40[b*]	38.24	31.55[a]	46.57
	D	119.47	110.63	76.26	98.04	17.24	37.93
IV	A	53.45[b]	25.19	11.20[b]	14.67	30.22[a]	46.02
	C	60.47[b]	33.20	17.07[b*]	22.20	27.11[a]	44.55
	D	128.42	122.59	86.15	109.12	13.18	34.02
Total	A	57.79[b]	32.51	14.00[b]	23.67	32.00[b]	46.67
	C	62.93[b*]	43.18	19.27[b**]	34.49	26.00[b*]	43.88
	D	178.50	220.13	134.15	210.22	13.82	34.54

A = adults; C = children; D = Down syndrome
* = $p < .05$; ** = $p < .01$

Adapted, by permission, from G.A. Chiarenza, 1993, "Movement-related brain macropotentials of persons with Down Syndrome during skilled performance," *American Journal on Mental Retardation* 97(4): 449-467.

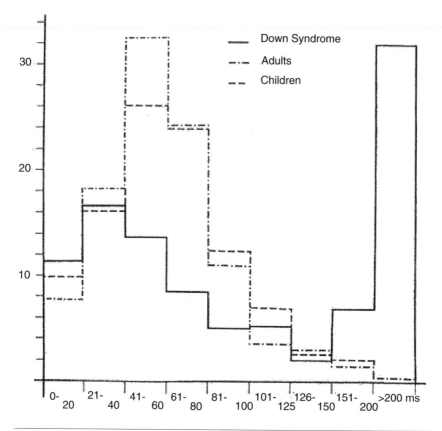

Figure 14.2 Percentage of "performance time" of subjects with Down syndrome, adults, and children in the nine time intervals.

Adapted, by permission, from G.A. Chiarenza, 1993, "Movement-related brain macropotentials of persons with Down Syndrome during skilled performance," *American Journal on Mental Retardation* 97(4): 449-467.

For the subjects with DS, practice produced only a partial improvement in the performance time, which remained steadily higher in all four blocks in comparison with the two control groups ($p < .01$). In fact, their performance time decreased from 261 ms in the first block to 128 ms in the fourth one, whereas it dropped from 70 ms to 53 ms in the CA control group and from 68 ms to 60 ms in the MA control group.

The performance accuracy for the participants with DS showed the same course: the performance shift decreased from 214 ms in the first block to 86 ms in the fourth. In the CA control group it fell from 22 ms to 11 ms, and in the MA control group from 22 ms to 17 ms. Comparison of the performance shift in the subjects with DS in the four blocks with that of the two control groups was consistently significant ($p < .01$). Moreover, in comparing the two control groups, the adults were found to improve their accuracy with practice more than did the children: their performance shift did not differ from that of children in the first block, whereas it considerably diminished in the second one ($p < .05$) and retained this advantage in the following blocks. The target performance rate of the subjects with DS was steadily lower than that of the other two groups: 12% in the first block and 13% in the fourth one against 31% ($p < .01$) and 30% ($p < .05$), respectively, in the CA control group, and 22% ($p < .05$) and 27% ($p < .05$), respectively, in the MA control group. No significant differences were found in the target performance rate between the two control groups in any of the four blocks, although the adults had a significantly higher target performance rate than the children ($p < .05$) (table 14.1).

Electromyography

The EMG of the left forearm muscle group did not show any significant difference in the three groups as regards the amplitude before and during the movement and the rise time. For the subjects with DS, the EMG of the right arm related to the arrest of the sweep was not different in amplitude before and during the movement in comparison with the other two groups. In contrast the rise time was slower in comparison with both control groups, with a significant difference ($p < .05$) between the subjects with DS and the MA control group.

Movement-Related Brain Macropotentials

Remarkable differences were found in MRBMs during all four motor periods (see figure 14.3, on page 336). In the premotor period, the BP was present as a negative deflection in the frontal, central, and precentral regions in both control groups; the amplitude and the area of BP did not differ in a statistically significant way except for Pz ($p < .01$), where the amplitude value was higher in adults. For the subjects with DS it was absent or showed a reduced amplitude in all recording sites. There were statistically significant differences in BP between the subjects with DS and the control groups at all recorded cerebral areas, except for FPz when compared to the CA control group, and for FPz and Pz when compared to the MA control group. The results of the BP area comparison of subjects with DS and adults were the same as those for amplitude (Pz: $p < .01$; Fz, Cz, RPC, and LPC: $p < .05$). In subjects with DS and in children, too, results of the BP area comparison proved to be statistically similar to those regarding the BP amplitude, except for Fz and LPC (table 14.2). The BP onset did not differ in the two control groups, whereas it could not be recorded and measured in the subjects with DS because of the poor or insignificant amplitude of the potential.

In the sensory-motor period, the MCP was clearly present in control subjects in the central and precentral regions. In the subjects with DS, MCP was absent or showed a significantly reduced amplitude in all cerebral areas compared with the CA control group (Fz, Cz, Pz, RPC, and LPC: $p < .01$; FPz: $p < .05$) and in the frontal,

Table 14.2 MRBMs of Subjects With Down Syndrome and Two Control Groups (Means and SD)

In this table, the superscript a or b indicates a significant correlation between the subjects with Down syndrome and the control group in question. The asterisks indicate a significant difference between the two control groups.

		FP		FZ		CZ	
		M	SD	M	SD	M	SD
BP							
Amp.	A	1.65	4.34	-6.52[b]	5.01	-8.33[b]	6.22
	C	3.15	4.89	-4.41[a]	6.99	-9.25[b]	7.59
	D	1.67	6.22	0.58	5.05	-0.16	4.89
Area	A	370.95	1332.94	-1090.41[a]	1073.42	-1657.03[a]	1421.66
	C	941.39	1261.16	-1054.68	1661.59	-1771.81[a]	1641.04
	D	1061.77	2152.90	508.00	1567.65	318.55	1865.01
MCP							
Amp	A	0.86*	5.22	-13.95[b]	6.50	-15.07[b]	7.78
	C	3.64	5.94	-6.09[a]**	8.50	-11.45[b]*	10.98
	D	2.09	9.59	1.27	8.40	0.53	6.81
N_{100}							
Lat.	A	113.70	20.12	120.27	19.53	118.34	21.61
	C	121.70[a]	20.21	119.48	19.66	118.47	17.89
	D	104.16	8.50	109.30	14.16	109.05	7.92
Amp.	A	7.77**	3.22	15.86**	5.89	17.82**	10.38
	C	12.62	4.64	22.19[b]	6.98	26.04[b]	7.60
	D	7.59	6.30	11.12	7.16	13.60	7.53
P_{200}							
Lat.	A	192.81*	15.48	210.61	21.88	211.16*	15.91
	C	210.44	23.50	223.05[b]	18.80	266.55[a]	26.76
	D	210.06	23.50	195.73	25.87	201.73	31.19
Amp.	A	7.70	5.54	8.08	6.21	8.18	7.96
	C	6.97	7.42	5.84	9.56	7.65	12.90
	D	6.97	13.25	4.05	11.24	5.60	11.38
SPP							
Lat.	A	525.80	126.32	507.33	102.18	501.88	98.90
	C	537.09	99.18	539.41	99.84	501.74	65.34
	D	532.55	88.71	521.10	72.88	532.38	77.31

A = adults; C = children; D = Down syndrome subjects

Adapted, by permission, from G.A. Chiarenza, 1993, "Movement-related brain macropotentials of persons with Down Syndrome during skilled performance," *American Journal on Mental Retardation* 97(4): 449-467.

	PZ		RPC		LPC	
	M	SD	M	SD	M	SD
A	-7.10[b]	4.74	-8.96[b]	4.73	-8.36[b]	4.88
C	-0.68**	7.66	-6.51[b]	6.56	-5.02[a]	6.50
D	1.13	4.18	0.06	4.39	0.89	5.18
A	-1641.59[b]	1241.66	-1468.81[a]	1086.28	-1519.90[a]	1227.94
C	-568.91	1872.87	-1342.44[a]	1333.52[a]	-954.48	1345.34
D	1063.66	1261.20	436.25	1541.84	1158.62	2303.43
A	-10.94[b]	4.70	-15.49[b]	5.75	-14.57[b]	6.06
C	3.19**	8.32	-7.33[b]**	9.45	-6.27[b]**	10.40
D	1.81	4.87	0.88	6.34	1.98	7.47
A	123.02	25.25	116.83	22.33	119.72	20.45
C	127.61[a]	25.18	117.57	18.81	116.91	16.95
D	112.71	5.06	108.33	10.80	111.22	11.29
A	14.53**	5.30	17.17**	7.10	15.91**	7.10
C	22.03[b]	10.57	25.34[b]	7.29	23.32[b]	6.46
D	11.64	5.42	13.36	6.99	12.55	8.01
A	219.00	18.91	211.50	19.25	213.83	18.95
C	232.51	27.38	219.27	27.05	227.00[a]	28.37
D	210.34	33.41	210.56	28.21	201.82	27.20
A	10.24**	5.25	7.50	5.68	7.80	5.53
C	25.24[b]	10.86	5.08	9.71	6.09	9.92
D	9.28	8.31	4.91	9.58	5.15	11.02
A	497.82	79.89	516.05	99.34	509.72	97.08
C	495.27	45.70	516.75	81.92	510.70	79.83
D	508.85	66.15	515.70	48.99	507.82	62.05

* = $p < .05$; ** = $p < .01$

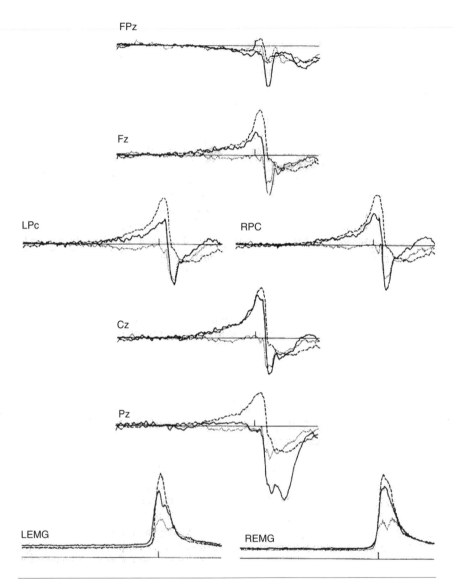

Figure 14.3 Grand average of rectified EMGs and movement-related brain macropotentials of subjects with Down syndrome (thick solid line), adults (broken line), and children (solid line). In this and in the following figure, the vertical bar in each trace indicates the instance of the computer trigger. Negativity is upward. Time scale is 3,200 ms.

Adapted, by permission, from G.A. Chiarenza, 1993, "Movement-related brain macropotentials of persons with Down Syndrome during skilled performance," *American Journal on Mental Retardation* 97(4): 449-467.

central, and precentral areas compared with the MA control group (Fz: $p < .05$; Cz, RPC, LPC: $p < .01$).

The two groups of normal subjects were also different from each other. In fact, the MCP amplitude was larger in the CA control group in all cerebral regions (Fz, Pz, RPC, and LPC: $p < .01$; FPz, Cz: $p < .05$). The latency of MCP with respect to the EMG onset did not differ in adults and control children, whereas in the subjects with DS it was impossible, because of the reduced MCP amplitude, to find a peak latency that could be measured with respect to the EMG onset. The absence or reduction in MCP, as well as other potentials, will be discussed later. However, they should not be attributed to a jitter effect related to the performance variability, since, as shown in figure 14.4, the grand average of rectified EMGs and MRBMs related to the target performance of all the three groups confirms the absence of MCP in the subjects with DS.

The latency of N100 was always shorter in the subjects with DS in all recording sites, when compared to both the MA control group and the CA control group. The difference was significant only for FPz and Pz ($p < .05$) between the subjects with DS and the MA control group; the two control groups did not differ from each other. Since the measurement of the N100 amplitude depends on the amplitude of BP, it was impossible to carry out a statistical comparison.

In the motor completion period, the latency of P200 was not significantly different between the subjects with DS and the adults. The children presented a P200 latency significantly higher than that of the subjects with DS in the frontal (Fz: $p < .01$) and in the central and left precentral regions ($p < .05$). In the children, P200 had a larger amplitude in all cerebral regions; the differences, with respect to both the adults and the subjects with DS, were statistically significant in all recording sites ($p < 0.01$). The lowest amplitude values were found in the group of the participants with DS.

In the postmotor period, the SPP was present as a positive deflection on all cerebral regions in all three groups, but with a lower amplitude in the subjects with DS. The latencies of this potential were not significantly different in the three groups. The amplitude of SPP measured from the baseline was not significantly different in the three groups, except for Pz between subjects with DS and children (table 14.2). When a comparison was made with SPP amplitude values measured as the difference from the P200 peak, the SPP amplitude of the adults was significantly greater in all recording sites ($p < .01$) compared to the subjects with DS and the children, except for Pz when compared to the children. The SPP amplitude of the children was not significantly different from that of the subjects with DS.

Discussion

Successful performance depends on a correct and accurate temporal sequence of ballistic bimanual and self-initiated movements. The limited temporal range of actions forces temporal and motor programming of the whole task. Moreover, as

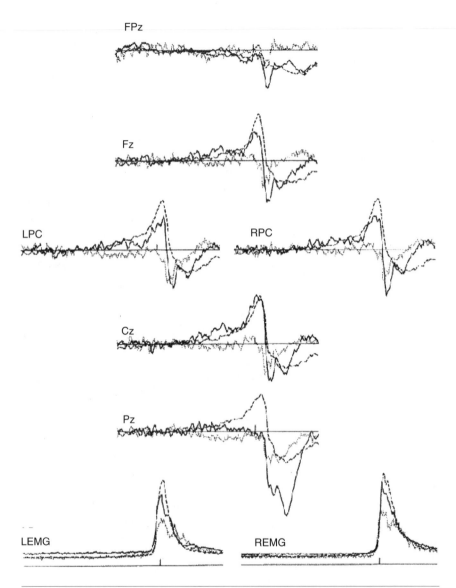

Figure 14.4 Grand average of rectified EMGs and movement-related brain macropotentials related to target performance of subjects with Down syndrome (thick solid line), adults (broken line), and children (solid line).

Adapted, by permission, from G.A. Chiarenza, 1993, "Movement-related brain macropotentials of persons with Down Syndrome during skilled performance," *American Journal on Mental Retardation* 97(4): 449-467.

subjects can evaluate the result of each test in real time via visual feedback, they are also able to compare each performance with the preprogrammed motor strategy and change it in the most suitable way to reach the target.

The preparation of an effective movement sequence involves the development of a central clock that controls the temporal course through afferent and efferent systems (Hirsch & Sterrick, 1964; Rosenbaum & Patashnik, 1980). The performance improvement of this clock depends in part on the presence of proprioceptive and exteroceptive feedback regarding the performance accuracy. However, it does not eliminate the need for motor programming (Rosenbaum, 1983), which plays a fundamental role in the organization of the temporal sequence of movements. On the other hand, motor programming depends on a higher age-related synaptic efficiency of the central nervous system (Craik, 1947). In fact, the interval between two consecutive movements often has been found to be shorter than the time required for the proprioceptive and exteroceptive feedback of the first to act as a trigger of the second (Lashley, 1951).

The performances of the participants with DS in our investigation suggest that the development of this central clock proceeds with difficulty. The subjects with DS demonstrate considerable difficulty in carrying out the bimanual movement in the correct temporal sequence. They were found to be steadily slower in executing the task compared to both control groups. They showed the highest rate of trials with performance time above both 60 and 200 ms. Moreover, their performance time decreased greatly from the first block to the fourth, but the target performance rate remained practically unchanged and below that of the controls.

The children showed the highest increase in the target performance rate as the task proceeded, even though they did not reach the values of the adults. The adults did not improve target performance rate with practice, which was already high in the first block, but they showed a greater increase in their performance accuracy compared with the children.

The performance accuracy of the participants with DS showed the same behavior as the target performances: the performance shift remained on steadily higher values throughout the trial. Therefore, the adults executed the task more speedily and accurately throughout the test. The children proved able to utilize experience, progressively improving their performance, even though they did not reach the level of the adults. The participants with DS were consistently below the other two groups in both accuracy and speed. Not only were they slower and less accurate, but they were also unable to benefit from practice, unlike the two control groups that were matched on mental or chronological age.

These findings agree with several previous studies showing that perceptual-motor functions of subjects with DS appear to be greatly impaired in comparison of subjects with the same chronological or mental age (Cratty, 1969). The difficulty in maintaining equilibrium (Pesch & Nagy, 1978), the markedly prolonged reaction time (Berkson, 1960), and the inability to carry out rapid movement sequences (Frith & Frith, 1974) are some of the perceptual-motor functions of which subjects with DS display poorer performances than subjects affected by other forms of mental retardation. Furthermore, persons with DS have particular difficulties in carrying out tasks involving a temporal component and when the sequence of movements must be programmed so as to make the resulting action coincide with an external event (Henderson, Morris, & Ray, 1981). To make it possible, in fact, it is necessary for the movement to be programmed according to precise spatial and temporal parameters. The specific problem of motor programming in persons with DS seems to lie predominantly in the temporal component and not in the spatial one (Henderson, Morris, & Frith, 1981).

In parallel to motor performances, MRBMs also showed significant differences between subjects with and without DS. The BP is characteristic of the premotor period (Kornhuber & Deecke, 1965) when the organization of ideokinetic elements for the execution of the movement takes place (Chiarenza et al., 1982; Chiarenza et al., 1983). Its clinical and neurophysiological characteristics make it an important index of cortical maturation. The BP appears, in fact, at about the age of 7 years in the frontocentral regions, and it progressively increases in amplitude up to adolescence, when it reaches the values seen in adults (Chiarenza, 1986a). It is absent or has a low amplitude in various clinical situations: chronic schizophrenia (Chiarenza, Papakostopoulos, Dini, & Cazzullo, 1985), Parkinson's disease (Deecke, Englitz, Kornhuber, & Schmitt, 1977), dyslexia-dysgraphia (Chiarenza et al., 1986), and learning disabilities (Chiarenza et al., 1982).

In the current study, the BP was present in the two control groups, with a greater amplitude in adults, whereas it was absent or greatly reduced in all cerebral regions of the subjects with DS. Warren and Karrer (1984) showed that during the execution of unskilled movements, the BP is missing or appears as a positive deflection in young adults affected by mental retardation. The absence of BP in participants with DS could therefore indicate the presence of a programming failure of perceptual-motor performance, both simple and complex.

It has been assumed that the BP is a cholinergic potential: its absence in subjects with DS would therefore agree with the microscopic and histochemical findings that showed a remarkable deficit of the central cholinergic system in subjects with DS (Kitt et al., 1984; Perry et al., 1985; Price et al., 1982).

During the sensory-motor period the MCP was absent or had a reduced amplitude in the subjects with DS. This potential is considered to be an index of reafferent sensory activity: it represents the elaboration in precentral and frontal regions of the kinesthetic information related to the executed movement (Papakostopoulos et al., 1975; Papakostopoulos & Crow, 1984). Since suitable proprioceptive information is of fundamental importance for the preparation and the correct execution of movements, the lack of elaboration of this sensory feedback, expressed by the MCP, could be responsible for the poorer capacity for temporal organization that subjects with DS show in carrying out complex motor acts.

Animal experiments (Dubrovsky & Garcia-Rill, 1973) and observations of patients with damaged posterior spinal columns have shown that total or partial deafferentation prevents the temporal control of a motor sequence. Furthermore, it is important to note that in the same experimental situation, subjects over 60 also show slower performances and a steadily reduced MCP amplitude (Papakostopoulos & Banerji, 1980). Given that macro- and microscopic investigations are in agreement in showing an early onset of anatomopathological signs of cerebral aging in subjects with DS, the reduced amplitude of MCP could indicate a poor cortical reactivity to the reafferent sensory information.

Sensory neurography of the median nerve performed bilaterally in 6 children with DS (aged 11-16 years), compared with 10 healthy controls of similar age, proved to be significantly subnormal in the group with DS. Moreover, sensory nerve action potentials were also of lower amplitude (Brandt & Rosen, 1995). Brandt and Rosen suggested that an impaired peripheral somatosensory function should be added to previously known symptoms associated with DS. The results also support previous findings of poor performance in children with DS on tests of tactual perception. Therefore, the lower amplitude of MCP in children with DS compared with adults could reflect not only a central deficit but also a peripheral impairment of somatosensory function.

The N100 wave is considered the cerebral response evoked by the appearance of the sweep on the oscilloscope. Its latency is shorter in subjects with DS, but in this study it was significantly reduced only for FPz and Pz when compared with the group of children. This result is in agreement with those studies of BAEPs by Squires, Buchwald, Liley, and Strecker (1981) and in contrast with those of cortical ERPs by Bigum et al. (1970), Marcus (1970), and Gliddon et al. (1975). These discrepancies can be attributed mainly to the different experimental paradigms used by these authors, their experiments being externally paced.

The shorter latency of N100 for the subjects with DS on the task in this study could be attributed to a deficit in the central mechanisms responsible for the perceptive elaboration of sensory input. An analogous interpretation has been suggested for the flat recovery function of wave V of the BAEPs of the subjects with DS (Otto et al., 1984; Squires et al., 1981).

The P200 is considered to be one of the late components of somatosensory potentials (Chiarenza et al., 1983), and its latency was greater in children than in the other two groups, with no significant difference between subjects with DS and adults. As the latency of P200 has been found to decrease with age (Chiarenza et al., 1983), these findings would indicate that for subjects with DS, the neuronal systems subtended by this potential have reached a maturation comparable with that of normal adults, whereas the neuronal systems are still relatively immature in 10-year-old children. The lower amplitude of P200 in participants with DS could be an index of reduced elaboration of reafferent sensory input. This result is in agreement with other investigations of late sensory and cognitive components of cerebral-evoked potentials in subjects with DS (Squires et al., 1979).

The presence of SPP on all recorded brain areas in subjects with DS and the fact that its amplitude was similar, except on Pz, to that of subjects with the same mental age, but lower than that in subjects with the same chronological age, could indicate that subjects with DS are able to recognize and evaluate the results of their perceptual-motor performances but that they do not manage to use such experience to improve their performances.

In fact, other than elaborating movement strategies, the SPP is present only when the subject can also evaluate, from time to time, the result of his or her performances and utilize the acquired knowledge to change or to influence future actions (Chiarenza, 1986a; Papakostopoulos, 1978a). If the possibility for evaluation is lacking, the SPP does not appear (Papakostopoulos, 1980; Papakostopoulos et al., 1986). This potential has peculiar developmental characteristics: it is always present in the parietal regions and appears at the age of 9-10 years in the frontocentral regions. With age its amplitude in these areas increases until it reaches adult amplitude in adolescence, whereas the latency decreases (Chiarenza et al., 1983). Children under 10 years are likely to be unable to elaborate complex strategies based on formal and probabilistic thinking (Chiarenza, 1986b). These results agree with, and extend to self-paced tasks, the previous observations of Karrer and Ivins (1976b), Squires et al. (1979), and Lincoln et al. (1986) with P300 experiments.

There is evidence to support the assumption that all surface-positive slow potentials, such as SPP and P300, originate from the hyperpolarizing inhibition of pyramidal neurons and the electrotonic diffusion of postsynaptic inhibitory potentials to apical dendrites (Creutzfeldt, Lux, & Watanabe, 1966). The physiological tone of the cholinergic component of the ascending activating reticular system projecting toward thalamus and cortex is thought to play a predominant role in the genesis of such positive potentials (Marczynski, 1978). Since the SPP is considered a potential produced by cholinergic systems (Marczynski, 1978), its low amplitude might reflect the cortical and subcortical cholinergic deficit shown by histochemical and microscopic studies in persons with DS (Perry et al., 1985; Price et al., 1982). Furthermore, these findings would suggest the SPP and BP are generated by different neuronal systems, both because they are differently distributed on the scalp and because they are differently involved in DS.

In conclusion, the pathological structural organization of the CNS, from brain stem to cortex, may be responsible both for the poorer performance of the participants with DS in this perceptual-motor task and for the abnormalities of MRBMs that are the electrophysiological equivalent.

Conclusions

Analysis of the performances during the execution of a perceptual-motor, self-initiated task shows that persons with DS have greater difficulty in organizing correct temporal sequence of ballistic movements. Moreover, they are relatively slower in performing the task because of a defective timing of motor sequences.

From a neurophysiological point of view, these behavioral aspects express themselves in a reduced preparation of the movement (absent or very low BP), a lack of elaboration of the reafferent somatosensory information (absence of MCP), and a reduced capacity for evaluating the outcome of the performance (presence of low SPP).

References

Balazs, R., & Brooksbank, W.L.B. (1985). Neurochemical approaches to the pathogenesis of Down's syndrome. *Journal of Mental Deficiency Research, 29,* 1-14.

Ball, M.J., & Nuttal, K. (1980). Neurofibrillary tangles, granulovacuolar degeneration and neuron loss in Down syndrome: Quantitative comparison with Alzheimer dementia. *Annals of Neurology, 7,* 462-465.

Barnet, A.B., & Lodge, A. (1967). Click evoked EEG responses in normal and developmentally retarded infants. *Nature, 214,* 252-255.

Benda, C.E. (1969). *Down's syndrome.* New York: Grune & Stratton.

Berkson, G. (1960). An analysis of reaction time in normal and mentally deficient young men. *Journal of Mental Deficiency Research, 4,* 51-77.

Bigum, H.B., Dustman, R.E., & Beck, C. (1970). Visual and somato-sensory evoked responses from mongoloid and normal children. *Electroencephalography and Clinical Neurophysiology, 28,* 576-585.

Brandt, B.R., & Rosen, I. (1995). Impaired peripheral somatosensory function in children with Down syndrome. *Neuropediatrics, 26,* 310-312.

Burger, P.C., & Vogel, F.S. (1973). The development of the pathologic changes of Alzheimer's disease and senile dementia in patients with Down's syndrome. *American Journal of Pathology, 73,* 457-468.

Chiarenza, G.A. (1986a). Development of sensory motor and cognitive processes: Movement related brain macropotentials in children. In V. Gallai (Ed.), *Maturation of the CNS and evoked potentials* (pp. 236-246). Amsterdam: Elsevier.

Chiarenza, G.A. (1986b). Electrophysiology of skilled performances in children. *Italian Journal of Neurological Sciences, 5*(Suppl.), 155-162.

Chiarenza, G.A., Papakostopoulos, D., Dini, M., & Cazzullo, C.L. (1985). Neurophysiological correlates of psychomotor activity in chronic schizophrenics. *Electroencephalography and Clinical Neurophysiology, 61,* 218-228.

Chiarenza, G.A., Papakostopoulos, D., Giordana, F., Guareschi-Cazzullo, A. (1983). Movement related brain macropotentials during skilled performances. A developmental study. *Electroencephalography and Clinical Neurophysiology, 56,* 373-383.

Chiarenza, G.A., Papakostopoulos, D., Grioni, A., Tengattini, M.B., Mascellani, P., & Guareschi-Cazzullo, A. (1986). Movement related brain macropotentials during a motor perceptual task in dyslexic and dysgraphic children. In W.C. McCallum, R. Zappoli, & F. Denoth (Eds.), *Cerebral psychophysiology: Studies in event related potentials* (EEG Suppl. 38, pp. 489-491). Amsterdam: Elsevier.

Chiarenza, G.A., Papakostopoulos, D., Guareschi-Cazzullo, A., & Giordana, F. (1980). Movement related brain macropotentials during skilled and unskilled actions in children. *Riv Ital EEG Neurofisiol Clin, 3,* 507-512.

Chiarenza, G.A., Papakostopoulos, D., Guareschi-Cazzullo, A., Giordana, F., & Giammari Aldè, G. (1982). Movement related brain macropotentials during skilled performance task in children with learning disabilities. In G.A. Chiarenza & D.

Papakostopoulos (Eds.), *Clinical application of cerebral evoked potentials in pediatric medicine* (pp. 259-292). Amsterdam: Excerpta Medica.

Chiarenza, G.A., Tengattini, M.B., Grioni, A., Ganguzza, D., Vasile, G., Massenti, A., Albizzati, A., Papakostopoulos, D., & Guareschi-Cazzullo, A. (1984). Long latency negative potentials durante un compito percettivo motorio. Caratteristiche evolutive in bambini normali. *Riv Ital EEG Neurofisiol Clin, 7*, 538-541.

Colon, E.J. (1972). The structure of the cerebral cortex in Down's syndrome. A quantitative analysis. *Neuropädiatrie, 3*, 362-376.

Craik, K.J.W. (1947). Theory of the human operator in control systems. *British Journal of Psychology, 38*, 56-61.

Crapper, D., Dalton, A.J., Skopitz, M., Scott, J.W., & Hachinski, V.C. (1975). Alzheimer degeneration in Down syndrome. Electrophysiologic alterations and histopathologic findings. *Archives of Neurology, 32*, 618-623.

Cratty, B.J. (1969). *Motor activity and the education of retardates*. Philadelphia: Lea & Febiger.

Creutzfeldt, O.D., Lux, H.D., Watanabe, S. (1966). Electrophysiology of cortical nerve cells. In D.P. Purpura & M.D. Yahr (Eds.), *The thalamus* (pp. 35-55). New York: Columbia University Press.

Deecke, L., Englitz, H.G., Kornhuber, H.H., & Schmitt, G. (1977). Cerebral potentials preceding voluntary movement in patients with bilateral or unilateral Parkinson akinesia. *Progress in Clinical Neurophysiology, 1*, 151-163.

Delabar, J.M., Theophile, D., Rahamani, Z., Cettouh, Z., Blouin, J.L., Prieur, M., Noel, B., & Sinet, P.M. (1993). Molecular mapping of twenty-four features of Down syndrome on chromosome 21. *European Journal of Human Genetics, 1*, 114-124.

Dubrovsky, B., & Garcia-Rill, E. (1973). Role of dorsal columns in sequential motor acts requiring precise forelimb projection. *Experimental Brain Research, 18*, 165-177.

Dustman, R.E., & Callner, D.A. (1979). Cortical evoked responses and response decrement in nonretarded and Down's syndrome individuals. *American Journal of Mental Deficiency, 83*, 391-397.

Elbert, T., Lutzenberger, W., Rockstroch, B., & Birbaumer, N. (1986). Response outcome influences the Bereitschaftspotential. In W.C. McCallum, R. Zappoli, & F. Denoth (Eds.), *Cerebral psychophysiology: Studies in event related potentials* (EEG Suppl. 38, pp. 248-250). Amsterdam: Elsevier.

Ellingson, R.J., Eisen, J.D., & Ottersberg, G. (1973). Clinical electroencephalographic observations on institutionalized mongoloid confirmed by karyotype. *Electroencephalography and Clinical Neurophysiology, 34*, 193-196.

Ellingson, R.J., & Peters, J.F. (1980). Development of EEG and daytime sleep patterns in trisomy-21 infants during the first year of life: Longitudinal observations. *Electroencephalography and Clinical Neurophysiology, 50*, 457-466.

Ferri, R., Bergonzi, P., Colognola, S.A., Musumeci, S., Sanfilippo, P., Tomassetti, A., Viglianesi, A., & Gigli, G.L. (1986). Brainstem evoked potentials in subjects with mental retardation and different karyotypes. In V. Gallai (Ed.), *Maturation of the CNS and evoked potentials* (pp. 369-374). Amsterdam: Elsevier.

Ferri, R., Del Gracco, S., Elia, M., Musumeci, S.A., & Stefanini, M.C. (1995). Age, sex and mental retardation related changes of brainstem auditory evoked potentials in Down's syndrome. *Italian Journal of Neurological Sciences, 16*, 377-383.

Foit, A., Grozinger, B., & Kornhuber, H.H. (1982). Brain potential differences related to programming, monitoring and outcome of aimed and non-aimed, fast and slow movements to a visual target: The movement monitoring potential (MMP) and the task outcome evaluation potential (TEP). *Neuroscience, 7*, 571-581.

Frith, U., & Frith, C.D. (1974). Specific motor disabilities in Down syndrome. *Journal of Child Psychology & Psychiatry & Allied Disciplines, 15,* 293-301.

Galbraith, G.C., Gliddon, J.B., & Busk, J. (1970). Visual evoked responses in mentally retarded and nonretarded subjects. *American Journal of Mental Deficiency, 83,* 341-348.

Gigli, G.L., Ferri, R., Musumeci, S.A., Tomassetti, P., & Bergonzi, P. (1984). Brainstem auditory evoked responses in children with Down's syndrome. In J.M. Berg (Ed.), *Perspectives and progress in mental retardation: Vol. 2. Biomedical aspects* (pp. 277-286). Baltimore: University Park Press.

Gliddon, J.B., Galbraith, G.C., & Busk, J. (1975). Effect of preconditioning visual stimulus duration on visual-evoked responses to a subsequent test flash in Down's syndrome and nonretarded individuals. *American Journal of Mental Deficiency, 80,* 186-190.

Grunewald, G., Grunewald-Zuberbier, E., Homberg, V., & Netz, J. (1979). Cerebral potentials during smooth goal-directed hand movements in right handed and left-handed subjects. *Pflügers Archive fur die Gesamte Physiologie, 381,* 39-46.

Hansford, R.G. (1983). Bioenergetics in aging. *Biochimica et Biophysica Acta, 726,* 41.

Harris, W.S., & Goodman, R.M. (1968). Hyper-reactivity to atropine in Down's syndrome. *New England Journal of Medicine, 279,* 407.

Henderson, S.E., Morris, J., & Frith, U. (1981). The motor deficit in Down's syndrome children: A problem of timing? *Journal of Child Psychology and Psychiatry, 22,* 233-245.

Henderson, S.E., Morris, J., & Ray, S. (1981). Performance of Down syndrome and other retarded children on the Cratty Gross-Motor Test. *American Journal of Mental Deficiency, 85,* 416-424.

Hirsch, I.J., & Sterrick, C.E. (1964). Perceived order in different sense modalities. *Journal of Experimental Psychology, 67,* 103-112.

Johnson, R. (1986). A triarchic model of P300 amplitude. *Psychophysiology, 23,* 367-384.

Kakigi, R., & Shibasaki, H. (1991). Middle-latency somatosensory evoked potentials following median and posterior tibial nerve stimulation in Down's syndrome. *Electroencephalography and Clinical Neurophysiology, 80,* 364-371.

Kakigi, R., & Shibasaki, H. (1993). Scalp topography of somatosensory evoked potentials following median and posterior tibial nerve stimulation in Down's syndrome. *Brain Topography, 5,* 253-261.

Karrer, R., & Ivins, J. (1976a). Steady potentials accompanying perception and response in mentally retarded and normal children. In R. Karrer (Ed.), *Developmental psychophysiology of mental retardation* (pp. 361-417). Springfield, IL: Charles C Thomas.

Karrer, R., & Ivins, J. (1976b). Event-related slow potentials in mental retardates. In W.C. McCallum & J.R. Knott (Eds.), *The responsive brain* (pp. 154-157). Bristol, UK: Wright.

Kitt, C.A., Price, D.L., & Struble, R.G. (1984). Evidence for cholinergic neurites in senile plaques. *Science, 226,* 1443-1445.

Knapp, E., Schmid, H., Ganglberger, J.A., & Haider, M. (1980). Cortical and subcortical potentials during goal-directed movements in humans. In H.H. Kornhuber & L. Deecke (Eds.), *Motivation, motor and sensory processes of the brain: Electrical potentials, behavior and clinical use. Progress in brain research: Vol. 54* (pp. 66-69). Amsterdam: Elsevier.

Kornhuber, H.H., & Deecke, L. (1965). Hirnpotentialänderunger bei Willkürbewegungen und passiven Bewegungen des Menschen: Bereitschaftspotential und reafferente potentiale. *Pflügers Archive, 284,* 1-17.

Lashley, K.S. (1951). The problem of serial order in behavior. In L.A. Jeffres (Ed.), *Cerebral mechanism in behavior.* New York: Wiley.

Lincoln, A.J., Courchesne, E., Kilman, B.A., & Galambos, R. (1986). Auditory ERPs and information processing in Down's Syndrome children. In W.C. McCallum, R. Zappoli, & F. Denoth (Eds.), *Cerebral psychophysiology: Studies in event related potentials* (EEG Suppl. 38, pp. 492-495). Amsterdam: Elsevier.

Mackenzie, R.A., Creasey, H., & Huang, C.Y. (1983). Neurophysiological evidence of aging in Down's syndrome. *Clinical & Experimental Neurology, 19,* 139-146.

Mann, D.M.A., Yates, P.O., & Marcyniuk, B. (1987). Dopaminergic neurotransmitter systems in Alzheimer's disease and in Down's syndrome at middle age. *Journal of Neurology, Neurosurgery & Psychiatry, 50,* 341-344.

Marcus, M.M. (1970). The evoked cortical response: A technique for assessing development. *California Mental Health Research Digest, 8,* 59-72.

Marczynski, T.J. (1978). Neurochemical mechanisms in the genesis of slow potentials: A review and some clinical implications. In D.A. Otto (Ed.), *Multidisciplinary perspectives in event-related brain potential research* (pp. 25-35). Washington DC: US Environmental Protection Agency.

Netz, J., Homberg, V., Grunewald-Zuberbier, E., & Grunewald, G. (1984). Event-related changes of fast rhythmic EEG activity in a positioning movement task. *Annals of the New York Academy of Sciences, 425,* 483-488.

Ohara, P.T. (1972). Electron microscopical study of the brain in Down's syndrome. *Brain, 95,* 681-684.

Otto, B., Karrer, R., Halliday, R., Horst, R.L., Klorman, R., Squires, N., Thatcher, R.W., Fenelon, B., & Lelord, G. (1984). Developmental aspects of event-related potentials: Aberrant development. *Annals of the New York Academy of Sciences, 425,* 319-337.

Papakostopoulos, D. (1978a). Electrical activity of the brain associated with skilled performance. In D.A. Otto (Ed.), *Multidisciplinary perspectives in event-related brain potential research* (pp. 134-137). Washington DC: US Environmental Protection Agency.

Papakostopoulos, D. (1978b). The serial order of self-paced movements in terms of brain macropotentials in man. *Journal of Physiology, 280,* 70-71.

Papakostopoulos, D. (1980). A no stimulus, no response event-related potential of the human cortex. *Electroencephalography and Clinical Neurophysiology, 48,* 622-638.

Papakostopoulos, D., & Banerji, N. (1980). Movement related brain macropotentials during skilled performance in Parkinson's disease. *Electroencephalography and Clinical Neurophysiology, 49,* 93.

Papakostopoulos, D., Cooper, R., & Crow, H.J. (1975). Inhibition of cortical evoked potentials and sensation by self-initiated movement in man. *Nature, 258,* 321-324.

Papakostopoulos, D., & Crow, H.J. (1984). The precentral somatosensory evoked potential. *Annals of the New York Academy of Sciences, 425,* 256-261.

Papakostopoulos, D., Stamler, R., & Newton, P. (1986). Movement related brain macropotentials during self-paced skilled performance with and without knowledge of results. In W.C. McCallum, R. Zappoli, & F. Denoth (Eds.), *Cerebral psychophysiology: Studies in event related potentials* (EEG Suppl. 38, pp. 261-262). Amsterdam: Elsevier.

Perry, K.E., Curtis, M., Dick, D.J., Candy, J.M., Atack, J.R., Bloxham, C.A., Blessed, G., Fairbairn, A., Tomlinson, B.E., & Perry, R.H. (1985). Cholinergic correlates of cognitive impairment in Parkinson's disease: Comparisons with Alzheimer's disease. *Journal of Neurology, Neurosurgery & Psychiatry, 48,* 413-421.

Pesch, R.S., & Nagy, D.K. (1978). A survey of the visual and developmental-perceptual abilities of the Down's syndrome child. *Journal of American Optometry Association, 9,* 1031-1037.

Price, D.L., Whitehouse, P.J., Struble, R.G., Coyle, J.T., Clark, A.W., Delong, M.R., Cork, L.C., & Hedreen, J.C. (1982). Alzheimer's disease and Down's syndrome. *Annals of the New York Academy of Sciences, 396*, 145-151.

Ropper, A.H., & Williams, R.S. (1980). Relationship between plaques, tangles and dementia in Down syndrome. *Neurology, 30*, 639-644.

Rosenbaum, D.A. (1983). Central control of movement timing. *The Bell System Technical Journal, 62*, 1647-1657.

Rosenbaum, D.A., & Patashnik, O. (1980). A mental clock setting process revealed by reaction times. In G.E. Stelmach & J. Requin (Eds.), *Tutorials in motor behavior* (pp. 1-14). Amsterdam: North-Holland.

Schafer, E.W.P., & Peeke, H.V.S. (1982). Down syndrome individuals fail to habituate cortical evoked potentials. *American Journal of Mental Deficiency, 87*, 332-337.

Schmid, R.G., Sadowsky, K., Weinmann, H.M., Tirsch, W.S., & Poppl, S.J. (1985). Z-transformed EEG power spectra of children with Down syndrome vs a control group. *Neuropediatrics, 16*, 218-224.

Scott, B.S., Petit, T.L., Becker, L.E., & Edwards, B.A.V. (1981). Abnormal electric membrane properties of Down's syndrome DRG neurons in cell culture. *Brain Research, 254*, 257-270.

Skinner, J.E., & Lindsley, D.B. (1971). Enhancement of visual and auditory evoked potentials during blockade of the nonspecific thalamocortical system. *Electroencephalography and Clinical Neurophysiology, 31*, 1-6.

Squires, N., Aine, C., Buchwald, J., Norman, R., & Galbraith, G. (1980). Auditory brain stem response abnormalities in severely and profoundly retarded adults. *Electroencephalography and Clinical Neurophysiology, 50*, 172-185.

Squires, N.K., Buchwald, J., Liley, F., & Strecker, J. (1981). Brain stem evoked potential abnormalities in retarded adults. *Advances in Neurology, 32*, 129-139.

Squires, N.K., Galbraith, G.C., & Aine, C.J. (1979). Event related potential assessment of sensory and cognitive deficits in the mentally retarded. In D. Lehmann & E. Callaway (Eds.), *Human evoked potentials applications and problems* (pp. 397-413). New York: Plenum.

Straumanis, J.J., Shagass, C., & Overton, D.A. (1973). Somatosensory evoked responses in Down syndrome. *Archives of General Psychiatry, 29*, 544-549.

Takashima, S., Becker, L.E., Armstrong, D.L., & Chan, F.W. (1981). Abnormal neuronal development in the visual cortex of the human fetus and infant with Down syndrome. A quantitative and qualitative Golgi study. *Brain Research, 225*, 1.

Taylor, K.J. (1978). Bereitschafts potential during the acquisition of a skilled motor task. *Electroencephalography and Clinical Neurophysiology, 45*, 568-576.

Vaughan, G.H., Jr., Costa, L.D., & Ritter, W. (1968). Topography of the human motor potential. *Electroencephalography and Clinical Neurophysiology, 25*, 1-10.

Warren, C., & Karrer, R. (1984). Movement-related potentials in children. *Annals of the New York Academy of Sciences, 425*, 489-495.

Weinberg, H. (1980). Slow potentials related to initiation and inhibition of proprioceptive guided movements. In H.H. Kornhuber & L. Deecke (Eds.), *Motivation, motor and sensory processes of the brain: Electrical potentials, behavior and clinical use. Progress in brain research: Vol. 54* (pp. 183-188). Amsterdam: Elsevier.

Wetterberg, L., Gustavson, K.H., Backstrom, M., Ross, S.B., & Froden, O. (1972). Low dopamine-beta-hydroxylase activity in Down's syndrome. *Clinical Genetics, 3*, 152-153.

Index

About the
Contributors

Gil Lúcio Almeida graduated in physical therapy and earned his master's degree from Universidade Federal de São Carlos, Brazil. His PhD and post doctoral training focused on child development and motor control at Iowa State University, University of Illinois at Chicago and Rush Medical Center. He and his graduate students have been conducting clinical research on several motor dysfunctions. These studies have also been supported by Fundação de Amparo à Pesquisa do Estado de São Paulo and Conselho Nacional de Pesquisa - CNPq - Brazil. He teaches graduate and undergraduate courses in neurophysiology and motor control at the Universidade Estadual de Campinas. During his free time Gil loves to scuba dive.

   Rosa M. Angulo-Kinzler is an assistant professor in the Division of Kinesiology at the University of Michigan. She earned her double major PhD in Neural Sciences and Human Performance at Indiana University. Her research interest focuses on understanding how different extrinsic and intrinsic factors cooperate to facilitate motor skill acquisition and improvement in performance. Currently, she is exploring a novel paradigm designed to improve control of leg movements in infants and collaborates in three other projects: (1) looking at the effects of treadmill training on motor activity in infants with and without Down syndrome, (2) investigating the effects of context on infants' locomotion patterns, and (3) examining the effects of iron deficiency anemia in infants' motor activity.

   J. Greg Anson is a senior lecturer in Kinesiology in the School of Physical Education at the University of Otago, Dunedin, New Zealand. He earned his PhD from Penn State University. He is a Fellow of the American Academy of Kinesiology and Physical Education and a member of the Society for Neuroscience. His research focuses on the use of fractionated reaction time to examine the effects of health and disease on neuromotor processing. Leisure activities include kayaking on the magnificent harbors and lakes of New Zealand.

   Judith L. Charlton is Senior Lecturer and Research and Graduate Studies Coordinator in the Institute of Disability Studies, Deakin University, Melbourne Campus. She completed her PhD studies in 1987 at the University of Waterloo, Canada, under the supervision of Professors Eric Roy and Ronald Marteniuk. The broad aim of her research is to explore mechanisms and neurological bases of movement control in people with cognitive, sensory, and physical disabilities across the life span with a view to developing effective assessment tools and programs to enhance movement efficiency and independence in daily living.

Giuseppe A. Chiarenza is Director of the Unit of Child and Adolescent Neuropsychiatry at Rho Hospital - Azienda Ospedaliera "G. Salvini," Garbagnate (Milan, Italy). He is a medical doctor specializing in child and adolescent neuropsychiatry and neurology. His research field is focused on the psychophysiology of learning disabilities and mental retardation. He has founded the Italian Society of Psychophysiology and is currently the Vice President of the International Organization of Psychophysiology and of the Federation of the European Psychophysiology Societies.

Romeo Chua is an assistant professor in the School of Human Kinetics at the University of British Columbia. He received a PhD specializing in human motor control from Simon Fraser University. His research interests lie in the areas of cerebral specialization and motor control in Down syndrome, the visual control of movement, and dynamical systems analyses of perception-action coordination. He is funded by the Natural Sciences and Engineering Research Council of Canada and the U.S. National Institutes of Health. An avid Star Trek fan, Romeo also enjoys basketball, tennis, and reading.

Daniel M. Corcos is a professor of Kinesiology and Psychology at the University of Illinois at Chicago, and a Professor of Neurology at Rush-Presbyterian-St. Luke's Medical Center. He earned his PhD in motor control from the University of Oregon. He has received five grants from the National Institutes of Health including a Research Career Development Award. In his free time, he enjoys running, playing soccer, and coaching youth soccer.

Cynthia L. Dulaney is an assistant professor in the Department of Psychology at Xavier University. She earned her PhD in cognitive psychology from the University of Alabama and completed a postdoctoral fellowship at the University of Memphis. Her research interests include attention and memory in individuals with mental retardation and in older adults.

Digby Elliott is a professor in the Department of Kinesiology at McMaster University. He received his PhD in experimental psychology from the University of Waterloo in 1983. In 1997 he was listed by Current Contents as one of the most published authors in psychology. His current research is funded by the Natural Sciences and Engineering Research Council of Canada and the U.S. National Institutes of Health. In his free time Digby enjoys water sports, reading, and playing cards.

Sandra M.S. Ferreira is a master's student at "Universidade Estadual Paulista," Rio Claro, Brazil. She has received a grant from Fundação de Amparo à Pesquisa do Estado de São Paulo and is doing research on motor control in individuals with Down syndrome at the Motor Control Laboratory "Universidade Estadual de Campinas," São Paulo, Brazil. She enjoys spending her free time with her family.

Gerald L. Gottlieb is a research professor of NeuroMuscular Engineering at the Boston University NeuroMuscular Research Center. He holds BS and MS degrees in Electrical Engineering and a PhD in Physiology from the University of Illinois. He is a Fellow of the Institute of Electrical and Electronic Engineering and of the American Institute for Medical and Biological Engineering. Supported by the National Institutes of Health since 1976, he has studied various aspects of human motor control. In his free time, he enjoys a variety of physical activities associated with the conversion of potential to kinetic energy.

Matthew Heath is a PhD candidate in the Department of Kinesiology, University of Waterloo. His doctoral work is funded by the Natural Sciences and Engineering Research Council of Canada. In 1998, he received the Down Syndrome Research Foundation Young Scientist Award for his MSc work examining cerebral specialization in adolescents and adults with Down syndrome.

Elfriede Ihsen is Senior Lecturer and Discipline Leader of Psychology at Swinburne University of Technology at Lilydale. She completed her PhD in 1988 at Monash University in Melbourne under the supervision of Professor R.H. Day. Her expertise is in experimental and developmental psychology with an emphasis on the development of perception and action in children with disabilities, especially those with congenital blindness or vision impairment and children with intellectual or learning disabilities. She is also interested in researching the impact of age-related visual and physical declines on functioning.

Anne Jobling is a lecturer in Special Education at the Schonell Special Education Research Centre at the University of Queensland, Australia. She has had long-term involvement with significant research on Down syndrome at the Centre and is currently a codirector of that research program. Although her research has involved individuals with Down syndrome of all ages, she is particularly interested in motor development, health, and physical activity. She has written over 50 book chapters and papers as well as presenting at numerous conferences in Australia and overseas. With qualifications in both physical education and special education, she has been involved in the promotion of sport participation and the development of coaching education programs for people with intellectual disability for more than 20 years.

Thomas W. Kernozek is an assistant professor in the Physical Therapy Department at the University of Wisconsin at La Crosse, the director of the Strzelczyk Biomechanics Laboratory, and a research consultant for Gundersen Lutheran Sports Medicine. He has a PhD in Biomechanics from the University of Minnesota, an MS degree from Illinois State University, and a BS degree from SUNY Cortland. Dr. Kernozek has published research manuscripts in *Gait and Posture*, *Archives of Physical Medicine and Rehabilitation*, the *Journal of Athletic Training*, the *Occupational Therapy Journal of Research*, and *Medicine and Science in Sports and Exercise* related to gait and seating.

Mark L. Latash is Professor of Kinesiology at the Pennsylvania State University. He earned his PhD in Physiology from Rush University in Chicago. He has been using the study of movement as a tool to understand how the healthy and disordered central nervous system works. In these endeavors, he has been supported by NIH, Whitaker Foundation, American Paralysis Association, National Multiple Sclerosis Association, and other funding agencies. He is a member of the Society for Neuroscience, American Society for Biomechanics, and the Society for Neural Control of Movement. He likes to play soccer, guitar, tennis, and chess, and to hike in the wild.

Barbara M. Lavelle is a PhD (Disability Studies) student with the Institute of Disability Studies, Deakin University, Melbourne. Under the supervision of Dr. J. Charlton and Dr. E. Ihsen, Barb is investigating the movement patterns of children performing sequencing tasks involving prehension. In addition to a developmental focus, her research looks at childhood coordination disorders and their impact on motor control parameters.

Annick Ledebt is a postdoctoral research associate in the Faculty of Human Movement Sciences of the Vrije Universiteit in Amsterdam. She earned a PhD in France in the field of physiology and biomechanics of movement. Her general interests concern the acquisition of motor skills in children. Her specific research focus on independent walking constitutes an interesting natural paradigm to study different aspects of a long-lasting developmental and learning process.

Nádia F. Marconi is a master's student at the Institute of Biology, Department of Physiology, "Universidade Estadual de Campina," São Paulo, Brazil. She graduated in Physical Therapy in 1996 and is now studying control of reversal movements in individuals with Down syndrome in the Motor Control Laboratory. She has a fellowship from Fundação de Amparo à Pesquisa do Estado de São Paulo. In her free time she likes to work out and dance.

Eliane Mauerberg-deCastro is a professor of adapted physical education, motor behavior, and teacher preparation in the Department of Physical Education at the State University of São Paulo at Rio Claro, Brazil. She earned her doctorate in psychobiology from the University of São Paulo at Ribeirão Preto, Brazil. In 1988 she pioneered the establishment of outreach programs in which she and her students provide hands-on adapted physical activity services to people with disabilities in schools, hospitals, and institutions. In 1993 she founded the Laboratory of Action and Perception to conduct research in motor behavior and to study developmental changes in individuals with and without disabilities. She is the cofounder and editor-in-chief of the *Brazilian-International Journal of Adapted Physical Education Research* and was a founding member of the Brazilian Society of Adapted Motor Activity. She enjoys working with her students and program participants, traveling, house remodeling, and gardening.

Grant A. Mawston is a physiotherapist practicing in Hamilton, New Zealand. He received his BPhEd and BPhty degrees from the University of Otago, New Zealand. He is an avid soccer player and a regular participant in the national league competition.

Mark Mon-Williams is a lecturer in the School of Psychology at the University of St. Andrews, Scotland. He has just completed a research fellowship in the Perception and Motor Control Laboratory at the University of Queensland,

Australia. He receives grant support from the Engineering and Physical Science Research Council of the UK, the National Health and Medical Research Council of Australia, the Motor Accident and Insurance Commission of Australia, and Action Research medical charity in the UK. He is a hill runner.

T.K. Pitcairn is a senior lecturer in the Department of Psychology of the University of Edinburgh. In his previous existence he was an ethologist and worked at the Max-Planck-Institut fur Vehaltensphysiologie near Munich, Germany. Since coming to Edinburgh his research has been in the areas of social development and the understanding of facial expression. In his real life he rock climbs, skis, and paraglides.

Tjasa Planinsek is an assistant in the Faculty of Education at the University of Ljubljana where she receives grant support from the Chancellor Foundation. She earned her master's degree in adapted physical activity in 1996 from Katholieke Universiteit Leuven. She is a tennis coach and works with wheelchair tennis players. In her free time she enjoys tennis and skiing.

Geert Savelsbergh is a lecturer in the Faculty of Human Movement Science at Vrije Universiteit. He is the head of the research department Perceptual-Motor Development, part of the Research Institute for Fundamental and Clinical Human Movement Science, both situated in Amsterdam. Since 1999 he has served as editor-in-chief of the journal *Infant Behavior & Development* and was recently appointed as Visiting Professor at the Manchester Metropolitan University in the UK.

Paolo Stagi is a medical doctor specializing in child and adolescent neuropsychiatry and neurology, and in neurophysiopathology. He is working, mainly as a clinician, in the Unit of Child and Adolescent Neuropsychiatry at Rho Hospital - Azienda Ospedaliera "G. Salvini," Garbagnate (Milan, Italy).

Phillip D. Tomporowski is a research associate at the University of Connecticut in the Department of Sport, Leisure, and Exercise Sciences. He received his PhD in experimental psychology from the University of Mississippi. He has served as a psychologist for the Alabama Department of Mental Health and as an associate professor at the University of Alabama. His research interests include individual differences in intelligence and the study of developmental disabilities. He was a recipient of the Lilly Teaching Fellowship and U.S. Air Force Research Scientist Fellowships.

Charli Tortoza is currently pursuing his master's degree at the "Universidade Estadual Paulista," Rio Claro, Brazil. He is studying motor control in individuals with and without Down syndrome in the Motor Control Laboratory at "Universidade Estadual de Campinas - UNICAMP" São Paulo, Brazil. His research is supported by "Fundação de Amparo à Pesquisa do Estado de São Paulo." During his free time Charli enjoys playing with his son Eric.

John van der Kamp is a post-doc fellow at the Faculty of Human Movement Science at the Vrije Universiteit, Amsterdam. His PhD is in human movement sciences and deals with the information-based regulation of interceptive timing. In his free time he enjoys squash and hiking through the lowlands of the Netherlands.

Richard Van Emmerik is an assistant professor at the Exercise Science Department, University of Massachusetts at Amherst. He received his master's degree from the Vrije Universiteit in Amsterdam, the Netherlands, and his PhD from the Department of Kinesiology at the University of Illinois at Urbana-Champaign. He is also a fellow of the Royal Dutch Academy of the Arts and Sciences. His research background is in motor control and learning and focuses on understanding coordination of balance and gait in individuals with movement disabilities (such as in Parkinson's disease, stroke, and Down syndrome). He likes to chase squash balls and his two children.

Michael G. Wade is Professor and Director of the School of Kinesiology at the University of Minnesota. He earned his PhD in Kinesiology from the University of Illinois. Over a research and teaching career spanning almost 30 years, Wade has received federal and state support for his research on better understanding the perceptual-motor skills of individuals with a variety of developmental disabilities. He is a fellow of the American Association for Mental Retardation, a fellow of the American Academy of Kinesiology, and in 1994 was the inaugural Gray Research Fellow at the Department of Human Movement Science at the University of Western Australia. He is also past president of the North America Society for Psychology of Sport and Physical Activity. In his free time Wade enjoys playing golf, cooking, reading, and recreating with his family.

John P. Wann is a reader in the Department of Psychology at the University of Reading, England. He was awarded his PhD from the Applied Psychology Unit at the University of Cambridge. He receives grant support from the Engineering and Physical Science Research Council of the UK, the Australian Research Council, and Action Research medical charity in the UK. He is a cyclist.

Daniel J. Weeks is an associate professor and the Graduate Chair in the School of Kinesiology at Simon Fraser University. He earned his PhD in experimental psychology from Auburn University. He receives grant support from the Natural Sciences and Engineering Research Council of Canada and the U.S. National Institutes of Health. In 1996 he received the Distinguished Scholar Award from the North American Society for the Psychology of Sport and Physical Activity. In his free time he enjoys hockey, weight training, euchre, and playing the drums.

Timothy N. Welsh is a PhD candidate at McMaster University. In addition to his research interest in the perceptual-motor behavior of individuals with Down syndrome, he also conducts studies of visual selective attention and bimanual coordination. In his spare time Tim enjoys being involved in sports, both as a hockey player and as a coach in a Special Olympics bowling league in Toronto.

Jennifer G. Wishart is a developmental psychologist, holder of the first established chair in special education in Scotland, and is attached to Moray House Institute of Education, the University of Edinburgh. She did her undergraduate and postgraduate degrees at Edinburgh then worked for over 20 years as a contract researcher in the Psychology Department. Her research has been funded by the UK research councils and Down syndrome charities, and she is currently research advisor to the Scottish, UK, and European DSAs. In her other life, she enjoys traveling to countries with vineyards, eating good food, and walking her English pointer.

About the Editors

Dr. Daniel J. Weeks

Daniel J. Weeks, PhD, is an Associate Professor and Graduate Chair in the School of Kinesiology at Simon Fraser University in British Columbia, Canada. He has been conducting research in the area of perceptual-motor behavior in persons with Down syndrome for nearly fifteen years.

He receives grant support from the Natural Sciences and Engineering Council of Canada (NSERC) and the U.S. National Institutes of Health (NIH). His work has been published in numerous scholarly journals and texts, including the *Journal of Experimental Psychology; Canadian Journal of Experimental Psychology; Experimental Brain Research; Journal of Motor Behavior; Psychological Research;* and *Down Syndrome: Research and Practice.* He is on the editorial board for the *Journal of Motor Behavior* and *Behavior Research Methods, Instruments, & Computers.* Dr. Weeks sits on the Board of Directors for the Canadian Down Syndrome Research Foundation & Resource Center and is a member of their Research Forum. He is also a member of the Psychonomics Society and the North American Society for the Psychology of Sport and Physical Activity (NASPSPA). In 1996, he received the Early Career Distinguished Scholar Award from NASPSPA.

Dr. Weeks resides in Port Coquitlam, British Columbia, Canada, and enjoys fishing, drumming, and euchre.

Romeo Chua, PhD, is an assistant professor in the School of Human Kinetics at the University of British Columbia, and a research supervisor for the Simon Fraser/ McMaster University Down syndrome project. Over the past several years he has participated in collaborated research efforts of perceptual-motor behavior and functional cerebral specialization in persons with Down syndrome.

He receives grant support from NSERC and NIH. Dr. Chua is a member of the NASPSPA and the Canadian Society for Psychomotor Learning and Sport Psychology (SCAPPS). In 1996, he received the Governor General's Gold Medal from Simon Fraser University and the Young Scientist Award from SCAPPS in 1992.

Dr. Chua and his wife Brenda reside in Vancouver, British Columbia, Canada. He enjoys reading, music, and tennis.

Dr. Romeo Chua

Digby Elliott, PhD, is a professor in the Department of Kinesiology at McMaster University. His current research is funded by NSERC and NIH.

In the past 18 years, Elliott has published more than 100 peer-reviewed journal articles and been co-editor on two books. In 1997, he was listed by Current Contents as one of the most published authors in psychology. He is on the editorial board for the *Journal of Motor Behavior* and belongs to the NASPSPA and SCAPPS. He was president of SCAPPS from 1997 to 1998.

Dr. Elliott and his wife Elaine reside in Dundas, Ontario, Canada. He enjoys skin and scuba diving, jogging, and reading in his spare time.

Dr. Digby Elliott

OTHER BOOKS FROM HUMAN KINETICS

Motor Control and Learning: A Behavioral Emphasis
(Third Edition)
Richard A. Schmidt, PhD, and Timothy D. Lee, PhD
1999 • Hardcover • 512 pp • ISBN 0-88011-484-3
$59.00 ($88.50 Canadian)

A major text in the field of motor behavior written by two of the leading researchers.

Motor Behavior and Human Skill
Jan P. Piek, PhD, Editor
1998 • Hardback • 448 pp • ISBN 0-88011-675-7
$49.00 ($73.50 Canadian)

Provides a lively and varied forum for analyzing the many theoretical approaches used to understand motor control, motor learning, and motor development.

Neurophysiological Basis of Movement
Mark L. Latash, PhD
1998 • Hardcover • 280 pp • ISBN 0-88011-756-7
$45.00 ($67.50 Canadian)

The only contemporary comprehensive textbook on the neurophysiology of voluntary movement.

Progress in Motor Control, Volume 1
Bernstein's Traditions in Movement Studies
Mark L. Latash, PhD, Editor
1998 • Hardback • 408 pp • ISBN 0-88011-674-9
$49.00 ($73.50 Canadian)

Sets a new standard as the leading state-of-the-art account on motor control.

To request more information or to order, U.S. customers call 1-800-747-4457, e-mail us at **humank@hkusa.com,** or visit our website at **www.humankinetics.com.** Persons outside the U.S. can contact us via our website or use the appropriate telephone number, postal address, or e-mail address shown in the front of this book.

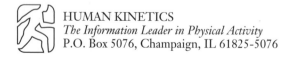
HUMAN KINETICS
The Information Leader in Physical Activity
P.O. Box 5076, Champaign, IL 61825-5076